An Economic Theory of Greed, Love, Groups, and Networks

D1630529

Why are people loyal? How do groups form and how do they create incentives for their members to abide by group norms? Until now, economics has only been able to partially answer these questions. In this groundbreaking work, Paul Frijters presents a new unified theory of human behavior. To do so, he incorporates comprehensive yet tractable definitions of love and power, and the dynamics of groups and networks, into the traditional mainstream economic view. The result is an enhanced view of human societies that nevertheless retains the pursuit of self-interest at its core. This book provides a digestible but comprehensive theory of our socioeconomic system, which condenses its immense complexity into simplified representations. The result both illuminates humanity's history and suggests ways forward for policies today, in areas as diverse as poverty reduction and tax compliance.

PROFESSOR PAUL FRIJTERS is a professor of Economics at the University of Queensland. He was elected "Best Economist under 40 in Australia" by the Economic Society of Australia for 2009–2011, and his work consistently ranks in the top 4 percent of downloaded and cited economic research in the world. Professor Frijters has undertaken research in a wide variety of fields, including happiness and well-being, migration in China, behavioral economics, and health economics. The findings of his research feature regularly in the global media.

GIGI FOSTER is a senior lecturer in the School of Economics within the Australian School of Business at the University of New South Wales. Her research focuses primarily on decisions related to human capital, with a particular emphasis on social influence and behavioral economics.

000000682889

An Economic Theory of Greed, Love, Groups, and Networks

PAUL FRIJTERS WITH GIGI FOSTER

CAMBRIDGE
UNIVERSITY PRESS

CAMBRIDGE UNIVERSITY PRESS
Cambridge, New York, Melbourne, Madrid, Cape Town,
Singapore, São Paulo, Delhi, Mexico City

Cambridge University Press
The Edinburgh Building, Cambridge CB2 8RU, UK

Published in the United States of America by Cambridge University Press, New York

www.cambridge.org
Information on this title: www.cambridge.org/9781107678941

First published 2013
Reprinted 2013

Printed and bound in the United Kingdom by the MPG Books Group

A catalogue record for this publication is available from the British Library

Library of Congress Cataloguing in Publication data
Frijters, Paul.
   An economic theory of greed, love, groups, and networks / Paul Frijters
   with Gigi Foster.
      pages   cm
   Includes bibliographical references and index.
   ISBN 978-1-107-02627-8 – ISBN 978-1-107-67894-1 (pbk.)
   1. Avarice.   2. Economic man.   3. Reciprocity (Commerce)   4. Social groups.
   5. Social networks.   I. Title.
   BJ1535.A8F75 2013
   306.3–dc23   2012043730

ISBN 978-1-107-02627-8 Hardback
ISBN 978-1-107-67894-1 Paperback

Contents

Figures

Preface

GIGI FOSTER

During my undergraduate days, while studying the materialist science of economics together with its more flowery cousins, philosophy and political science, I kept the following translation of a quotation from Dostoevsky's *Brothers Karamazov* pinned above my desk:

Give up your gods and come worship ours, or else death to you and your gods!

At the time, I saw this as a comment on the negative power of organized religion. Displaying the quotation was for me both an affirmation of the comparatively pacific nature of atheism and an expression of horror that beliefs alone could lead to material destruction. My horror, as with most people's, was both self-righteous and the product of ignorance.

As a budding economist and a firm utilitarian, however offended I was by the apparent irrationality of faith, I still perceived something good in it. I could not ignore its pacifying influence on the down-trodden, an observation offered only with heavy negative moralistic overtones in the standard canon. Yet many vexing questions continued to reverberate in my mind, to which I found no satisfactory answers in anything I read. Why did smart people allow themselves to believe in the demonstrably false? Why could they not be shaken by rational arguments? Why did they engage in seemingly ridiculous activities, such as prayer, and why did they brainwash their own children and others into performing these activities as well? Why did this brainwashing regularly work? Why might it feel good to believe in falsehoods? How personally committed was I to rejecting this potential stream of good feeling on the basis of the intellectual barrenness of its source, and was my rejection itself not a blatant violation of my own professed utilitarianism?

The science of mainstream economics captured my mind and my career by quantifying and explaining so much of human behavior using one simple framework. But economic theory as taught to me did not go far enough, and the links depicted in my liberal-arts education between economics, philosophy, political theory, and other social sciences (chiefly psychology, anthropology, and sociology) were not developed or mutually consistent enough, to satisfactorily answer questions such as these.

Several years ago, I accepted Paul Frijters' offer to collaborate on the production of a book like this, which marks a key milestone in what is now a longer-term joint project. A central goal of this project is the development of a tractable theory that comprehensively and with minimal internal inconsistency explains the governing dynamics of social and economic life. Questions such as those above as well as many others are being directly addressed in this project. Paul began this work independently, laboring for twenty years mostly without acknowledgment and at great personal cost to construct the basic intellectual framework that currently underpins the project and is presented in this book. By the time I joined him, therefore, most of the pieces of the puzzle we present here were already identified. What I have contributed is mainly glue, polish, some rejigging here and there, and above all a new source of energy to help put the pieces into place. I thank Paul for seeing the potential in our collaboration. It has been immensely rewarding, both personally and intellectually, to be of assistance in this way and to see something so much larger than myself take shape.

Naturally, as with any significant undertaking, there have been costs to joining this project. First and most obviously, it is highly time- and labor-intensive to produce a book. These costs have been borne not only directly by me but also indirectly by my husband Michael Baker and our children, Sienna and Neil, without whose unending support I could never have committed to such a venture. From a career perspective too, there have been costs: the academy of economists by and large does not reward the production of broadly reaching books such as this one, but rather the production of "high-quality" journal articles. This is the main reason why books like this are rare.

A longer-term cost that has come from working on this book is a loss of innocence. The story told here offers such a powerful microscope into the inner workings of humans that looking through it can trigger fundamental personal change. As a prime example, while the prospect of understanding the genesis of love is intellectually compelling, actually witnessing the demystification of the love mechanism is also shocking on a personal level. One must find a way to carry on after this experience as a normal individual, despite having deconstructed love (and hence one's own loves) into constituent parts that are laid bare. More generally, a strong element of conscious will gradually becomes crucial in maintaining the health of one's inner life, as the pillars of that inner life are gradually exposed.

What this book contains in relation to the realm of the heart is hence not a message for cowards. Part of the book's message is that the "realm of the heart" is broader than common understanding would suggest. I expect that most readers who are open enough to read to the end will have a negative emotional reaction to at least one part of the story told – a reaction that many will quickly rationalize on intellectual grounds – because in this book, sacred cows of one breed or another are slaughtered regularly and without ceremony. Established wisdom in many disciplines is not taken at face value, but rather examined with single-minded intent, and what are deemed the useful bits are surgically excised. By implication, the remainder is merely offal. There is no dignity in this, which will offend those for whom established wisdom has become part of their own identity and is therefore something to be revered. Given the constraints of space, and notwithstanding scores of references, we also cannot pay homage to each previous thinker who has had an idea that could be shown to support the various lines of argument put forth. I cannot offer an apology for what will be perceived as the book's insufficient reverence, but I do recognize the need to ask the reader to be patient and forgiving.

I believe that the story we tell in this book heralds a new dawn in social science. An enhanced version of the economic view of man is built, defended, and used to explain at a fundamental level the supporting features of a modern economy; the process of technical advancement and the ultimate sources of economic growth; the roles of faith, power, competition, and collaboration in our economies; how the symbiotic relationship between the public and private sectors has emerged through the process of social development; gender relations, political manipulation, and the natural tendencies of academic disciplines; the variable longevity of different types of social group structures; and the nature of culture. Our story nominates a minimum set of individual and social building blocks required to make sense of both our daily lives and our socioeconomic structures in a cohesive manner. It points out the awesome strengths and the inherent weaknesses of our current societies and provides a foundation on which to conceptualize economic, social, moral, and psychological health, and predict our future as a social species. An avalanche of supporting research findings and real-world examples – shocking, comic, and banal – are drawn from throughout the world and across time. Centuries of thought are drawn upon, meaning that some of the explanations offered will already be known to the reader, while others will be either the result of new combinations of familiar material, or else entirely novel. Because it is a work in progress, frontiers are described that I hope will lead to rigorous debate in established circles and stimulate the research agendas of young people. Extensions and applications in dozens of areas are immediate. Reading this story for the first time will be, at worst, extremely uncomfortable and, at best, the ultimate intellectual thrill.

No science can progress without continued rejuvenation of its theoretical backbone. One of my hopes for this project in the longer term is to make the story in this book, as it continues to evolve, fully at one with the canon of mainstream economics, for the sake of the continued intellectual vitality of economics and social science more broadly. In this sense, helping to construct this book has been above all a religious endeavor with the pursuit and dissemination of truth in social science as the god. My religiosity in this regard has defeated my rational utilitarian impulses, as I am not at all sure that the dissemination of this book will increase total happiness.

I hope that you approach this book with an eager and open mind, ready to engage. My best advice to you for coping with its messages on an emotional level is to allow yourself to love, and to retain your belief in a few benign falsehoods. Without them, you are not truly human.

Acknowledgments

PAUL FRIJTERS

This book has been an intellectual journey full of the best things in life: companions who traveled along for parts of the way; generous benefactors whose gifts and encouragements paid for the endeavor; and a supporting home environment to rest the weary legs. In terms of co-travelers, I have been privileged to have met many academics who read the early scribbles, participated in subprojects and grants, and who coauthored papers and books on aspects of the overall problem. In many ways, the endeavor has fed off their thoughts and insights. If there are any I fail to mention below, know that it is not due to lack of appreciation but the sheer volume of company that they are in.

In the 1990s my fellow travelers included Alexander Tieman, Bernard van Praag, Susan van Velsen, Sheldon Grant-Levy, and Frans van Winden.

In the 2000s my fellow travelers included Ada Ferrer-i-Carbonel, Raquel Fonseca, Jack Pezzy, Benno Torgler, Dirk Bezemer, Uwe Dulleck, Gert Frijters, Bas van der Klaauw, Andrew and Catherine Grey, Juan Baron, Michael Shields, Andrew Leigh, Mary Morgan, Joop Hartog, Robert Gregory, Xin Meng, Robert Haveman, Barbara Wolfe, Penelope Baldwin, Angus Maddison, Bruce Chapman, Raja Junankar, David Johnston, and the Horne family. Their encouragements, criticisms, suggestions, and ways of looking at human behavior all strongly influenced the directions taken.

Some of my PhD, Honors, and Masters students have also been coaxed into joining the journey for a few years. I owe particular thanks to Redzo Mujcic, Harry Greenwell, Tony Beatton, Nemanja Antic, Debayan Pakrashi, Cameron Murray, and Melissa Bond.

Special thanks go to my academic colleagues Malathi Velamuri, Jack Pezzy, Xander Tieman, and Hannu Virtiainen, who sacrificed a large slice of their academic time towards the project, tirelessly poring over every argument and spreading good rumors about it.

I of course thank my supporting writer, Gigi Foster, for her unwavering enthusiasm and belief in the venture.

I also thank my research assistants over the years: Jacinta Holloway, Ben Hancock, Amalia Savini, Daniel Quiggin, Hiau Joo Kee, Fernando Ramirez, Su-Min Lim, Miriam Carter, Cara Fioravanti, and Cassandra Davies, for their determination to source each and every niggly fact, often contacting outside academics to get resolution on the finer points of noneconomic disciplines.

As the end came nearer, the number of people involved grew rapidly. In the last few years numerous people have provided useful comments on the manuscript and on its presentation, including Nicholas Gruen, Andrew Schuller, Geoff Harcourt, Sugata Marjit, Michael Baker, Marco Faravelli, Bill von Hippel, Ryan Manuel, Deirdre McCloskey, and Gabriele Gratton. Thanks to Manuela Torgler for the illustrations!

No long journey can be undertaken without external sponsors paying the bills. In this sense, I have been very fortunate that several funding agencies have in the last twenty years given me money to keep plodding forward. Thanks go to multiple grants from the Australian Research Council as well as from the Gruen Foundation. Indirectly, grants from the World Bank, the Ford Foundation, the Dutch and Australian Ministries of Social Affairs, and the several universities I have worked at have also subsidized this project.

The team at Cambridge University Press that took on the task of molding this project into publishable form has been amazing. The editor, Chris Harrison, and his team of anonymous but very supportive referees gave many impulses that shaped this project for the better.

Then my friends and family: the main idea in the book, which is that ideals, love, friendship, joy, and compassion play a big role in daily life alongside the greedy impulses to gather and control, is of course largely informed by introspection and by those we love around us. If you doubt this, simply ask yourself: have you never done anything out of kindness for others? Have you always secretly tried to get the most for yourself without a real care for your partner, your children, your country, or your job? Surely not. Kindness at the daily individual level can be observed all the time, both within ourselves and in others. The little kindnesses and the big ones. The anonymous donation to charity and the sacrifice of a second car in favor of a better education for our kids. The donor card that saves a life when we are dead and the drought aid we give to farmers. The smile given to a beggar and the lives laid down for the homeland in times of war. We breathe love every day of our lives, even when there are no others to observe us doing it.

Since these matters form a large part of this book, it is in a very direct way that the loves of my life have informed this book, and I need to thank both family and friends for showing me the difference between love and greed. Thanks go in particular to my wife Erika Turkstra and our three kids Robert, Carmen, and Jasmine, but also to all my other family members and friends, including many of the colleagues above. I dedicate this book to you.

Introduction and preview

Introduction

Society routinely asks broad questions of economists and expects fairly all-encompassing answers. Are trade barriers good or bad? What is the role of private enterprise? How involved should government be in regulating industry? A reasoned yet simple answer to any of these questions must depend on some aggregate view of how a country works. Whatever the particulars, each question is a "system" question that touches upon so many aspects of the whole economic and political system that its answer inevitably requires some explicit or implicit overarching story.

For example, one cannot answer the question on trade barriers without some implicit equilibrium framework in mind, together with an implicit understanding of how trade barriers come to be politically sponsored. Likewise, one cannot provide the *raison d'être* of private enterprise without a fairly complete picture of the roles of other actors in the economy, such as consumers and government, and the dynamics in operation between these different actors. Policy makers and students routinely present economists with simply stated questions that nonetheless have only imprecise answers, due to being underpinned by a plethora of implicit ideas and possibilities. The reasonableness of any simple answer to such a question depends upon the reasonableness of the answerer's underlying aggregate view.

The goal of this book is to offer such an aggregate view. The starting point of the book is to take the principles of mainstream economics at face value. Layers of selected ideas are then added and integrated with the mainstream economic view, relating to the roles of loyalty, groups, power, and networks. What results is an enhanced view of how society works that increases the number of phenomena covered, and deepens the existing story.

1

The groundwork laid by economics

The dominant aggregate view of economists is roughly as follows. Humans are primarily motivated by greed, and competition between greedy individuals leads each of them individually to specialize in doing what they do best. At the aggregate level, this dynamic leads to a condition of balance, in which all opportunities for mutual advancement have been depleted as long as some benevolent rule-setter forces people to abide by property rights and contract law. Competition amongst a large number of individual actors within such an institutional framework produces an optimal outcome for society as a whole in terms of productive efficiency, and therefore should be encouraged on the grounds of maximizing social surplus. The very structures of society itself, such as our parliaments and our notions of fair play, can likewise be seen to have survived a long-fought competition – not amongst individuals, but amongst institutions and ideas, in which those that were more appealing to the innate wishes of the population as a whole survived.

Relying on this overall view of society allows economists to abstract from specific situational factors and deliver simple, fairly general answers to the broad questions they are routinely asked. Trade barriers, most economists would claim, give a monopoly to domestic suppliers at the expense of domestic consumers, and deliver aggregate efficiency losses. Private enterprise exists so that greedy individuals have incentives to discover the most efficient means of producing existing goods and discovering new goods. Government should regulate industry when market imperfections, such as entry barriers, information asymmetries, or externalities threaten the ability of the unimpeded market to deliver the socially efficient allocation of resources.[1]

---

[1] I here temporarily ignore concerns about the trade-off between efficiency and equality (cf. Okun 1975). It is true that economists often make the theoretical distinction between maximizing the size of the economic pie (termed "allocative efficiency") and distributing it, where the latter is seen as a normative issue that could potentially be addressed via taxes and transfers (preferably nondistorting ones). Yet, while economists often pay lip service to the possibility of transfers to losers from policy changes, such that everyone would benefit from increases in the economic pie (i.e., so that such increases are Pareto-improving), full transfers seldom occur in reality. It would be fairer to say that economists worry mainly about the size of the economic pie, while leaving its distribution to politics. In this book, this political process is itself taken as part of the subject under study.

The holder of such a stylized "mainstream economics" view will advocate those forms of competition that lead to optimal specialization, and will advocate mechanisms that allow for orderly transitions of institutions along the lines of optimal fitness. The holder of such a view will analyze the material incentives of every actor involved in a problem, and will generally try to solve the problem by realigning those individual incentives with what is optimal for society as a whole, often through exploiting the power of greed-based competition amongst individuals. The policy advice of the economist boils down to a set of answers to the following sequential questions: "How does the socially optimal outcome differ from what we have now; who currently benefits materially from which aspects of the current situation; and whose material incentives can we change such that their individually optimal choices will coincide with what we want them to do from a social welfare perspective?"

This is a powerful and intuitive way of looking at any problem. It is also a view that has been highly successful in influencing thought in both the public and private sectors, as witnessed by the dominance of the language of economics in policy circles, international institutions, and business. In terms of the ability to generate simple stories that can be grafted on to many different situations to deliver simple advice, it is hard to think of a more successful and useful view that has come from the social sciences.

The mainstream neoclassical view of economics sketched above depicts "Homo Economicus" (economic man) in isolation, living each day only to satisfy his greedy desires through the pursuit of material wealth. This atomistic and materialistic view of humanity has, over its long life, come under fierce criticism for being demonstrably simplistic. Economic insiders know that people do not just care about money; they know that people are not always experts at calculating what is in their own best interests; they know that historical accident has as much to do with existing institutions as those institutions' supposed "economic fitness"; and they know that competition does not just happen in a vacuum, but requires the existence of quite culturally specific institutions in order to appear. The main task in this book is not to remind the reader of all the inadequacies of the stylized mainstream economic view. Rather, I want to recognize its great value in providing people with simplified stories and solution strategies, and then to expand the mainstream view by adding important elements not currently included.

Loyalty and groups

The first element I wish to add to the mainstream economics view is an understanding of the crucial role of love and loyalty in generating behavior, both at the micro-level and the macro-level. This will require offering a working definition of loyalty, and then asking why people are loyal – considering loyalty to families, countries, clans, and other groups as all essentially the same type of phenomenon.[2] This question is critical if we are to make sense of why people care for their children, fight for their country, do not coordinate on defrauding the tax authorities, by and large follow the constitution, and so forth. It is contended in this book that economics has not incorporated satisfactory answers to any of these questions into its mainstream view, notwithstanding the economic literature on altruism and groups.

The inclusion of love and loyalty will lead more broadly to a consideration of how the power implicit in social groups can influence behavior. I will illustrate how groups form initially, and how they manage to create the incentives for group members to abide by group norms. This again is an area that traditional mainstream economics has been unable to illuminate, yet it is demonstrably important in influencing the behavior of groups of people in aggregate. This analysis ultimately seeks to explain and thereby predict the existence and behavior of important groups in modern economies, including the "citizens" of the nation state, the "faithful" in religions, the self-identifying members of ethnicities, unions, and other clubs, and so on.[3]

---

[2] Many authors have used the word "altruism" to describe the behavioral reflections of love and loyalty. As Ackerman (1996) argued in her review of attempts to incorporate altruism in economic analyses (p. 701), "Altruism ... cannot be understood within the standard economic framework. Theoretical progress requires a richer conception of individual utility functions and a base in cognitive psychology that incorporates the power of ideas and emotions in motivating behavior." I fully agree with this statement, and use the word "loyalty" to denote the abstract foundation of altruism as typically understood. In this book I also address "loyalty" directly rather than "altruism" because this offers broader conceptual scope: people can be loyal to abstract ideas (as well as people), whereas the notion of "altruism" typically is associated only with loyalty to people.

[3] These behaviors were squarely in the realm of what many early contributors to modern economic science (e.g., Adam Smith) considered worthy of attention; see Harcourt (1995) for further discussion.

Trade networks

The first observation I make about trade networks is that they are a crucial component of the modern economic system of production and exchange. While this idea is accepted in some economic circles, standard economic practice – often stated as part of an assumption of zero transaction costs – is to presume that everyone can instantaneously trade with anyone else and can switch trading partners at zero cost. Reality is more complicated. People and organizations live, produce, and exchange in trade networks of limited size, where relations are specific and where one cannot exchange one relation for another without significant cost. For instance, a car company relying on a trade network of suppliers that deliver different automobile components cannot instantaneously obtain, say, its windshield wipers from an alternative supplier. Such a change would take time to implement, since it would require that alternative supplier to develop specific knowledge in order to suit the customized requirements of the car manufacturer: that windshield wiper has to be made of specific material, must conform to specific standards, and must fit onto specific components made by others. It takes time and resources to comply with such demands. Similarly, consumers, financiers, doctors, and any number of other professionals depend upon the individuals and organizations in their current network when making their production and consumption decisions.

Even if they were not a crucial element in the economy, trade networks are a particular type of social group, and therefore should be included in this book for the sake of providing a complete treatment of groups and their dynamics. Yet there is also one remaining, more insidious reason to include an analysis of trade networks. Such networks form the main conduit between changes in the material circumstances of individuals and in their behavior as political actors in other existing groups. As such, an understanding of trade networks will be a crucial element in answering the questions of how and when major political and economic institutions emerge.

Organization of the book

This book is organized to follow the train of thought shown above. The preview following this introduction provides an illustrative summary of where the book is heading, by presenting a set of stylized questions that will be addressed. These questions range from those that mainstream economics already considers "core business" to questions that lie at the periphery of present-day mainstream economics.

In Chapter 1 of the book, I review in more depth the mainstream story of economics. This chapter outlines the main overall story that "we" economists teach our students, and illustrates its great relevance in generating implications for how the world is run and how it should be run. This first chapter paves the way for the ensuing chapters by noting contentious areas where extensions to the existing aggregate story might be fruitful.

Chapters 2 through 4 then delve into the main concepts with which the economists' story outlined in Chapter 1 will be enhanced. Chapter 2 explores the concept of loyalty, also termed love. Chapter 3 considers questions relating to groups and power. Chapter 4 analyzes network formation, drawing on the collapse of networks in the wake of the dismantling of the former Soviet Union in order to illustrate the economic and political role of networks.

Chapter 5 draws the strands of the previous chapters together and presents an augmented overall story of how our economic and political systems work. This chapter includes a novel heuristic for tackling socioeconomic questions based on this augmented story. This heuristic is then applied to the questions introduced in the book's preview. The book concludes by reviewing what has been added to the aggregate view of economists, as well as noting some elements of socioeconomic life that are still not well integrated.

To the best of my knowledge, with one exception,[4] none of the specific observations or individual theoretical arguments in this book is new. Each can be found in some other discipline and/or in some previous time period, which are duly referenced. The novelty of the book is in the explicit attempt to bring many diverse strands of thought together to form a single overall view. In that regard, each of Chapters 2 through 4 is in itself a novel perspective on one aspect of the problem, while the main point of innovation is the synthesis in Chapter 5.

---

[4] I believe that the unified description of the nature of love and loyalty, embodied in the Love Principle presented in Chapter 2 – while derived from observations many have made previously – is itself new.

Preview

In this Preview, I first describe the context from which this book emerges, to clarify its scope and intended aims. Several applications are then introduced that can be directly analyzed through the lens of the unified view that will ultimately emerge. This is followed by a reflective discussion of the methods applied in order to construct and arrive at this unified view, and a final statement of purpose for the book as a whole.

The view of economics in this book is as a discipline ultimately driven by the need of policy makers and the rest of society for advice on how to deal with perceived problems.[5] By "problem," I mean a facet of economic, social, or political life in which different decisions can be made that may lead to dramatically different outcomes in terms of overall social welfare. What policy makers or society consider to be an "economic problem," and therefore one for which they turn to economists for advice, is itself the outcome of perceptions and competition: self-interested economists plying their trade will naturally seek to expand the set of problems about which they dispense advice, and thereby gradually encroach on the territory of other social scientists, such as anthropologists, psychologists, or sociologists. Social scientists from other disciplines will naturally do the same. The question of what is an "economic problem" therefore has an answer that shifts with the political winds.

To determine what should count as the main territory of economists, I reviewed the surveys of professional economists run over the years, with a particular focus on the surveys of members of the American Economic Association with which many economists, both American and non-American, are affiliated. In addition, I reviewed the twenty-five most popular introductory textbooks in economics currently available, as selected by Lopus and Paringer (2011) for their chapter on economic textbooks in *The International Handbook on Teaching and Learning Economics*.

The textbooks unanimously agree that the modern "territory" of economists minimally includes problems surrounding material

---

[5] This is similar to the view espoused in Harcourt (1982).

trade-offs. Typical examples of trade-offs presented to students are whether to fund policy A or policy B, or whether to consume X or Y. This consensus is at the forefront in the three most popular textbooks: Mankiw's (fifth edition) first and fourth principles of economics are that "people face trade-offs" and "[p]eople respond to incentives." The first chapter of McConnell et al., which apparently is the most widely sold economics textbook ever and is now in its nineteenth edition, is similarly about scarcity and choices; Samuelson and Nordhaus (nineteenth edition) also name scarcity and trade-offs as belonging to the central concepts of economics. New textbooks run the same line: Stone (2011) proffers (p. 12) as key economic ideas that "choice and scarcity force tradeoffs" and that "opportunity costs dominate our lives." Textbooks of intermediate vintage (e.g., Boyes and Melvin [eighth edition]) similarly place scarcity and choice at the center of their definitions of economics.

These economic textbooks, as well as the questions posed in the surveys of economists, address trade-offs concentrated in the wealth-generating part of the economy: production and exchange. The dominance of these domains as the source of the typical decision problems on which economists are consulted means that, by and large, policy questions in these domains define mainstream economics.

Under each ensuing subheading in this Preview, I provide a brief sketch of a problem – whether residing in or out of the traditional "territory" of economics – and then give a quick summary of how mainstream economics would view and then proceed to solve the problem. In each case, I then sketch the augmented view of the problem that subsequent chapters will work towards. These problems are only briefly introduced here, but will resurface again throughout the book. They range from those that will be intimately familiar to any practicing economist to those that, while amenable to economic arguments, will not be easily recognized as traditional economic problems.

International trade

A key question facing policy makers is whether they should catalyze or hinder international trade. This is the main question addressed by Adam Smith in his most famous book, published in 1776. This book, *The Wealth of Nations* (Smith 1776), directly addresses the political question of whether government should interfere in agricultural trade – wheat, in particular.

Hindrances placed on trade by policy makers can take the form of tariffs on imports or exports, quotas on the number of goods that are allowed into the country, or quality requirements on imports that effectively block them. The archetypal situation is that policy makers in a particular country are asked by that country's domestic producers to protect them from cheaper imports via implementing one or more such hindrances. Typically the argument made by the domestic producers is that this interference by policy makers will "save jobs."

The mainstream economic answer to the question of whether to implement such hindrances is a resounding "no," regardless of the type of hindrance. As Winters, McCulloch, and McKay (2004) observe (p. 72) in their review of trade liberalization, "[m]ost economists accept that, in the long run, open economies fare better in aggregate than do closed ones, and that relatively open policies contribute significantly to development."

The main argument behind this stance is that in any voluntary trade, both trading partners know what they are doing and therefore are both benefitting from the exchange. In the case of international trade, the importing consumer gets the good at a better price than he would otherwise have to pay (or a higher-quality good at an equal or lower price), while the exporter also receives a better price than he could get elsewhere. Any alternative price that could be gotten elsewhere is interpretable – under the assumption of competitive markets – as the cost that others would face in order to produce the same good. The very observation that consumers prefer a cheaper foreign supplier therefore signals that domestic producers' actual comparative advantage lies elsewhere than in producing the good in question.

Economists who observe domestic suppliers lobbying policy makers for protectionist policies view this situation as an opportunity to create additional social surplus by rearranging the economy. The domestic economy could grow larger in the long run if suppliers currently making tradeable goods that cannot compete with foreign imports would stop making them, and would instead produce those goods in whose production processes they have a comparative advantage. Through this lens, hindrances to imports merely impoverish one's own country in the long run, both by preventing domestic consumers from getting a better deal, and by preventing domestic producers from reorienting themselves towards production processes in which they have comparative advantages.[6]

Naturally, mainstream economists admit some exceptions to the standard case above, mainly to do with failures of perfect competition. We know that trade barriers can be beneficial to the domestic country if the foreign competitors in question have a large degree of market power, and domestic demand is somewhat elastic; we know it is possible, in a situation with large upfront costs, that temporary trade barriers might give the domestic industry a required window of opportunity in which to establish itself as the world leader in an industry and reap monopoly rents itself; and so forth. Chang (2010) provides an entertaining review of such exceptions, for this case as well as other policy areas addressed by mainstream economics.

Despite these exceptions and many others for which economists have fully developed models, economists make up a solid bloc in favor of freer international trade, and as such applaud free trade agreements, unilateral reductions in tariffs, harmonization of tax rules in order to facilitate free trade, and similar initiatives. Working towards freer trade is an activity that occupies many policy economists inside trade ministries, foreign affairs ministries, and international organizations. There are of course economists working for the "other side," i.e., economists who argue against trade liberalization, either because their employer requires them to argue against freer trade or because they genuinely think that one of the exceptions applies.

However, surveys amongst American, English, and Australian economists show that freer international trade is something that the vast majority of economists applaud. In the original survey of American Economic Association (AEA) members in 1977 (Kearl, Pope, Whiting, and Wimmer 1979), some 97% of the responding economists agreed with the statement that "tariffs and import quotas usually reduce general economic welfare," and only 16% of those who agreed did so with some provisions. Fifteen years later, a general survey (Alston, Kearl, and Vaughan 1992) of American economists, including those in business, academia, and government positions, found that 93.5% agreed

---

[6] Although not the central goal of domestic policy makers, foreign suppliers' welfare is also higher in the absence of import restrictions. Symmetrically, domestic suppliers are better off in the absence of export restrictions.

with the same statement. An international survey of French, German, Austrian, and Swiss economists (Frey, Pommerehne, Schneider, and Gilbert 1984) found that 89.7% of respondents agreed with the same statement. A 2011 survey of Australian economists, which I helped to initiate and run,[7] found (p. 6) that about 60% of respondents agreed with the fairly strong statement that "Australia should unilaterally reduce all artificial barriers to international trade including subsidies, tariffs and import quotas," while only 26% disagreed with that statement. The AEA survey from 2007 (Whaples 2009) found (p. 343) that 83% of economists agreed that the US "should eliminate remaining tariffs and other barriers to trade," a stronger statement than that used by Kearl et al. (1979) and thus unsurprisingly slightly less strongly, though still overwhelmingly, supported by responding economists. Across the dozens of surveys of economists, there is no other question on which the consensus in the profession appears so strong the world over. This consensus is also reflected in the assertions made in popular textbooks, with a typical statement being "trade is a win-win situation" (Baumol and Blinder 2009 [eleventh edition], p. 5).

On this problem, the unified view at which this book will arrive is almost exactly the same as the mainstream economic view, and hence the advice it offers on this problem is virtually identical. The little this book adds is some further understanding of why industries that campaign for import protection do not phrase their requests for protection in terms of being shielded from the choices of their own domestic consumers, but instead appeal to some imagined benefit to the country as a whole from implementing protectionist policies. Within mainstream economics this type of appeal is sometimes called "cheap talk," and seen as a pretense that smart voters and politicians should see through in an instant. It should be clear by the end of this book that such pretense is a vital ingredient in successful political lobbying. For now, I merely note that the pretense is directed towards a particular audience: domestic voters and politicians.

---

[7] This survey was managed by Richard Hayes on behalf of the Economic Society of Australia, and the instrument and average responses are available at www.ecosoc.org.au/files/File/CC/Survey%20summary%205%20categories.pdf.

Competition regulation

What should policy makers do with an organization that dominates a market for a particular good, particularly when that good has no close substitutes? The classic nineteenth-century version of this question was what to do with Standard Oil, the domestic oil monopolist in the United States run by the Rockefeller family. Modern versions of this question revolve around the market power of companies such as Microsoft (software) and De Beers (diamonds), and often take the form of whether or not to allow the merger of competing firms.

The mainstream economic position on market power is that it should be diffuse whenever possible. In those cases where a monopoly is inevitable because of strong cost advantages for sole suppliers (which is the case with computer platforms or other networks, such as water distribution), then the state should either be the monopolist itself or should regulate a private monopolist so that it does not overcharge, undersupply, or otherwise extract excess surplus from the sale of its goods to consumers. The underlying principle is to try to push the allocation of surplus from realized transactions back towards what would result in a competitive market.

The strongest policy instrument available is to force the monopolist to break up into competing firms. Standard Oil was forcibly broken up into several oil companies in order to generate more competition and lower prices, and similar break-ups were proposed for Microsoft in the late twentieth century but never implemented. Minimizing the amount of market power held by any one private company, in order to obtain a more palatable allocation of surplus to consumers, has been the main rationale for why many governments are the sole owners/suppliers of national defense, railways, highways, passports, water, and even health care (Arrow 1963): it is thought that private suppliers of such goods and services would overcharge and undersupply, and successful regulation is deemed to be difficult in these areas.

The same basic reasoning has led mainstream economists to advocate and work within competition regulation authorities, such as the Antitrust Division of the Department of Justice and the Federal Trade Commission (FTC) in the US, the Australian Competition and Consumer Commission (ACCC) in Australia, and the Office of Fair Trading (OFT) in the UK. In every advanced economy there are similar government bodies charged with preventing monopolies from arising. These authorities can block mergers and acquisitions, and often can even break up existing monopolies. Additionally, anticartel legislation is in place in countries throughout the world to prevent private companies from coordinating such that they behave "as if" they were monopolists. The explicit rationale is always the same: private companies coordinating on increasing the price asked from consumers is a bad thing for the country as a whole, because it would reduce overall welfare by comparison to the competitive ideal.

As with international trade, the number of nuanced deviations from this mainstream economic position is huge. For example, matters get incredibly complicated, both theoretically and practically, when there is more than one good at stake. In the case where the good in question is merely part of a set of goods needed to obtain a final consumable package – such as when the good is a CD produced by a domestic monopolist, and a foreign monopolist makes the CD players – it is suddenly not at all clear that one would want to break up the domestic monopolist supplying one link in the chain: that might well increase the power of the monopolist in another part of the supply chain, which might not be subject to domestic policy. Difficulties also arise when the production of a good involves long-term investments that are hard to observe and that interact with the investments made by other companies.

Yet, despite the many nuanced exceptions to the rule, the basic opinion of mainstream economists on the issue of market power is that one perennially strives to increase the level of competition in the provision of a good whenever one can, and otherwise to regulate any existing monopolist such that it behaves as if it has competition.[8]

---

[8] This is evident both in economic textbooks and in surveys of economists. A typical example from the former is Mankiw's seventh principle of economics: "Governments Can Sometimes Improve Market Outcomes. When a market fails to allocate resources efficiently, the government can change the outcome through public policy. Examples are regulations against monopolies and pollution" (Mankiw 2009, p. 11).

Surveys of economists paint the same picture: in Kearl et al. (1979), 85% agreed with the statement that "Antitrust laws should be used vigorously to reduce monopoly power from its present level." 87.5% of the economists in the international survey reported by Frey et al. (1984) agreed with the same statement, and only 12% of Australian economists (most of whom were educated in the US and Europe) in 2011 disagreed with this statement.

The view proffered in this book is again identical to the mainstream economics view, but I will point out some of the issues hidden from this mainstream view. As with trade barriers, those who lobby in favor of continued unregulated private monopolies invariably argue that the existence of these monopolies somehow benefits society as a whole and not just themselves, which is puzzling because such pretense "should" (from the economists' viewpoint) be transparent, hence pointless, and therefore not a behavior that we observe. Moreover, there is the question of why one should trust the regulators, and then in particular why one should trust *economists* as regulators. When the whole rationale of regulation rests on the fact that one does not trust the regulated monopolist to do the right thing for society as a whole, why should one trust that the regulating economist will do the right thing for society as a whole? This question only deepens if one reflects on the fact that the regulators are legally supposed to work in support of the well-being of the country as a whole. What kind of entity then is this "country-as-a-whole," and why is a regulator in practice bound to its well-being? In other words, who regulates the regulator? Of course, no one person does. There is an implicit trust in the way that economists as a group monitor themselves and are trained, and it is this trust that underpins society's trust in them as regulators. This dynamic is important to understand, if only to have an idea of the limits of "benevolent regulation."

Environmental regulation

The classic environmental policy question faced by society is what to do with entities that pollute some public space with their activities. Examples include industries that pump dangerous toxins into the air as by-products of what they produce, individuals who pollute the public space with their garbage, and countries that over-fish the oceans to the extent that global fish stocks are threatened, to the detriment of all other countries' fishing industries.

The mainstream economic approach to this problem is to identify the underlying market imperfection that yields the undesired outcome, and then – similarly to when correcting monopoly situations – to enforce the cheapest incentives-based solution that returns society as nearly as possible to what would result from a competitive situation.

With regard to pollution by a domestic producer, for example, the market imperfection is that no one owns the air into which the polluter discharges his toxins, meaning that there is no one with whom the polluter can trade the right to pollute. One solution to this market imperfection is to create "emissions rights," and to sell such emissions rights to polluters, allowing them then to trade in these new rights. This has occurred in Europe and the US to manage emissions of sulfur dioxide. Another, in-principle equivalent solution is to charge the polluter the marginal cost of his pollution as borne by the rest of society, so that the polluter has an incentive to reduce his level of pollution to the socially optimal level: that is, such that at the last unit of pollution produced, the societal value of an extra unit of pollution is exactly zero. This is more or less the main tactic of governments in advanced economies in managing industrial waste disposal. It is also one of the main policy options for dealing with the problem that burning fossil fuels is warming the planet.

In the case of personal garbage, there is more than one market imperfection. First, there is no clear owner of the public space that individuals pollute. Second, the cost of monitoring the garbage-disposal behavior of all individuals is prohibitive. This implies that it is not feasible to create a garbage emissions market or to cost-price marginal garbage, because people will simply ignore any such grafted market system and pollute anyway. As a second-best solution, policy makers typically choose to make garbage disposal essentially costless for individuals by setting up a system where people simply have to put their trash outside their houses, whereupon it is collected and disposed of communally by the local government. In order to encourage recycling, governments have begun to promote social norms of garbage separation, such as when they ask the public to separate their plastics from their vegetable garbage. This appeal to ideals is not part of the mainstream economic approach, but economists do recognize the problem that high monitoring costs would make it difficult to maintain a garbage market.

In the case of international fishing, the mainstream economic observation is that no one owns the productive input, in this case the oceans. This results in a tragedy-of-the-commons problem whereby no individual country has an incentive to leave any fish for any other country even if, when this approach is taken by all countries, stocks become so low that future fishing is endangered. Individual countries will argue, rationally, that if they do not fish the last fish then someone else will. The first-best economic solution to this market imperfection is to create ownership over the fish in the oceans. Failing that, the second-best solution is to come to an international agreement about who is allowed to fish where and for how large an amount. However, the monitoring costs of enforcing such agreements are high (as with personal garbage) because there is no international police force capable of following and protecting fish anywhere they go. As a result, third-best solutions have also come into play, such as agreements between countries about special zones where no one is allowed to fish, and which they can agree will be under the protection of a particular country or authority.

In regard to these types of problems, this book will again agree in the main with the position of mainstream economics and therefore with mainstream economic advice. Yet in this problem we are starting to encounter phenomena outside of the traditional purview of economists – in particular, social norms. Social norms have a role to play in regard to garbage collection, and even in regard to industrial waste disposal: governments make appeals to their citizens and firms to "do the right thing" in terms of waste, and it should surprise any economist to see just how positive the response to such appeals is. Separated garbage collection is now the norm in many countries, with social stigmas attached to noncompliance.[9] This has the material effect of reducing the cost of garbage collection and disposal.

Social norms are also at play in regard to many other environmental issues, such as keeping forests, river beds, or parks clean and maintained. Just think of honesty boxes in national parks, or the environmental volunteerism evidenced by Clean-Up Days. These examples bring into greater focus that humans belong to groups with standards and behavioral expectations to which they somehow feel bound. Although mainstream economics has no place for this dynamic, there seem to be such things as appeals to these "group ideals" to which many people truly respond, and which moreover can generate aggregate responses that significantly reduce the material costs of attaining good societal outcomes. Clearly, groups cannot just ask their members for anything, or else there would be no need for competition regulation.

---

[9] Viscusi, Huber, and Bell (2011) note the existence and relevance of these social norms in the case of water-bottle recycling in the US, though they argue that their predictive effect is entirely captured by the policies that change the economic incentives. Since the policies they study still do not make it worthwhile from an individual cost-benefit point of view to recycle, their findings mean that state-wide laws probably reflect social norms held at the state level.

Questions then arise about the sources and limits of group ideals themselves and of individuals' compliance with them.

Voting behavior

Elections are an important part of political systems in many countries, both for governments and for many groups within and between countries. People vote for the leaders of their national government and their local government, their staff representatives on the boards of large organizations, and the leaders of their professional societies. Voting is believed to deliver representatives who are anchored somewhat to the wishes of their electorate, and as such voting is seen as a vital input in discovering the material interests of the voting population. Voting is therefore something that governments generally wish to encourage, and policy makers may be asked to recommend interventions that would increase voter turnout. Some countries, such as Australia, fine citizens who do not vote, and others simply set up polling places and entreat people to come.

From an economist's viewpoint, the main question surrounding voting is why people bother to vote at all. There is a clear effort cost associated with voting. In some countries, such as the United States, people have to pre-register to vote, and then have to make the time to actually go to a designated polling place and cast their votes, sometimes waiting in line before being able to do so. The effort cost per capita is easily on the order of several hours per election, for which the shadow value in terms of lost income can easily reach hundreds of dollars for a given voter.

Yet, particularly in the case of large elections involving millions of voters, the odds of making a difference to the final outcome is absolutely minuscule – i.e., on the order of one in a million or less. No rational, purely self-interested person should therefore bother to vote at all, but nevertheless millions of people do bother to vote in elections all across the world. Bartels and Brady (2003) summarize the large political science literature on this phenomenon (p. 157): "The primary lesson from the three-decade attempt to explain the paradox of voting ... is that narrow self-interest is too weak to account for a great deal of political participation."

Turnout is not the only puzzling aspect of the electoral system. Political parties rely on millions of volunteers, who give up years of their lives in order to campaign for their parties, and who are often highly educated people with high potential earnings and great demands on their time (Freeman 1997). Given the minuscule odds of reaching a sufficient number of voters that they can honestly claim to have made a difference, why do these volunteers bother?

Mainstream economics has recognized this puzzle for a long time, but it has had great difficulties fitting observed voting behavior into its central story. In an early attempt to explain voting with classic economic arguments, Downs (1957) appealed to the idea that people can rationally justify voting if they believe they have a good chance of changing the result of an election. This type of explanation has since been regarded as unsatisfactory because of the implausibility of believing one is pivotal if millions of others also vote; hence, other explanations were sought. Harsanyi (1977) explained voting (p. 650) by appealing to the idea that people get utility from behaving in accordance with internal moral standards, via what could be described as a "warm glow." Blais (2000) similarly appeals to a notion of civic duty when explaining voting. Feddersen and Sandroni (2006) formalize this further in a model that has a role for both costs and a warm glow of voting. Others, such as Faravelli and Walsh (2011), argue that voting occurs because individuals care about the policy that others have to endure and thus invoke a paternalistic group-oriented utility to rationalize voting. Benabou and Tirole (2006) similarly appeal to nonselfish motives when they observe more broadly (p. 1652) that "[p]eople commonly engage in activities that are costly to themselves and that primarily benefit others. They volunteer, help strangers, vote, give to political or charitable organizations, donate blood, join rescue squads, or even sacrifice their life for strangers."

These papers and many others show how mainstream academic journals have in recent decades turned to nonmaterial motives as an explanation for voting. Yet, these explanations are incomplete, taking existing groups as given without wondering how individuals become attached to them, or else invoking a potentially limitless amount of altruism towards the rest of society that is incompatible with their everyday, "normal" greedy behavior. Why individuals should get a warm glow from voting and not from, say, washing their neighbor's car every Saturday, is unclear. As a result, the dominant "altruism" explanations have not yet been incorporated into broader economic thinking: they take for granted many aspects of the phenomena that need explaining.

The view this book will work towards is that individual voters have myriad idealistic and group-oriented motivations that make them vote and volunteer, and hence that voting and volunteering behavior is not motivated by a conscious perception of direct economic benefit. Rather, individuals care about their own ideals and opinions, and they view the act of voting or political volunteering as a signal of this care. What is more, they truly identify in some measure with political groups, and they vote as an expression of their group identities. Admittedly, these very ideals, opinions, and political groups can form around shared material interests, such that there is still an "ultimate" personal material benefit associated with activities like voting and volunteering. Nevertheless, this association with material interests is indirect and an individual would still not vote from the perspective of his conscious, material cost-benefit calculus. So, even for the person who consistently votes for policies in his material interests, the voting act itself is still a reflection of idealism and group identification.

Tax-paying behavior

Taxation too lies at the core of the system of governance of any country, and is understandably a fixture in many scholars' definitions of government. On one extreme, Rousseau envisaged taxation in terms of a "social contract" between the taxers and the taxed, whereby those who tax should do so in the name and for the ultimate benefit of those paying the tax (Rousseau 1762). In Rousseau's vision, which is more or less the dominant view today, the taxers represent society, and collected taxes are spent on things that enhance the health and wealth of that society. Other scholars instead view taxation as a form of theft by the powerful, legitimized by state propaganda (Charles 1993). On this question, policy makers may seek advice regarding how to increase tax compliance.[10]

Yet from an economic standpoint, the most fundamental question in the analysis of tax-paying behavior is not why tax compliance is

---

[10] They may also seek advice about how much tax to levy in different scenarios, or what type of tax to levy, in which case the recommendations of economists can come in quite handy.

not perfect. Rather, it is why so many individuals and organizations willingly pay so much tax, and do not put substantially more effort into avoiding or minimizing their taxes. In their review of the earlier literature, Andreoni, Erard, and Feinstein (1998) posit (p. 819) that "[e]conomists have traditionally modeled tax cheating as if it were adding one more risky asset to a household's portfolio. However, many households comply more fully than is predicted by this approach." Similarly, Frey and Meier (2004) remark (p. 1717) that "[m]any important activities, such as charitable giving, voting, and paying taxes, are difficult to explain by the narrow self-interest hypothesis."

Accordingly, Frey and Meier (2004) and Torgler, Schneider, and Schaltegger (2009) pose tax compliance as a puzzle to economists because the odds of being found to have avoided paying tax are extremely low, and moreover, the punishment for being found to have avoided taxation is also fairly minor in many countries.[11] From a simple cost-benefit point of view, then, self-interested individuals in advanced economies should be paying much less in taxes than they are. This puzzle casts a significant shadow on the ability of mainstream economics to deliver sound recommendations about how to increase tax compliance.

As added evidence that tax compliance is not well-explained by material incentives, Slemrod (2007) reports that the penalty for detected tax evasion had no effect on the compliance levels in the studies he reviewed. The stylized finding is that it is not so much the size of the fine but more the probability of detection that is a deterrent for tax evasion, which makes no sense from a material cost-benefit point of view.

As with voting, the somewhat older mainstream economics view was that observed tax compliance is a simple function of incentives.

---

[11] This assertion is not entirely uncontested. Slemrod (2007) notes that even though the possibility of a tax audit is typically lower than 1 percent for nonbusinesses and the fines are no more than 10 percent of the evaded amount of tax, various forms of observable income can only be hidden by additional effort that would raise suspicion. Most importantly, labor earnings within large organizations are administered by those organizations and cannot easily be hidden by the worker. While this may be true, the same workers display far more tax compliance with respect to their dividend earnings, rent, capital gains, and other more easily hidden sources of income than would make sense given the regime of low detection rates and fines. Indeed, Slemrod (2007) acknowledges that the levels of tax compliance with respect to corporate income, rent, royalty, capital gains, and other forms of income are too high from a pure cost-benefit point of view.

According to this view, more people will comply with tax regulations if the odds of being found to be dishonest are increased (Allingham and Sandmo 1972). There is certainly a clear relation between the ease with which taxes can be evaded and the degree to which they are evaded (Klepper and Nagin 2000). Yet the puzzle of high overall compliance remains.

To explain high tax compliance in the face of low material incentives to comply, several papers in economics have tried to argue either that individuals misperceive the true probabilities of being found out (Sandmo 2005) or that there is some hidden benefit to paying taxes, such as in terms of signaling to neighbors (Posner 2000). However, paying taxes is even more difficult than voting behavior to rationalize on materialistic grounds because the costs of paying taxes are so formidable: on average, governments collect approximately 35 percent of their nations' income in taxes. For most taxpayers, this implies a cost associated with tax compliance that is far larger than the cost of voting. The degree of irrationality and/or the amount of signaling value required to explain the high degree of observed tax compliance as simply a reflection of material self-interest are therefore daunting enough to invalidate these explanations.

It is more in the behavioral economics literature on tax morale that we see arguments invoking notions of social norms, such as "reciprocity towards the state," or other explanations not grounded in material self-interest, such as "tax-paying habit."

Scholars in this behavioral economics literature have sought evidence that people's identification with the spending plans of the state is related to their level of tax compliance. Typical empirical approaches in this literature involve randomly sending taxpayers letters telling them about how taxes are spent, or earmarking taxes to pay for something specific (see, e.g., Torgler et al. 2009). An important stylized fact in this literature is that tax compliance is far greater in countries with strong internal identification with the government as a whole (such as the countries of northwest Europe, where governments are seen as "legitimate") than in countries where that identification is lacking, such as in Russia or countries in Latin America. Frey and Meier (2004) explicitly appeal to the idea that reciprocity within groups is required to explain tax compliance behavior.[12]

---

[12] In his review of models of reciprocal behavior, Sobel (2005) (p. 392) defines reciprocity as "a tendency to respond to perceived kindness with kindness

The dominant explanation of Aldrich (1993), Frey and Meier (2004), Benabou and Tirole (2006), and Torgler et al. (2009) is quite similar to what I will argue in this book. Both voting and paying taxes, I will argue, are intimately related to the loyalty that individuals feel towards the groups they are part of, as well as to the social norm within those groups that paying taxes is a form of reciprocity that is reasonable to expect of group members.[13]

In my story, coercion is initially required in order to achieve tax compliance of populations, as reflected in the heavy fines and constant monitoring that were needed to induce compliance when taxation was first introduced as a regular phenomenon by royal courts in Europe. Many tax revolts occurred over the centuries. Yet, in time, populations did start to self-identify as groups, complete with elected and otherwise "legitimate" representatives, and paying taxes became "the right thing to do." Adhering to this social norm is now, like voting, a form of showing loyalty to internal notions of proper behavior, taught and encouraged by our formal education systems and by the communities in which we grow up. What started as very reluctant compliance with the demands of those who held the swords became a habit of thought over time that only needs minimal monitoring to be sustained in the modern age.

The low levels of punishment for tax noncompliance in modern economies derive from the implicit interpretation that noncompliance mainly stems from mistakes or ignorance of the tax law.[14] Low fines reflect a social norm around this generous interpretation: the group as a whole expects that even those found to have evaded or avoided taxes did not really mean to do so, and should therefore not be punished too harshly for their mistakes. As such, the present system of low monitoring and low punishment accompanies an equilibrium of social norms through which the majority of the real monitoring and punishment is not actually accomplished by tax authorities, but by the whole society, in which tax evasion is held to be something shameful.

---

and perceived meanness with meanness and to expect this behavior from others."

[13] See also Bolton and Ockenfels (2000) on the central role of reciprocity within groups.

[14] In the present day, compliance is not just about low levels of tax evasion, which is illegal, but also about low levels of tax avoidance, which is not illegal but can still be socially frowned upon.

It is worth repeating that tax compliance is not a peripheral issue in the workings of modern economies. On the contrary, getting people to pay taxes is probably the single most important ingredient supporting our entire system of governance, and as such it is astounding that mainstream economic thinking does not include a coherent story for why individuals are so tax compliant.[15] Indeed, in none of the twenty-five most popular economic textbooks is the topic of tax morale or tax compliance a chapter.[16]

Returning to the original policy question, what recommendations should be given to those wishing to increase tax compliance? While a student naïvely following the mainstream economic textbook story would opt for an increase in monitoring and punishment of non-compliers, the story in this book would advise that only as an initial step. I argue that the real key to continued tax compliance is to maintain the degree to which the taxed can identify with the taxers via "nationhood activities" such as televised inaugurations, swearing allegiance to the flag at school, national sporting events, and the like. Punishing tax evasion then serves simply to maintain the social norm of tax compliance by publicly reprimanding those who too obviously flout the norm.

---

[15] One might claim that property rights are, if not as important as tax compliance, at least a close second in terms of fundamental ingredients required for our socioeconomic system to function. Property rights are inventions of large groups, and are explicitly enforced by group institutions such as the police and the courts. Yet they are also embedded in social norms of respecting other people's property, as well as by habits of thought: we are taught to be comfortable with the idea that not everything is ours. The history and development of property rights has been discussed in countless books inside and outside of economics (e.g., Weber 1922, Weber 1923, Hirschman and Vaughan 1983, Bowles 1998), but as with tax morale, fully understanding property rights involves concepts that lie outside the purview of mainstream economics, such as power and social norms. My review of economic textbooks uncovered none that start with this problem or incorporate a sensible answer to it in the overall view of the economy presented to students.

[16] The topics of tax incidence and the size of tax revenues are of course mentioned in most textbooks, but those topics do not really address the question of how to increase or maintain tax compliance. The only textbook I found that briefly mentions the problem of tax compliance is Tucker 2010 (seventh edition), which spends pages 352–357 on "The art of taxation," but still includes no interpretation of what high tax compliance means for how we should view our societies.

Symbolic expenses

I define symbolic expenses as costs paid towards a cause in the absence
of a realistic story in the minds of those paying about how the expense
is going to materially affect the cause. Symbolic expenses, which can
take the form of money or effort, can most easily be identified as such
with the benefit of hindsight and distance. Obvious examples include
the sacrifices that the ancient Greeks made to their gods supposedly in
order to bargain for favors from them, or the more modern Chinese
practice of burning fake money supposedly in order to bring good luck
to loved ones. All known ancient societies had some form of sacrifice,
ranging from the neolithic farmers of Eurasia, who sacrificed their own
sons and daughters apparently in an attempt to buy good harvests, to
the rain dancers of Africa whose livelihoods depended so clearly on
rain. Every known modern society still retains some practices that are
clearly sacrificial in nature, such as tossing coins into wishing wells to
buy luck, or praying to an unseen entity for miracles. Another modern
example is the "40-Hour Famine" initiative promoted by the charity
World Vision, in which participants were asked to fast for forty hours
on August 17–19, 2012, in a show of solidarity with hungry people in
Africa.

The connection of symbolic expenses to a policy objective is less
obvious than in the case of prior examples, but to the extent that policy makers are interested in the efficient allocation of resources, they
might wish to reallocate expenses that are not producing a clear benefit.
If symbolic expenses are truly a pure waste, then it should be a natural core activity of economists to say publicly that they are wasteful
and to argue against them. However, perhaps surprisingly, mainstream economics has almost nothing to say about symbolic expenses.
Symbolic expenses are not mentioned in any of the twenty-five most
popular textbooks, including those that make space for "heterodox"
approaches, nor are symbolic expenses mentioned in standard surveys
of economists.

As a result, mainstream economics lacks even the categories into
which one could fit many symbolic expenses. To fast for forty hours
without creating a direct material benefit for oneself or anyone else
would not even be classified as altruism, since there is no obvious
benefit of the fasting to anyone else. It would be entirely possible for
a freshly minted PhD graduate in economics never to have heard of

such phenomena or to have wondered why they are observed, apart from being fed the universal line that "economists do not argue about tastes" and that any such frivolities are hence not part of any economic problem.

Yet it is not "tastes" but rather a type of implicit exchange that is involved, since those making these expenses make them, in their minds, in order to get something back. Ancient neolithic people surely did not sacrifice their own children because they enjoyed seeing their loved ones die. They probably thought that it was the only way they could buy good harvests and thereby prevent even more catastrophic loss of life. Similar things can be said for the contributors of other symbolic expenses: they believe that some unseen entity will reciprocate their expense with some favor.

A few mainstream economists have recognized the existence of symbolic expenses and tried to rationalize them. A well-known example is the theory of Iannaccone and Berman (2006), who hypothesize that large symbolic religious expenses are like club entry fees, where the clubs are religious sects and the entry fees ensure that only people who truly wish to cooperate with each other and thus are prepared to pay the fees will end up in the club. Bearing in mind the types of symbolic expenses often made by worshippers and the benefits offered by organized religious sects, this theory implies that some worshippers will forgo sex before marriage in order to gain entry to a club whose members jointly organize jobs, education, and child care. While this is an ingenious explanation for some sacrifices, it does imply that people do not truly believe the stories they tell about their own sacrifices, e.g., that sex before marriage is "against God's wishes." Also, this theory cannot explain the phenomenon of people making symbolic expenses without anyone seeing their sacrifices, which does happen regularly, as evidenced by anonymous church donations or private prayer. In short, it does not fit the psychology and widespread use of sacrifices, though it may well be an apt description of the economic role of sacrifices in particular religious groups.

What makes symbolic expenses especially intriguing is that one cannot always say for sure which expenses are really symbolic, and hence just how widespread symbolic expenses really are. One reason for this is that one cannot argue about the extent to which a current expense is symbolic without upsetting those who make the expense. Which devout Christian wants to hear that lighting candles in the church will not soothe anyone in the afterlife; which devout Buddhist will be happy to be told that living well will not result in coming back as a higher life form; and which devout Muslim wants to hear that the 10 percent of his income he pays to charity will not lead to a spot in heaven? The same is true of those making sacrifices towards causes outside the realm of religion. Which fervent environmentalist wants to hear that introducing a subsidy for renewable energy might harm the environment because it encourages the further destruction of forests to make way for biofuel production?

I will not argue that any of these expenses is necessarily purely symbolic, but they are without doubt important examples of substantial contributions towards unseen abstractions made by large numbers of people who cannot point to a visible, realistic mechanism via which they will lead to the desired outcome. Each is a faith-based expense, which is seen by the person making the expense as a kind of *quid pro quo* between himself and the unseen entity that is supposed to reciprocate the sacrifice by handing down a favor.

It is entirely possible that symbolic sacrifices form unrecognized parts of many "normal" expenses made by both individuals and governments. Private school tuition fees are a good example. Are the parents who pay these fees making a symbolic expense towards their own internal notion of what parents should do for their children, in the absence of a realistic idea that the expense is actually going to help? This would only be true in the case that the alternative education, such as free state school, is just as good, and where there is no other visible benefit. This is difficult for an outsider to verify. It is thus possible that some private school fees are purely symbolic expenses, and even that the parents themselves might know that they are symbolic, but it would be virtually impossible for an outside observer to argue convincingly that such an expense is symbolic rather than a rational investment to materially help the child.

Many examples of symbolic expenses can be found in the political whims of a population. A population may, for example, support raising taxes in order to "do something about the health crisis." It is quite probable that the vast majority of the population has no idea how the tax increase is actually going to improve health outcomes, and also quite probable that in reality the increased health expenditures will just end up as increased salaries for those already in the health industry, without resulting in an improvement in any health outcome.

The rule of thumb I offer is that an expense is probably symbolic in character if the individual making the expense neither knows nor cares about the actual mechanisms via which the expense is supposed to have its beneficial effects. I will argue that this is because the person already believes, whether consciously or unconsciously, that the expense will have a payoff. It is then the job of the economist to argue that the group making the expense has better things to do with its resources, or at least to subvert the process so that the headline expenditure is far greater than the actual expenditure.

The self-image of economists

A question for any science is whether the outside image of its activities and the self-image of its practitioners are consistent with its own theories of how the world works.

Economists clearly comprise a recognizable group, with educational institutions, social norms dictating proper behavior (e.g., no overt rent-seeking), expectations that people do the right thing for the group (e.g., helping in the peer review process), and an array of societies and elections of leaders into those societies.

Moreover, the dominant point of view taught to young economists is that one should think in terms of what is optimal for society as a whole. Economists are supposed to work out the "first-best" solution that a benevolent "social planner" would enforce; we are supposed to see market imperfections with an objective eye and either inform the proper authorities of their existence or actively campaign for an optimal solution. While we are rarely taught explicitly how we should view ourselves, I would say that the implicit self-image of the mainstream economist is that of someone whose main professional objective is to discover the truth about the economic system or some aspect of it, so that he may ultimately advocate policies that improve the welfare of society as a whole.

Naturally, many economists take subtly different positions. For some, such as the chief economists of commercial banks, the group whose welfare they have in mind is not society as a whole, but the company or organization for which they work. For others, such as retired academics writing their last books, there are few other goals but the pursuit of truth.

A singularly problematic aspect of this self-image is that truth-obsession and do-gooder attitudes do not feature in the models we economists have of the rest of society. If the economist is such a noble person, or at least not someone only motivated by the income he earns by being an economist, then what accounts for his commitment to truth-seeking and welfare maximization? Moreover, where else do truth-obsession and do-gooding appear in our economies, and why have we economists not modeled these aspects of humanity?

One possible answer is to see economists as the sole exceptions to the rule – that is, to take economists themselves outside of the set of phenomena one attempts to explain via economic theories. Another possible answer is that most economists are lying through their teeth when they claim to be truth-seeking or interested in maximizing social welfare, and are instead indeed just maximizing their personal gain, as their models predict that they should. This explanation still requires some unknown reason why economists then feel they need to justify themselves by arguing that their purpose is to benefit society as a whole.

It gets worse. The type of economist who depicts the rest of the world as being inhabited by agents who are rational and have complete information is, by implication, redundant. Instead of working out how the economic system works, such an economist could simply walk up to the first person on the street and ask him how the economy works, the probability distribution of interest rates next year, and so on. This may seem an exaggerated example, since many such economists claim to assume only that agents behave "as if" they are rational, but this claim implies an appeal to some unknown and un-modeled process via which individuals' actual behavior happens to coincide with what they would do if they truly were rational, without exploring whether irrationality in the absence of this unknown process would lead to different results. If the standard economic agent exhibits irrationality, why do mainstream economists not model it explicitly?

There is, in sum, a certain amount of fudge involved in on the one hand viewing society as being made up of greedy and clever individuals, while on the other hand viewing oneself as a useful truth-seeker who works for the ultimate benefit of society as a whole. This book reconciles these two phenomena by adopting the view that economists form a "reciprocal group" of "somewhat equals," that itself creates ideals (social norms) of transparency and truth-seeking that match the role that economists play within the larger groups in which they operate.

It is the perceived success of economists-as-a-group that gives the individual practitioner his status and makes him comply with the behavior necessary for him to continue to be recognized as part of that group. At the group level, a somewhat evolutionary process of competing subgroups and competing disciplines steers the group of economists towards those ideals and aggregate opinions that are in its best material interests, giving rise eventually to the adoption of ideals that are ultimately self-serving in terms of the robust continuation of the group. At the individual level, many a practitioner actually believes in the group ideals and acts accordingly, which in turn keeps honest all those economists for whom the group ideals are nothing more than fluff.

I will argue in this book that economists are just one of many reciprocal groups in society, each of which has its own ideals that more or less fit its role in society as a result of the type of evolution of ideals sketched above. Individuals belong to many groups at the same time, and actively search for groups that advance their interests, slowly becoming more fervent members of a group in some circumstances and slowly losing their fervor in other circumstances. Rather than being the exception, economists are normal people: what goes for economists goes for others.

The task ahead

The object of this book is to explain the core aspects of our socioeconomic system. This core includes not only the problems that mainstream economics already successfully addresses, such as those involved with trade, regulation, and the optimal treatment of lobby groups. It also includes our system of taxation, our political structures, and the scale and efficacy of symbolic expenditures. Within the explanation provided, our own actions as social scientists must make sense as an integrated part of the whole, rather than being seen as an exception. The story constructed must furthermore make sense of the major historical developments involved in shaping the institutions we now have, such as the way in which taxation arose, and the way in which we moved from autocratic political structures that favored small elites to the current dominant structure in which those in power are more or less held to account by their populations, both via elections and via social norms.

To construct such a story and have it ultimately hang together as one piece of cloth, I will incorporate into the existing mainstream economic framework the concepts of love, groups, power, and networks. Such concepts have been talked about and discussed for centuries. The challenge in writing this book has been to incorporate them in such a way that they do not lead to the loss of what has been gained in mainstream economics by ignoring them.

Perhaps the most significant piece of the puzzle that I will add is a theory of the genesis of love. I will argue in this book that humans have an almost unshakeable propensity to believe that anything they cannot directly control, but which they nevertheless believe to be capable of doing something useful for them, is amenable to a bribe. This belief extends to entities that are unseen and might not even exist. This contention will form a cornerstone of the theory of love in this book. I will argue that we love people and entities because our unconscious mind has tried to strike an implicit bargain with them. This basic tendency will be argued to play a key role in the development of groups and group ideals. Just as mainstream economists, including myself, would argue that our greed colors everything we do, so too will I argue that our innate tendency to believe in the reciprocity of the unseen or otherwise uncontrollable is present in almost every sphere of human life.

Methodological considerations

It is not obvious how to approach these broad topics. One could imagine building up a mathematical model from first principles; constructing a broader macro-model with the aim of providing falsifiable predictions at the potential cost of being wrong at the micro-level; or embarking on a major literature review in which average opinions are distilled around a set of pre-chosen topics. Each of these choices comes with an inherent value system.

I have made methodological choices for this book based on the nature of the ideal theory being targeted, the feasibility and inherent biases of different research processes, and the inherent morality of each process and its likely result.

The ideal theory
The approach I take is positivist and empirical in the sense that I look for consistent stories that can describe and predict phenomena of interest. I will thus be looking for a description of loyalty that is descriptive

of loyalty relations seen in reality, as well as predictive of the means by which one can engender loyalty in individuals and whole societies. Similarly, I will be looking for stories that describe and predict group formation, that describe and predict power dynamics, and that describe and predict network formation.

The ideal theory hence is one that explains and predicts phenomena of interest, that is potentially falsifiable in a Popperian sense but survives such tests, and that has prescriptive power useful for decision makers. Furthermore, all aspects of the ideal theory would fit together to form a logically consistent whole, and the relation between each aspect of the theory and every other aspect would be clear and testable.

The actual process and the ensuing theory

The ideal of an internally consistent, falsifiable, single model incorporating all of the phenomena discussed above will not be reached in this book due to the range and complexity of the phenomena addressed. Yet, the ideal of reaching falsifiable conclusions and generating internally consistent stories of how concepts relate to each other and predict phenomena of interest still permeates the endeavor. The method I use is a blend of logical empiricism, analog reasoning, and pragmatism.

Pragmatism underpins the limited scope and integrability of the various substories in the individual chapters: I cannot give a falsifiable, internally consistent mathematical model whose constituents could all reasonably be measured and that combines all of the elements I wish to combine. At best, I can generate mathematical models that combine a few elements to mimic some of the real-world phenomena I am trying to capture, and some of these models are given in Chapter 6. The best I can offer, in addition to proofs of concept for each of the substories (love, groups, power, and networks), is an outline of how these substories combine to explain the grander phenomena that arise from them.

This pragmatism is no more than a reflection of the situation in which we already find ourselves in social science. All we currently have are consistent stories about small parts of our societies, and vaguer stories about how the smaller parts fit together in an overall view. Almost any two different models in economics formally clash. For example, the mainstream model one uses to analyze the competition between two firms will differ in its assumptions from the model one uses to analyze the effect of interest rate rises on house prices. While they formally clash and are mutually inconsistent, both models can nevertheless incorporate some basic concepts such as wealth maximization and rationality. Whether to apply the model of competition or of inflation depends on the object of analysis. There is an implicit background heuristic that determines which model comes to mind when one is faced with the phenomenon of interest. This itself is a form of pragmatism, in that "we economists" rely on pattern recognition to decide which model is deemed appropriate for which circumstance.

Another example of pragmatism in economics is the market demand-and-supply cross that appears in all the major introductory economic textbooks. That market cross comes with a story about excess supply or demand when prices are above or below equilibrium, causing the "invisible hand" of the market to readjust prices so that there is neither excess demand nor excess supply. Yet, the market cross is incompatible with Walrasian general equilibrium theory, wherein only the intersection of the demand curve and supply curve has an interpretation: all the other points are out of equilibrium and thus cannot be interpreted. Put simply, the market cross does not exist in general equilibrium theory. This inconsistency, which arises because there is no actual mechanism in general equilibrium theory for price formation, will only become clear to economists after many years of training. One can interpret this inconsistency in two ways: either general equilibrium theory is a poor codification of the much older ideas behind the market cross, or else the market cross is a convenient but imperfect didactic tool for introducing the ideas in general equilibrium theory. Nevertheless, both general equilibrium theory and the market-cross story share similar substories, embodied in their assumptions about agents and market interactions.

One should see the theories in this book in the same way. The individual theories on greed, love, groups, and networks are each designed to fit particular core observations, but only when simplified and joined in particular ways can they be used to explain bigger phenomena.

Another aspect of the approach followed in this book is analog reasoning, which comes into play when devising the individual theories themselves. Candidate theories to capture love, groups, power, and networks were generated by viewing those concepts through different potential metaphors. The final metaphorical representation for each concept was selected based on its fit to the core phenomena targeted by that concept, as well as the ability of the theory generated using that representation to help in the wider endeavor. By and large, only the final theory for each concept is presented in this book, rather than all the metaphors and associated theories that were tried and discarded along the way.

As an illustration of analog reasoning, suppose one wants to model the economic phenomenon of labor migration. One way to view labor migration is to think of it as a flowing river. Within that metaphor, one can appeal to concepts that capture the key aspects of flowing rivers. For argument's sake, take the key image of a flowing river to consist of gravity, a fluid, and some resistant surface.

In the context of migration, the role of gravity can be taken up by "wage differences," the role of fluid can be taken up by "home populations," and the role of the resistant surface can be played by "migration institutions." By then making appropriate assumptions about those aspects of the phenomenon, one can come up with mental models that mimic migration flows, "explained" by the concepts of wage differences, populations, and institutions. One can mold this stylized representation into a mathematical model and estimate parts of it. Yet the way one came up with the idea that wages, populations, and institutions were the key aspects to model was first to envisage labor migration as a flowing river.

The flowing river analogy can be further expanded. By seeing gravity as a kind of composite force pulling on the fluid, one can re-imagine the role of gravity to be played by many different concepts that mimic gravity. One could thus replace the role of wage differences by that of "cultural proximity" or "relative peacefulness." One can even think of gravity as a factor that itself has various components and thus encompasses all three candidates at once (wage differentials, cultural proximity, and peacefulness).

Working out the parallels between a flowing river and labor migration is but a single possibility. There are many more potential metaphors, which lead one to think of different models.

One can, for example, think of labor migration as a form of hunting, in which case the core roles to fill are very different. Suppose one takes the basic image of hunting as one of hunters, prizes, and snares. Within an economic model of migration, the role of hunters would be taken up by companies wanting to hire workers; the role of the prize that motivates the hunter would be played by the productivity of potential migrants; and the role of the snare would be taken up by labor contracts. As with the flowing river analogy, the hunting analogy can easily be formally modeled, expanded in many ways, and tested. One can even run the hunting metaphor against the flowing river metaphor by comparing their respective abilities to generate a model that explains actual migration flows, or enlightens a research audience about the process of migration. Yet other metaphors that come to mind when thinking of international labor migration might be those of conquering armies, or spreading diseases, and the usefulness of these could be evaluated in similar fashion.

In sum, there are many ways in which one can frame an initial phenomenon, and many resulting ways in which one can generate concepts to explain and predict it. In principle, one can line up many metaphors and evaluate which one is best in terms of predicting the core phenomenon originally targeted, or in the sense of whether the concepts used fit in with other phenomena one would also like to explain.[17] It is precisely those two criteria, i.e., the ability to fit the core phenomena originally targeted by the concept, and the ability to fit in with other theories used for other problems, that have guided my selection of theories for each core concept.

Selecting core concepts from the social science literature

Once one has hit upon a set of core concepts with associated core phenomena one wants those concepts to explain, the processes of analog reasoning, pragmatism, and positivism explained above can be used. But how are the core concepts themselves chosen? Why are greed, love, groups, and networks taken to be the prime concepts, rather than other major concepts in social science, such as, say, identity, social norms, institutions, and human capital? How do the concepts presented as "core" relate to the apparently more subsidiary concepts?

The answer is that what this book presents as the core concepts to add to the existing one of greed were selected by trial and error. There was no reason at the outset to designate the concepts of love, groups, and networks as core, rather than any of the many dozens of equally prominent concepts in social science. It was purely a question of which minimal set of concepts generated the maximum gain in terms of reasonably explained phenomena, and in terms of the ease with which

---

[17] Gilboa, Postlewaite, Samuelson, and Schmeidler (2012) also discuss the nature and value of analog reasoning in economics.

the group of concepts themselves fit together. The choice is thus purely an *ex post* one.

Each core concept itself is approached as if one neither is an economist nor has any larger agenda as to the phenomena outside of the single concept. This approach, taken in each of the chapters, is a form of "temporary ignorance" that helps to avoid the temptation of starting with what is considered accepted wisdom in some discipline and then pressing other questions into that mold whether or not they really fit.

Potential core concepts are then weeded out when one suspends that temporary ignorance and evaluates how well each of the candidate concepts describes a target set of core phenomena, the degree to which they clash with other concepts already deemed necessary to explain other phenomena, and their out-of-sample performance with regard to phenomena one was not initially targeting with the concept in question.

This also implies that while the book does not present separate theories of social norms, freedom, identity, institutions, and so forth, along the way all such concepts were extensively reviewed for their suitability as core concepts. Many other such concepts indeed have a natural place in this book, for they arise organically from the interplay amongst the concepts designated as core. The distinction between core concepts and other existing concepts is not meant as an implicit judgment on the innate usefulness of different concepts.

As an example, the organization of violence will turn out to be a crucial part of group power, as one might expect. The only reason I do not present a lengthy treatise on the organization of violence is that such a viewpoint simply turned out not to be very fruitful when seeking to explain many phenomena. There is, for example, a relationship between the organization of violence and the self-image of economists, and even one between the organization of violence and sacrificial behavior, but the relationships are very convoluted and not intuitively clear. Yet, from the concepts of greed, love, groups, and networks, it should be clear by the end of the book how organized violence relates to all of the examples above, and more. Similarly, along the way, institutions, social norms, identity, and many other concepts will be placed, implicitly or explicitly, in the overarching story.

The reason not to discuss all of the potential sets of core concepts is that there is simply no point in regurgitating all of the mental activity that led to this book. Doing otherwise would simply waste the reader's time in wading through all the failed combinations, or the thoughts that were silly, clearly untrue, or plain useless with the benefit of hindsight. Instead, I mainly present the story as it unfolded *ex post facto*. The core concepts that are claimed to "do the job" themselves suggest where the main caveats lie in existing mainstream economic stories, and what the best evidence is for alternative stories.

In order to see how my final result relates to the existing literature, each chapter on a core concept contains sections dedicated to discussing the most prominent ways in which existing literature treats that concept, as well as the similarities and differences between the view I offer and those offered by prior thinkers.

The morality of the endeavor

How does the process explained above relate to the criticism made by philosophers of logical positivism and modern economists such as Mark Blaug and Amartya Sen? Blaug (1985) and Sen (1988) denounce the claims of detachment often made by economists and call for a more ethical approach to economics, in which economists recognize more openly that they are political actors.

Where this book is unashamedly and somewhat radically positivist is in its rejection of any recognized *ex ante* moral viewpoint as the "right way" of looking at something. Not only that, but I have sought stories involving an explanation for the existence and direction of moral feelings, without in any way saying beforehand that this or that moral viewpoint is "right."

Yet the book is also unashamedly ethical in that the problems looked at are not random. I have not spent my intellectual energy on counting the number of grains of sand on a beach, but rather on trying to understand the politics of international trade, the motivations behind symbolic expenses, the realistic policy options to reduce the severity of recessions, the how and why of migration in China, and other affairs of humans.

The choice of how to spend one's time is inherently ethical, and in my case driven to a large extent by what economists as a group have taken on as their "core business." By not spending time on other phenomena, "economists" are implicitly saying that those phenomena are not important enough to merit their time, which is explicitly or implicitly a judgment of value, or at the minimum a recognition of the limits of their territory.

The goal of this book – to generate stories that do a good job of describing and predicting major socioeconomic phenomena at minimum intellectual cost – is somewhat postmodern in that the goal itself inherently accepts that economics plays a role inside "society" from which its practitioners ultimately derive their status and income, and that there is value in performing this role better.

Moreover, as Sen and Blaug would both urge economists to do, I wish to say something of use, which in turn does imply a conscious rational judgment that it is actually beneficial to overall well-being to have a better understanding of our socioeconomic system. In this sense, both the choice of subject and the decision to disseminate are inherently moral choices.

PART I

Greed and love

1 | *Individual materialism, organizations, and power: The view from mainstream economics*

All that interests me is money.
> – Salvador Dali, quoted in Frey (2003), p. 7

This chapter reviews the mainstream economic treatments of the following broad concepts: the atomistic economic agent, the competitive forces that give rise to organizations, the defining features of trade networks, and the nature of power. For brevity, what is outlined below simply summarizes the mainstream view presented in the most popular textbooks for undergraduate and graduate students within the discipline of economics.

The goal of this chapter is to demonstrate the great predictive strength of the mainstream economic view, but it will also point out explicitly the "black boxes" that this mainstream view does not fully capture. The main point of the rest of the book is then to fill in these black boxes.

1.1 Homo Economicus: Humans as individual rational wealth maximizers

The basic workhorse model of human motivations in modern economics contends that humans are mainly motivated by greed and rationally weigh different options for resource allocation. According to this view, an individual behaves as an "individually rational agent," trying to attain maximum personal benefit from limited material resources. George Stigler expresses the mainstream view thus: "Man is eternally a utility-maximizer – in his home, in his office (be it public or private), in his scientific work – in short, everywhere" (taken from the Tanner Lectures, quoted in McKenzie 1983). Whenever there is conflict between what satisfies Homo Economicus ("Economic Man") and what satisfies others, Homo Economicus will choose the satisfaction of his egocentric needs (Pettit 2001). In the extreme, Homo Economicus would totally destroy the well-being of others if it meant receiving even the tiniest bit of personal profit.

Despite the apparent selfishness of Homo Economicus, this model of humanity is not completely without moral appeal, because it by necessity contains an open-minded view of humans. Personal profit is mainly generated through exchange, and hence Homo Economicus is dependent upon suppliers, consumers, business partners, and even competitors for his own profit maximization. For this simple reason, all other humans are viewed by Homo Economicus merely as entities that have the potential to be directly related to his business, and therefore his behavior towards others is entirely dictated by circumstances. The atomistic economic agent is thus untainted by preconceptions or stereotypes: he does not judge his fellow humans on any basis other than their usage value. Kirchgassner (1991) characterizes Homo Economicus as possessing a "disinterested rationality" – not knowing, for example, envy nor gloating. This is a morally positive view of humanity, in the sense that it presumes the possibility of making Homo Economicus comply with any desired moral code merely by shaping his material incentives in that direction. This "morally adaptable" feature of Homo Economicus is made clear in Holler (1983) (p. 78, translated):

Contrarily to the man in baroque or rococo, who just seeks to satisfy his appetites, Homo Economicus is a calculator of happiness; he counts, measures, weighs, and decides. Even the most disparate aims and means are subject to his calculations. Nothing is excluded. On the contrary! Among the subjects of his calculations we find the most human and most noble, as love and heroism. Homo Economicus never boggles. He does not know any given world order and therefore acknowledges none. Thus he can perform his calculations on the grounds of every imaginable world order. As he is by definition neither a hero nor a saint, it is by definition not excluded that he be a hero or a saint. Nothing can prevent him from being the one or the other – and he does not have to feign or to deny himself. The only condition in pursuing his aims is that he chooses his means deliberately and at the same time is conscious of the positive or negative effects this decision has on his other goals, taking them into consideration in his decision as well. Homo Economicus is not distinguished by the quality of his aims, but by the transparency of his actions.

The singular importance of material motives in economic thinking about Homo Economicus is usually traced to Jevons (1871), and it has remained, together with its implied moral ambiguity, a strong tenet in current economic thinking.[1] One cannot overestimate the extent to which materialist explanations are ingrained amongst economists in particular. No matter how strange the cultural institution, economists will by and large construct a material explanation for it. Some clear examples of "economic explanations" of supposedly cultural phenomena are provided in one introductory economics text (Frijters, Dulleck, and Torgler 2009) and reproduced here almost verbatim:

1. Cultural inhibitions against eating cows in India. A standard economic explanation for this inhibition is that it prevents people from eating their productive future capacity when times are bad. In India, cows are a source of income and food for many people (producing milk) and are a source of transport and farming aids (producing oxen, which are used to pull carts and plow fields). They are also strong animals, able to survive famine and thus unlikely to compete with humans for food during times of scarcity. This cultural inhibition therefore protects the society's long-term survival and wealth-maximization potential by squelching "transient urges" to eat cows when food is scarce.
2. Cannibalism in meso-America in pre-Columbian times. The explanation for this offered by historical materialists is that other sources of protein were scarce, and hence these people were just being efficient with the available stock of protein.
3. Constantly changing European rules on the food labeling of Australian beef. The standard reason for this offered by mainstream economists is that these regulations are part of an attempt by the European agricultural lobby to prevent competition from Australian beef, thereby preserving their own incomes.

What underlies economists' conviction regarding the fundamental importance of materialist motives? Mainly, observation. Examples

---

[1] The basic argument that material considerations are amongst the primary movers of human behavior is also firmly established in other disciplines, though not as centrally as in economics. In the tradition of historical materialism in Marxism, sociology, and anthropology, the importance of material considerations is not even confined to individual behavior. In its most radical form, historical materialism holds that in order to understand many societal institutions (often referred to as the societal "superstructure"), one should ultimately look at the material incentives of those controlling these institutions.

abound of how people respond powerfully to material incentives in practice. Quoting directly from the same textbook (pp. 10–11):

1. Merely a week after the Russian tsar Peter the Great imposed a heavy tax on wearing beards in 1698, there was barely a whisker to be seen in the country.
2. In the Middle Ages, the Muslims modified Roman poll taxes by reducing rates and limiting their application to non-believers. It is said that this tax policy brought more converts to Islam than the sword or the Koran.
3. While guaranteeing a minimum price for wool, Australia maintained overproduction of wool in the late '80s and early '90s, thus keeping its own farmers happy while driving international wool prices down. Such a strategy is evident in the agriculture sector all around the world.
4. Prior to unification, the average age of East German women at the birth of their first child was 22.7, as opposed to 28.3 for West German women. Following unification, reproductive behavior in the eastern and western parts of Germany converged within a decade. The reason? After unification, labor markets in former East Germany underwent drastic restructuring and unemployment increased significantly. East German women were at a higher risk of unemployment and had lower chances of returning to the labor market after being unemployed than their male counterparts. This discouraged women from having their first child until later in life, because once they left the labor force for maternity leave it would be more difficult to regain employment. This induced a trend amongst East German women to have their first child later.
5. Statutory regulation of shopping hours in New Zealand, spanning 1892 to the late 1970s, limited shop trading hours during the week and banned trading on weekends. This was labeled as "culture." However, when women started entering paid work in greater numbers at the end of the '60s, they demanded longer shop trading hours and trading on weekends. Their demands led to the deregulation of trading hours in 1977, showing both how personal beliefs changed with material incentives and how public decisions were eventually changed.
6. When the European nations supported their farmers by providing export subsidies, the borders between countries saw the

phenomenon of trucks laden with agricultural produce crossing the same border in different directions dozens of times per day, simply to claim the same subsidy many times over.

As Pettit (2001) stresses, the belief that people are self-centered materialists directly informs policy: "It may be behind the assumption of economic policy-makers and institutional designers that no proposal is plausible unless it can be shown to be 'incentive-compatible': that is, unless it can be shown that people will have self-regarding reasons for going along with what the proposal requires" (p. 80).

The dominance of the wealth-maximization motive in explaining economic actions also underpins much of the material in introductory economic textbooks. As discussed in the Preview, the three most popular undergraduate economic textbooks (Mankiw 2009, McConnell, Brue, and Flynn 2011, Samuelson and Nordhaus 2010) pose the economic problem as one of making choices in a situation of material scarcity. The same is true of all twenty-five textbooks highlighted by Lopus and Paringer (2011). Tucker (2010) (p. 5) typically defines economics as "the study of scarcity and choice." Sexton (2011) (p. 47) echoes this definition and adds that "[p]eople respond to changes in incentives." Hubbard and O'Brien (2009) (p. xiv) have as one of their three key economic ideas that "[p]eople respond to economic incentives."

The wealth-maximization motive permeates standard textbooks and mainstream economic thinking more deeply than just via the definition of the economic problem and the assertion that people respond to material incentives. The explanation of opportunity cost, for example, is usually made in terms of forgone earnings or alternative forms of material consumption. Particular types of economic agents are furthermore depicted as *solely* interested in money, such as profit-maximizing firms, wage-maximizing job seekers, or "rent-seeking" political interest groups. All of these depictions can be summarized by the simple idea that humans, to a large degree, behave like wealth-maximizing individuals.

1.1.1 Homo Economicus in historical perspective

Homo Economicus emerged as an intellectual idea in the Enlightenment period. In the early Middle Ages, materialism was seen in society as strongly immoral, making it virtually impossible to talk about materially oriented humans in any but derogatory terms. At that time, Homo Economicus had the reputation of being akin to an unpleasant adolescent, and church doctrine was heavily imbued with the idea that it should counter men's evil nature by continuously advocating pious behavior (Ritzmann 1999).

Not until the thirteenth century did it become possible for upstanding citizens to suggest that humans "normally" act in their own material interests. Self-love started to be tolerated by dominant clerical scholars such as Thomas Aquinas, who was influenced by the Greek philosophers: "If a man desires a secular good in an inordinate manner, this arises from his not loving himself in an ordinate way: to love someone means to wish him good: therefore it is obvious that sin arises from inordinate self-love" (Aquinas 1935, p. 398). The key novelty in this quotation is that some degree of self-love ("loving himself in an ordinate way") is seen as reasonable and even desirable.

Over the centuries, the concept of Homo Economicus has been heavily criticized, and some scholars long ago predicted that the concept would be abandoned in favor of the idea that humans are motivated by social and political concerns rather than by purely material considerations. It was prophesied that Homo Economicus would be replaced by his rivals and opponents from the vast family of "homines," such as "Homo Sociologicus" and "Homo Politicus." Homo Economicus was insulted, being famously labeled a "pleasure machine" (Bentham 1954, Earnshaw 1997, Locke 2002), an "infamous fellow" (Verspagen 2002, Vromen 2008), and many other colorful appellations. Merquior (1991) summarizes opinion at the time as viewing Homo Economicus as a "vile materialist," an "ignoble maniac," and a "fanatic of sordid passions."[2] Nonetheless, the concept has survived until the modern day, and still dominates introductory economic textbooks.

Whether Homo Economicus is a reasonable depiction of the main mental activities and motivations of humans has been hotly debated within economics. Many economists felt that what was important was

[2] By the same token, economists have been scathing about the alternative simplified views of humanity on offer. Some economists regarded Homo Sociologicus as a "conformist enslaved by conventions" (p. 73 of Brunner and Meckling 1977), who "is not an evaluator, any more than ants, bees and termites are evaluators" (p. 552 of Meckling 1976).

less whether the internal psychology of humans was being adequately captured, and more whether the ensuing predictions of the Homo Economicus model fit reality. Dahrendorf (1968) remarked many years ago in this respect (p. 92):

In economic theory the protracted argument over whether a Homo Economicus who permanently weighs profits and losses is a realistic image of man's economic behaviour has been decided: literal realism is quite unnecessary so long as the theories based on the model provide powerful explanations and useful predictions.

This view has appeal, in that it absolves the economist of the need to defend the indefensible. After all, it is undeniable that Homo Economicus does not contain a perfect description of how humans behave. How could one possibly claim that greed is the reason that people pray, hug their children, give to charity, or defend their country in wartime? Taken at face value, the quotation above implies that historical debates about whether or not humans "really" consciously maximize their material wealth are irrelevant to the predictive value of the Homo Economicus model. The model still retains value if indeed humans often act directly to further their wealth, and particularly if many of their other motivations also lead them to behave in ways that make it appear that they are maximizing wealth. More generally, a modern economist can simply bypass any request to explain behaviors such as prayer and philanthropy by pointing out that the Homo Economicus construct was never meant to explain everything, but rather to explain a large amount of economic behavior using a very simple rule of thumb.

Yet, the view that Homo Economicus was never meant to be a realistic description is also problematic because taken to the extreme, it then becomes a dead-end theory. If one already relinquishes the idea that Homo Economicus captures psychological realism, and merely defends it by pointing to the behavioral predictions it generates, then it becomes very hard to make further intellectual progress. How would one add to the Homo Economicus construct? What would be the starting point from which to build when trying to explain divergences between the predictions of the Homo Economicus view and reality? In order to extend the Homo Economicus view of the world, one has no choice but to take it literally and from that basis try to add to it. Having added to it, one can once again judge the result on its predictions.

1.1.2 Generalizations of Homo Economicus

The early economists knew that they were abstracting from the complexities of human behavior. They knew that greed could come from several underlying psychological motives, were keenly aware that humans are motivated by more than greed alone, and many hoped that we would one day develop a more realistic yet still workable view of humanity. This is where the difficulty has been: there have been thousands of extensions to the Homo Economicus view of the world, but it has simply proven too difficult to generate a more realistic view of humanity that is also analytically tractable.

An important attempt at generalization is the preference approach of standard abstract microeconomic theory that is exemplified by Pareto (1906), Samuelson (1938), and Samuelson (1950). Within that theory, individuals are not motivated by greed for explicitly material goods, but simply have "preferences over bundles of goods." These bundles can be anything, including goods consumed by others (a form of "altruism"), or highly immaterial services (such as prayer). Behavior simply arises from people choosing what they prefer. Extended to such an abstract level, economic theory encompasses almost any view of human motivations.[3]

The difficulty with this abstract view is that it is simply too broad and nonspecific. There is not a single known example of any scientist measuring a full preference set (Van Praag and Frijters 1999, Clark, Frijters, and Shields 2008), nor is it reasonable to expect that anyone ever will measure a full preference set in the absence of mind reading. To map a full preference set one must know not only what people choose in reality, but also what they would have chosen in various alternative states of the world that did not materialize and hence cannot directly be observed. To truly know what an individual would have chosen in all the millions of states of the world that could arise daily but do not, as is strictly necessary for the measurement of preference sets, is properly seen as an economist's utopia (Clark et al. 2008, section 2).

---

[3] I do not here equate the economic literature on utility maximization with that of preference theory, although the two are often conflated. The key difference is that unlike with preference maps, there are candidate empirical measures for utility, such as happiness, which can be analyzed to yield empirically defensible insights and clear policy prescriptions (Clark, Diener, Georgellis, and Lucas 2007). One can also argue that from a psychological perspective, it is more realistic to see a reward function as primary and preferences as secondary.

As with nearly all important lines of thought in economics, the frontier of this subfield has progressed beyond the fundamental contributions of its progenitors that are found in student textbooks. In a recent handbook on these matters, edited by Anand, Pattanaik, and Puppe (2009), the contributing authors show how they have extended the classic preference model of Samuelson and the expected-utility model of von Neumann–Morgenstern (von Neumann and Morgenstern 1947) in many directions. Modern generalizations of preference models allow for various "irrationalities," including hyperbolic time-discounting, uncertainty about probabilities, state-dependent utility, partially unobserved goods, rank-dependent utility, and so forth.

1.1.3 Limitations of existing generalizations of Homo Economicus

While these extensions allow for incredibly sophisticated and rich behavior at the abstract level, they almost by design move economists' intellectual efforts even further from the world of scientific observation. The statistician wishing to truly implement such models at a macro-level would not only have to find a full preference map, but would also require a full map of how subjective probabilities relate to objective probabilities; a full accounting of the differences across people and circumstances as to their valuations of the future (in order to pin down different discount rates); a complete description of each individual's current situation (to allow for "state-dependent" utility); and so on. While the extensions to the 1950s Samuelson model thus "fit" the anomalies observed in laboratory experiments that violate that model, and in that sense attempt to address the rift between theory and data, they do so at the cost of adding even more layers of unmeasurable abstractions. This might insulate the resulting generalizations from empirical falsification, but it also prevents them from generating sharp predictions and policy advice. Almost anything goes, or can be argued to.

The core problem with the main existing generalizations of Homo Economicus is thus that they are demonstrably too broad to be falsifiable, and hence, too broad to be useful to practitioners. As a result, in actual empirical work by economists, one will not find the preference-based view of humans as it appears even in its basic form, let alone any of its more generalized forms. Rather, a much simpler view of humans is taken as the basis of measurement and choice. For example, scholars interested in explaining unemployment routinely view individuals as caring about money and just one other thing, namely leisure (for a review, see Frijters and Gregory 2006). Trade-offs then arise between income and leisure, and from observing individual choices, one can try to work out how much individuals care about one versus the other. The thousand other things that an abstract micro-theorist might think are relevant are simply swept under the carpet.

In other applied subfields of economics, the individual is similarly reduced to someone motivated by only two needs (or to a one-dimensional linear index of motives), one of which is almost always material greed. Examples abound in the published economic analysis of morality, guilt, sex, climate, and so forth: applied work nearly always examines an explicit or implicit trade-off between one of these "goods" and material wealth. Thousands of estimates exist of the "shadow value" of things like "housing amenities," "good weather," "mental health," "passive smoking," and so on (Van Praag and Frijters 1999, Mervin and Frijters 2012). Standard infinite-dimension preference-based microeconomic theory is hence largely irrelevant to empiricists, who instead reduce individual motivations to a much more manageable number of dimensions for the sake of tractability.

Preference-based theory is also irrelevant for much of applied theory, such as that developed in regulation economics and macroeconomics. When applied theorists analyze particular markets or examine business cycles, they cannot start from the presumption that individuals have preference maps. Typically, individuals are either modeled as being completely materially oriented, such as when they run the profit-maximizing firms that dominate the macro- and micro-theories of markets, or else modeled as caring only about two things, such as consumption and leisure.

In sum, the main value of general preference theory is as an umbrella model that aids in thinking about specific simplified models. Mainstream modern economics in practice does not adhere to a single model, but rather offers a collection of simplified and hence tractable models that contain overlapping assumptions, at the core of which are the model of Homo Economicus and its implications for the mechanics of perfect markets. Economists may allow that motivations other than greed may matter in the short run, but the mainstream view is that all non-material considerations gradually become eroded when they run contrary to materialistic incentives, and that for this reason they do not truly matter in the long run. The gauntlet is thereby laid down for others to develop workable models of human behavior that explain more than is explained by the Homo Economicus construct.

1.1.4 The core problem

How then should one build on this construct to address its lack of explanatory power in some important areas, without falling into the trap of chasing a fully realistic view where thousands of phenomena matter simultaneously, or devolving to hopelessly broad generalizations? I argue that one should try to add a select few elements, captured by workable and defensible rules of thumb, that can account for most of what is left unexplained by the Homo Economicus view. That is the problem tackled in this book. To this end, we must first enumerate the observed behaviors and aspects of the socioeconomic system in which economic actors make their choices that can be explained by the Homo Economicus view, and then determine where additional elements are required in order to fill in the gaps.

1.2 Socioeconomic phenomena explained by the Homo Economicus view

1.2.1 Competition and organizations

Within standard economic thinking, greedy individuals compete against one another in markets. In these markets, greedy consumers try to buy goods for the lowest price possible, and greedy producers try to sell goods for the highest price possible. If all producers are selling the same thing and all consumers know all the prices being offered, then the consumers are first going to buy goods from the seller with the lowest prices, then from the seller with the second-lowest prices, etc., until consumers cannot find any seller who is prepared to sell his goods for a price low enough that the consumers want to buy them. Following this process to its natural conclusion, such a market exhibits a tendency – termed by Adam Smith "the invisible hand" – for the prices at which transactions occur to adjust to the lowest price at which any seller who makes a transaction is willing to supply his goods to the market, and equivalently, the highest price that any consumer remaining in the market is willing to pay.

The remarkable thing about a market where all prices have converged to the price of the lowest-price seller is that, at this price, a "spontaneous order" arises in which the "right" people produce the "right" goods. This means that sellers who must sell for a high price make no sales, and are hence driven out of the market. These will be the sellers for whom producing the good has a high cost. Conversely, consumers who do not want the good as much as others, and hence are not prepared to pay as high a price as other consumers will, do not buy the goods. This then means that the lowest-cost producers end up producing the goods and selling them to the consumers who have the greatest willingness to pay for the goods. This is called an efficient outcome, in that it is not possible to generate more gains from trade: no producer can produce another unit of the good at a price low enough that any consumer wants to buy it.

The archetypal free-competition or laissez-faire world of the economist is one in which the process above operates in many markets at the same time: all goods are sold in competitive markets, with many buyers and sellers who all have complete information regarding prices. In this laissez-faire world, every potential producer ends up producing the thing he is relatively best at producing, because supplying that good will earn him the highest profit across all possible profit-seeking activities that he could undertake. Conversely, each consumer ends up with the bundle of goods he values most out of all bundles he could afford. This final situation is called an "equilibrium" (denoting the concept of balance) because it denotes the point at which no further profitable trades are possible: no producer or consumer wishes to change his behavior.

The astounding aspect of this spontaneous order is that it requires no specific organization to tell people what to produce and what to consume, or what prices should be. The prices that emerge naturally from markets are all that is needed to make people realize what they are best at (i.e., the productive activity that will make them richest), and these signals arise purely from the invisible hand of individual greed. It would be extraordinarily difficult for any economic planner to second-guess these signals and arrive at the same system of allocation. This is the basic reason why economists advocate free markets, and has been a basic train of thought motivating much of economic policy making across the world for the last few centuries.

The economists' ideal of perfect competition that delivers optimal outcomes naturally yields ready-made policy advice one can apply when deviations from this ideal state are observed in real markets. The general form of this advice is to do what can reasonably be done to push the market in question towards the ideal state of perfect competition. Some reasonably easy-to-observe deviations from the perfect-competition ideal include an insufficient number of buyers or sellers; barriers faced by producers to charging for the use of the good; and imperfect information on the part of buyers about the quality of the good.

Regulation authorities in the real world spend their time removing barriers to "normal competition," through such activities as breaking up monopolists, organizing funds for the production of public goods, enforcing quality signals, and so on. This is clear evidence that the idea of perfect markets is not one that mainstream economists believe blindly to hold in all real-world circumstances, but rather that it is taken to be a reasonable description of what is attainable, and provides an underlying causal theory as to how to move towards the best outcome. The aggregate story is one of predictable forces reflecting individual greed, and clear optimal and suboptimal social outcomes.

A particularly relevant implication of the mainstream view of competition concerns the size of organizations in which people combine to produce and consume goods. The size of organizations will naturally tend towards efficiency in a perfect market, in the sense of delivering the lowest production cost per unit of goods produced. All "returns to scale" (reductions in per-unit production cost as the scale of production increases) are exhausted by each efficient organization, and the advantages of becoming even bigger are outweighed by the disadvantages, which mainly involve the difficulty of coordinating large organizations.

The reasoning for this is simple. If an organization is bigger than the efficient size for a given production process, then entrepreneurs could make more profit by setting up smaller organizations. If the organization is smaller than the efficient size, then entrepreneurs could increase total profit by joining two organizations, perhaps through a merger or takeover. Competitive pressures in equilibrium thereby cause existing organizations to be the efficient size.

This remarkable prediction of the effect of competition on organizational size fits many actual organizations in the world. Manufacturing firms are very large because of returns to scale: the unit cost of production keeps falling as the manufacturing plants grow and the production process is divided into smaller and smaller steps. Restaurants usually operate on a smaller scale because the per-meal cost reductions achieved by producing fresh food in bulk quickly fade as the scale of production increases. State bureaucracies are very large because the cost advantages of larger armies and larger bureaucracies are huge, making it efficient to have defined countries.

The combination of competitive markets and the realities of different returns to scale in the production of different goods are thus capable of explaining the size and structure of many organizations. This is but one example of the great applicability of economic thinking. In this particular example, only greed plays a role as a human motivation: given the realities of the production process for different goods, no individual motivation other than the pursuit of material wealth is needed to get exceptionally clear predictions on how large organizations are going to be.

The story above is not useful only in explaining the size of existing organizations; it also yields rules of thumb as to what to expect in the future. For example, economists know that internet-based activities are by and large characterized by increasing economies of scale. Applying the logic above then immediately yields the prediction that almost any single productive activity on the internet is subject to monopolizing tendencies. Absent external interference, a single dominant supplier of each internet-based "product" is likely to emerge. One should expect the emergence of a single dominant search engine, a single dominant gambling site, a single dominant auction site, and so on. Economists are indeed already designing institutions to optimally regulate internet businesses (Brady 2003, Sidak 2006, Baumol, Cave, Cramton et al. 2007).

1.2.2 Institutions

Although not made explicit in the simple ideal of "perfect markets," individuals' greed itself implies that a variety of institutions are implicitly required to support the operation of free markets. If people will do anything to increase their material wealth, as implied by the Homo

Economicus view of humanity, then why would they simply accept offered prices? Why would they not, for example, steal products or production technology, kill competitors, or in some other way seek a market advantage through dishonest or immoral behavior? The existence of institutions is a necessary condition for such behavior not to occur on a regular basis. Many past and contemporary authors have argued in this vein that institutions prevent chaos and arbitrary behavior (Smith 1776, North 1990, Ostrom 1990, Kasper and Streit 1998).

Institutions include formal ones such as parliaments, legal systems, education systems, state governments, and so on, as well as informal ones such as notions of fairness and adherence to the laws of the land, conventions, and internalized rules and customs. The importance of informal institutions should not be understated.[4] One can have the most beautiful constitution in the world, but if populations take no notice of it, then it is an irrelevant piece of paper with no more significance than a toilet roll with inscriptions. Formal and informal institutions in combination are important in the running of our societies, as together they form the rules of the game to which people adhere. They constrain the possibilities for opportunistic behavior in human interactions.

Despite the absence of explicit institutions in the traditional formulation of free competition, one can apply the logic of competition itself to derive natural implications about the rise and survival of institutions (in somewhat like manner to deriving the implications of competition for organizational size). Mainstream economics views institutions as very similar to competitive firms: they arise in the competitive arena of politics, and hence must ultimately prove to lead to lower costs than their competitors in order to survive. Through this lens, institutions observed today should be, amongst all providers yet tried, the lowest-cost providers of whatever has proved to be useful in supporting individuals' interactions and otherwise the pursuit of their objectives (Kasper and Streit 1998).

Hayek (1979) is a good example of an economist who argues for the innate "fitness" of economic institutions (pp. 149–150):

Though our civilization is the result of an accumulation of individual knowledge, it is not by the explicit or conscious combination of all this knowledge

---

[4] The importance of informal rules was recognized as far back as Confucius (*c.* 2,500 years ago), who emphasized the importance of rituals.

in any individual brain, but by its embodiment in symbols which we use without understanding them, in habits and institutions, tools and concepts, that man in society is constantly able to profit from a body of knowledge neither he nor any other man completely possesses.

Diverse social scientists have argued that institutions at different levels arise from an evolutionary process rather than a conscious top-down process. Easterly (2007), in trying to explain the failure of foreign economic experts to influence the actual policies of developing countries, notes (p. 331): "institutions may emerge much more from the social norms and spontaneous arrangements of many actors than from the dictate of some expert from above (Dixit 2003)." Weber (1922) envisaged the state itself as the victor in a brutal and violent struggle for dominance (p. 154, partially translated): "A compulsory political association with continuous organization (*politischer Anstalt-betrieb*) will be called a 'state' if and in so far as its administrative staff successfully upholds a claim to the monopoly of the legitimate use of physical force in the enforcement of its order." The state, with its taxation system, army, and police, was in Weber's view simply the winner of centuries of struggle between smaller violent entities. It "won" because it was able to "deliver" violence (read: preservation of order) more effectively than its competitors, and as the winner it "earned" what is called a monopoly of violence. In politics, this is still the dominant definition of the state, and the dominant view of how states emerged.

One can also envisage competition between institutions within the state. For example, notions of fairness that diminish the wealth of the population are presumed to be gradually discarded for more "useful" notions of fairness that also deliver economic benefits. Inefficient government institutions are gradually displaced by more efficient ones because entrepreneurial politicians manage to get elected by promising to change the inefficient institutions, and to some extent are held to those promises. The operation of a competitive market, it can be argued, is visible even here: the marketplace for politicians begets political entrepreneurs looking to "weed out" high-cost institutions. According to this view, the long-term outcome of this competitive process is that a country and, in the long run, the whole world, ends up with the lowest-cost institutions.

One can make similar criticisms of this stylized story as one can of competitive markets for goods as traditionally considered. One set of criticisms revolves around information. How does a given person know which institutions are inefficient, and hence which changes to vote for? How does a politician know which institutions are inefficient, and even if he did, how could he convince an unknowing electorate? More broadly, since politicians are themselves supposedly out to maximize their own wealth rather than the wealth of the whole country, why would they be keen to change inefficient institutions anyway? Who actually has the job of determining within countries what works and what does not work? Broader still, what upholds the competition within politics in the first place – i.e., what upholds the democratic rules of the game? After all, democracy is not something that has always existed, and is not the only system of government in the world. Why do we still have wars and violent break-ups of large countries unless we are clearly not yet in "equilibrium?" These and many other questions have been posed of the mainstream economic view of institutional evolution.

The mainstream economic view of institutions as arising from an interplay between greedy individuals is hence incomplete. The steps between greed and institutions must be taken via concepts other than those encased in the Homo Economicus view, and it is by no means a foregone conclusion that these other concepts will end up being irrelevant in the long run.

1.3 Love: The first addition to the mainstream view

I will argue in Chapter 2 that one main element missing from the materialistic view of humans is their love, both for other humans and for their beliefs. Love is defined as a form of unconditional loyalty, and will be said to be present whenever a person would be willing to help advance the interests of the object of his love, even if the object of his love would not notice the help and even if the loving person would receive no observable reward.

Social theorists have long argued that love might be an important human motivation. In his *Theory of Moral Sentiments*, Adam Smith – frequently seen as the founding father of economics as a discipline – talks about various "virtues," including love and sympathy, as cornerstones of individual behavior. He argues (p. 9): "Howsoever selfish man may be supposed, there are evidently some principles in his nature, which interest him in the fortune of others, and render their happiness necessary to him, though he derives nothing from it except the pleasure of seeing it" (Smith 1759). The phenomenon Smith describes here is very close to the definition of love in this book. Other classical thinkers too allowed for such a concept. Even a celebrated pragmatist like Machiavelli acknowledged the role of love, for example when he wrote in a letter that he loved his country more than his soul (Guicciardini and Moulakis 1998). Building on these ideas, I will propose a theory for how and why love arises, so as to truly integrate love into the mainstream economic view of human motivation.[5]

This integrative task is complicated by the fact that unlike the "goods" traditionally analyzed by economists, loyalty cannot be bought, and is not tradeable in the open market. Looking at commodities such as loyalty, trust, or honesty, Arrow (1974) stresses (pp. 23, 26): "they have real, practical, economic value; they increase the efficiency of the system, enable you to produce more goods or more of whatever values you hold in high esteem. But they are not commodities for which trade on the open market is technically possible or even meaningful."

I expect to see love as a major player involved in almost every facet of an individual's decision making. Love within families should be a central reason for what parents do for their children and what dynasties do over time. Love within companies should be an integral part of how teams of people actually get things done within organizations, which is completely in line with the argument of Simon (1991) (pp. 34–37): "pride in work and organizational loyalty are widespread phenomena in organizations…Willingness of employees at all levels to assume responsibility for producing results – not simply 'following rules' – is generally believed to be a major determinant of organizational success." I also expect love to be an important ingredient in understanding

---

[5] Modern mainstream economics by contrast sometimes recognizes bonds of love, but only as a tacked-on component of people's preferences or as part of the constraints they face. A typical example is the study by Meer and Rosen (2009), who argue that charitable giving has been seen by many previous economists as due to a combination of greed and altruism. These authors found that alumni of American universities were much more likely to donate to their alma mater if they had children who might attend there, which suggests that the donations are not solely guided by a love for the universities but also by the motive to buy entry for their children. Since plenty of donations were made by childless alumni, however, the authors conclude in favor of a combination of motives behind charitable giving.

the operation of large groups, including ethnic, religious, and nationalistic groups. I expect to see a role for love in explaining why individuals uphold the institutions of law and democracy, and hence for it to play a pivotal role in setting the "rules of the game" to which Homo Economicus acquiesces.

The argument that love plays a role in the political system is not new. Love has been previously recognized as an important ingredient in the viability of the Rousseauian social contract between the taxers and the taxed (Torgler et al. 2009). The viability of the tax-and-spend system depends not only on society's capacity to inspire fear in those who have to pay taxes, but also on its capacity to develop amongst the taxed a feeling that their tax compliance is "the right thing to do," which by necessity requires some bond between the taxers and the taxed. How such bonds are developed and maintained is thus a crucial issue in understanding taxation, which as argued previously lies at the heart of the economic system.

As one might expect, loyalty to groups is a major element of study in other social sciences, particularly sociology. However, even there, there is a strained relation between models of self-interested humans and observations on self-sacrificing behavior. As Brewer (1991) remarks (p. 475), "most of our theories are inadequate to account for much human action in the form of collective behavior. The self-interested, egocentric view of human nature does not explain why individuals risk or sacrifice personal comfort, safety, or social position to promote group benefit (Caporael, Dawes, Orbell, and van de Kragt, 1989)."

While the mechanism underlying the genesis of love is an area mainly untouched to date by social science, existing research already contains a wide variety of concepts that are strongly related to love. Other-regarding preferences, emotional attachment, altruism, self–other merging, social preferences, group loyalty, empathy, selflessness, and many other terms appear regularly in the literature of economics and other social sciences. A brief note is in order regarding how these prior terms relate to love as defined in this book.

Some prior terms are completely absorbed by my concept of love, such as the term "altruism" as used by Becker (1974) to describe the feelings parents have towards their children. I certainly would call these feelings love, and the parent–child relation is a key point of departure for the theory of love in this book. I prefer the word love over "altruism" because the word love is more easily applied to describe loyalty towards unseen abstractions, such as gods or ideals, whereas "altruism" is more normally reserved for bonds between humans.

Other prior terms are fully included in my definition of love, but require clarifying side notes. For instance, Andreoni (1989) (p. 1447) talks about "warm-glow" altruism, by which he means forms of altruism that make the person who is altruistic feel good about his altruistic acts. This phenomenon is also called love in this book: it is not considered separately because the "warm glow" is not an observable reward (the reward is only internal). I will allow for both love towards a person and love for an act, and either may be associated with what Andreoni (1989) calls "warm-glow" altruism.

Finally, some prior terms are only partially included in the definition of love used in this book. An example is the term "emotional attachment," which is favored by many psychologists to describe altruistic bonds such as those between parent and child. Positive emotional attachment is viewed as love in this book as long as the attachment is accompanied by a willingness to help the object of attachment, which is not always the case. One can feel an attachment to something and yet have no willingness to help further its interests, such as when one feels good about the success of a sports team but has no corresponding willingness to actively support it.

1.4 Power

Most people would freely admit that power plays a role in various aspects of our socioeconomic system, yet its formal treatment in economics is scant. Before sketching the addition to the Homo Economicus view that I suggest in this area, some general remarks about power are in order.

One might define power as influence over the thoughts and actions of other individuals.[6] Weber (1922) thus defined power (*"macht"*) as

[6] Many alternative views of power are to be found in the literature, each quite explicitly associated with particular views on how societies work. Lenin's view, embedded in the question of "who governs whom," is mainly that power is defined in reference to a class struggle between groups. The following definition, from Dahl (1957) (pp. 202–203), comes closest to what is meant by individual power in this book: "A has power over B to the extent that he can get B to do something that B would not otherwise do." Another dominant line of thinking is to equate power with the main thing that can be attained with power, i.e., access to resources.

the possibility of subjugating the behavior of another to one's will. This definition is agnostic about whether power can be held by individuals outside of any social context (such as when one thinks of power as pure physical strength), or whether power is instead mainly a group phenomenon that cannot be meaningfully analyzed without also adopting a view of group processes (such as when one thinks of power as accruing to a position within a group). Machiavelli used a variety of undefined terms such as *potente, autorità, forza*, and *imperio* when discussing power (Dahl 1968). Some political scientists have explicitly bemoaned the difficulty of working with the concept of power – e.g., Lukes (1986) (p. 17): "in our ordinary unreflective judgments and comparisons of power, we normally know what we mean and have little difficulty in understanding one another, yet every attempt at a single general answer to the question has failed and seems likely to fail." It is not easy to give a satisfactory definition of power. The sheer diversity in the types of people who seem to have power and the contexts in which they are operating make it difficult to simplify power into a workable construct.

As noted above, economists too have found power to be a fuzzy concept, and by and large have not examined it in much detail.[7] This is perhaps unsurprising, given the inherently egalitarian view of humans implicit in both the notion of single-minded individual wealth maximization, and the classless ideal of the free market. No one actor has more prima facie potential than another; all are equals in competition and free to pursue their independent greedy interests. Economics simply presumes when required that individuals and institutions have power, without wondering about the source or limits of that power.

One stream of economic research that considers a limited form of power focuses on the cost side of specific transactions between parties in which power could be relevant (see, for example, Harsanyi 1962). A typical analysis in this vein might proceed as follows: "In order to control Y, X uses some of his resources. How far X is willing to go depends on his opportunity cost of controlling Y. Similarly, Y has a next-best use of resources embodied in what she is unable to do if she

---

Parkin (1971) captures this view as follows (p. 46): "[T]o speak of the distribution of power could be understood as another way of describing the flow of rewards."

[7] There are some exceptions, such as Galbraith (1984). Also, while mainstream economics has spoken at length of market power, it has left alone the question of authority and the origin of the rules of the game, which I wish to address directly.

complies with X." Yet again, however, such a language and approach reduces power to simply "an alternative use of resources" that takes the majority of the more interesting power relations in society as given and immutable.

In recent decades, the mainstream economic analysis of power has shifted towards focusing on the link between power and information. Whereas Stigler (1961) could still write that "One should hardly have to tell academicians that information is a valuable resource: knowledge is power. And yet this occupies a slum dwelling in the town of economics" (p. 213), a generation later the *Handbook of Game Theory* could devote whole chapters (McMillan and Rothschild 1994, Ausubel, Cramton, and Deneckere 2002) to bargaining power arising out of information advantages, drawing on a long line of papers in the intervening period (e.g., Harsanyi 1967). This handbook reflects a large literature whose essential idea is that a person with superior information can manipulate those who have inferior information. Better-informed people, it is argued, have better outside options, know when to make take-it-or-leave-it offers, and have superior information about the actual value of interactions, which all lead more-informed individuals to prosper at the expense of less-informed individuals.

What is the prima facie evidence supporting this view? States, churches, schools, parties, and multinational corporations have indeed heavily controlled information flows throughout history. If you can make other people believe something, then you can influence them, a point strongly made by Foucault (2002), who argued that power can become amplified if used to shape the way people think about their world. For example, if you can make a population believe that you are the rightful ruler of a country because you have access to lines of communication, then you might indeed actually become and remain the ruler of that country. On a more individual level, if you know the value of a good and someone else does not, then your exchange with that other person will more likely benefit you than the other person. Within this view, power is essentially about the amount of knowledge that you possess relative to others, your ability to gather knowledge, and your ability to disseminate knowledge to others.

One criticism of this view is that in perfect markets, everyone possesses all the information there is and hence there are no individuals more powerful than others. Another criticism is that there is no clear role in this view for prior personal beliefs, such as religious beliefs, in generating power for particular individuals (e.g., popes). Such beliefs are by necessity treated as the unexplained outcome of prior processes. The many historical instances of populations ignoring the media messages of dictatorial regimes are also hard to reconcile with the most simple version of the "power = information" paradigm: if power were only about the control of information, then those with the largest amounts of information and the ability to disseminate it (such as dictators) should automatically have control over many others (such as their populations). To my knowledge, there is no aggregate view of the economic system that includes an explicit role for power as arising from information asymmetries.

The most damning critique I can make of the "power = information" paradigm is that it does not capture that power which derives purely from positions within groups. The police officer who resigns his position has the same information just before and just after his resignation, and will know the same people, yet at a stroke will have lost much of his power. The same goes for a head of state, a CEO, or a church leader. We intuitively know that the power wielded by figures of authority derives in the main from the power of the whole institution of which they are a part, and that they are but the temporary holders of that group power. Further, it is not individual or even group information asymmetry that underpins that group power in the short run: "the police" as a group entity has power, even if "the police" knows less than any other group or individual. I return to this theme below.

1.4.1 The individualistic approach to power

One strong line of thought in social science holds that power exists at the individual level and can be measured. This would allow one to say, for example, that individual A has one unit of power, while individual B has two units of power. Early views of power reflect this desire to quantify and individualize power: Russell and Brittan (1938) defined power as a quantitative concept, namely the production of intended effects; Weber's view that power is the possibility of imposing one's will upon the behavior of others allowed for power to be conceptualized and held at the individual level (Weber 1922), although in practice he also considered power in the form of collective will; and Dahl (1986) saw a powerful individual as someone who could carry out his own will, despite opposition or resistance. Harsanyi (1962) also took an individualistic approach to power, in which the key question revolves around the cost of control, implicitly equating power with resources.

Within this individualistic approach, one can try to define characteristics of power such as its magnitude, distribution, scope, and domain. Resources, skills, motivations, and costs have been suggested as key characteristics that explain and describe power (Dahl 1968). Power as an *über*-concept is then not only defined by the level of resources available, but also by whether power is actually exercised, whether individuals have the skills to exercise power, and whether individuals are motivated to use the resources to increase their power. The social science literature has seen many attempts to measure the power of interacting individuals (see, for example, Simon 1953 and Dahl 1968), which generally follow the notion that where X and Z have power over Y, the power of each is measured by the amount of change in Y that is attributable respectively to X and Z. The greater the change in Y, the greater the power of X or Z; X exerts more power than Z if he induces more change in Y.

One difficulty in such attempts to assign numbers to the efforts people make to influence others is that individuals have many wishes, and exert their influence via many different channels: people are not loyal only to one object or cause, nor do they resort only to direct one-on-one manipulation. Rather, individuals operate within groups (families, work environments, clubs, and so on) and can influence others via these groups.

A broader problem with the individualistic approach is that power includes outcome and process characteristics that shape and are shaped by existing structures. As made clear in the examples of the police and the pope, power is embedded within public institutions, quite apart from the individuals who populate those institutions at any point in time. Government institutions such as the army or the tax administration exercise power through activities such as commanding armies and taxing people. Large private organizations exercise market power, power to invest or produce, and power through ownership. Schools, churches, political parties, and the media exercise power by influencing opinions. Power is wielded at any point in time and through various means by a vast array of individual players, from politicians and religious leaders to fashion and business leaders. Yet the individual who wields power as a school headmaster or police officer would not have the same power if he did not hold that position within the socioeconomic structure. This implies that the power people wield because of their positions inside institutions is ultimately derived from the source of power of the whole institution.

1.4.2 Group power

The key difficulty in understanding power is that the power of one person is almost never independent of the power of others.[8] The power of the legal courts is not independent from the power of the police, since without the police, courts are powerless. Yet, without the courts, the power of the police is greatly diminished. The same goes for the power held by almost any person in society. A politician is only powerful within a political system, and would be powerless without constitutions, parliaments, state executives, laws, and enforcement agencies. The power of a religious leader depends upon the power of the media outlets via which he reaches the faithful. The power of a fashion guru would disappear without a fashion industry.

Many sociologists have recognized the group nature of power, and in particular the group nature of representative power, i.e., the power of "leaders." Schermerhorn (1961) (p. 6) wrote that "[a]uthority ... has a superindividual quality since it embodies norms or values of an entire group or the society at large." Foucault (1986) (p. 234) also advocated a group lens when discussing power, writing "[i]t is never localized here or there, never in anybody's hands, never appropriated as a commodity or piece of wealth. Power is employed and exercised through a net-like organization. And not only do individuals circulate between its threads; they are always in the position of undergoing and exercising this power."

Power has thus remained in social science a fuzzy "group phenomenon," in which we see that social-psychological phenomena such as "the trust of the general public in official institutions" must play a large role. According to this view, it is basically meaningless to say that X has some amount of power and Y has some other amount of power. Such statements only make sense if one takes a collection of group relations as immutable and given, and moreover overlooks the

---

[8] This is not true of resources, for example, whose value to their owner is essentially independent of whether others also hold resources.

reality that the dominant power relations in modern societies are not between one individual and another, but rather between individuals and groups.

1.4.3 Groups and power: The second addition to the mainstream view

Power and groups comprise the second main "black box" that this book addresses. The main break I will make with most of the traditions discussed above is to include an explicit recognition that the forms of power important to our socioeconomic system are group-based. This point of view is not unique, however. Canetti (1984), for example, explicitly recognized power as solely a group phenomenon. It has also been observed that man is a group animal whose self-image is inextricably linked to the groups of which he is part (Sen 1985), and that any analysis of power is thus derivative of an analysis of groups.

What is the value to an economist of adopting notions of groups and group power? It is that we can then tackle questions such as why individuals and groups accept outside power when they are driven out of markets or in other ways fail to advance themselves through market transactions. Why do such individuals not complain, resort to violence, or try to simply grab others' resources? How is it possible that millions of individuals, who are members of powerful groups (religions, ethnicities, countries) and who are innately group animals with strong passions and violent tendencies, interact peacefully in markets, accepting both implicit and explicit rules of the game? On a related point, what motivates those who uphold the rules of the game? Having answers to such questions is crucial to understanding why our economy works. I will argue that the answers revolve around groups and power, with group loyalty being a key element in both.

Economists have examined these questions before, but mainly in the far past. The "loyalty equilibrium" needed for market forces to play out was foremost in the minds of early economic philosophers. Hume (1740), for example, referred to three important laws underlying modern economies: the "stability of passion," the "transference of property by consent," and the "performance of promises" (p. 578). These laws are offered as prerequisites for market economies to work, which naturally leads to the follow-up question of how these market prerequisites came to be. Smith (1776) too was acutely aware of the importance of groups, and how the consent of groups was a vital pre-requisite for markets. Yet as Furuboth and Richter (1998) ask, how did the "pre-established harmony" emerge?

In mainstream economics today, the notion of "adherence to rules of the game" and the issue of group power that lies behind this adherence are almost never discussed. When such matters are discussed, groups are frequently not even mentioned. It is well-accepted that individual property rights give individuals discretionary power over resources; contract laws enforce the deals individuals make; and an intricate set of rules helps to prevent smaller groups of individuals from defrauding others (for example, by colluding over prices or quantities). Yet these fundamental rules are all highly dependent on groups. Alchian (1967) argues (pp. 2–3): "In essence economics is the study of property rights ... the question of how property rights should be defined and exchanged, and on what terms." Yet it is *groups* that give out and maintain property rights and contracts, not individuals. It is "the police" and "the justice system" that back up these rights, not Policeman A or Judge B. It simply does not make sense to think of property rights as existing or being adhered to outside of an overarching group construct. Moreover, it is people's loyalties within this group construct that produce their adherence to property rights and thereby prevent our socioeconomic system from descending into a chaos of unfettered resource-grabbing. If economics is the study of property rights, then economists must accommodate groups.

Loyalty is a recognized component of the group dynamics of a whole country. Loyalty to the state, in the form of patriotic fervor, is a prime motivator for most soldiers defending democratic countries, as well as for policemen and others who serve the state. Even totalitarian regimes try to actively generate loyalty towards their regimes in order to maximize their power over the population under their control (Wintrobe 2006). Arendt (1970) notes on this topic (pp. 67–68) that

no government exclusively based on the means of violence has ever existed. Even the totalitarian ruler, whose chief instrument of rule is torture, needs a power basis – the secret police and its net of informers. Only the development of robot soldiers, which, as previously mentioned, would eliminate the human factor completely and, conceivably, permit one man with a push of a button to destroy whomever he pleased, could change this fundamental ascendancy of power over violence. Even the most despotic domination we know of, the rule of master over slaves, who always outnumbered him, did not rest on superior means of coercion as such, but on a superior organisation of power – that is, on the organised solidarity of the masters.

The importance of groups and the loyalty towards them that gives rise to group power are widely recognized in social science. It is not that there are no theories on groups, power, and loyalty – quite the opposite in fact, there are hundreds of them – but that these elements have not to my knowledge been integrated into the overall story of mainstream economics. What I seek to offer is a simple, stylized understanding of group behavior and group power. Loyalty is a key component in both.

1.5 Networks and market frictions: The third addition to the mainstream view

A network can be reasonably defined as a facilitator of exchange. The "perfect competition" ideal of mainstream economics has no obvious use for networks, however, as it presumes that consumers know all price–good pairs on offer, and that the market simply somehow reaches the lowest price at which the lowest-cost seller is willing to sell. In this ideal conception, "the market" is a social phenomenon in which everyone is linked to everyone else in a kind of overarching supernetwork.

Yet in reality, individuals search for goods, buyers, and suppliers within networks of limited size, and moreover the type of network within which someone searches has implications for the ultimate market behavior he will exhibit. Individuals who search for goods and partners within small, highly informal networks (such as families and villages) will behave quite differently from individuals who search within large anonymous networks (such as the internet). Anonymous large networks resemble the overarching supernetwork presumed by mainstream economics much more closely than do small, informal networks. In the latter, various informal institutions such as trust and reciprocity are significant inputs into any transaction, whereas in large anonymous networks, transactions can be made purely on the basis of mutual needs and regulated only by formal, mutually accepted rules.

It has been seen as problematic that markets should be represented in mainstream theory as having no search element, when in so many real-world transactions, search is an obvious antecedent to exchange. Underscoring this, Coase (1937) states (p. 390):

> In order to carry out a market transaction it is necessary to discover who it is that one wishes to deal with, to inform people that one wishes to deal with and to what terms, to conduct negotiations leading up to a bargain, to draw up the contract, to undertake the inspection needed to make sure that the terms of the contract are being observed, and so on.

Yet in the earliest models of markets, such as those in the work of Leon Walras at the end of the nineteenth century, the problem of how market transactions actually came about was simply presumed to be solved by a form of magic. Walras presumed that there was an all-knowing auctioneer who simply told everyone the competitive prices in all markets, and all individuals abided by this pronouncement (Walras 1874, Daal and Jolink 1993).

Since that time, mainstream economics has put significant effort into finding realistic mechanisms by which markets actually reach equilibrium. One dense collection of such attempts lies in the literature on what is called the "tatonnement process" (Dreze and de la Vallee Poussin 1971), which nonetheless has not managed to solve this problem without invoking new problems. In particular, it is difficult to come up with a process of how people search for prices and exchange partners without there being some cost to this search. Yet as soon as there are search costs, some people might rationally choose not to search more than once, and hence might end up buying goods at a price that is very high. This in turn might mean that not all sellers remaining in the market are in fact low-cost sellers, which in turn means that markets might not be so efficient. Hence the usual results on the desirability of market institutions start to unravel once one allows for search costs.

Pissarides (1990) describes in great detail how the problem of having to search for trading partners, as workers do when looking for jobs, usually produces the unfortunate situation that the resulting prices and observed trades are not the prices and trades that would be optimal for society as a whole. This basic observation spawned a thriving literature on search and matching that has examined the importance of search frictions in explaining the behavior of markets, including the roles of clubs, search intermediaries, reputation mechanisms, and contracting limitations. This literature has generated interesting results, such as that if search costs are high enough, then it might be socially optimal not to have markets at all but to simply have a communist system under which a single organization collects all relevant information once, and then tells everyone else what to do. In such a system, the (high) search costs are only borne once.

Other problems regarding how markets reach prices and how transactions occur are also addressed in the literature. Even if there is no cost associated with finding trading partners, it is not clear how one can reach a single "market price" following the chain of steps outlined previously without some actual sales being made at nonequilibrium prices. Unfortunately, as with costs of finding trading partners, as soon as one allows for the notion that not all actual sales are made at the final "correct" price, many of the nicest results about the optimality of free markets disappear.

Real-world markets involve not only search costs but many other costs, borne both by individuals and by society as a whole, that are not captured in the idealized "free competition" view. Bargaining and decision costs – e.g., costs associated with obtaining legal advice or making any information gathered useable – and supervision and enforcement costs involved in monitoring, protecting, and enforcing contracts (Williamson 1985, Furuboth and Richter 1998) are prime examples. Beyond individual market transaction costs are the broader costs of setting up, maintaining or changing an organizational design (including a political system), and running a system. Costs of measuring, monitoring, and enforcing compliance can be quite substantial, and are all completely ignored in the mainstream view of perfect markets. All of the above types of costs as a group are commonly called "market frictions."

I present in Chapter 4 a rule-of-thumb solution to the omission of market frictions from the mainstream economic view of perfect competition, in which remedies for market frictions are treated as knowledge in which agents can invest. The argument is that individuals invest in their networks of sellers, clients, and friends in order to collect information about the prices and quality of goods and jobs. The bigger a person's network, the more specialized that person can become, and hence the more productive he will be. This means that markets are inextricably linked with particular types of social groups – networks – that are subject to the economic calculus of gains and losses. Where this view differs from other similar arguments is that I will go on to link networks to political processes, thereby linking markets to political outcomes through the mechanism of market frictions. Networks will turn out to be not only facilitators of exchange, but also core ingredients in the diffusion of political power.

1.6 Conclusions

In summary, the mainstream view of humanity and its social structures offered by economics has proven to be a powerful tool for understanding the world. The stylized view is fairly coherent and self-congratulatory: greedy individuals end up producing what they are best at through the invisible hand of the market; their institutions and organizations arise from competition between institutions, leading to the lowest-cost institutions and organizations being observed in equilibrium; the resulting rules and social norms promulgated by institutions take advantage of all possible returns to scale and incorporate all externalities; the political process is similarly a competitive one, leading politicians to propose optimal changes; and "we economists" exist in order to tell politicians and other decision makers where their individual and collective best interests lie.[9]

The elements I wish to add to this standard view have all been individually recognized as important, and have been discussed at length in economics and in other social science literatures. They have simply not been incorporated into an overall integrated view of how our economic system works. The "black boxes" identified in the preceding discussion have been argued by economists either not to truly exist or not to be truly important. Power, networks, and love/loyalty have essentially no role in the mainstream economic view. Networks are implicitly irrelevant because markets are frictionless and instantly reach optimal prices. Power is implicitly unimportant because each individual consumer, seller, and politician is seen as powerless and thus must take the ultimate rules of the world as given. Love and loyalty may be important for small-level consumer choices, but have been seen as irrelevant to how firms and countries operate.

---

[9] In the most radical version of the mainstream story, however, "they" already knew what was optimal before "we" did.

One might wonder why it is necessary to, at a single stroke, incorporate more than one concept into mainstream economics. Why not write one book about love and mainstream economics, then another one about groups, love, and mainstream economics, and so forth?

The reason to opt for a big push on several fronts is the problem identified by Kahneman (2003) when he reflected on the gap between economics and psychology over the preceding thirty years. He writes (p. 162): "Has the gap been narrowed in the intervening 30 years? A search through some introductory textbooks in economics indicates that if there has been any change, it has not yet filtered down to that level: the same assumptions are still in place as the cornerstones of economic analysis." Kahneman points to the problem that while it is relatively easy to acknowledge the limitations of mainstream assumptions and to ask mainstream economics to acknowledge those limitations, it is far harder to see how the main story can be changed to incorporate other insights without losing much of the usefulness of the original story. He goes further when he concludes his review by saying,

Much has happened in the conversation between economics and psychology over the last 25 years. The church of economics has admitted and even rewarded some scholars who would have been considered heretics in earlier periods, and conventional economic analysis is now being done with assumptions that are often much more psychologically plausible than was true in the past. However, the analytical methodology of economics is stable, and it will inevitably constrain the rapprochement between the disciplines. Whether or not psychologists find them odd and overly simple, the standard assumptions about the economic agent are in economic theory for a reason: they allow for tractable analysis. The constraint of tractability can be satisfied with somewhat more complex models, but the number of parameters that can be added is small. One consequence is that the models of behavioral economics cannot stray too far from the original set of assumptions. Another consequence is that theoretical innovations in behavioral economics may be *destined to be noncumulative* [italics added]: when a new model is developed to account for an anomaly of the basic theory, the parameters that were modified in earlier models will often be restored to their original settings.

It is the practice of restoring all other parameters to their original settings that would make it a futile endeavor to push for just one additional concept in mainstream economics. There are already hundreds of additional concepts that have been incorporated independently in various sub-literatures. Yet these independent additions do not survive the filtering that takes place when translating the thinking of an entire discipline into the story presented to economics students in their first years of study, nor do they typically retain the insights gained from the addition of other non-standard concepts. Fudenberg (2006) (p. 694) recognizes this problem and urges behavioral economists to "devote more attention to the foundations of its models, and develop unified explanations for a wider range of phenomena."

What goes for the discipline of economics as a whole also goes for subfields within it: too many additions make each sub-story unworkable. Easterly (2007) (p. 329), for instance, accuses the academic industry that has sought the "determinants of growth" of trumpeting no fewer than 145 different right-hand-side variables found to be significant in growth models. He similarly criticizes that subfield for having "too many" theories (p. 330), and partially blames the plethora of development theories for the general failure of top-down experts to have made any noticeable difference to the development of poor countries. As a result, Durlauf, Johnson, and Temple (2005) advocate building models that constrain the effects of other variables on growth and development to flow through a very limited set of factors of production.[10] In this spirit, for each of the areas considered (love, power, groups, and networks), I will aim for relatively parsimonious stories.

Chapter 2 examines the concepts of love and loyalty, from which preliminary implications are drawn for the concept of power. Chapter 3 then presents a taxonomy and analysis of archetypal group types and considers the important features of power relations within and between groups. Chapter 4 illustrates how networking is at the heart of the market economy. Chapter 5 then combines the networking view of market economics with what we have learned about love, power, and group types into an overall view of how our socioeconomic system has evolved and functions.

---

[10] Chapter 4 of this book takes up the challenge of expanding the set of factors of production to allow a stronger role for policy while still constraining the problem to a manageable dimension, essentially augmenting the standard list with one additional factor (links between agents), though the inclusion of that factor quite radically changes the interpretation of other factors.

2 | *Love: The missing building block*

Selfish materialism is extremely powerful in explaining many of our laws, our customs, our politics, and our choices as consumers. Yet, as discussed briefly in the previous chapter, selfish materialism alone cannot lead to the kind of human organizations we see in reality. Love is an additional core motivation that I wish to define, dissect, and finally incorporate into the economic view of human nature, our organizations, and our societies more broadly.

Loving something or someone is defined, in this book, as caring about that thing or person regardless of any observable reward. One loves if one is willing to sacrifice oneself for someone or something, even if no one is aware of that sacrifice and even if there is no tangible reward. This willingness comes about because loving actions invariably bring a sense of internal warmth to the individual who loves. The mechanism I propose that creates this sense of internal warmth is that someone who loves has effectively redefined the other as part of himself, and therefore feels rewarded when the object of his love is nurtured, as if he himself is being nurtured.

By this definition, one truly loves one's children if one feeds them, clothes them, hugs them, educates them, and invests in them, even if one detests all of these activities and even if the children never give anything back. You truly love another person and are therefore altruistic towards him when you willingly go out of your way to ensure that he is happy, even if he does not love or even know you. Similarly, you truly love a god when you revere and worship that god, even if that god never smiles upon you or acknowledges you. Love is a form of unconditional loyalty. For this reason, I will use the words love and loyalty interchangeably throughout this book.

Many examples illustrate that some form of loyalty, rather than only selfish materialism, must be at play in the workings of our societies.

Consider independent judges, who are supposed to uphold laws. If independent judges were motivated solely by material considerations, they would all be corrupt and their verdicts would be up for sale. One may suggest appointing someone to monitor judges' conduct, and indeed some countries do that. To monitor judges only moves the problem to the next level, though: those responsible for verifying the actions of independent judges would themselves be corrupt if selfish materialism were their only motivation. The person who in turn monitored the first-hand monitor of judges would also be corrupt. If people's actions were guided only by direct self-interest, then one could turn nowhere for a truly independent and reasonable assessment of whether or not a law had been transgressed. It would all be a matter of who bribed whom the most; no incorruptible watcher would be watching the watchers (Seuss 1973).

Yet independent judges do exist, and they are not all corrupt. For example, in 2001/2002, the high court judges in Zimbabwe vetoed the actions of their own government that illegally imprisoned opposition leaders. Several high court judges were subsequently forced out of office in the ensuing three years by the dictatorial regime, including the Chief Justice Guybbay (Irwin, Maguire, Martin, Martin, and Poswa 2004).

Other examples of adherence to ideals are likewise difficult to reconcile with pure selfish materialism. In 1982, for example, a vast alliance of churches, union leaders, lawyers, doctors, journalists, and students in Suriname protested against the military coup of 1980 (*Report on the Human Rights Situation in Suriname* 1983). On December 8th, after repeated warnings by the military dictatorship to cease their cause, the leaders of the protest movement were rounded up and shot. The perpetrators have to this day not been punished: the main military leader of the coup, Desi Bouterse, was in fact elected president of Suriname in 2010. The Suriname example is just one of about forty such cases highlighted in a 1983 report by the Inter-American Commission on Human Rights (*Report on the Human Rights Situation in Suriname* 1983).

Honorable men and women can hence be found amongst independent judges and "civic society" members. Not all people in civic society are bound by their oaths and their ideals, but a surprising number are. What holds for judges and civic leaders also holds for other professionals who make up the backbone of the state apparatus, such as independent central bankers, independent industry regulators, some of the military, and the people who draw up constitutions.

Such people are often amongst the first to resist a dictatorial takeover or some other insult to the ideals upheld in a free and democratic state.

We can also observe the presence of loyal men and women in any large organization. The loyalty of such individuals to a set of ideals keeps the rest honest. Thus, any theory of large human organizations needs to explain how such loyalty to ideals or values is formed and sustained. Not only is this a crucial question from an academic standpoint, but an understanding of loyalty is also important for all those who wish to manipulate people and situations. Any actual or would-be ruler, spiritual leader, bureaucrat, manager, or policy advisor has a strong interest in knowing how to induce loyalty in practice. In this chapter, I examine what circumstances induce it, and how we can manipulate others and ourselves into loyalty.[1]

2.1 The plan of the chapter

In the first part of this chapter, I lay out a general theory of love from the bottom up, by starting with the kind of empirical data that should be relevant to understanding the phenomenon of love. I gradually build up to a general theory of love, expressed in a statement about causality that implicates the core driving forces of love. I call this statement the Love Principle. This expositional approach requires that for the first part of this chapter, the reader temporarily forgets everything he knows about economics, and instead simply considers, as a stand-alone question, the puzzle of how love comes about.

Once a simple theory of love has been distilled from stylized data, the chapter continues by linking that theory to existing findings about love from across the social sciences, still ignoring the question of how a theory of love can be married with the view of mainstream economics. I then analyze how individuals experience desire and power, which are the two phenomena most implicated by the Love Principle as causal factors in the development of love. Finally, the chapter returns to the main theme of the book by examining how love differs from the existing Homo Economicus framework, and how one can conceptualize

---

[1] This chapter presents in condensed form the material in an unpublished booklet entitled "The Love Principle." That work was completely focused on the subject of loyalty, and thus included more detail than required here.

a combination of the two. It is there that I consider the evolutionary origins of both love and greed.

Below I start my investigation of love by telling several "love stories." These stories – which form the data on which to base the theory of love – are stylized examples that tell of how human love blossoms in many different situations.

2.2 Love stories: Our loves and how they come to be

2.2.1 *The loyal soldier: Break 'em down and build 'em up*

This story tells of how, everywhere in the world, soldiers become loyal to their fellow soldiers and to their army's values in general.[2]

Consider the tactics used by the US Army, and indeed by most modern armies, to transform a naïve, selfish 18-year-old into a front-line infantry division soldier ready to die for his unit. The essence of the training manual, as, for example, discussed on p. 157 and ensuing of Whitworth (2004) and put into historical context by Athens and Ulmer (2003) (pp. 109–110), is that you first "break them down" in order to then "build them up." In phase one, the trainers physically and mentally exhaust the recruit. They create physical stress through physical exertion, lack of food, and lack of sleep. They aggravate the mental distress caused by lack of sleep by a continuous bombardment of insults, disparaging remarks, and exposure to danger. In short, they take away all sense of control from the recruit and make him feel weak. This deprivation of control brings the recruit to the point where he feels desperate and is in great mental distress.

In such a state of mind, the recruit is eager to grasp onto anything that will alleviate the pressure and bring back a sense of control. In response to this distress call, the army (in phase two) offers group cohesion, army loyalty, and the ethics of obedience as a means of regaining control,

---

[2] I do not wish to claim that an army wins the loyalty of all of its soldiers. Some are more successfully trained than others. Some drop out before they are trained. Others simply "do their time" and are not particularly loyal to anything other than themselves. There are thus many exceptions to the statement that "many recruits are turned into loyal army soldiers during their training." Similar nuances can be brought to bear on many of the statements to come, but to mention them in each case merely fills pages without adding understanding. I proceed without repeating such disclaimers after every example.

while demanding an end to selfishness. Authorities punish the unit as a whole for signs of individual disobedience, which means that pressure towards obedience within the unit is added to the outside pressure. The weaker the initial sense of identity, the more quickly the recruit gives in, partially jettisoning his former identity for one that incorporates the desired values. The stronger the initial sense of identity, the longer this process takes. If trainers induce too much stress, they run the risk of the recruit committing suicide or derailing in some other way. There is an appropriate amount of stress depending on the degree to which the recruit needs to be changed, whether the recruit believes he has an alternative to accepting the army's implicit offer, and so forth.

The usual outcome of this type of training is compliance. This can be achieved in a matter of months, and is a procedure that is virtually identical the world over. Bourquin (1979), for example, describes the procedure used some 200 years ago by the drill sergeants of Shaka Zulu in South Africa:

[The Zulu Warrior] had to be capable of enduring any amount of hardship. The cow-hide sandals, in normal use on account of the many thorns and stony terrain, were regarded by Shaka as an encumbrance which impeded the speed and sure-footedness of his soldiers. His armies had to learn to march barefoot and, to test whether the soles of their feet were sufficiently hardened, they had to dance at times on ground covered by thorns.

From the army cohorts forged by Shaka Zulu in South Africa 200 years ago, to the marines in Russia today – from infantries in Latin America to the army droves of China and the front-line soldiers of the US – young men in their millions and from highly diverse backgrounds have been effectively indoctrinated by the simple procedure described above. It is one of the most astonishingly replicable feats of social engineering that exists, and it provides a basic recipe for how humans form loyalties and how they can thereby be manipulated.

2.2.2 *The loving child*

This story relates to how most young children are brought up to be loving members of their family and of their community; how they are made to adhere to norms of behavior; and how they eventually come to believe in concepts of right and wrong.

Children are brought up to adopt values and to form bonds with others very much like soldiers are trained to be loyal to their unit. A common strategy pursued by parents and carers is that the small child, who has precious little control over anything that happens to him, is rewarded for making desirable adjustments in behavior and values. The small child is rewarded for starting to smile, walk, and talk, and for being altruistic towards other family members. The rewards include the satisfaction of both physical and mental needs. The child is punished for noncompliance, where punishment can take a physical form but can also include the withholding of gratification of mental needs, such as when parents do not hug the child or are coarse with him. Most children comply, as a means of gaining control over their environment and obtaining the rewards.

After a while, the rewards for these desired behaviors stop. For example, the child is no longer rewarded for walking or talking, and instead these behaviors are taken for granted. It is effectively demanded of the child that he adopt the desired behaviors until they become second nature. Rewards and punishments are then handed out for the next layer of desirable behaviors and values, until finally the child becomes an independent entity, no longer under the direct control of his carers. In the process, however, he has become what is known as a "socialized human" who possesses a desired set of behaviors and values, as well as loving himself and his parents/carers.

Note the timing involved here: what one first has to induce an individual to change into, by confronting him with a demanding power that is capable of satisfying needs, subsequently becomes an integral aspect of the identity of that individual and no longer needs reinforcement. The individual has come to love the very behaviors and values that were initially demanded from him. The individual has also come to love those who set these demands upon him.

A system of rewards and punishments operates within schools as well, where both teachers and peers demand changes in the individual, more or less explicitly.

2.2.3 The love for our children

This story relates how parents or carers come to love the children (or other dependents) they care for. It also tells of the circumstances under which carers do not love the ones in their care.

Children often wield power over their parents long before birth. Finding a partner with whom to have children, getting pregnant, and dealing with all the tribulations of pregnancy and birth are extremely time-consuming and emotionally demanding activities. In this sense, an infant takes up a lot of energy and time even long before it is born, just as if it were an independent power demanding attention. Infants are also a tremendous source of joy for many parents and carers. They can make carers feel valuable, loved, and therefore part of a larger group. Their youth also holds a promise: children can, after they have grown up, care for their parents and perpetuate the beliefs of the parents into the future.

Birth itself is a love booby trap. By the time she goes into labor, a woman is in great physical discomfort and suffering from lack of sleep. The contractions of labor then last on average for about twelve hours, weakening and tiring the mother even more. Nature plays another trick on the female body in the form of manipulating internal levels of oxytocin, a chemical that acts as an emotional stimulant, making it easier to form emotional bonds.[3] Oxytocin levels greatly increase in the months leading up to birth, and reach heightened levels during the pains of labor (Insel 1992). This primes the mother to be at her most emotional when birth takes place, which carries the possibility of the mother being very loving (as well as very angry!) towards anyone around at that time. Thus programmed to be very emotional, many mothers indeed initiate a strong bond of love for the child during and immediately after birth.

The baby too is emotionally aroused as a consequence of the highly stressful birth process, making it possible for the baby to quickly imprint upon the smell of the mother, which helps it find the nipple (Klaus 1998). The infant is much less subject to a love booby trap because infants can accept different carers (and nipples) very quickly, largely because they cannot form long-term memories, so babies are simply not capable of loving a particular person forever from the time of birth. Lindquist (1945) for example finds that four-to-five-month-old infants were unable to recognize their mothers

---

[3] The main evidence that oxytocin is useful in bonding comes from laboratory studies on rats and sheep, where increased levels of oxytocin in the brain were found to lead to more distinct maternal behavior (Fahrbach, Morrell, and Pfaff 1984, Kendrick, Keverne, and Baldwin 1987).

more than five days after last seeing them. Mothers, however, are truly booby-trapped to love their infants: weakened by the experience of birth, their emotions primed by chemical stimulants, and full of good wishes towards the infant, most mothers are sitting ducks for love.

Fathers are snared to a much lesser degree. Most importantly, they are not subjected to elevated oxytocin levels, extreme physical pain, or extreme mental stress directly before and at birth. Despite this, many fathers are still weak and stressed at birth. The stress does not stop there: the constant attention and care demanded by infants keeps all parents and carers on their toes. In particular, the loss of sleep involved in feeding and caring for an infant during the first few months of its life is extremely stressful for most parents. As long as parents feel they cannot avoid their caring tasks, they are at the mercy of the baby's whims: small though it may be, the baby effectively wields tremendous power over both of its parents. The infant achieves a situation of exhaustion in its parents similar to that achieved by an army platoon commander drilling his soldiers. No wonder infants are usually loved by their parents.

Loving one's children is not, however, inevitable. Carers can opt not to care for their children. They can abandon them, give them up for adoption, or refuse to spend much time with them. Such situations can arise when carers refuse to acknowledge the power of their children. These carers will love their children less, at least on average. Thus, just as having children can be a conscious choice, binding oneself to one's children can also be a choice: one can choose consciously to put oneself into a position where one is vulnerable to love.

2.2.4 The love of a fan

A fan will rejoice at the highs of his hero and be sad when his hero eventually falls from the limelight. Even after the hero dies, some fans remain committed devotees. Well-known examples of this phenomenon in the West revolve around such stars as Elvis Presley, Marilyn Monroe, and Babe Ruth. Unseen and often unrecognized by his hero, a fan may keep empathizing with his hero and remain a loyal follower until the day he himself dies.

Of the many people who become loyal fans of a given hero, most are young, and most are in some sense weak. The typical hardcore fans are the youngster desperate to grow up and leave home; the young adult having a hard time in his or her work or private life; and the sick in general. Such people, not coincidentally, exhibit some core characteristics similar to the soldier undergoing military training. They are in some sense feeling low, and are faced with some outside power that they cannot control and that appears extremely desirable. In the case of the fan, part of the perceived desirability of the hero is the fan's wish to be himself the hero: the fan partly lives the life of the hero by identifying and empathizing with the hero.

No better illustration can be found of the love of a devoted fan than in the words of a particular hero. In a BBC interview in 2004, a famous Indian actress, Preity Zinta, said:[4]

Karl Marx said religion is the opium of the masses. But in India, movies are religion. And only in India do Gods have competition from actors and, yes, cricketers. I had a glimpse of the power of the moving image and actors very early in my life. There was a mythological television serial on the Hindu epic Ramayana which was a huge hit in the 1980s. People from neighbouring villages would descend on our farm home to catch the soap religiously. Every Sunday morning had a set time table. At 8:30 sharp, people would arrive, greet my grandparents, take off their shoes, step towards the television set and bow in front of it as they would to a deity. At 9:00 all eyes would be glued to the telly as they sat in pin drop silence and experienced God ... After six years and 17 films in the business, I am getting a taste of what being a film star in India is all about. It is a high that is higher than cloud nine. It is the toughest job in the world, it is crazy and at times it is also scary. Fans come in various shapes and sizes and people will do anything to come close to their favourite star. Temples are built in our names. Fan letters flood our mailboxes and the love is unconditional. Sometimes the love and the adulation can make you feel so humble and close to God. Recently, I met a little girl who was dying of leukemia and had expressed a desire to meet me.

All the themes of this chapter are here: the notion of love as unconditional attachment, the desirability and power of the person adulated, and the close similarity between the love for a hero and the love for a deity.

---

[4] This passage was taken from a transcript of the British Broadcasting Corporation (BBC) interview on June 22, 2004 with Preity Zinta, "Bollywood" actress.

2.2.5 The faith of a hermit

This next story illustrates how many people find spirituality by putting themselves in situations where the conditions for love apply. Spirituality is a form of love: a spiritual person greatly loves his god, spirit, or idea.

Consider the search for spirituality in medieval Europe, as researched in great detail by Besse (1910). In order to liberate themselves of earthly considerations, devout young men in search of god would give all their worldly belongings to the church and seclude themselves in isolated regions where they had to live off the land by surviving on wild game, berries, plant roots, and so on, washing and drinking from cold streams. The lack of comfort they experienced was meant to purify their souls, making them more receptive to contact with god.

The hermit is at the mercy of nature's forces like no other. The hermit suffers cold when it freezes, and hunger when little grows. The hermit's weakness makes the supposed controller of nature (god) look strong. Nevertheless, the hermit is still human, and so part of him still craves to survive, and to experience warmth and the comfort of a secure life. Reports of hermits who eventually told their stories to traveling writers indicate that they did attain spirituality, in the sense of often finding themselves in awe of god's work. Many claimed to have been sent visions of god or his messengers, and the history of medieval Europe is full of cases where the visions of hermits were taken to be true.

The acknowledged "hermit hero" in medieval European Catholicism was Francis of Assisi, who lived in modern-day Italy from about 1182 until 1226. He advocated a return to simple living. The Franciscan order that he spawned is built upon a philosophy of poverty and devotion to god. To this day, Francis is revered as the patron saint of animals and the natural environment because he himself lived very simply. For the purposes of this book, the most relevant thing about St. Francis is the connection between poverty and simplicity that he advocated, on the one hand, and the elevated level of spirituality he claimed to have achieved himself and that he claimed others would achieve, on the other.

The example of St. Francis is also interesting in that his cause was taken up by the Catholic church. Balk (2008) tells the following about how the pope found a use for St. Francis:

The legend is that when St. Francis stood before Innocent III in 1209, wearing his coarse serge garment tied about the waist with a cord, and begged the great Pontiff to approve his movement, he was at first rejected. But while the Pope lay sleeping the night after his meeting with Francis, he had a dream of the Lateran shaken and falling, and a poor beggar holding it up with his shoulders. This beggar he recognized: it was Francis of Assisi. Innocent understood that the new Order would be a pillar of the Church ...

Medieval Europe is not the only place where this basic recipe for spirituality has been practiced. Many revered prophets and "sons of God" have secluded themselves, living a frugal life in order to find spirituality. Both Jesus and Buddha are portrayed as having spent time living in extreme simplicity. In current Indian culture, there are still hermits who deliberately free themselves from their worldly possessions and seclude themselves in search of spirituality, partially because living a secluded and spiritual existence (termed *Vanaprastha*) is seen as one of the four stages of life in Hinduism.

The famous Indian preacher of tolerance and nonviolence, Mahatma Gandhi (1869–1948), also advocated simple living. He spent many of his later years in austerity, even when imprisoned, where he sewed his own clothes and tilled his own food. He urged others to do so in order that they too would experience spirituality. He was in a sense an Indian hermit: as Chakrabarti (1993) (p. 53) states, "Gandhi makes an in-depth approach to spiritualism through the education of austerity primarily because in his vision of a new world of spiritual regeneration he cannot do away with the blessings of simplicity and austerity."

So too are there Chinese hermits, who are religious men who live simply. According to Balcom (2004) (p. 137), "the place of the religious hermit in Chinese culture continues to be deeply ingrained." Wise, holy men who weaken themselves in various ways (e.g., through narcotics use, physical pain, and social deprivation) in order to become close to nature or "spirits" believed to be powerful are also a feature of Aboriginal culture in Australia and in African cultures: Pratt (2007) discusses the role and lifestyle of shamans in Africa, and many of his examples fit the examples of other cultures. Similar practices related to attaining greater spirituality through deliberate self-deprivation can be found in the indigenous cultures of North and South America. Pritzker (1998) (pp. 467–477) discusses the role of deprivation in achieving spirituality in various tribes of North America, while Vitebsky (1995) (p. 46) describes similar processes for South American cultures.

In sum, the "hermit recipe" appears in some form in most known cultures. The recognized path to spirituality is finding a situation where one is vulnerable due to being at the perceived mercy of the god or spirit one is attempting to approach. In most cases, there is an element of conscious choice, in the sense that the person wishing to love more or less consciously seeks to make himself weak while beholding a force he perceives as powerful, and thereby puts himself into a similar situation as the army recruit or the laboring mother.

2.2.6 The love for our partners

This story is about the love for our romantic partners. Two kinds of happy accidents are discussed: love at first sight and the love that grows between partners over time.

The good news about love at first sight is that it exists. Sternberg and Weis (2006) list the attributes connected with being in love (p. 88): "Lovers experience extreme energy, hyperactivity, sleeplessness, impulsivity, euphoria, and mood swings." From neuroscientific studies (Marazitti, Akiskal, Rossi, and Cassano 1999), it has furthermore been found that people in the early stages of romantic love have similar levels of a particular neurotransmitter (platelet 5-HT) as people with obsessive-compulsive disorder, suggesting that the internal experience of strong romantic love is akin to that of being obsessed.

Love at first sight towards prospective partners also fits in with the love stories above. It usually involves the young: generally, older people are wary from experience and will consciously work against experiencing love at first sight. Love at first sight often occurs on emotionally charged occasions, and the object of love is invariably desirable. Love at first sight does, however, fade over time. Some researchers have claimed that "the butterflies" leave after seven years, but this is not a holy number that holds for everyone. Some people report falling in love with a different person every week. They combine a high ability to believe in someone new again and again (gullibility) with very rapid fading of the influence of love (low power endurance).

While some of us fall in love with our partners the moment we set eyes on them, for many others love grows over time. Cautious about losing themselves, some people start relationships by simply desiring things of another person, such as sex, warmth, security, or self-esteem, without any emotional feelings for the other whatsoever. Over time it becomes clear whether or not the other can continue to meet these needs and desires. If so, then an awareness of the power of the other gradually develops. Often unexpectedly, we start to fear that the other may leave us, or when our partners are away, we suddenly miss them and discover feelings for them. Like love at first sight, love that develops over time comes as a surprise: few of us anticipate, as we start out in a relationship, fearing the loss of our partner or coming more and more under his power.

Our own desires build this trap for us: as we become more and more trusting, we let our guard down and thereby allow ourselves to become vulnerable. We are then weak in the sense of accepting that the other has some emotional power over us that we cannot directly command. We suddenly find ourselves in almost exactly the same situation as the soldier finds himself in the army, or as the hermit does when beholding his god: we behold the demands and power of the other from a position of weakness. Those who give in to the power of the other start loving their partners over time. Those who reject this – who simply refuse to be vulnerable – essentially refuse to allow themselves to love.

A love partnership is one in which the love of both requires the two individuals to submit mutually to the power of the other. However, there are some partnerships that never develop into love and are at heart a form of mutual possession, where both individuals simply derive some use from the other. This occurs when both feel themselves to be so powerful that they refuse to be vulnerable towards the other. Being that strong leads one to expect many things from the other, and leads one to think that one does not have to submit to the other's wishes. In such cases, both partners have exceedingly high expectations as to what the other will do for them, but neither will get or give much love.[5]

2.3 Analysis: Love and the Love Principle

What common elements exist in the love stories above? First, love comes as a surprise to the individuals involved: while they can

[5] Some sociologists argue that increased expectations in relationships are important in explaining higher divorce rates in industrialized countries (e.g., pp. 247–248 of Segrin and Nabi 2002).

manipulate the degree to which they are vulnerable to love, they cannot simply choose to love something. As Sternberg and Weis (2006) state (p. 88), love is involuntary. How can people then love if they do not consciously choose to do so? The only possibility is that there must be such a thing as an unconscious mind involved in love.

A second key point is that love is not, by and large, given to things under one's command. While they may get pleasure from them, people do not worship water bottles, pens, chairs, or anything else they feel they control themselves. Love apparently involves feeling weak (i.e., unable to wield control) in relation to the thing or person being loved.

A third key point is that the object of love is believed to be able to satisfy some overt or hidden desire.

These thoughts are summarized in the following description of love's genesis that I henceforth refer to as the Love Principle:

Love derives from the attempt of the unconscious mind to bargain with something that is believed to be capable of fulfilling desires and that is perceived to be too powerful to be possessed by direct means.

The first part of the Love Principle states that the genesis of love is an act of which we are not consciously aware, which means love is not a direct choice. Love can only indirectly be chosen by the conscious mind, such as when we consciously decide to put ourselves into a situation where the Love Principle applies: i.e., in which we greatly desire something and where the object that we believe to be capable of satisfying that desire is perceived to be too powerful to control directly.

The first part of the Love Principle also embodies the timing issue so crucial to the development of love. Love starts as an attempt by the unconscious mind to bargain with something or someone else. The implicit offer is effectively, "If I give in to your power over me by including you in the set of things I care for, then you will give me what I desire." The unconscious mind expects to be rewarded for this offer of love. However, once initiated by the unconscious mind, love migrates to the conscious mind in the sense that the object has become part of the self-image of the individual (what is loved has become part of what the lover cares for), meaning that the welfare of the loved entity starts to be a goal in and of itself within the one who loves. The conscious self thereby becomes the slave of the previous decision of the unconscious mind to make an implicit deal: it cannot easily undo the love response initiated by the unconscious mind. This is also why first impressions are so important in matters of love: once hooked by the unconscious mind, the conscious becomes bound.

The second part of the Love Principle points out that we only fall in love with something that we believe is capable of satisfying a desire. Naturally, different people desire different things, meaning that different things can be loved. For the majority of the human race, however, this bluntly means that we do not easily love the ugly, the old, or the weak because they cannot normally give us the things we want. There are circumstances in which we yearn for the nod of the invalid, the gratitude of the old, or the approval of the weak. But by and large, our dreams concern achieving things that are hard to achieve: e.g., having sex with the strong and beautiful, having control over many others, and feeling the admiration of the crowd. Unless we have learned to love them in the past, the presently powerless (and therefore undesirable) are more often despised than loved.

The third and final part of the Love Principle is about power. The unconscious mind is a cold calculator and simply refuses to love what it believes it can get by dominating (owning) rather than loving. We do not love a computer when we believe ourselves to be the computer's master rather than its slave. We do not love a weak suitor who will blindly do whatever we tell him. We may take love from such weaker entities, but we only invest our love when we believe we cannot dominate.

A key facet of the Love Principle is the faith that the unconscious has in the reciprocity of the entity with which it is trying to strike a bargain. Whether or not the entity exists, is human, or has reciprocated in the past, the unconscious is prone to believing that the entity is reciprocal. This assumed reciprocity of the entity with which we are trying to bargain is perhaps the most surprising element of our love response, and I discuss this phenomenon in more detail below.

The Love Principle summarizes the mechanics behind each love story discussed above. The soldier desires acceptance and a sense of control from a powerful army bureaucracy; the child desires many things, including food, warmth, and security, from a powerful parent who has guided it to expect rewards for compliance; the loving parent desires many things, including future security and a sense of belonging, from a child who controls the parent's life to an incredible degree; the hermit is weak and hungry in the sight of his god's power. All implicitly believe that the entity to which they are giving their love will reciprocate.

The Love Principle fits the most common forms of love that many of us experience in our lives – so while it may not be the only thing that can explain our loves, it does explain a variety of facts fairly simply. To my mind, this is the mark of a good theory. However, it is important to acknowledge that every example and element of the supporting evidence above is open to alternative interpretations.[6] Thus, when I say that the Love Principle fits a given observation, I do not mean that the Love Principle is the only thing that can explain something. The validity of the Love Principle lies in its fit to known cases and its predictive applications. Above all, it is the fact that a large set of quite diverse examples can be explained by the Love Principle that should be seen as its supporting evidence, which can then be compared against the evidence in favor of alternative theories that might similarly be thought to explain the same diverse set of facts. In much of the remainder of this chapter, I will delve into further implications and underlying processes to see whether the Love Principle fits other observations, and whether humans have the mental hardware that would make something like the Love Principle possible.

As a final note, in light of the stories and Love Principle above, what is *not* true love? One characteristic that is sometimes associated with love, but is distinct from it, is conscious possessiveness. Those who care for their romantic partner only if that other person is faithful and kind in return, for example, do not love but possess. Such possessive people have a partner like a child has a toy that can be discarded the moment its usefulness expires. It is true that we take care of our possessions and are willing to fight for our territory. However, that care stops the moment we believe that the possession has lost its usefulness. So, consciously protecting what we own is thus not the same as true love. Similarly, those who only care for their god if that god "gives something back" do not truly love their god. Those who care for their country only as long as it provides for them do not truly love: they are not true patriots. Possession and love are thus two very different things.

2.4 The basic science of love: Introduction and preview

I now remove the blinds between the analysis so far and the academic literature by discussing the evidence relevant to love that has been

---

[6] Such ambiguity is not unique to this case; interpretational ambiguity is a perpetual pest when it comes to theorizing in the social sciences.

amassed by science. Insights on love have been contributed by different scientific disciplines for at least the last hundred years. For the sake of brevity, only the most important such insights are discussed here.

From neuroscience, the science that maps the structure and function of the human brain, we have been shown how to understand emotions biophysically, how love relates to emotions, and how emotions and conscious choices interact inside our brains. From ethology, the study of animal behavior, we have learned about the "attachments" (the word used by ethologists to describe what we call love in humans) that are possible in the animal world. Studies of primates have been especially useful in revealing what kinds of attachments, such as those between parents and offspring, have a long evolutionary ancestry. From evolutionary biology, the science of the evolution of species, we have gained an understanding of how the things we love and the circumstances under which we love help us to survive and prosper in normal circumstances. This field therefore illuminates how love relates to the "survival of the fittest" concept. From cognitive developmental psychology, the study of how children grow up to be mentally functioning adults, we have learned about the circumstances under which children form normal emotional attachments to care-givers, and those in which their emotional development stalls. From studies of happiness and attachment in adults, we have learned about the long-term effects of love. In sum, we have gained a wealth of observations from the sciences that can help to both guide and test our ideas about the nature and genesis of love.

Given all of these readily accessible scientific insights, why did I not begin this chapter with them rather than with a collection of less scientific-seeming "love stories?" The main answer is that scientific disciplines are severely handicapped with regard to how they can research love. No psychology lab is allowed to put the amount of pressure on its subjects that an army officer is allowed to exert on his recruits. No neurologist is allowed to keep subjects inside a magnetic resonance imaging (MRI) machine continuously for ten years, which is roughly the time window parents and schools can use to induce love and loyalty in children. No happiness researcher is allowed to take away all of a subject's material possessions in order to observe whether that person then becomes more spiritual. The essential ingredient lacking in basic science is power. Neither do scientists have the power over their subjects that those same subjects face elsewhere, nor has science so far invented a way to measure the extent and source of the actual powers any particular individual faces on a day-to-day basis, partially because individuals themselves often do not realize the powers under which they live. For these reasons, basic science is almost useless when it comes to understanding the circumstances under which real people form loving relationships, which in turn become part of the bedrock of modern society. It is an area of scientific inquiry in which the tools of modern science are of very limited use.

Another issue that hampers science in its analysis of love is the level of analysis. Much of science deals with either basic phenomena, such as the question of what an emotion is, or high-level phenomena, such as the demographic trends in the world. The Love Principle is positioned in between the basic level and the aggregate level, neither directly leading to predictions at the aggregate level nor obviously following from a single phenomenon at the basic level. As a result, the connection with both basic phenomena and high-level aggregate findings has to be fleshed out *ex post* rather than derived *ex ante*. It is medium-level observations that lead me to believe that something like the Love Principle must be true, but the question remains whether it fits what we know at the more basic level and whether it leads to aggregate phenomena that we can observe and therefore use to validate it.

What basic science can thus offer is a way to think about how the phenomenon of love fits in with evolution, basic desires, and basic mental and psychological processes. While some insights from scientific inquiry can help us to hypothesize about the genesis of love, its strongest role can therefore be seen as helping us understand the mechanics, consequences, and correlates of love once that love is established.

The next few sections briefly review large areas of the human condition that science has helped us to explore and that are important to our understanding of love.

2.5 The human brain

In order to understand many of the insights relevant to love that have been contributed by neuroscience, a short summary of the basic structures involved is first required.

The basic unit of mental activity is the neuron, of which the brain has about 10 to the power 11, each of which on average is connected to some 7,000 other neurons via synapses. The way information is shared across these neurons is via electrical or chemical impulses: a given neuron may send a message that excites other neurons to also fire impulses, or conversely that inhibits them, making them less likely to send further impulses. The simplest picture of the brain that emerges is a self-feeding system of waves of impulses being passed along, exciting or inhibiting other impulses.

Neuroscience tells us that the enormous number of neurons in the brain are organized into many separate functional centers with different tasks – such as the processing of a certain type of information (such as visual, auditory, or emotional) – and that these different centers interact in specific ways. One center is concerned with attaching emotion to what is heard. Another center attaches emotion to what is seen, and further subdivides seen objects into those that are animate and those that are inanimate. The emotional centers in particular are situated in certain physical places (specifically, the thalamus, the basal ganglia, and the hypothalamus) and have direct connections both to our senses and to our higher-order reasoning centers, which are located in the prefrontal cerebral cortex.

Damage to a specific one or more of these centers directly translates into odd behavior. The close examination of hundreds of cases of individuals with particular forms of brain damage has provided a wealth of scientific insight in this area. For example, we have learned that lesions to the "lateral hypothalamus" result in a person becoming placid and unemotional, whereas lesions to the "medial hypothalamus" result in highly excitable behavior that includes the individual becoming quick to anger. In the first instance, impulses that would normally generate an emotional response never reach the emotional centers; in the second instance, the countervailing impulses that normally temper one's emotional responses never reach the emotional centers (p. 746 of Kandel, Schwartz, and Jessell 1991). Neuroscientists have also closely examined what happens within mentally healthy people's brains when they are faced with specific tasks, such as listening to something or solving a puzzle, further helping to build up a reasonably good idea of which parts of the brain do what, and how they interact.

The picture that emerges from the Kandel et al. (1991) and Kandel, Schwartz, and Jessell (2000) textbooks on neuroscience is that the brain is a storytelling machine with multiple layers. All of the basic information flowing into our brains from our senses and our self-reflection gets broken into small pieces for analysis by the various neural subcenters, after which our analytical centers concoct interpretations of the facts presented to them, based on past experiences. Multiple stories may easily be created, which leads to odd possibilities, such as that the left side of the brain believes something different from what the right side of the brain believes. People are capable of saying they cannot see a ball in front of them (according to the message emanating from one side of the brain) while picking up that ball at the same time (according to the message emanating from the other side). The possible interconnections involved even in simple tasks, such as speaking a sentence, are so numerous and complex that we social scientists need simplified representations in order to make progress in understanding human behavior for the purposes of a book like this.

A metaphorical representation that I will exploit henceforth is that of the brain as a giant railway network where information is analyzed in the stations (clusters of neurons), and the railways (axons ending in synapses) are the lines of communication between the stations. Each station concocts a tiny story based on the information it receives, and feeds that story through to other stations. The brain is in this sense one very powerful reasoning and, potentially, excuse-providing machine.

2.5.1 *The conscious and unconscious mind*

We may possess a vast railway network inside our heads, but we are not directly in charge of which trains are running at any given time. Evidence of the existence of some level of our brains that we do not directly control has been contributed over the decades by many natural and social sciences. Different terms have been used for this level of the brain, most commonly "subliminal," "unconscious," and "subconscious"; I will generally refer to it as the unconscious.

Clean examples of phenomena regulated unconsciously are things such as the heart rate, blood pressure, growth, and eye focusing. The conscious mind clearly relates to the analytical part of our brains' activities, and as such is directly involved in strategic games, analyzing new information, the creation of new music and literature, and mulling over the advantages and shortcomings of different ways of looking at the world. Many mental activities are more of a blend, initially involving more of the conscious mind but gradually taken up automatically by the unconscious. Walking, talking, dancing, and other such often-repeated activities fit into that category. One way of seeing this is that the trains and stations of the brain must compete for the attention of the conscious mind, and thus must generate story-lines that appear to be novel, dangerous, and/or potentially rewarding enough to require the conscious mind's attention.

Neural science has taught us that desires and perceptions can be manipulated unconsciously. For instance, Byrne (1959) examined sub-liminal messages and emotional responses by giving subjects short visual cues intended to elicit a desire to eat. One group of his subjects was exposed to flashes of pictures, lasting no more than 1/200th of a second, of the word "beef." These visual cues were so brief that individuals had no conscious memory of being given the cues: i.e., when asked, they would not be able to say what they saw. Yet, the group shown the pictures was markedly more likely to be hungry and to accept an offered sandwich than control-group subjects who had not been shown the pictures. While this process resulted in an unconscious triggering of desires, this did not mean that subjects were successfully led to a partic-ular course of action in order to fulfil those desires. The subjects shown the flashed "beef" picture were no more likely to choose a beef sand-wich over any other sandwich, compared to the control subjects. This shows that desires can be subliminally increased without involvement of the conscious mind, but that these desires are not easy to direct.

In other studies, researchers have found it possible to alter people's relative judgments subliminally, such as by using short visual cues that tell subjects which of two lines is longer or which of two weights is heavier. Theus (1994) reviewed this literature and concluded that while there was sufficient evidence to suggest that perception could be changed and emotions could be aroused subliminally, there was much less evidence that individuals could be manipulated to change their choices in any particular direction.

Love and the conscious/unconscious division

Studies looking at human subjects who reported being in love have found that these subjects' brain patterns are similar to those of individu-als with obsessive disorders who cannot stop thinking about something (e.g., cleanliness). When normal humans say they are "in love" with a person, it therefore means that their conscious minds are constantly preoccupied with the object of their love. They are addicted to those thoughts much like we can imagine being consciously obsessive about trying to learn a new dance.

The basic mechanisms that determine whether we want to dance, and how we should activate muscles in order to do so, are mostly unconscious. Yet some of the important steps are taken consciously: for example, we consciously decide to drive to the dance lesson, and actively direct the memorization of dance movements. I contend that in love too, the unconscious desires something, whereas the conscious mind assesses the power of the person or the idea that captures our attention. If our conscious mind decides that the person or idea we desire is already under our control, then the unconscious ceases its involvement. If not, then the unconscious mind puts a love program on the tracks. This is accompanied by constantly focusing on the object of desire and by alerting the conscious mind insistently of the benefits of the desired person or idea. Our obsessive attention to what we are learning to love is in effect a symptom of an unconscious mind busily teaching us to love someone or something that cannot be easily obtained. The conscious can actively resist by trying to divert the attention of the whole brain to something else, and by suppressing emotions, but it cannot alter the desires of the unconscious. The individual in this sense faces limited choices about what to desire and what not to desire. It is not merely the case that our unconscious alerts the conscious of things it desires, such as food or drink. The unconscious itself is activated by things of which we may be unaware even on reflection, such as pheromones in the case of sexual attraction.

However, any particular love we have acquired can, like other things we learn in later life, change in nature or importance over time. Just as we can learn to walk and talk differently in later life, it is possible for us to consciously redirect our emotional centers to reject old loves or adopt new loves. Adults can unlearn their loves learned in childhood. Ever the adaptors, we can consciously decide to put ourselves in situations that lead our unconscious into reducing its love for one thing or increasing it for something else.

2.5.2 The neural "love program"

Drawing on this very basic understanding of the brain, we can begin to be more precise about what love is. Research by neuroscientists tells us that love for other individuals produces automated emotional

responses of which we are not usually consciously aware. We emotionally color what we see, hear, smell, or touch, and it is thus a normal
response to automatically experience positive feelings when we see or
hear our loved ones. If, due to some form of brain damage, we do not
feel that automated response, we become confused because we miss an
internal response that we expected to feel. Individuals with a particular
form of Capgras syndrome (an affliction corresponding to a particular
form of brain damage) can thus be convinced that they see an imposter
when they are beholding their own mother, simply because the brain
connections that normally provide an automatic emotional response
when seeing their mother are severed.

Love is hence connected to emotions, but it is not itself an emotion. Izard (1992), recognizing that love was not itself an emotion,
called love "a complex affective-cognitive network." To love, defined
previously as being willing to sacrifice oneself for something regardless of any observable reward, is like being automatically subject to
the activation of a program of emotional responses when exposed to
certain stimuli. Hence when one says "I love Robin," this means that
seeing, helping, protecting, and being with Robin are activities that
activate positive emotions: being exposed to these stimuli automatically
sets certain trains on the track. Seeing Robin hurt likewise automatically activates negative emotions: other trains then run. What I claim
distinguishes loving from "liking" or other affectionate responses is
the requirement that with love, even being an unseen and unrecognized helper of Robin automatically activates positive emotions. Liking
could mean simply, for example, that positive emotions are activated
by seeing or being with Robin.

Development of the neural love program

Despite their best efforts as documented in many thousands of studies, researchers have not found conclusive evidence that humans are
pre-programmed to love anything in particular. A child needs to be
stimulated to develop the ability to love, which we can think of as
possessing developed neural programs ready to produce automated
emotional responses to stimuli (such as other people or ideas) – or,
metaphorically, possessing the ability to set a "love program" on
the tracks. Unlike goslings, for example, human babies are not pre-
programmed to imprint on the first thing they see that moves. Also,
unlike many animals, humans do not necessarily love forever whatever

they bonded with in childhood. There is essentially no evidence that humans naturally love anything forever, which is why psychologists avoid the term "imprinting" in preference for terms such as "emotional attachment" when speaking of humans. Because we do not form immutable attachments to anything in particular, Lorenz (1959) essentially concluded that humans specialize in nonspecialization.

However, like other primates, humans need to be stimulated to learn how to love as young infants. If we are not exposed to other people who stimulate us to respond to them in an emotional way, then we simply do not allocate the mental space to the "love program" train network that we otherwise would. Kandel et al. (1991) in this vein discuss (p. 946) "critical periods" in the development of behavior in humans in which we learn (or do not learn) how to become socially and emotionally competent.

Results from an early study analyzing the importance of childhood learning for later emotional behavior are reported in Spitz (1945) and Spitz (1946). Spitz compared the development of infants raised in a foundling home for abandoned children with the development of children raised in a nursing home attached to a women's prison. Both sets of infants were raised in a clean environment and were provided with adequate food and medical care. The babies in the nursing home were cared for by their mothers, who were prison inmates. The infants in the foundling home were raised by nurses, each of whom was responsible for seven infants. Another major difference in the environments faced by the two sets of babies was the amount of external sensory stimulation they received. In the prison nursing home, the infants were able to see out of their cribs and observe the activity in the ward, while in the foundling home the babies' cribs were covered by sheets, which were used to keep the babies quiet and docile. Hence, the foundlings lived in relative sensory and social deprivation compared to the babies in the nursing home.

At the age of four months, the infants in the foundling home scored better than those in the nursing home on several developmental tests, suggesting that genetic factors did not favor the infants in the nursing home, which is as one would expect given that their mothers were in prison. At twelve months of age, however, the motor and intellectual performance of the children in the foundling home had fallen far below that of the children in the nursing home, with many developing what is now known as anaclitic depression. The children in the foundling home were withdrawn, showed little curiosity or gaiety, and were prone to infection. At the ages of two and three years, the children in the nursing home tested as similar to those raised in the homes of normal families, while the development of those in the foundling home had been delayed. Only two of twenty-six foundlings were able to walk and speak, and even they could only say a few words. Their ability to function socially was similarly impaired.

One way to conceptualize the development of our capacity to love is to say that we are born with nascent neural train stations and tracks that have the potential to become the infrastructure used in love programs, but that infrastructure will not become large and active if we are not stimulated to build it up as young infants. This does not necessarily mean that such stations and tracks can only be built if we are ourselves loved, but it does mean that they will not develop if we are not prompted to use them. Fortunately, because the vast majority of humans have experienced a providing carer who stimulated them to love her in early childhood, we should be able to assume the existence of a ready-made "love program" in most people. This means that it should be possible to develop a fairly universally applicable understanding of how that program is activated.

2.6 Emotional development and regulation

The development of emotional behavior in humans occurs in many different stages and calls upon many different abilities. An infant first displays primary emotions, then starts to recognize them in others, leading to simple mental models of how others react. This leads in turn to the development of secondary emotions that depend upon those mental models, and finally to the development of complicated emotional behavior based on social norms and an increased understanding of the reaction patterns of other individuals and whole groups.

2.6.1 Emotional development

Our primary emotions appear earliest and are associated with culturally universal facial expressions. Fear is the classic primary emotion, but anger, joy, distress, and disgust are also already observed by twelve months of age. Interest, joy, physical distress, and disgust appear to be present at or shortly after birth (Izard 1977). Anger can be seen as early as four months, and surprise at six months (Charlesworth 1969, Stenberg, Campos, and Emde 1983).

By the end of the second year of life, the secondary emotions begin to appear. These include embarrassment, guilt, shame, and pride (Lewis and Michalson 1983, Lewis, Sullivan, Stangor, and Weiss 1989). These are referred to as secondary emotions because they require a recognition of how others react to us, meaning they are emotional derivatives of developing the ability to see ourselves through the eyes of others. A secondary emotion such as embarrassment requires building a simple mental model of how others might perceive us, which is quite a high-level abstract task. An important element in this higher-level ability is the ability to interpret the behavior of the adult as emotional behavior, something that Thompson and Goodvin (2005) call "social referencing." It involves recognizing basic emotions in the facial and body expressions of others, and requires that the two-year-old is capable of understanding that others might not feel the same way that he feels. In order to experience something like embarrassment, a child also needs to understand what is expected of him: the child needs to be able to evaluate his own behavior against the social norms of the group, implying in turn that by age two, children start to become aware of social norms.

While very young children are unable to truly empathize, by the time they are toddlers this appears to change. Zahn-Waxler (2000) documents that toddlers are able to react with concerned attention to their mother's distress, an ability that continues to develop through childhood. Thompson and Goodvin (2005) also document that toddlers "discover" the possibility that individuals employ deception by displaying emotions contrary to what they are actually feeling.

Throughout early childhood, the ability of children to read the emotions of others keeps improving. Gnepp and Chilamkurti (1988) argue that by middle childhood, children begin to understand how personal background, experiences, and personality can yield unique emotional reactions. Lewis and Michalson (1983) comment on how children learn to read others and suggest that people obtain their knowledge of situationally specific emotions (the emotions that others feel in particular situations) from three sources: direct observations; the reported experiences of others (including, for example, information contained in books); and empathetic processes.

Throughout their childhood, children also learn about cultural differences. They learn to recognize not only that certain types of emotional behavior are desirable in their own culture (such as that being angry or glad is acceptable at certain times, and not at others), but also that different cultures have different types of expected behaviors (Cole, Bruschi, and Tamang 2002).

What Thompson and Goodvin (2005) and similar studies furthermore make clear is that the basic emotions themselves do not markedly change over time. What changes during the course of childhood is not the content of any given emotion itself, but the mental space taken up by the centers that activate particular emotions. To see what this means, consider anger. The feeling of being angry is hardwired: one is born with the ability to be angry, and the hot-headed aggression activated during anger never truly changes in character throughout one's life. The same holds for the feelings of jealousy, pride, joy, fear, and many other specific feelings: the nature of these internal experiences is given from birth.

Hence, the emotions activated by love are given at birth. What is acquired after birth are changes in the sensitivity to the circumstances that lead to these emotions. So, for example, one can allow oneself to get angry for many reasons, or one can learn not to become angry over many things. One can similarly be jealous of everything and everyone, or one can learn not to activate the feeling of jealousy often. The learned skill of controlling one's emotions is termed "emotional regulation."

2.6.2 Emotional regulation

Thompson and Goodvin (2005) note (p. 442) that just after birth, babies experience strong swings in emotions, which only gradually become more modulated and controlled in infancy, as "maturational advances occur in adrenocortical activation and in parasympathetic regulation." In the toddler and childhood years, humans learn to control their emotions more and more, which is reflected in the brain by the development of more and stronger connections between the relevant brain regions: the child learns to suppress emotions when needed, and activate them when allowed.

Some children start to display emotional self-regulation as early as age four, as witnessed by conscious efforts not to hurt others when others can be expected to be hurt from continued "normal" behavior

(Cole 1986). These efforts mean that the child is able to recognize trade-offs between his own joy and others' pain, and has developed the ability to choose against his immediate gratification. This latter skill derives from learning to consciously suppress the intensity of his own desires. As Thompson (1994) argues, learning how to turn our own emotions "off" is a very useful trait to have from an evolutionary perspective. When we perform complex abstract tasks, such as calculating sums or considering new ideas, it would be handy to be able to "turn off" our emotional centers so as to minimize distractions (p. 408, Thompson and Goodvin 2005).

Emotional regulation is accomplished when the conscious part of the brain releases chemicals that numb our emotional centers. Inhibiting our emotions is thus a conscious decision, but it is only available to us after we have learned how to activate it. Families and schools are prime examples of places where we learn to discipline our minds in this way.

2.6.3 Is attachment in children related to power and desire?

Two child-study findings stand out in illuminating what generates a normal love response. The first important finding from child studies is the fact that reciprocity is not a required ingredient in initiating the love response. Children can display love towards those who do not love them back. The clearest evidence on this point derives from studies of abused children. Even children with horrific histories of abuse by their parents tend to love the abusing parents. Phelan (1995) for instance documents the cases of daughters who were victims of incest, including the mental difficulties of the incest victims in coping with their competing emotions towards their incestuous fathers. Stevenson (1998) highlights how one of the major dilemmas surrounding abused children is that many of them in later life still, at some level, love the parent who abused them and find it hard to let go of that love. Rather than only loving those who care for them well, it appears that children are vulnerable to the activation of love towards any person who holds power over them.

The second clear and useful finding of behavioral studies comes from the examination of interactions between machines and children. Children do not develop love for machines that automatically provide for them. Toys, "food machines" (such as refrigerators or microwaves), and "warmth machines" (such as central heating) are perceived by children as "powerless," and by and large do not generate a sustained love response even though they are steady providers of things that children want. This lack of a love response towards inanimate providers is probably itself a learned trait, i.e., children do not love automatic providers because they are not taught to fret over automatic providers but are instead taught to see them as powerless.

These basic observations fit the predictions and precepts of the Love Principle in that they illustrate the important roles of power and desire in the activation of love, as well as further affirming the curious unimportance of actual reciprocity in a love response. The apparent ability of the unconscious to maintain belief in the reciprocity of the entity with whom it seeks a bargain is very reminiscent of Stockholm syndrome, which describes a tendency of captives and abductees to develop strong emotional ties and allegiance to whomever captured them.

2.7 Categorization and emotional activation

Two mental abilities are of particular importance in understanding the nature of human love: our ability to categorize objects, and the activation of our emotions by stimuli.

2.7.1 Categorization

Psychologists have suggested that humans are prone to divide the world into categories of "us" and "them," whereby the "us" group consists of those with whom we recognize a shared trait. Tajfel, Billing, Bundy, and Flament (1971) demonstrated that this trait need not be at all meaningful outside of the categorization framework itself. They ran several experiments with classrooms of schoolchildren who were divided into completely arbitrary groups (e.g., by telling the children that they shared some meaningless trait, such as that they would all overestimate the number of dots presented in a screen whereas the other group would underestimate the number of dots). Those groups were then allowed to interact. Group members were asked to divide an amount of money over group members and nongroup members, as well as to assign some punishment to group members or nongroup members. Tajfel and his coauthors found that no matter how the groups were selected – i.e., whether groups were given meritorious labels (such as "more accurate") or neutral labels – the individual members displayed strong group-oriented behavior. Students would assign the vast bulk of the available wealth to group members, and would punish non-group members. These experiments have since been replicated using many other ways of dividing groups, such as randomly sorting students into red groups and blue groups. The same basic findings were produced by Harnad (2005).

"Categorization theory" has since been extended to incorporate the notion that people constantly put everything and everyone observed into mental boxes, i.e., abstractions, simply because this process allows us to digest a lot of information quickly.[7] This argument makes a lot of sense. Every one of the ten snapshots taken by the eyes and processed by the brain every second will contain several hundred objects, which means that we must deal with identifying something like 100,000,000 objects every day. The fact that we manage to do this without pausing for at least a second or two at every object means almost inevitably that we must have some method of stowing away or entirely dismissing the vast majority of these objects extremely quickly, leaving only a few for our attention to dwell on.

The role of categorization in love

One "stowage area" in our mental system of categorization that is particularly important in matters of love is the box of "me." This box includes everything associated with "the things and people that feel like part of me." This box, containing our self-image and identity, is crafted from many steps of recognition and emotional reactions to that recognition.

Our ability to access the box of "me" can be interrupted. For example, Keenan, Nelson, O'Connor, and Pascual-Leone (2001) describe cases of patients in whom the left and right sides of the brain were anesthetized consecutively. Individuals whose right brains (where facial processing takes place) were anesthetized could not recognize their own faces, even though they could still verbally describe the features of their

---

[7] Tajfel (1969) concludes (p. 82) that categorization "introduces simplicity and order when there is complexity and random variation" and "can help us to cope only if fuzzy differences between groups are transmuted into clear ones, or new differences created where none exist."

own faces because the speech centers are mainly located in the left side of the brain.

Our self-image, like every concept we create or confront, is no more than a story told by several stations in our brain to its other stations. This particular story takes the form of a map of what and where we are. There is a center in the brain called the posterior parietal cortex, which houses our awareness of where and what we are (see p. 1091 of Squire, Berg, Bloom, du Lac, Ghosh, and Spitzer 2008). When we reach for a mug of coffee standing on a table behind us without looking over our shoulders, we use this mental map of where we are situated in a wider space. If access to this map is subdued or numbed, it is actually possible for us to believe that we are not inside our bodies or heads, or indeed that we are not even human.

Our ability to believe ourselves to be outside our own bodies, most easily experienced in dreams, can also be activated by chemicals or strong emotions when we are awake. Blanke and Dieguez (2009) review the many instances known to us of diseases, such as epilepsy, in which people have out-of-body experiences. A well-known example is the shell shock that soldiers experience. A soldier who has lost a limb will often look at the place where that limb was supposed to be, but will feel that he is not looking at himself. His shock produces an out-of-body experience, which arises from the fact that the center responsible for constructing his mental map is deliberately numbed at that moment by other centers. Another well-known example occurs during medical operations. Muldoon and Carrington (1951) describe how, during surgical operations, the drug-induced mental state we experience often leads to numbing of the center responsible for making us feel inside ourselves, in which case we can feel ourselves to be floating above the operating table.

Our potential to escape our mental maps of who and where we are means that we have the capacity to believe that we are partially someone else, as sometimes is evident in dreams. There is a strong likeness between loving others, on the one hand, and partially dissociating ourselves from our internal maps of who we are, on the other. I argue that loving others is essentially equivalent to incorporating others into our own sense of self.

When we truly identify with someone else, we can say that we love that person because we want ourselves to do well (mentally, spiritually, socially, and physically). We simply count the loved one as being part of ourselves. The ability of humans to believe that others make up a part of themselves is also what makes a hero (or other person whom we would like to be) desirable when beheld by our unconscious minds: not only do we want to be them, consciously and/or unconsciously, but we unconsciously believe we can actually be them. When we empathize with others, such as when we feel an instant connection with starving children shown on television in another part of the world, this feeling emanates from our definition of them as, to some extent, part of ourselves. We then care for them unconditionally, as we care for ourselves.

In support of this contention, there is direct evidence that we are able to react emotionally to circumstances affecting others in the same way as we would react to them if they affected us personally. Mervin and Frijters (2012) for example found in a large Australian data set that followed 20,000 individuals for ten years that, on average, the mental health of married partners was affected by the life events of their spouses about 10 percent as strongly as it was affected when those same life events befell themselves. If a friend of one partner died, for instance, or if the partner was fired or promoted, this affected the second partner's mental health about 10 percent as much as if the important event had happened directly to the second partner, all else equal. Mervin and Frijters (2012) also review many other papers in the medical and social science literatures that find very similar results.

Combining what we know from neural science with categorization theory yields the implication that loving something or someone involves thinking of that person or thing as belonging to the "me" box.[8] The things we love ignite the automated emotional responses that make up the love program: when we either observe the person or thing we love, or think the thing or person we love is doing well even if we do not see them, we feel a positive emotional response.[9]

---

[8] However, humans can develop love for others even if they do not love themselves. One way of understanding this is to say that we are capable of separating the part of ourselves we hate ("me") from the part we love ("my loves") in our categorization system.

[9] A personal example from the supporting writer of how this pervades life: when my youngest child lost her furry teddy bear, which we had encouraged her to love, we told her not to cry because the teddy bear was probably happily on holiday and she should be happy that the teddy was doing well.

A final general point to make regarding categorization is that humans continually re-categorize things. The mental boxes we carry around are not fixed but updated with new information and new uses throughout our lives. We update our ideas of what a car is, what a tree looks like, and so on, and make room for new abstractions when we encounter new phenomena such as the latest electronic gadget. This extends to social abstractions, meaning we continually reinvent ourselves and the boxes we belong to, allowing us to form new social bonds. For love, this means that the box of "me" also gets continually rewritten towards the powers around us, notably ourselves, but also any other power we confront. Our mental flexibility inevitably involves a continuous fading of any previous love.

2.7.2 *The role of emotional activation and regulation in love*

Combining the idea of categorization with a basic understanding of emotional learning and mental processes allows a more subtle formulation of what love is. We can think about love inside a human brain as an automated emotional response to an image, sound, smell, or idea that we feel to be a positive part of our self. When we care unconditionally for another person, we are in a sense caring for that positive part of our self: we experience anger when our loves are wronged and experience joy when things go well for them, just as if the events had happened to a self-loving "me."

If love is intimately tied up with emotions, both in terms of the underlying desires that initiate love and in terms of the processes that are activated in a love response, then what we know about emotional activation becomes relevant to understanding love. From the Love Principle one would expect that individuals are more likely to initiate love when more emotionally active. Particularly from the point of a manipulator, we want to see what kinds of circumstances make individuals more emotive and whether more emotive occasions are indeed disproportionately involved in emotional bonding.

Thompson and Goodwin (2005) note that emotional activation itself combines activity in those regions of the brain that are very old from an evolutionary point of view, such as the limbic system and the hypothalamus (which simpler mammals also have), with activity in the more sophisticated, "newer" parts of the brain such as the frontal cortex, which is disproportionately large and developed in humans relative to any other species. It also involves hormonal activity that is itself regulated by many parts of the brain. Emotional activation is hence an incredibly complex phenomenon.

One basic finding is that our emotions can be aroused as a package. A trivial illustration of this is that we are more emotional all-round when we are awake than when we are in a coma. A more salient illustration is what happens to a woman during labor: the oxytocin induced by labor supercharges the emotional centers, which is why labor is so often accompanied by anger.

Another finding, important to any would-be manipulator of the affections of individuals, is that it is comparatively simple to emotionally charge people. One normal route is physical exertion. After heavy exertion, during which our bodies produce emotionally stimulating chemicals, we are more liable to experience emotions than at other times. This helps explain the bonding that takes place amongst men in armies, and the widespread use of sports clubs and dance clubs as hunting grounds for partners.

Another avenue to emotional charging is the intake of specific neural transmitters, which work by stimulating or repressing one or more areas of the brain. Like some naturally occurring hormones, the active ingredient in most illegal drugs (cocaine, heroin, XTC) supercharges both the emotional centers and several other brain centers (often those involved in vision, which explains the hallucinogenic properties of some drugs). Breiter, Gollub, Wesskoff et al. (1997) examined the effects of cocaine on brain activity in human subjects, and found changes in many areas of the brain associated with emotions. In particular, they noted a deactivation of activity in the amygdala, which reduced the ambient level of fear. They also noted an increase in activity in the ventral tegmentum, the area responsible for producing dopamines in the brain, which is a main source of the euphoric feelings generated by cocaine. For XTC (MDMA), Vollenweider, Gamma, Liechti, and Huber (1998) found that recreational doses produced increased emotional sensitivity.

It also appears that the degree to which we are liable to become emotionally active depends on the influence of body cycles (most notably the menstrual cycle in women), sunlight (higher emotional activity is present during the start of summer), and various naturally occurring smells, sounds (Juslin 2001), and visual stimuli. Moos, Kopell, Melges, Yalom, Lunde, and Clayton (1969) showed in a study of fifteen females that their self-rated anxiety and aggression peaked at the start of the menstrual cycle, while their "pleasantness" peaked mid-cycle. Harmatz, Well, Overtree, Kawamura, Rosal, and Ockene (2000) found that the mood of normal people is best in the late spring/early summer due to exposure to sunlight.

We can actively seek circumstances that are emotionally rousing if we want to love. We can also choose to avoid such situations. Just as a person trying to quit smoking can choose to avoid exposure to smoking imagery when he wants to prevent himself from relapsing, so too can we purposefully avoid situations that are more likely to catalyze a love response. Emotional regulation also has implications for the type of circumstances in which one can expect people to initiate love. Few love programs are set upon the tracks while the would-be lover is doing a complicated mathematical problem.

Fear

Fear works differently from our other emotions. Fear prepares the brain for action (fight or flight) and puts the body on high alert by readying the muscles for action, diverting blood from non-essential activities to those bodily systems involved in fight or flight, and preparing the conscious mind to analyze the situation without further emotional distractions. In limited doses, this stress improves mental performance (Thompson and Goodvin 2005), though in very high doses, stress can paralyze the body and the mind such that an individual is actually less capable of meeting a threat. Laughter is known to be a very strong fear-reducer, which is why humor is very important in the game of love: reducing fear paves the way for other, more positive emotions to be activated.

2.7.3 Summing up the basic science of love

Based on the scientific evidence presented so far, we should understand any particular love as an emotional reaction program that, like all programs, can be altered in later life. Starting to love, which is a form of accepting something as a positive internal image, means that we have unconsciously decided to accept something as part of our self in order to satisfy our deeper desires. Feeling those deeper desires requires emotion, and hence can only take place when the brain is emotionally charged – that is, at a time when the unconscious rather than the conscious mind decides what emotions come to the fore. Emotional charging itself is highly predictable and hence highly manipulable.

We have also learned that our underlying ability to love needs practice: infants who are given no social stimulation become almost catatonic and unable to form social relations. The "love programs" that we begin with (often towards our parents) and that develop in later life require strong participation by the unconscious mind. Some involvement of the conscious mind, particularly its ability to evaluate stimuli and its abstractive capacity, is also required in order to experience particular loves.

A note on the presumption of reciprocity of the love target

The primary remaining caveat to this story of love is a lack of hard evidence regarding how the tendency of the unconscious to believe that some outside power is reciprocal is actually mentally coded. How can such a tendency be so universal? Is it even possible to hardwire such a tendency? I discuss this frontier before moving to a fuller discussion of the more well-documented phenomena of desire and power.

According to the theory of love as presented here, a human tendency to presume reciprocity on the part of an outside power is required in order to explain sacrificial and religious behavior, and to make sense of the "surprise" aspect of love. Yet, without an actual mechanism to point to, it may well be that it merely *appears* that humans have such a tendency, and that more analysis would reveal a more complicated story that would not rely on such a tendency. For the sake of scientific rigor, it is important to speculate somewhat on what else could fill this gap. If there is no way in which such a tendency could arise or be hardwired, then the Love Principle as stated above must be, at a minimum, too simplistic.

Two main possibilities arise based on the literature reviewed above. The first is that the presumption of reciprocity is not a hardwired tendency but merely a heuristic learned very early on in our lives as young babies. The second is that the tendency is hardwired. Each of these possibilities is discussed in turn.

Young babies are in the odd position that they do not know the language of their carers, might not even recognize them as belonging to the same species, and have no way of knowing *ex ante* what strategies for manipulation might work. In short, babies face powers they do not understand that seem to be responsible for all the good and bad things

in their lives: food, warmth, comfort, hugs, songs, cold, thirst, and so
forth. Both good things and bad things will initially come to the baby
as a surprise, and the "baby scientist" will try to figure out what is
happening and how to get more of the good and less of the bad. The
baby's means of manipulation are very simple: screaming, some limited
eye and mouth movement, and, over time, other conscious movements
of limbs and other parts of the body that he learns to recognize as
his own.

One mechanism through which a tendency to presume reciprocity
might arise is that young babies hit upon this tendency, or heuristic,
as a means of explaining to themselves how their surroundings react
to them. If they smile, they are rewarded; if they start to walk, they
are rewarded; if they keep screaming, their carers get annoyed; if they
make too much movement when being changed, they stay cold for
longer; if they spill food, it gets lost; and so forth. Almost any consistent
reaction to him by his carers can be viewed by the baby as a form of
reciprocity, complete with a mental model of what the outside powers
apparently want. A baby thus learns that his environment rewards and
punishes him for his behavior and, by forming a mental model of what
the unknown seems to want, the baby develops the useful heuristic of
presuming reciprocity from his environment.

This potential mechanism for the emergence of an automatic presumption of reciprocity on the part of an outside power is consistent
with the finding that babies who are not stimulated do not develop an
ability to interact with others, and thus do not learn how to love. This
would mean that the Love Principle is not a universal law in the sense
of holding for all humans, but merely fits most humans, since most
of us were stimulated and treated consistently enough in childhood
that we developed the presumption-of-reciprocity heuristic much like
we developed heuristics for eating, walking, and language. If true, this
would mean that there should be particular areas and connections in
the brain that encode this heuristic, and future research should be able
to find them in normal humans but not in others.

The other possibility is that the tendency to presume reciprocity is
in some way hardwired, meaning that all babies today are born with
it because it was selected as advantageous via eons of evolution. One
possible route to this possibility would be if our perception of the division between our sense of self and our sense of the outside environment
is blurred in particular ways.

An intriguing possibility in this line is suggested by research on hyper-religiosity and, more generally, on brain activity and spirituality. Urgesi, Aglioti, Skrap, and Fabbro (2010) studied patients who had had parts of their brains removed or damaged as a result of cancerous tumors. These authors concluded (p. 316) that there was evidence of a connection between damage to certain parietal areas and changes in both one's sense of self and one's religious tendencies: "Damage to posterior parietal areas induced unusually fast changes of a stable personality dimension related to transcendental self-referential awareness. Thus, dysfunctional parietal neural activity may underpin altered spiritual and religious attitudes and behaviors."

What studies like this suggest, but certainly do not yet conclusively prove, is that our sense of self as a spatial entity is involved in a love response and that changes in that spatial sense of self might lead to changes in our "natural" degree of devoutness towards outside powers. As reviewed above, one of the functions of the parietal lobe is to generate a mental map of where we are in relation to other things, both physically and emotionally. Perhaps, with certain types of brain damage, we start to think of ourselves as smaller and less significant than we actually are, leading us to think of the outside as bigger and more powerful. Perceiving ourselves as relatively weaker than before, we then – by the Love Principle – naturally become more devout.[10]

One further step is then required. Imagine not only that our perception of relative power changes with certain types of brain damage, but that our perception of the division between "self" and "the outside" is blurred to begin with. There might essentially be two levels of self-awareness: the "normal" or more conscious notion of oneself as being within a particular body, but also a sense of oneself as a quality applying to all things that appear to be "powerful and desirable" in one's mental map. Someone who perceives there to be an outside power from which he wants something may then, as part of the love response, begin to perceive himself to be in part outside his own body – to be in fact part of the "outside power" that is perceived. Knowing and caring for the self, an individual would naturally then assume that the outside power (also partly the self) also knows and cares for him.

---

[10] Greed, similarly, can potentially be mentally coded in relation to a mental map, for instance as an act of grabbing and holding: to be greedy is to grab (Otte 2007).

The hypothesis is then that we essentially perceive our relation with the outside power as in part a relation with our own self. An expectation would develop of perpetual caring and good feeling towards us on the part of the outside power: if it were possible for this power to reward us, we know it would (because if it were possible for us to reward our self, we would). Therefore, giving to this outside power is perceived to be the same as giving to our self. Our sacrifices towards that outside power then make that outside power – our self! – better nurtured, and hence more able to give back to us, following what we assume is its natural tendency. This then is a presumption of reciprocity of the outside power: the more we nurture it, the more it will nurture us. If we do not nurture it, then it will be unable to nurture us.

What speaks in favor of this hypothesis is not only the fact that spirituality can become greatly amplified by specific forms of brain damage, a finding that is difficult to explain using the baby-heuristic theory mentioned above, but also that it helps to explain how and why we anthropomorphize the unknown. It even suggests an actual mechanism for the perception of power. Power could be perceived by the individual as a kind of physical space: more powerful things take up more space in our mental maps, and anything powerful to some extent becomes tainted with our notion of self. The logical corollary is that our own "complete" self changes as that mental map changes: not only does the outside partly become us, but we partly become the outside. This then gives rise to a single story explaining the concept of territory (we "own" things because those things "are us"), transcendentalism (our gods are "us outside of ourselves"), and the presumed reciprocity of the unknown. It also explains our lack of true examination of the characteristics and wishes of the worshipped power: we do not doubt that our gods and other loved ones will be reciprocal towards us, because in doing so they are simply sharing their resources with themselves, i.e., with us.

To some extent, the two theories above are competing possibilities that cannot both be true. If the tendency to believe in the reciprocity of outside powers is a heuristic learned by babies faced with consistent carers, then there should be many people without this tendency and there should be particular places in the brain that house this heuristic. If, on the other hand, the theory of "love as a blurred mental map subject to distortions regarding the nature of the self" is true, then the tendency to presume reciprocity should be almost universal. Further, we should also be able to see the activation and involvement of mental maps in our perceptions of power, our sense of ownership, and our lack of introspection concerning the behavior of the unknown.

Future research in these areas will hopefully point to one or the other of these explanations as the correct one. At this point I favor the mental map hypothesis, mainly because it has the potential to explain many other phenomena that we were not originally looking to explain. Henceforth, the book simply proceeds as if the Love Principle holds true, viewing love as a form of re-categorization of the self that is brought on by outside stimuli.

2.8 Revisiting the Love Principle from an individual perspective

Armed with a better understanding of how love might work at the cognitive level, I now dissect the core ingredients for the love response as individuals experience them: desire and power. Psychologists and sociologists have large literatures on each concept, and only the main points are highlighted below. The main aims of this section are to be more precise about what is meant by desire and power, and to see whether what is known about these two phenomena fits the theory being advocated here.

2.8.1 Introduction to desire as experienced by the individual

Humans desire a great many things. We have basic desires such as hunger, thirst, a desire for warmth, a desire for sex, a desire for control over our surroundings, and many more desires that we are born with and never completely shed. Other desires are shaped during childhood and by life experiences, and differ across cultures and time.[11]

---

[11] The relation between desire and "needs" is complex. At the most basic level, humans experience pleasure from a variety of basic stimuli, including warmth or a full belly, which reach the brain via the senses and internal pathways. Chemical stimulation from drugs also follows this process. Such stimulation increases the level of dopamine in the brain, which in areas such as the nucleus accumbens (the "pleasure center") is experienced as pleasure. Our evaluation of reality is also related to several emotions, including fear, anger, and jealousy, which also have direct connections to our levels of pleasure. By contrast, various sensations are experienced as unpleasant, including pain, shame, and cold, and these involve several systems in the brain, making it hard to speak of a simple "pain–reward"

Nevertheless, scientists have discovered remarkable commonalities across culture and experience in those of our desires that are related to the attractions we feel for other people and for ideas. The available scientific evidence about these common aspects of desire can be categorized into three broad areas: the physical realm, the social realm, and the spiritual realm. Since most of us already acknowledge the role and importance of physical desire in matters of love, I omit a detailed discussion of that category here. The basic rule of physical desire is that we are physically attracted to what is likely to lead to healthy offspring at times when we are most capable of producing healthy offspring ourselves.

2.8.2 Social desirability

Social desirability is most immediately relevant to generating love for potential partners. It captures those aspects of a perceived potential mate that relate to the expected access of hypothetical offspring one might have with that mate to the necessities of life. This link has almost without doubt been an important evolutionary driver behind the human love program: powerful providers (both male and female) can be expected to take better care of eventual offspring. Social success is very similar to social status, as both capture the basic notion of being securely seen as part of and important in a group. In the eyes of the beholder evaluating a potential mate, such an image not only bodes well for any hypothetical offspring, but also holds more immediate promise for the beholder: a mate with high social status would bring his partner greater social status, and more secure group membership.

Social desirability is the most culturally dependent factor of desirability. This is because social success, which is what carries the ability to provide offspring with what they need to prosper, is mainly a function of what a whole group of people thinks, rather than what any

system. One can think of a "need" then as something without which individuals feel a lack of pleasure and an excess of some type of discomfort (including the mental anguish of uncertainty, loss of self, or confusion), while one can think of "desire" as the motivation to experience more pleasure and less pain. Yet, since the mechanisms through which we experience pleasure are built up over our lives and can vary from culture to culture, there is no clear hierarchy of either needs or desires, nor do all humans desire the same things. For example, anger can become addictive, and pain, inflicted either on oneself or on others, can become related to pleasure.

individual thinks. This makes it possible for social desirability to be entirely self-fulfilling. By this, I mean that some things are only desirable because everyone in a given clan or country thinks they are desirable. Examples include what styles are in fashion; whether one should sport a large earring (as do the Tuareg tribesmen of the Sahara) or nose-bone (as do some Papua New Guinea tribes); whether one should eat caviar for lunch (as do rich Westerners); how much and what type of flattery one should offer, and so on. What is seen in a particular society as a sign of being "with it" on any of these matters is entirely dependent on the local culture, and it is thus hard to give any reliable rules for what will remain fashionable and what will not.

There are some constants in social success, however, which are not subject to the whims of group opinion. Wealth and influence are robustly socially desirable, and are often objectively visible to some extent. Anything that ensures a stream of resources that can meet basic needs is also naturally desirable. Signals of wealth such as fur coats, expensive jewelry, expensive cars, high-priced food, high-priced holidays, and so on can all be objects of desire in themselves that ultimately derive from the attractiveness of social success.

Baumeister and Leary (1995) (p. 498) link the appeal of social status to a need to belong: "need for power may well be driven by the need to belong, as we suggest later. Likewise, people prefer achievements that are validated, recognized, and valued by other people over solitary achievements, so there may be a substantial interpersonal component behind the need for achievement." They argue that high-social-status people are able both to enjoy and to confer on others a greater sense of belonging, which contributes to the desirability of social success.

There is quite likely a gender-specific component to social desirability. Darwinian theory suggests that females – who invest more of their effort into offspring than do males – should choose males who are ready and able to expend their own effort in raising their offspring, and thus should prefer males who are in possession of valuable resources.

Buss (1989) finds some evidence for this Darwinian theory. In a cross-cultural study of thirty-seven cultures, Buss found that females valued characteristics such as "good financial prospects," "ambition," and "industriousness" more highly than men. Similarly, Townsend (1989) and other studies revealed that women, more than men, prefer criteria to do with wealth and status that are closely linked to resource acquisition.

Voland and Engel (1990) and Bereczkei and Csanaky (1996) document that, in both industrial and pre-industrial societies, women who marry higher-status men have more surviving children than those who marry lower-status men. These studies suffer from potential reverse causality, in that it is likely that the healthier women in a given group marry the higher-status men, but their results are still indicative. Also in line with Darwinian theory, men appear to find wealth less important in women. Townsend and Levy (1990) find that they are more concerned with the physical attractiveness of potential mates, which is a signal of fertility.

There is also a part of social desirability that is not related to wealth and is almost free of culture. Traits in this area include empathy, charm, and more generally the ability to read, anticipate, and fulfil our various desires. An important mental desire that these traits can fulfil is our wish for high self-esteem. People who can make us feel good about ourselves by praising us, for example, thereby fulfil one of our desires and show us they can keep fulfilling that desire in the future too. Similarly, when someone is able to guess what we really want at any point in time, then that person signals an ability to read our desires and thus an ability to satisfy them better than someone who cannot read our desires. In short, social aptness is a desirable trait.

2.8.3 Spiritual desirability

The general rule under this heading is that an idea is spiritually desirable if it can aid in the gratification of one or more mental needs. This criterion is satisfied by ideas that make us feel good about ourselves, that console us, that offer us a reward in an unknown future (including an afterlife), that make us feel we have a sense of control when in daily experience we have none, and so forth.

A series of examples from everyday life illustrates how this works.

- To a person who feels continuously oppressed by family, work, or the government, ideologies in which he is greatly valued are very seductive. Thus, the notion that someone powerful (a god, a country, a tribe, or "nature") cares about him even if he does not see that entity is very seductive.

- To the person who thinks little of himself, the idea of being seen as beautiful and powerful is very seductive. Thus, the idea of belonging to a powerful group (an army, a nation, a bureaucracy, the intelligentsia) is very seductive.
- Feelings of emotional security can be very seductive to those who feel very insecure. Hence, those whose lives are at the mercy of the weather, or those who fear being poor or alone, will derive comfort from worshipping nature or god.
- Ideologies that make one feel part of a movement that forces others into doing things, for good or for bad, make one feel in control and are thus inherently desirable. Hence, the idea of basic human rights, the idea of an all-loving god, and the idea of being part of a superior country or group are very seductive to all those wanting to feel superior, valued, and loved.

Proponents of desirable ideas invariably claim that their particular ideology is true and will ultimately be victorious. This is in accord with the Love Principle, which requires a belief by the one who loves in the desirability ("truth") and power ("victory") of the love object. Yet it is impossible to believe in the power and desirability of something if one does not even believe it exists. Thus, the belief that a potential love target exists is a prerequisite for love towards that object to develop. Importantly however, the Love Principle does not require that the love target *actually* exists. Someone believing himself to be valued by a nonexistent supernatural power is receiving a real mental benefit, in the form of increased self-esteem.

The malleability of belief

Psychologists have used many terms to refer to the tendency for people to believe whatever they want: cognitive dissonance, self-serving bias, *ex post* rationalization, and many other florid labels. Each of these terms can be unpacked to reveal extensive and nuanced theories, but the core observation of all of them is that people, whether intelligent or not, have an astounding capacity for ignoring the truth if the truth gets in their way. For instance, as verified in dozens of experiments, those who are unsuccessful at a game of skill invariably claim they had bad luck, whereas those who were successful claim they simply played better. People who were randomly given gifts and then asked which, out of a whole range of possible gifts, they thought was most valuable tended to claim that the gift they happened to have was the best. They followed the simple reasoning of, "If I have it, it must be the best." In experiments (Vaughn, Tajfel, and Williams 1981) where individuals were randomly assigned into red and blue groups, those who happened to have been selected into the red group afterwards claimed that those in their group were "objectively" better and nicer than those in the blue group. Symmetrically, those people who happened to be selected into the blue group thought that those in the blue group were "objectively" better. These are just a handful of results from the thousands of psychological experiments carried out that illustrate the many weird and wonderful things that people can be led to believe, and the circumstances leading to such beliefs.

A clean example of a human belief in nonexistent entities is the existence of multiple religions. Though some religions allow for the possibility that other gods exist, these are rare and certainly do not include the two biggest religions, Christianity and Islam. From the perspective of any given believer, it must then also be true that the majority of the world's religious believers believe in nonexistent gods. From the perspective of the atheist who does not believe in any form of religion or spirituality at all, more than 90 percent of the world's population is deluding itself. Hence, whomever is right, it is a given that most humans believe in nonexistent entities: only a fraction can possibly be right; the majority must be wrong.

Exactly the same holds for patriotism. In questionnaires that ask people whether their country has a culture superior to that of any others, a sizeable fraction of respondents answer affirmatively.[12] Whoever is "objectively right," it is a mathematical certainty that most people who believe in the cultural superiority of their own country must be wrong, at least if we think of superiority as something that can be judged on universal standards.

What goes for religion and patriotism can be extended to all ideas and spiritual beliefs. Whether it is a belief in karma, a belief in inner

---

[12] Surveys on such attitudes are held regularly. For example, the Pew global attitudes survey of 2011 (see www.pewglobal.org/2011/11/17/the-american-western-european-values-gap/) asked respondents in five developed countries whether they agreed or not with the statement that "Our people are not perfect, but our culture is superior to others"; 49% of US respondents and 47% of German respondents agreed with this, while only 32% of British and 27% of French respondents agreed.

equilibrium, a belief in alien intervention, or a belief that Elvis and Hitler still live, holding a belief that is similarly held by only a small proportion of the world immediately implies that the vast majority of the world's people believe in things that do not exist or that are untrue (e.g., "there is no such thing as karma").

To the truly calculating love-seeker, the main message from this analysis is that trying to convince others of a single truth is part and parcel of the game of love. Objective truth has absolutely nothing to do with it. In order to convince others of something, one must appeal to the desirability of the idea and the perceived power behind it. Once others are convinced of the desirability and power of the target, they will make up their personal truth themselves as they go along.[13]

2.8.4 Introduction to power as experienced by the individual

As touched upon in the introduction to this book, power is the ability to influence people, and through them, events. Many things can wield power. The power of religion moves people to follow certain rules; the power of music draws individuals into dancing together; the power of good food induces individuals to go in search of it and to consume it; the power of football makes hordes of individuals spend their Sunday afternoons in a certain way. All of these powers, each of which offers desirable things, can be passionately loved by humans.

---

[13] It is not easy to allow oneself to doubt whether deeply held beliefs are possibly wrong. Perhaps this is therefore the place to express a sentiment that I attribute to Erasmus on these issues: the inescapable fact that the vast majority of us strongly believe in things that are not true is not a reason to despair, but makes one re-evaluate the importance of truth. The ability to fool ourselves makes us love things outside ourselves. It leads us to care for others we would otherwise fear and avoid. The religious zealot is often willing to spend much of his life helping others via charity and good works. The philosopher in effect spends his life trying to equip others with a way to live harmoniously with each other. The patriot is willing to hand over a large fraction of his earnings to the state in the form of taxes, which are used to educate and feed people, most of whom the patriot never sees. The believer in human rights spends his life in the service of the happiness of others by working tirelessly against dictatorships. Does it really matter if most of these believers are most likely wrong about the objective truth of their beliefs? Arguably not. Judge them rather on the happiness and resources that their beliefs and their consequent love bring to others, than on the objective truth of their case. Another way of putting this same sentiment that the supporting writer offers is that in light of the mountains that can be moved via the mechanism of belief, truth itself – while revered by some as a god – is, in many specific instances, not objectively more powerful than any other idea.

The precise type of power we are concerned with in this section relates to the capacity of an individual to withstand (i.e., refuse if it does not suit him to comply with) the demands of others, and to force others to comply with his own demands. Naturally, these two capacities do not always go together. It is possible for a person to have the perceived ability to withstand the demands of others but to lack the ability to force others to comply, as in the case of a weak but stubborn grandmother. It is also possible for a person to have the ability to force others to comply, but to lack the (mental) ability to refuse the demands of others, as in the case of a physically strong but mentally weak person.

Power does not only reside in the hands of individuals. Groups can wield a power no individual could wield. Obvious examples are armies, or whole nations, which can collectively do what no single individual in an army or nation can. Power is also a matter of perception. As long as a person thinks he cannot resist a demand and thus complies with the demand, power is wielded by the demander. This holds even if there is no actual physical power to back up the demand. Hence, someone who obeys the perceived commands of laws, a religion, or a country, when he would not do so of his own free will in the absence of those external perceived entities, is under the power of the entities whether or not the entities have any actual physical control over him. Indeed, as one could infer from religious belief, it is not even necessary for an entity to exist for its power to be perceived. A completely imaginary entity, such as a nonexistent alien from outer space, can be perceived by a given individual as exerting great power over him. It is important to include such possibly nonexistent entities in our conceptualization of power, because we so often give our love to things that no one else observes.

I will examine more closely in later sections of the book the inner workings of political power as a group phenomenon. Here, I look at power from the perspective of a person who experiences it, and briefly discuss the various actors that wield power, ordered according to how directly humans experience that power.

2.8.5 Physical power

Naked, physical power is experienced by nearly all of us in early childhood. Our carers are usually physically able to force us to do many things: to eat, to go to bed, to change our clothes, and to be quiet. We are physically dominated. As we grow up, physical power becomes less important to many of us because the laws under which we live limit the use of physical power. Still, we as young individuals are often subject to physical domination at school, in the army, on the sports field, and within the home.

2.8.6 Mental power

Whereas physical power ultimately relates to the ability to physically demand and reward someone, mental power relates to the ability to demand and reward mentally. Being mentally strong is not the same as being smart. Being smart is about understanding the world and thereby realizing how best to influence it, but being smart is not about being able to resist external demands. One can be very smart and still be the slave of everyone else. One can also be very limited intellectually and yet have the great mental strength of being able to resist the demands of others. Mental power is as much about independence of spirit as it is about understanding what is asked of oneself.

In contrast to physical power, mental power is not directly observable and hence to some extent must be guessed at by others. A person's strength of will, self-confidence, and independent ability to choose for himself are only truly revealed as we observe him over time. When we only have a limited time to assess someone's mental strength, we mainly rely on that person's body language to make the assessment. Studies of body language, such as by Argyle (1975) and Knapp, Mark, and Hall (1992), find that body language is related to culture and time. Hand signals in particular mean something different in different cultures, which many tourists find out to their peril. For example, making an "O" with the fingers means "OK" amongst scuba divers, but is the sign for sexual intercourse in Turkey.

One cross-cultural commonality of body language is that anything that looks fearful appears weak (Kudoh and Matsumoto 1985, Meeren, van Heiknsbergen, and de Gelder 2005, de Gelder 2006). Defensive (fearful) body language is comprised of all body positions that appear closed, such as folded arms, crouched walking and sitting positions, eyes gazing down at the floor, and bowed heads; overtly agreeing very quickly with those in authority; taking advice that is offered without questioning it; changing one's mind continuously; and speaking fast or with frequent hesitation. By contrast, confident (fear-less) body language signals mental strength, and includes all body positions that appear open, such as open arms, stretched body posi-tions, walking upright, looking people in the eye, and head held high; and talking slowly but steadily.[14] Speaking with short pauses, in which you appear to think things through, can be taken as a sign of strength if you are seen to reflect on what you are about to say. It makes you look sincere, as if you are prepared to listen and reason, and are men-tally secure enough to question what you previously thought. This only holds in measure though: when you are too easily swayed and brought to pause, you appear weak.

Gullible people will by and large observe these signals and take them at face value. Management courses and courses in self-confidence are often about teaching the participants methods of mimicking these signs of strong behavior.

2.8.7 *Group power*

Group power is a very difficult form of power to understand because it is built upon beliefs, and these beliefs are often unobserved. Worse, unlike in the case of mental power where at least one can observe body language and make an estimate of the degree of mental power held by another person, there are few clear signals that point to people's actual beliefs. A simple example can illustrate the problems this creates for analyzing group power.

The concept of group power may be thought of as being embodied in a leader, such as the commander of an army or the director of a com-pany. His word goes, and that is the end of it. But why? Why cannot someone who is told to do something by the CEO simply ignore the

---

[14] This is often seen as a sign of authority. The former French president, François Mitterrand, is a famous example of this. When he was still an up-and-coming young socialist politician he spoke swiftly, including as many arguments in his speeches as possible. But once he was elected president of the French Republic in the 1980s, his speech slowed down. At the end of his fourteen-year reign, he spoke at half the speed of his younger self, perhaps due to some mental slowdown but alternatively perhaps as a deliberate attempt to appear stately. He mimicked a king who does not demean himself by giving the twenty reasons for his decision, but who informs his subjects in a gentle and fatherly way of the main reason for his decision and then continues with the task of ruling his country, leaving the details to lesser mortals.

request, as if it were given by a helpless child? The answer is that orders from above are followed because the person being ordered expects someone else to punish him if he disobeys: the person in the army disobeying a commander risks being shot, and the person disobeying a company director risks being fired. Yet those consequences are enforced by others, not the commander or the director himself. Hence, the power of the initial order flows from the fear (on the part of the one being ordered initially) that someone else will follow an order to punish someone who does not follow an order. This fear is encouraged by the appearance of power that a leader upholds. It is not coincidental that the emblems of royal power for most European monarchs are physically powerful animals such as lions, dragons, bears, and eagles.

However, this merely begs the question: why does someone who is ordered to punish someone else for disobedience actually follow that order, instead of just ignoring it? This second-round order will only be followed because this second-round person, in turn, would fear that yet another person would punish him for not punishing the transgressor. This hypothetical chain could go on forever. At the end of the day, what makes an order powerful is thus the belief that somewhere in the chain of command, a sizeable group will actually indeed follow orders. As soon as a small group of people holds such a belief about others, then it is suddenly in the best interests of everyone else too to follow orders. Hence, the power of a leader is nothing more or less than the combined belief of all of the other individuals in his organization that he has power.

Importantly, this notion of power is entirely group-oriented and can apply not only to people, but also to ideas, organizations, countries, ideals, and many other things. The ideal of democracy can be powerful in the sense that people are prepared to fight for it, which can be simply because they believe there are others who are prepared to fight for it, and moreover prepared to reward other defenders or proponents of democracy (and punish the enemies of democracy). The same is true of religious organizations. When one believes there are very many others who are willing to support a religious organization, to punish those who do not support it and to reward those who do, then it becomes entirely logical to also support such a religious organization, at least outwardly. The religious organization is powerful simply because others believe it to be powerful.

As illustrated, the problem with analyzing group power is that it is extremely difficult to look inside people's heads and see what they believe about the power of other people and ideas. Group power is furthermore bound by the group in which it arises: the commander or director of Nation A's army has no power over the citizens of Nation B. What may be seen as a powerful idea, religion, or person in one group can be entirely powerless in another group that has different beliefs.

Examples of group power are almost infinite, but some examples are helpful in illustrating that group power is not always obvious.

- The power of the law. The law is made up of thousands of rules that people and organizations are meant to follow. If they do not follow a rule and are caught, offenders are liable to be punished. Of course, in practice, it is not so easy to catch those who break the law, nor is it always so easy to even know the law because no individual could possibly be aware of the millions of laws applying in any particular country. However, many basic laws are followed most of the time by people and organizations afraid to break the law. People and organizations pay taxes partially because tax authorities can check up on them. People abide by the most important traffic rules: most road users stop for red lights and do not drive drunk. The law is hence powerful in the sense that people and organizations feel compelled to obey it. The law can also satisfy desires because obedience to the law makes traffic safer, allows public services to be funded from taxes, and makes us feel safe from criminals. What gives the law its power? The answer is very clear: the power of the law lies in social beliefs. The taxpayer believes there is a chance of being caught by a tax auditor. The tax auditor believes that if he does not audit, he will be fired by his boss or prosecuted by the police. A boss will fire a tax auditor who does not do his job because he believes his chairman or colleagues will get him into trouble if he does not. The policeman does his job because he fears being fired or prosecuted if he does not. This web of beliefs stretches indefinitely. It is simply the sum total of social beliefs that the law is to be followed which gives the law its power. Without these social beliefs, the written laws of our countries are just pieces of paper with no more power than a paper napkin. As Thomas Hobbes pointed out, "Covenants, without the swords, are but words" (Hobbes 1651). In developed countries today, the "swords" and the beliefs that direct them are present, and give power to the law. Add to this the fact that the law can be interpreted as satisfying some of our core human needs, and one should not be surprised that there are people who love the law and who obey it not only out of fear of being punished, but also because they value it unconditionally.

- The power of money. Money can be used to buy goods and services from other people. This goes as much for the baker who sells his bread in return for the price of that loaf, as it does for the worker who sells his time to an organization in return for a wage. The reason that a baker or laborer accepts coins, bank notes, credit cards, and checks as payment is because they expect to be able to buy things with this money from other people. In turn, the people selling what the baker and laborer buy (e.g., flour, a house, or a bank loan) expect the money they receive to be able to buy things from other people. This web of beliefs, again, stretches indefinitely. As with the law, what makes money "powerful" is the joint belief of a whole society that money is powerful. When this belief is lacking, money loses its credibility and becomes worthless. This has happened in several countries throughout history. For the most part, however, people believe in the ability of money to purchase goods and services that they need and desire. This belief does bring with it the perception of power, because money is not easy to obtain. Hence, money also can be loved. Not only coins and bills, but anything else that is used as money, can be loved.

- The power of the idea of human rights. The power of an idea can be explained using the same type of argument. Human rights can be enshrined in law, in which case the argument that they have power is the same as that for any law. Even if the idea of human rights is not (yet) codified in a law, it can still have power. This occurs when many believe in and defend the idea of human rights. Believers will try to punish those who do not abide by the idea of human rights, and will try to reward those who do. The believers will make the followers feel they are part of the "good group" that is morally superior to other groups. Even nonbelievers can then feel forced to comply with the idea of human rights. Thus the idea of human rights can be powerful simply because it has fervent defenders. The idea is also capable of satisfying needs because it can give its followers a feeling of moral superiority. The idea of human rights can, therefore, be loved. The same reasoning holds for any ideology, religion, or common opinion:

what gives them power are the beliefs and loyalties of others. Their inherent ability to satisfy desires often takes the form of providing feelings of moral superiority and elevated self-esteem.

2.8.8 Out-of-sample predictions regarding love, desire, and power

The power aspect of the Love Principle would imply that the strong have greater difficulty falling in love than the weak: for the strong, most others are weaker than they are, and are thus able to be directly dominated. This is also why the weak are capable of such great love, which is in turn why weakness can be endearing. The weak are predicted to love many things, whereas the powerful can only bring themselves to love something even more powerful than themselves, such as a god, a whole country, or an ideology. This basic reasoning gives out-of-sample predictions that we can use to try to test the validity of the Love Principle.

First, we should see power itself to be an aphrodisiac, capable of drawing love; and second, we should see changes in the pattern of love whenever there are changes in the distribution of power.

On the first prediction, there is casual empiricism in the form of Henry Kissinger, who in answer to a query by Chairman Mao as to how he could gain access to beautiful women when he was fat and not very attractive, said: "Power is the ultimate aphrodisiac" (*New York Times*, October 28, 1973). More substantively, there is a long history of sociology that has made the same point as Kissinger, though perhaps less colorfully.

Baumeister (2001) made a detailed study of the relation between symbols of power and sexual attraction. One might observe that soldiers and sailors deliberately keep their uniforms on when they are out for romantic encounters. Popular magazines routinely detail the lives of the rich, powerful, uniformed, and famous, which fits in with the notion that humans are unconsciously attracted to powerful people and wish to be close to them.

The sociologists Sadalla, Kenrick, and Vershue (1987), quoting many other writers such as Charles Darwin, argue that women unconsciously sense the evolutionary benefit of having a powerful father for one's children. Women are attracted to power and the attraction includes strong sexual feelings. They fantasize about controlling that power, which is responsible for decisions that affect the lives of many others, including their own. Women (unconsciously) attempt to control the power that is able to satisfy many of their wishes, via initiating a love response. Men also marvel at the sight of power when they believe it can give them what they want. Robinson (2003) argues that men find power in their female partners sexually attractive, though there is not as much agreement on this as on the opposite relation. Men face power in other situations, however, and give their love to it in the form of loyalty. Loyalty to our bosses, to our country, and to our teachers are prime examples.

The second out-of-sample prediction is that a change in power leads to a change in the patterns of love. If a person becomes more powerful, he should become less attached to others and should start to defy powers he previously would have worshipped.

Western mythology provides wonderful examples of the arrogance of the powerful. In Greek mythology for instance, there are the stories of King Tantalus, a son of Zeus who dwelt amongst humans, who believed himself to be so powerful that he dared to serve the gods his own son for dinner to see whether they would notice. The gods were not fooled, and after this and several other brazen incidents, they devised an eternal torment for his arrogance. They placed him in water and near food but whenever he reached out for food or drink, the water and the food would move just beyond his grasp. Another king, Sisyphus of Corinth, also tried to outwit the gods (and on several occasions succeeded). He was punished by having to eternally roll a stone up a hill, only for the stone to roll down the hill just before it reached the top. One may note that in Greek mythology, as in most mythologies, only those with great earthly power are seen to defy their gods, perfectly illustrating the power aspect of the Love Principle.

The most extreme known example of an earthly power defying the gods is the Roman emperor Caligula, who believed himself so powerful that he directly challenged the gods by having his armies attack the sea and other symbols of the realm of the gods. Smith, Howitt, and Cassell (1857) (p. 9) relate the following story:

Caligula ... assembled an army on the coast of Gaul and embarked on board the imperial galley, from whence he issued orders to commence the attack against an imaginary enemy. Afterwards he informed his astonished legions that they had conquered the sea, and commanded them to gather up the shells upon the shore, the spoils of their bloodless victory, for which he afterwards decreed himself the honours of a triumph in Rome.

In more recent times, there have arguably been changes in the power balance between the genders and between the young and the old, which we should expect to have implications for love. The widespread perception that the old command less respect in Western societies than they used to (see, e.g., pp. 318–319 of Bond and Coleman 1993 or Sung 2001) could be explained by the Love Principle if the old are less powerful now than they used to be in previous eras. This is indeed almost certainly the case. It is no longer true that the elderly control who works on the land, as they used to; family elders no longer have the economic might to force their children to marry certain partners; family elders lack the legal and financial ability to prevent their children from moving to different places; the pace of change in the way we work now is such that children no longer turn to their elders for knowledge of how to do things (few ask their grandparents how to use the internet); and so forth. Hence, the power that the elderly hold over the younger generation is far less now than in centuries gone by. The Love Principle correctly predicts that the level of respect the elderly enjoy should therefore have decreased. Only those who currently have power because of their wealth, or those who wielded extraordinarily great power when they were young, still command respect when old.

The power aspect of the Love Principle also predicts that women would on average love more than men, but that they will have become more equal in their love as the genders have become more equally matched in terms of their political power. What speaks for this out-of-sample prediction is evidence on life satisfaction. Kohut, Stokes, Gross, and Speulda (2003) find that women are on average happier, or at least as happy, as men. Even in rural areas of India decades ago, or indeed in rural areas of China nowadays (e.g., Knight, Song, and Gunatilaka 2007), where many women have difficult lives and are often dominated by their men, aggregate happiness amongst women is at least as high as amongst men. The Love Principle offers an explanation for this. The weak can derive solace and some happiness from the well-being of those they love, whereas the strong lack this because they simply love less, and thus cannot derive as much enjoyment out of the well-being of others. Women in rural India and China are weaker than men, and therefore (by the Love Principle) more vulnerable to love: for example, they are more devout by most measures than their male family members. They simply love more than men, which provides a source of greater happiness, even though life was and in many cases still is brutally unfair to them.

What should also be true is that women should have become less attached to their men over time as their economic independence and hence their power relative to men has increased. One fact that speaks in favor of this prediction is the increase in divorce rates in Western countries over the course of the twentieth century, coupled with the stylized finding that the majority of divorces are instigated by women, who have gained in power over time and therefore adjusted their expectations upwards.

May (1980) and May (1988) thus directly blame the increased expectations of women for the increase in divorce rates. Riley (1991), citing copious anecdotal evidence on the wording of divorce petitions filed by women, claims that the increase in expectations had in fact already started by the late 1700s, as witnessed by an increase in words like "nuptial happiness," "love," and "affection," which replaced words about financial support and fidelity. Fals-Stewart and Lam (2010) similarly argue that divorces have become more common due to a shift in female expectations of marriage from those centering on the provision of necessities, fidelity, and duty to those concerned with intimacy, support, and companionship. Arguably, a key potential reason for this increase in expectations is the greater economic power of women.

2.9 Comparing love with greed

How does love, as explained above, compare with greed in terms of how it unfolds and how it motivates individual behavior in a particular instance?

The first model provided in Chapter 6 is a simple mathematical model of how one might conceptualize greed and love at the individual level. Here I give a simple verbal account, aided by the diagram in Figure 2.1 that summarizes the processes involved in greed and love.

The timing involved in the elicitation of the greed response is identical to that involved in the elicitation of the love response. Both processes begin with some desire held at the unconscious level. The person can also be consciously aware of the desire, but what makes the desire unconscious at heart is that the individual wants something

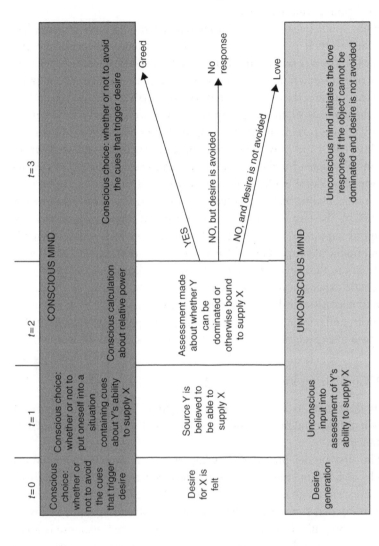

Figure 2.1 The processes of greed and love

and would keep wanting it even if he were to try consciously not to want it.

The individual must then experience an encounter with some entity, real or imagined, that the individual perceives as being able to satisfy the held desire. This source can have been consciously sought out, as is the case with speed dating for example, but it is also possible that the source is found by accident and indeed that the very presence of the source strengthens the degree of desire. What is depicted as a temporal sequence might thus very well involve an innate desire only becoming manifest when a source that appeals to the desire is encountered.

The next stage involves an assessment of the power of the encountered entity. This assessment directly involves the conscious mind, in the sense that the person can actively decide how much to acknowledge the power of the entity involved. For example, when one tries to bargain with a god of rain, one makes a somewhat conscious choice as to how much power is presumed to exist on the side of the god. One can choose not to believe in the existence of the god at all, thus denying it any power, or one can choose to believe in the god and that the god has some amount of power that merits a particular level of sacrifice (e.g., two rain dances, rather than one or three). In a similar way, one can somewhat consciously choose to deny the existence and power of many entities, including entities that clearly do exist.

The ensuing stage consists of a crude calculation as to whether or not the perceived entity can be dominated, and this is where the love and greed responses begin to diverge. An entity that in some way can be dominated directly is a candidate for eliciting a greed response. An entity that is completely dominated and that is simply forced to give up the desired goods, a situation that arises in theft or rape for example, is treated with contempt. An entity with whom one engages in direct, conscious exchange, such as a trading partner on the internet or in a shop, is treated as an entity that is dominated: a conscious bargain is made with the entity to give it something (money, return favors, labor time, and so on) in exchange for the thing that is desired (goods, wages, and so on).

By contrast, love arises when the individual calculates that the entity is too powerful to dominate. Still insistently feeding the conscious mind reminders about the held desire, the unconscious makes a "love bargain" with the entity. In the language of the neuroscientists, the entity that is deemed to be too powerful to dominate is obsessed over, and a process of creeping re-categorization takes place wherein the individual starts to think of himself as partially becoming one with the entity about which he obsesses.

How can the love program be stalled? One main tactic is to stay away from the cues that trigger desire, something made more possible when one has a good enough understanding of oneself to predict which cues will be most effective. Another tactic is to consciously reject notions of external power. A third approach is to build up one's own internal sense of power, so that one perceives oneself to be able to directly dominate outside forces in more situations.[15]

2.10 Why does love exist? An evolutionary perspective

Modern humans apparently arose in Africa (Templeton 2002) and derive from a long line of primates of which the vast majority also originated in the plains and valleys of Africa (Relethford 2001). The main psychological mechanisms of satisfying desires discussed above – greed and love – must therefore have proved themselves in the competition over sexual mates and resources in Africa in which our primate ancestors would have been engaged. And the evolutionary advantage must have held at the individual level, not merely have had group benefits, for evolutionary selection works at the level of the individual. What individual evolutionary advantages did the mechanisms of greed and love hold? Do we share them wholesale with other primates, or is there something uniquely human about the love or greed responses as we experience them?

At its core, the basic distinction between greed and love is the difference between dominance and submission. Dominant and submissive

---

[15] In the categorization suggested by Kahneman (2011), one can think of the love response as a default strategy when domination turns out not to be possible, a "system 1" reaction in his terms. The love response is still not entirely a default strategy, in the sense that there is still a choice element involved in whether or not to stay away from active cues. Also, unlike many of the examples in Kahneman (2011), the love response is not necessarily successful most of the time in the life of each individual. For a particular individual, the love response might well lead to one unrequited love after the other, meaning that love should not be seen as a heuristic that is usually successful and only now and then dysfunctional. I tend to see it more as a strategy, either stimulated in childhood or hardwired, that then becomes a somewhat immutable trait that is activated in later life by circumstance.

behaviors are readily observed in other social animals, such as dogs, horses, cattle, sheep, chickens, and almost any other animal that humans have domesticated. Like their wolf ancestors, dogs will fight with each other for the dominant position in a group, and the outcome of the fight determines which dog submits to the power of the other and which dog instead remains dominant (Fox 1971, Mech 2003). The dominant pack animal gets the advantages of that dominance, such as access to preferred sexual mates and food. These same advantages accrue to dominance within other animal groups.

While there is therefore an obvious evolutionary advantage to a dominance drive, the usefulness of submission, and thus of the love response, needs more explanation. For nonhumans, one immediate advantage of submission is that the submitting animal can survive in circumstances where it cannot dominate: it lives to fight another day. Maclean (1990) documents submissive behavior in reptiles, and notes how submissiveness is a strategy to avoid personal destruction (p. 235): "submissive display is the most important of all displays because without it numerous individuals might not survive." Ohem (1986) discusses the role and origin of submissive behavior in the context of facial expressions in mammals. He describes the ability to become submissive as one that allows for the development of a stable hierarchy within a group that would itself cause a marked decrease in confrontational encounters, if only as a by-product of the evolutionary selection of submissive behavior.

By accepting a subordinate role, submitting animals not only survive, but also get to share in other group benefits, such as safety in numbers and the advantages of joint foraging. This has been observed in many species, including Harris' sparrows (e.g., Rohwer and Ewald 1981). Waal (1996) notes this benefit in the context of groups of monkeys, in which there are also dominant and subordinate members. Ohem (1986) and Gilbert (2000) also extensively researched the social benefits of submissive behavior, pointing to reduced loss of resources spent in confrontation and in maintaining threats. Depending on how long the submission has to be maintained and the level of its implied reduced reproductive access, submissive behavior can be an optimal energy-conserving strategy for an individual.

Yet, particularly for males competing for access to females, submitting in perpetuity to other dominant animals would imply no access ever to sexual reproduction, which would make submissive behavior an evolutionary dead end. Subordinate animals can try subversively to have sex with females, but in social animal species in which sexual access is strongly aligned with being the dominant animal, presently subordinate animals eventually need to find a way to have a "second chance" at being dominant.

Christian (1970) suggests that one advantage of submission is the possibility that the submitter survives and thrives in the territory into which he is forced, thereby potentially becoming the progenitor of a large group of animals in a new territory. Submission would thereby be the evolutionary equivalent of a "long-shot second chance." However, this would only apply in extreme cases where submission is accompanied by outright rejection from the group territory. Perpetual submission for males might also be a reasonable strategy in certain unusual cases, such as where the dominant animal is close kin. It seems more likely, however, that there is an evolutionary benefit that flows not from perpetual submission but from temporary submission, and thus that we should expect evolution to favor some mechanism through which one's perception of the relevant power structure may change with time – allowing love to fade.

Amongst females, there is a more obvious evolutionary advantage in submitting to dominant animals: sexual submission to a strong male will enable a female's children to inherit some of the same traits (e.g., strength) that he possesses. Yet, females too would benefit in an evolutionary sense if their attachment to dominant animals could fade over time, making it more appealing to them to strike up new relations with new, potentially even more powerful mates.

Gilbert (2000) explores individual animals' optimal choices regarding whether to submit or try to dominate in many different situations. Distinguishing between nine different submissive defense strategies, ranging from immediate forms of submission (such as hiding) to more long-term forms of submission (such as admitting defeat), he finds that the most stable evolutionary strategies are a mixture of dominance and submission: i.e., to fight for crucial things and to give in on things that matter less.

2.10.1 *Dominance and submission in humans*

Much submissive behavior is associated with direct physiological changes. In human males, losing competitions causes sharp drops in the level of testosterone production, particularly in individuals whose levels of anxiety are very sensitive to status, i.e., socially anxious individuals (e.g., Maner, Miller, Schmidt, and Eckel 2009). This points to the role of testosterone in preparing one for a fight to obtain and/or maintain dominance, implying that the interests of a losing male are best served by a reduction in testosterone levels so as not to get sucked into fights he cannot win. If a socially anxious individual starts winning some competitions (for example, because the previously dominant individuals have died or have in some other way lost ground), his testosterone levels increase again.

Amongst humans and other primates, there are many benefits of submission other than eventual access to sex. There are immense evolutionary advantages for any individual in being able to function well in a group over long periods of time: pooling resources with others over extended time creates the possibilities of specialization, capitalization on returns to scale, and diversification of risk over many years. These in turn imply increases in either expected health (hence, fertility) and/or expected reproductive life span for any given group member. It is also true that one of the main reasons for the evolutionary success of humans as a species is our ability to have long-lasting relationships during which the young mature and are "educated" by the group.[16]

2.10.2 Evolutionary benefits of the love program

How does submission and, more generally, the human love program, help to support humans' long-lasting ties – which in turn support our modern societies?

Subtle differences in hierarchical position between younger and older males, and between males and females, would be created by the use of submissive strategies by some group members on some occasions, even within relatively egalitarian hunter-gatherer societies. These small hierarchical differences would assist in lowering the prevalence of confrontation, thereby making the group itself more stable and hence more attractive for individual members to be part of.

---

[16] Again, evolutionary pressures operate at the level of the individual, not the group. Hence, what is good for the group but not necessarily good for the individual will not be selected by natural evolutionary processes, but rather can only be a by-product of the evolution of traits based on individual advantage.

Yet, love is not merely a form of temporary submission; I have claimed above that love involves a true change in the internal self-image of the one who loves. It is thus a more complete form of submission, even though it is not perpetual because that internal self-image gets updated continuously. One of the possible evolutionary reasons for the development of that more complete form of submission relates to self-esteem. Within a social group, knowing full well that one is a subordinate animal involves a great deal of mental angst, and brings with it a high risk of depression (Gilbert 2000). This risk of depression itself makes evolutionary sense: since perpetual submission carries a great evolutionary cost, making submission an unpleasant state is a way of providing an incentive for the subordinate animal to "try again" in some way. Yet, when escape from a group is virtually impossible and a subordinate animal must therefore live with being subordinate for very long periods of time, the animal can become depressed and thus quite dysfunctional. One evolutionary "solution" to that problem is to allow the subordinate animal to more completely submit in the form of a change in its identity, thereby reducing the angst involved in the feeling of being subordinate. By loving what dominates us, we have re-asserted a sense of control over it and can thereby function with less mental anguish. Gilbert (2000) (p. 22) calls this an "affiliative" submission strategy.

Other advantages of loving also exist, beyond surviving a situation of sustained subordination. For example, the behavior that flows from loving someone else provides a way to send a signal that one is less of a threat and can thus be more trusted, which is helpful in all interactions involving a degree of hidden information and hidden action. Someone who is trusted will be more sought out as a partner with whom to have and raise children, which requires long-term investments. Someone who is more trusted will be more valuable as a partner with whom to share food and form a mutual defense against others. A loving individual will be perceived as more likely to return to his mate even if they are physically separated for long times, such as when hunting or even when lost, making him more appealing as a mate in the first instance. While these advantages actually accrue to the *appearance* of being trustworthy rather than being truly trustworthy, a love program can be important to have whenever there is a high degree of monitoring that makes "faking" difficult.

Another long-run advantage of the ability to submit is that it brings with it the ability to learn adaptively: the weak learn from the strong because they follow the strong rather than fight to the death. An ability to submit for longer periods (i.e., via a love program) would be especially important for species that have long childhoods, such as humans: during childhood there is much to learn, and little to dominate. Yet, even then, the individual would be best served by an ability to submit coupled with a reluctance to submit to weak others, because otherwise he would follow weak examples. Evolution for this reason should have equipped our children, and particularly our boys, with a fierce dominance drive that only strong influences can tame.

A final evolutionary advantage of love is that love can create stronger ties between us and our offspring: long gestation periods and long periods of learning become possible in the presence of stronger group attachments. This benefits both child and parent: the child learns more from the parent about how to survive, and the parent is able to influence the child's behavior once it becomes an adult, such as by influencing the child to allocate food to the parent's other children.

A greater ability to form social bonds with things that demand our attention thus increases our bonds with the next generation. There is a "programming" difficulty though in that a greater ability to form strong emotional bonds with an entity that demands our attention does not itself guarantee that such an ability gets "activated" towards our offspring and not towards someone else. Nature's "solution" to this problem in the case of females is to vary the hormonal balance around childbirth, i.e., to increase the receptiveness towards love around the time of childbirth. Combined with the immediate demands a child makes within the womb and as a newborn, these hormonal changes make a strong emotional tie between mother and baby highly probable.

The individual evolutionary advantages of love are hence a combination of forestalling extreme mental angst, signaling amongst adults, following the lead of the strong when young, and forming ties with the entities that carry our genes. There is a whole myriad of further group advantages to love, mainly in terms of group loyalty and the accompanying benefit in terms of competition over resources with other groups. Yet, from the point of view of the individual gene, such group benefits are externalities that cannot themselves give rise to love or sustain its presence over time.

A remaining question is why love should be initiated by the unconscious rather than the conscious mind. One might argue that if we were
consciously able to choose what and whom to love, then all the previously mentioned advantages would still be available, but mistakes
could be avoided by means of the superior analytical abilities of the
conscious mind.

The preservation of self-esteem provides a rationale for why submission must be unconscious rather than conscious: if we knew we
were submitting to something because we could not dominate, our
self-esteem would be hurt. An unconscious tendency to love an outside
power then provides both the advantages of submission as well as continued high self-esteem due to ignorance of the actual mechanism. As
a protection to our self-esteem, we would even after the fact not really
want to know why we love.

2.10.3 *Unique aspects of love in humans*

None of the advantages mentioned above are particular to humans.
The signaling, learning, and caring advantages of love hold as much for
humans as they hold for wolves, chimpanzees, horses, and elephants.
These animals too live relatively long lives in groups, and I would thus
argue that versions of the Love Principle are also likely to apply to the
bonds formed by such animals.

Is there something particular about human love for which one would
want to find an evolutionary reason? What appears most particularly
human is our ability to have strong emotional bonds to unseen abstractions. It is our bonds to gods, spirits, dreams, unseen large groups, and
so on that finds no or very little echo in the animal world. Dogs do
not carve out symbols of their gods and, apparently, neither did our
close relative in the hominid line preceding us, *Homo erectus*. These
earlier hominids did not use symbols, did not know ritualized burials,
did not erect any form of temples, and did not have much in the way
of aesthetics. All of these specific *Homo sapiens* behaviors are directly
relevant to the Love Principle, in that they can be seen as reflections of
attachments to gods, the dead, and abstract notions of beauty. Interestingly, Neanderthals, who have been argued by several authors to
have had a lasting influence on the human gene pool,[17] apparently did

[17] Recent, though still disputed, evidence puts this influence at 1–4 percent
of the human genome for non-African populations. See Krings, Stone,

engage in art and symbolism so probably also shared our ability to have relations with the unseen.

Psychologists have argued that human relationships with abstract entities help to establish and maintain group identities as well as group goals (Burkert 1983, Wilson 2002, Boyer 2008). The ability to love unseen abstract entities would then allow for stronger group ties than those seen in other animals, or even other hominids, though several of these benefits might be "accidental" from the point of view of individual evolution. Having relations with abstract entities might have advantages on average, but can be individually dysfunctional at times, such as when someone has a relationship with an unseen and nonexistent tree spirit.

Under this interpretation, *Homo sapiens* is more "dreamy" than *Homo erectus*, and this dreaminess improves our ability to function in groups beyond the degree seen in other animals. Following the arguments regarding spatial self-awareness in the preceding section on the science of love, one can interpret the dreaminess of *Homo sapiens* as a blurry distinction between others and ourselves – or, put another way, an ability to self-categorize within many different abstractions, including unseen ones. Given that the hominids from whom humans descended lived in small groups, there is a high probability that the specific dreaminess selected by our evolution would have mainly catalyzed a blurring of the distinctions between others in the group and ourselves. This does not hence merely support strong ties with those who are genetically close to us, but provides the framework for maintaining ties with a whole group.

An interesting difference found between men and women's cognitive functioning has relevance to this point. Schulte-Ruther, Markowitsch, Shah, Fink, and Piefkea (2008) (p. 393) claim that "[b]ehavioral studies suggest that females often perform better in emotional tasks than males." These authors go on to argue that women devote more mental capacity towards recognizing and predicting emotions, and that men are more prone to suffer from psychological ailments in which a lack of empathy is a key component, such as autism. Cahill, Uncapher, Kilpatrick, Alkire, and Turner (2004) similarly argue that both the usual

Schmitz, Krainitzki, Stoneking, and Paabo (1997) or Paabo (2003), or www.eva.mpg.de/neandertal/press/presskit-neandertal/pdf/PR_MPI_Neandertal_EN.pdf.

level of empathizing and the native ability to do so are higher in females. There is thus some, though of course not undisputed, evidence to suggest that men are more prone to tune out emotional signals and that females are more strongly affected by emotions. This does not mean that men make better thinkers and women are more emotional, but it does suggest that abstractions have a greater pull on male attention.

One face-value explanation for such a difference is to hypothesize that throughout our evolution, men were more often in positions that required quick reflection, such as fight-or-flight situations, while women had caring roles. Women thus needed to be able to read emotion more quickly, while men needed to tune out their emotions more often.

An alternative possible evolutionary mechanism for this gender difference is that a greater abstractive lure is a means of "ensnaring" men to form strong ties with their families. After all, for men there is no clear cue, like childbirth for women, to anchor an attachment to any particular offspring. Yet a man who did not possess the capacity to bond well with his children would not be seen by women as an attractive provider, and hence, a good choice of mate. Perhaps an evolutionary solution to that problem was to increase the degree to which men would be capable of bonding with abstractions, so as to make them care more for abstract notions of family and group ideals.

In terms of evolutionary timing, our ability to bond with abstractions probably came last. The group advantages of shared abstractions only become salient in animals who already have the capacity to develop and manipulate high-level abstractions, and where groups already are the normal social environment. This logic, combined with the finding that the hominids preceding us did not appear to engage in symbolism, means that the blurring of the distinction between abstractions and ourselves is probably the final piece in our social evolution. To create deities from real-life economic uncertainty reflects an extraordinary creative ability, allowing us to have reciprocal relations with the unseen (Fehr and Gachter 2000, Frijters and Baron 2012). To be quintessentially human is not to perceive clear differences between our paintings, our poems, our gods, our political ideals, our partners, and ourselves; we can love all of these entities with almost equal intensity.

In summary, I argue that there are sound evolutionary reasons for the development of an ability to love, and that what makes us particularly human is our creative ability to extend our love to highly abstract concepts.

2.11 Conclusions

This chapter described love as a form of submission, in contrast to greed as a form of dominance. It reviewed the scientific evidence in support of the development in humans of a capacity to love, where love is explained as the result of a bargain the unconscious makes with entities from which it wants something, but that are perceived to be too strong to be dominated.

In real life, numerous entities and our own desires demand our love constantly: our family, our teachers, our bosses, our preachers, our poets, our friends, the "norms of proper behavior" we live under, the fears we succumb to, our hopes for the future, the things we are asked to do in return for success in life; the list goes on and on. Whether or not we realize it, we are incessantly asked to love or give our support to something or somebody without observable, immediate reward. It is a practical impossibility to give in to all of these demands, yet never to succumb would mean to live without love. One important task individuals face is thus to manage the various demands for their loyalty, such as when a soldier must choose between his loyalty to his close family (who will often not want him to take major risks) and his loyalty to his army unit and his country (who may well order him to take major risks).

Engendering love in humans is not beyond our control: manipulating the love response can be learned. As such, one should expect any entity that survives for a long time, such as a country or a family dynasty, to work out how to engender loyalty in its members. In turn, the loyalty of individuals within such an entity gives rise to group power and the ability to erect elaborate structures upon the foundation of that group power. What kinds of groups have arisen in human societies, and how does power arise in such groups? These questions are taken up in the next chapter.

PART II

Groups, power, and the development of institutions

3 | *Groups and power*

The dominant groups in the world today are competing nation states, each containing millions of citizens living together more or less peacefully but still mainly striving for their own gain. Many other types of groups have also been mentioned in previous chapters, including religious groups, families, army units, and scientific disciplines. They play an obvious role in the fabric of our socioeconomic system. Yet how did all of these groups arise, why are some more dominant than others, and how do they relate to individual humans? The aim of this chapter is to develop a framework for how individuals relate to groups, how groups form, and what the connections are between political power and group entities.

3.1 A note on methodology and organization

One way to approach this question is to work from an initial picture of individual psychology, and infer from that psychology what kind of groups and associated power structures would most logically arise. However, this bottom-up approach has a fatal flaw for my purposes, which is that human psychology is so rich and complicated that almost anything could be argued to exist or to be impossible. From categorization theory alone, for example, one would be hardpressed to predict beforehand the basis on which individuals would categorize one another into groups. Why do we see the most dominant real-world groups forming around things like similarities in country of origin or cause, rather than around similarities in height, gender, or intelligence?

One might alternatively try to develop a theory of group formation based on the joint purpose of a group, such as defending something, nurturing something, thinking through something, or watching something. While such a classification scheme has some descriptive merit, it would also be seriously deficient for my purposes, because the classification itself does not lead to many useful insights on group power, on the relation between groups and more basic human psychology, or on the question of how groups evolved over time. A categorization based on group purpose hence lacks a natural link with mainstream economics and other social sciences: it would be a stand-alone descriptive classification. The same goes for categorizations based on age, size, or geographical location.

Another alternative approach is to start from a theory of human needs, where the main role of groups is seen to be the satisfaction of those needs. Yet this approach suffers from a similar indeterminacy. One could for example point to the existence of pride, and argue that pride itself would make hierarchical organizations impossible. One could alternatively highlight our ability to empathize with others, and argue on its basis for the possibility of a kind of "beehive" group based on love, where every actor acts purely for the good of the group. One look at reality reveals that neither of these hypothetical conjectures is correct, but one would be hard-pressed to guess this by merely examining individual psychology. Even projecting human development from the point of the first agricultural settlements, with a veil of ignorance and based purely on our historical ancestry as hunter-gatherers, one might conjecture that love-beehives would be just as likely to develop as the social structures that we see today.

Each of the bottom-up approaches sketched above lacks sufficient predictive power as to what kind of groups should or could exist in reality. Following any one of them would be rather like examining all of the individual components taken from a whole parking lot full of different cars (nuts, bolts, windshield wipers, pieces of rubber and metal, and so on), and wondering what kind of machines could be made with those components. It is of course possible that one could stumble upon the truth, but it is just as likely that one ends up with, say, airplanes or boats.

3.1.1 A pragmatic approach

I contend that in order to ensure one does not end up with airplanes or boats, one should start from lived reality. A close look at real groups will at once narrow the field of candidate theories, and provide opportunities to learn along the way about the human traits most important in the emergence and maintenance of groups. By peeking at the "cars in the parking lot" we can get a better idea as to how we should view the relative importance of and relationships amongst the individual components we have to work with.

The approach I take in the first part of this chapter hence mimics the approach taken to study love in Chapter 2. I take the many human organizations known today and in history, as well as the many applications of power seen today and in history, and look for common themes that would point to a particular overarching framework. Individual components are involved not as direct building blocks, but as part of an *ex post facto* check on the reasonableness of a candidate framework.

Unlike Chapter 2, which of necessity required an enumeration of different examples of human love, this chapter need not explicitly enumerate different examples of human organizations. This is because the discussion of love in Chapter 2 has already introduced many groups and hence sources of power, ranging from countries to families to armies. Every love story essentially also contained a story of one or more human groups. What this chapter offers is a minimum set of concepts – a theory – with which to tie the many instances of human groups and power together.

At its core, the task of developing this theory is one of pure pattern recognition. What is the minimum number of different *archetypal* group types we can postulate that, together, fit almost every organization we have encountered so far? What specific differences between these archetypal group types are needed in order to embed a story of political power within and between groups, in a way that matches how we see politics being played out in the real world, and to make the emerging taxonomy fit *ex post facto* with the theory of greed and love developed so far?[1] And how does

---

[1] Such an endeavor is not unique. Sprott (1958) similarly tried to classify groups into a small set of more or less typical types. He distinguished between permanent small groups (families, villages, and neighborhoods), experimental groups (temporary teams and work units), crowds, and "other" groups. While his main argument – that groups should be understood as a whole collection of arrangements between people (including social norms, expectations, rituals, histories, etc.) – is accepted wholesale in this chapter, I opt for a different and more parsimonious classification that more naturally includes the large groups that ultimately wield the most power, such as nation states and organized religions.

this hypothesized theory of groups fit what is known about human psychology?[2]

3.1.2 Preview of the chapter

In the first part of this chapter, I introduce a taxonomy of distinct archetypal group types, each of which is associated with different power configurations. The main group dichotomy presented is between reciprocal groups and hierarchical groups. The former is characterized by equal sharing within a group of individuals of equal power, and the latter is characterized by the members of one more powerful group or subgroup demanding the resources of the members of other less powerful groups or subgroups. At the most basic level, reciprocal groups make greater use of love and hierarchical groups make greater use of greed, although love and greed are both important in understanding each group type. The explanation of the distinctions between hierarchical and reciprocal groups will focus especially on how such groups function internally in terms of their social norms and the enforcement of those norms.

As explained briefly in Chapter 1, power has been defined variously in the literature. A good working definition for the purposes of this book is that power is the ability to influence the behavior of others. This naturally begs the question of where this ability comes from, and I will contend that the most important powers in our lives arise almost entirely from constructs relevant to groups rather than to individuals. In its simplest form, the power accruing to a group derives merely from the system of expectations by individual members within that group as to when to apply their aggregate physical and economic resources towards a common goal. References in this chapter to the "power of

---

[2] My approach takes as given that we are ultimately looking for a theory that ties in with mainstream economics and the love/greed dichotomy of previous chapters. There are many other lenses one could have in mind when looking at group processes, which in turn could lead to entirely different theories. A good example is found in the volume of sociological studies edited by Paulus (1980), in which one encounters such topics as "self-focused attention" within groups, and the "stresses of overcrowding." The first of these naturally leads to individual-level theories of shame and self-awareness, while the second leads to empirical questions about coping mechanisms and the frequency of awkward contacts. Theories arising from such topics are not so much in conflict with the endeavor in this chapter, but rather too tangential to use as a starting point.

individuals" will therefore usually refer to power that they hold because of some position they have within a group, and not because of traits they possess in isolation (such as physical strength or an ability to persuade others). Personal wealth and authority, for example, will mainly be viewed as being made possible by the social norms within groups, and therefore as derivative of group power.

Accordingly, my proposed taxonomy of group archetypes implicitly marries an analysis of groups with an analysis of power. It seeks to explain how group power is organized, and to clarify the limits of group power from the point of view of the individual.

After presenting and discussing this basic taxonomy, I draw out some of its many implications in order to illustrate its usefulness. This is followed by a discussion of the evolutionary origins of groups, and an analysis of how the group types presented relate to questions of economic efficiency, or in other words which types of economic problems are solved by different group types. The issue of how to manipulate individuals is then revisited with the archetypal-group theory in mind, in order to draw out the theory's implications.

Chapter 6 provides a micro-model in which the proposed archetypal groups arise, and in which violence, enforcement, redistribution, group membership, and the degree to which people feel part of a group are all endogenous. This micro-model is a direct copy of the model of groups, power, and freedom presented in Frijters and Foster (2010). Chapter 6 also revisits the model of Frijters and Tieman (1999). These latter authors considered how one could envision the evolution of nation states through the lens of a specific micro-model of local interactions.

The models in Chapter 6 thus show the interested reader how the concepts in this chapter might be translated into standard game-theoretical economic models. However, it is important to note that the approach I take to mathematical modeling is the opposite of the idealized economic approach, which is to find some set of first principles from which to build more complicated theories. I am skeptical that reality is sufficiently simple for the standard first-principles approach to be useful for my purposes. My approach in building these models is rather to start with higher-order phenomena and to find a minimum set of concepts and internal relations between those concepts sufficient to replicate those higher-order phenomena as they appear in particular contexts. Formal modeling using these concepts then provides an *ex post* consistency check that one indeed can replicate the higher-order behavior one was trying to explain by drawing on the proposed core concepts, plus a set of auxiliary assumptions made for reasons of mathematical tractability. Formal models are treated hence as proofs of concept, and descriptive of the wider theory, but neither complete nor predictive of actual current developments.

3.1.3 Reciprocity and punishment

The key concepts on which this chapter will draw are reciprocity and punishment, about which there are numerous contributions in the recent behavioral economics literature. These concepts will prove to be important in understanding the defining features of each group archetype.

The literature on reciprocity, of which the simplest definition is playing and expecting others to play tit-for-tat,[3] has accentuated the importance of reciprocity for nearly all human interactions (Bolton and Ockenfels 2000, Kolm 2008). Individuals behave reciprocally towards each other even when this is not in their immediate material best interests, such as when they anonymously return favors, offer fair wages, or contribute to public goods. Perhaps even more remarkable is that individuals have reciprocal relations with things that cannot be seen, such as their gods and their countries. Individuals give to and expect return gifts from these unseen entities, such as when they adhere to religious rules in the expectation of going to heaven, or when they volunteer for a war in the expectation of being cared for when they are in need. A recurring theme in research on reciprocity is the importance of equality and mutual consent as crucial elements in the ideals of the reciprocal group (Bowles and Gintis 2003). As I will argue later in this chapter, human reciprocity towards abstract common goals, as decided

---

[3] Sobel (2005) (p. 392) defines reciprocity as "a tendency to respond to perceived kindness with kindness and perceived meanness with meanness and to expect this behavior from others." While Sobel (2005) goes on to delineate different types of reciprocity, some corresponding to an innate sense of altruism towards others (called "intrinsic reciprocity" in his framework) and others to a well-understood self-interested strategy of behavior (called "instrumental reciprocity"), in this book I adhere to his main definition: a tendency to repay like with like, and to expect this from others. As such, the very concept of reciprocity immediately implies a social situation in which there are such things as others with whom one interacts, and of whose behavior one can hold expectations.

upon and adhered to by equal group members, features prominently in the origin and organization of the group type I call a large circle of reciprocity.

Another strong theme in the behavioral literature is the role of the threat of punishment in forcing people to follow group norms (Bowles and Gintis 2003, Dixit 2009, Nikiforakis 2010). Several behavioral economists have recently explored how the threat of violence is made credible by emotive attachment to ideals (Reuben and van Winden 2008, Hopfensitz 2009). They find in experiments that individuals whose ideals are violated react emotionally, leading them to punish the violator and thereby ensure the cooperative outcome that group members follow the ideal.

Obedience to real or imagined threats can also become a norm in itself, in which case the actual threat level can be quite low. An example of this is provided in the classic Milgram experiments (Milgram 1963) in which over two-thirds of Western laboratory subjects simply did what they were told when asked to inflict harm on others, even though they did not individually benefit. The revealed importance of the habit of obedience has been replicated for many countries and groups (Rosenhan and Mantell 1967, Shanab and Yahya 1978, Miranda, Caballero, Gomez, and Zamorano 1981, Burger 2009). Hierarchical organizations are thought to use implicit threats and the habit of obedience partly to ensure compliance with rules (Ouchi 1978, Radner 1992). A central aim of my group-type taxonomy and the associated model in Chapter 6 is to provide an explanation for how threats of violence and the habit of obedience arise and are maintained in different groups.

3.2 A taxonomy of group archetypes

I propose that there are five fundamental types of social groups, of which only one existed prior to the establishment of agriculture. Below I sketch archetypes of each group, since pure versions rarely exist in the real world, and then I discuss how actual groups are made up of combinations of these five archetypes.

3.2.1 Small hierarchies

An archetypal small hierarchy has a clear leader, a few of high rank, and a group of underlings, and includes not more than a few dozen individuals in all. All relations in the small hierarchy are defined on the basis of pure self-interest: the only combining element holding the group together is the material benefits of group membership, and consequent fear of desertion. The underlings follow their orders because of material self-interest (e.g., fear of punishment, or desire to rise in the hierarchy), while those of high rank have to maintain expectations of punishment and reward in all those below them in order to maintain their higher rank. A defining feature of a hierarchy is that those higher up in a hierarchy can ask unreasonable things of those lower down, and reasonably expect to be obeyed. In particular, higher-ups can ask lower-downs for compliance with rules and commands that are not in the interest of the whole organization, or even of the person in charge, yet there is still punishment for disobedience. Modern examples that come close to matching this archetype include the basic army unit, some criminal gangs, and some small private companies that are not based on family relations. Despite some hierarchical elements in gender relations within hunter-gatherer groups, small hierarchies were not fully developed before the establishment of agriculture.

3.2.2 Small circles of reciprocity

A small circle of reciprocity is comprised of a group of individuals who are in potential each other's equals, who know each other personally, and who have a recognized common goal that transcends their own personal well-being. The relations in this group are defined by the members helping each other out following implicit score sheets that are held in everyone's minds. Behavior is reciprocal in the sense that members receive gifts and return gifts, following the implicit score sheets, rather than being determined by hierarchical power structures and clear enforcement mechanisms. Small hierarchical differences flow from relative personal strengths or powers of persuasion, but group members see themselves as sharing a joint greater goal that typically transcends personal power differences and purely self-interested behavior. An archetypal example of a small circle of reciprocity would be a group of male hunter-gatherers who have the well-being and continuity of their whole group (including women, children, their ancestors, and their culture) as their joint goal. Of course each male in the group can still be primarily motivated by his personal well-being, but the group members share, or at least appear to share, the ideal of caring for the whole band. Modern examples that come close to this description include sports teams or teams of professionals who are part of collaborative groups, such as a group of senior scientists within an academic field or within the R&D division of a company. Such modern groups are characterized by reciprocal relations between more or less equal individuals, who to some extent share a higher ideal than merely their own well-being.

The ideals that define a small circle of reciprocity may only be passionately believed in by a small percentage of individuals within the circle. However, if the ideals that define a group are not too out-of-step with the material self-interest of the group members, then this heartfelt commitment by some percentage of the group binds the behavior of those who do not believe: all are held to the mental score sheet of favors as a sign of subservience to the group ideal. Those who do not believe have a strong incentive to pretend that they do believe.[4] We will revisit this dynamic later in the book.

3.2.3 Large hierarchies

A large hierarchy is defined by anonymous hierarchical relations across multiple layers, each one in charge of the one below and being commanded by the one above, with a single leader on top. A large hierarchy is too large for everyone to know everyone else personally. As in the small hierarchy, the defining characteristic of the large hierarchy is that each member is only interested in his own personal well-being and obeys orders mainly out of material self-interest. Pure modern

---

[4] This crucial observation, i.e., that what appears as reciprocal or "altruistic" behavior might in fact be merely compliance with social norms adhered to because of implicit threats by the group as a whole, has a long ancestry in sociological debates. Mauss (2002) (p. 94) investigated "gift giving" in many "more primitive" cultures and, quite in line with what is argued here, observes that "generosity and self-interest are linked in giving." As Komter points out, this is still the dominant position in the literature on gift giving (Komter 2005, Komter 2010), but there is a significant fraction of sociologists who claim that gift giving is "more altruistic," in the sense that the role of well-understood self-interest is far less dominant than Mauss claimed. This echoes the long debate as to whether greed really is a ubiquitous and unavoidable aspect of human nature, or instead is learned and strongly aggravated by particular circumstances. Economists, including myself, are firmly in the camp of the former. As argued in Chapters 1 and 2, greed is ubiquitous, a main and unavoidable feature of individuals, hardwired from eons of evolution, and barely manipulable.

examples of this type of social group hardly exist, as large hierarchies have mainly been relegated to history. An example from antiquity would be a large army of mercenaries, such as the mercenary armies of Hannibal or of the Roman Empire. Examples closer in time to today would be the early kingdoms of medieval Europe, such as that of the Plantagenets in England during their early reign. These were hierarchies that forced the population (mainly farmers) to pay taxes to them. One modern example that comes close to matching the archetype of the large hierarchy is a large, privately owned, privately run enterprise. Bureaucracies also have a layered structure, where one layer dominates another.

3.2.4 Large circles of reciprocity

Large circles of reciprocity are like small circles, but involving more people, and where the shared goal is an abstraction that only in a vague sense is the same for everyone. A good example of a large circle of reciprocity is those people who identify as part of a nation, and hold as a shared goal "the well-being of our country." Nationalism in this sense is an abstraction to which each subscribing person is supposed to owe some allegiance, and for which they can be asked to make sacrifices. In contrast with orders issued and obeyed in a hierarchy, demands made of individuals within large circles of reciprocity make sense (or at least appear to make sense) in terms of the ideals of the group: neither whim nor individual material self-interest is held above the ideal of the group as a whole. As with the small circle of reciprocity, heartfelt adherence to ideals by every group member is not required for a group to function as a large circle of reciprocity.[5]

---

[5] Frijters and Tieman (1999) argue that it does not actually take a large number of "true believers" to keep the mass of politicians and civil servants loyal to the overall good: all that is required is a sufficient number to make it perilous for the rest to be entirely selfish. The origin of "true believers" is there taken to be diverse. True believers may be a group that simply does not "recompute" at every moment and hence blindly follows current laws, thereby enforcing them for everyone. It may alternatively be that true believers are those who abide by the rationale of cognitive dissonance (Festinger 1957): *because* they have followed the laws so far, they truly believe in them. One can finally see the group of true believers as exercising a form of vanity, whereby they believe they are executing a design of higher moral value than that supported by the actions of others, making them derive direct utility from being loyal to the overall good. The role of true believers will be revisited later.

A good example of nationalism is English patriotism during World War I. A large group of individuals, mainly defined by where they or their relatives have spent most of their lives, self-identifies with the abstract notion of being "English." Each of these individuals is connected to every other one via this shared abstraction, leading each to expect certain behavior of every other member. This means to them that they feel beholden to a set of behaviors deemed to be "English," including loyalty towards England's main institutions, such as the monarchy and the rule of law. More generally, this concept of nationalism includes an explicit sense of reciprocity between the abstract notion of "England" and this group of individuals. This reciprocity includes the vague expectation that "if I defend my country, my country will look after me." Of course, in actuality, a country decides nothing. It is people who decide things, and the people making up the abstraction of "the country" cannot really be forced to honor any implicit bargain with the abstraction. Yet, in a broad sense, the expected reciprocity was indeed upheld in this case. During the war, while the women worked in the war factories, millions of men volunteered for the army. After the war, the "English population" not only took responsibility for looking after war veterans (hence in a sense "reciprocating" with those veterans) but moved further from hierarchy towards egalitarianism as its members began to be treated more and more like equals by other members, witnessed for example by the introduction of suffrage for women in 1918.

Nationalism defined within geographic borders is only one example of a large circle of reciprocity. There are many abstractions around which large groups have organized themselves in implicit reciprocal relations, including religions, cities, and professions. Modern religions, for example, nearly all explicitly incorporate the notion of reciprocity both within the group of believers and between the believers and the unseen entity. In relations between believers, most religions advocate adherence to what is known as the Golden Rule (of reciprocity): "do unto others what you would have them do unto you." Direct quotations from world scriptures are often used to press this point – e.g.,

- **Buddhism:** "Hurt not others in ways that you would find hurtful." (Tripitaka Udana-varga 5:18) (Buddha 30 BC)
- **Christianity:** "Therefore all things whatsoever ye would that men should do to you, do ye even so to them: for this is the law and the prophets." (The New Testament, Matthew 7:12) (*The Holy Bible* 1974)

- **Confucianism:** "Do not impose on others what you yourself do not desire." (The Analects of Confucius, 15.23) (Yu 1893)
- **Hinduism:** "One should not behave towards others in a way which is disagreeable to oneself. This is the essence of morality." (Mahabharata, Anusasana Parva, 113.8) (Vyasa 1896)
- **Islam:** "Not one of you is a believer until he desires for his brother what he desires for himself." (The Sayings of Prophet Mohammed, Forty Hadiths of an-Nawawi) (An-Nawawi 1997)
- **Judaism:** "What is hateful to you, do not do to your fellow men. That is the entire Law; the rest is commentary." (The Talmud, Shabbat 31a) (*The Talmud of the Land of Israel, Volume XI: Shabbat* 1991)

Reciprocity is also a fundamental component of the relationship between the believer and the unseen supernatural power of each of these major religions: the believer believes he will ultimately receive benefits from the power in accordance with whether he upholds the power's wishes. Those adhering to some set of divine rules go to heaven (or go up in the hierarchy of castes or levels of consciousness) after death, whereas those who have violated divine rules go to hell or to some other place of lower standing.[6]

What holds for religion also holds to a lesser extent for large professions, such as my own world of economics. Tens of thousands of economists have formed joint societies around the common goal of furthering economics as a profession, and a presumption of reciprocity is embedded in the peer review system.

Importantly, large circles of reciprocity take a long time to develop, and almost always include a host of supporting institutions, both

---

[6] Iannaccone (1998) reviews the literature on the economics of religion and concludes (p. 1491) that

[a]lthough beliefs lie at the core of every religion, economists have yet to say much about the formation of beliefs, religious or otherwise, nor have they given much attention to the process by which religions seek to shape people's beliefs and values. Although this issue is important in all economic settings, religion would seem to be the ideal testing ground for models of value change and belief formation.

I agree with this assessment. One of the major sources of external validation of the theories in this book has been the experimental paper by Frijters and Baron (2012) that links the basic content of religious stories with the Love Principle. These experiments will be discussed later.

formal (e.g., legal status of group members) and informal (e.g., linguistic and behavioral conventions). As with small circles of reciprocity, a defining characteristic of large circles of reciprocity is that no individual is deemed to be above the shared goal – not even a political leader. Not even the highest religious leader stands above the god of his religion, and not even the highest ruler within a nation stands above the needs of the nation. This is in fact the key aspect that differentiates a circle from a hierarchy, for in a hierarchy, the wishes of the leader top everything else. As a sign of subservience to the higher goal within circles of reciprocity, leadership within circles of reciprocity is almost never hereditary, but rather rotates amongst members based on some explicit set of rules. Virtually all surviving circles of reciprocity have developed rituals in which the power of the group is taken from the hands of one elite and placed into the hands of another. Elections, for example, can be understood as ritualized means of transferring the power of the group as a whole from one person or subgroup to another. Even within fairly small circles of reciprocity, such as medical associations or departments of scientists, group leadership is explicitly temporary.

In many ways, the modern world is at present dominated by various interlocking large circles of reciprocity formed around abstractions (nations, religions, great causes), with new abstractions emerging all the time. Other relations in society are then not immune to the possibilities for influence that become available by piggy-backing on the loyalties that emerge within these circles. For example, a relatively new abstraction is "the planet's ecosystem," with the explicit notion that "we" should care for the earth, which will then care for "us." Seeing the opportunity that this presents, an insecticide company in Australia has tried to cash in on the allure of the "green" abstraction by painting a green leaf on its bottles of fly spray, attracting the consumer like a moth to the proverbial flame.

3.2.5 Networks

Networks consist of functional lines of information and trade between individuals, without any power-based relations or shared ideals amongst members of the network. Having no "emotive" content makes them distinct from the other four types of groups. Members of networks are motivated by their material self-interest and make no attempt to hide that, but members' power relative to one another is either equal or simply irrelevant. Modern examples of pure networks include trade networks and networks of information.

The importance of networks for the story of power is that large networks can serve as the birthplace of future circles of reciprocity. The signatories of the American Declaration of Independence, for example, started out mainly as a network of traders and those who supported trade,[7] who shared ideas and relevant information for purely selfish reasons. This network transformed itself into a political movement, which invented new ideals (such as the idea of American independence) for essentially selfish reasons, and then these ideals began to lead a life of their own and form the centerpiece of a large circle of reciprocity (the American nation state). Another good example of this potentially formative role of networks is given by the merchant networks in the late Middle Ages in Italy, France, and England. These networks started as pure trading networks amongst entrepreneurs within and across countries, whose members were primarily interested in getting rich. Yet the size and importance of these networks grew with the growth of trade starting around AD 1000, and eventually these networks became the breeding grounds for the idea of "national citizenship" of these countries. When these networks became large enough, such as they were by the mid-eighteenth century in France, the shared ideals that had developed catalyzed the birth of a new large circle of reciprocity: e.g., the French nation state. That circle was powerful enough to overthrow the Bourbon royal family that had populated France's upper echelons ever since the fourteenth century.

3.2.6 Common elements of reciprocal and hierarchical groups

A common feature of the four "emotive groups" is that group identity itself is anthropomorphized by its members. As if it were human itself, the group identity begets a history, recognizable traits, and even a

---

[7] The majority (57 percent) of signatories were lawyers, and merchants were the next-most represented group, at 20 percent. As noted by Dignam and Galanis (2009) (p. 400), "on economic matters ... the values of the common lawyers and the merchant class coincided."

psychological character. Group members can talk about the identity of their group as if it were a living thing, with an origin and a destination. Families have stories about their "ancestry" and "roots"; ethnicities have stories about where their members came from, what rights and duties are carried by that ethnicity, and what its quintessential psychological characteristics are; companies have stories about their founders, traits that are particularly valued by the company, and what the company's role has been in different communities; countries have intricate histories, "national characters," and specific festivities; political ideologies have "founding authors" and specific behaviors with which they are associated (e.g., the right-wing political movement in the US is associated with prayer, support for traditional family types, and hunting). As a rule of thumb, the identities of reciprocal groups are far more elaborate and vibrant than those of hierarchical groups. This derives from the fact that the level of identification of group members with the abstract group identity is much higher in reciprocal groups than in hierarchical groups.

Emotive groups typically employ a set of "tricks" to enhance identification with the group as a whole, and to engender greater loyalty towards it. Oaths to joint ideals are a standard device, as well as initiation rituals and rites of passage between subgroups. Individuals can furthermore be assigned to specific recognized roles in the group, such as "leader," "nurturer," "arbiter," or "mentor." Each such position comes with a recognized set of expectations as well as some implicit borrowing of the power of the group as a whole towards particular purposes. Individuals can be encouraged to identify with their particular roles, which is an indirect means of becoming more loyal towards the group as a whole. Indirect loyalty of this sort is especially useful in hierarchical groups, such as when a "subordinate" is given a "duty" to get something done.

Another common feature of emotive groups, unlike networks, is that there is such a thing as group power. Emotive groups embody a joint physical, intellectual, and economic power that can be directed towards particular goals, including threatening or fighting with others. Emotive groups have recognized methods of creating joint expectations about the application of group power. In hierarchies, power is applied following direct orders from the top. In large circles of reciprocity, the direction about how to apply group power is provided by a recognized group process, such as a democratic vote, deliberation by a council of elders, or a religious ritual and interpretation. Group power is hence fluid. It can be borrowed, in that individuals can be understood in certain situations as representing some aspect of their group, in which case their actions carry the threat of retaliation by their group members.

As an example of this fluidity, consider a subordinate told by his superior to retrieve a pencil from a central storage unit. That subordinate, while merely having been ordered to do something, nevertheless borrows some of the whole group's power in order to overcome particular obstacles he may encounter while pursuing his objective (e.g., locks and guards): the subordinate can reasonably demand that others allow him to obtain and transport the item, as he is momentarily protected by the power of the group.

Yet, the power of the group as a whole stands or falls in direct proportion to the perceived or real loyalty towards group ideals and roles. There may be only a few true loyalists required to keep the rest in line, but if there is no real or perceived loyalty to anything, then everything said is cheap talk. We are back in the land of mainstream economics: there simply ceases to be a group.

3.3 Groups in practice

I contend that the five archetypes introduced above encompass almost every human relation we see today and in history. To illustrate this, I first provide several stylized modern examples, after which the emergence of the modern nation state is re-molded as the outcome of group struggle.

3.3.1 Modern organizations as melting pots of these five types: Large-group examples

As a first example, consider a large profit-oriented company, such as a car manufacturer in a Western country. Superficially, such a company is a large hierarchical group with explicit lines of responsibility: a CEO, upper management, lower management, and workers. But that company operates within the laws and norms of accepted behavior of the whole country: no executive manager would be able to whip his underlings or in any other serious way deviate from what is deemed "normal" by the rest of the country, and so the large group of reciprocity called "the country" in part determines the social life within the company. Moreover, the company itself contains many small circles of reciprocity that effectively hold particular parts of the company together, such as teams of design engineers or production workers who share a common goal.

Even the top senior management team itself will usually share, to a greater or lesser extent, the official ideal of being jointly responsible for the company, just as the board of directors will have such a stated ideal. Even though the real intent of the powerful people in these groups may be largely selfish, the explicit quid-pro-quo culture within the small circle of reciprocity that is senior management is strikingly similar to that of the hunter-gatherer males of 40,000 years ago.

The company's departments and work units typically have somewhat distinct identities, and their members also behave not unlike small bands of hunter-gatherers. Subsets of workers are organized into labor unions, which operate much like circles of reciprocity (a small circle if the union is company specific, or a large circle if the union extends to all workers in an industry). The company's divisions will often nevertheless include small hierarchies (such as administrative groups made up of members from different ranks). The whole company participates in business networks in which it trades, and political networks through which it lobbies. In this way, a large company can be seen as a somewhat hierarchical organization within the overall circle of reciprocity of the nation state, and consisting of a patchwork of small circles and small hierarchies.

The fact that a large organization is a political patchwork immediately illuminates why a senior manager faces monumental problems when trying to change anything in the organization. There are all kinds of separate groups with their own agendas, their own norms, and their own lines of communication. For change to occur, each of these groups must embrace that change or at least not resist it, which is unlikely to occur in the absence of great political skill on the part of the manager or his support staff. No large modern organization is truly "led" by any individual, for any movement away from the status quo requires large numbers of other individuals (all members of the organization's constituent reciprocal circles, plus the leaders of its constituent small hierarchies) to agree to that movement. A senior manager without extraordinary political skill is at best merely the "suggester in chief" regarding where the organization as a whole should go. Quite often, a senior manager will find himself no more than an "extractor in chief" of the wealth created by the whole organization, and one whose suggestions moreover are continuously sabotaged and/or ignored by the supposed underlings, who mainly pay lip service to the senior manager.

As another example of how a modern organization is composed of the five archetypal groups outlined above, consider a secondary school in a small village community within a Western country. As an entity that teaches the next generation the wisdom and ideals of the current generation, the school is strongly tied into the large circle of reciprocity of the whole country. As an integral part of the life of the village, the school will also play a role within the small circle of reciprocity defining the community itself. The ideals of those two circles manifest themselves in terms of how teachers, parents, and even pupils perceive the role and usefulness of the school. This means that in practical terms, no decision maker in the school can ignore the ideals of these circles and expect to command respect.

There will also be a small circle of reciprocity amongst the teachers within the school, upholding the ideals of the school itself and looking after its daily operations, using implicit score sheets to ask and perform favors within their circle. The existence of this small circle limits the degree to which the headmaster or Ministry of Education can treat different teachers differently, such as in the form of pay differentials. Since unequal pay goes against the egalitarian norms upheld within a circle of reciprocity, instituting pay differentials amongst teachers would incite significant political rebellion by teachers.

The school itself is also part of a hierarchy since it is beholden to the demands of a Ministry of Education, which determines parts of the curriculum. Within the school, there may also be a small hierarchy consisting of a headmaster in charge of administrative matters and matters of hiring and firing, and the (underling) teachers. There is a natural tension between that internal hierarchy and the circle of teachers, for while legally a headmaster might officially be in charge, the proper running of the school requires the goodwill of the circle of teachers, whose norms involve treatment as equals rather than as underlings.

Finally, the school as a buyer of books, roof repairs, uniforms, fences, sports equipment, and so forth is a part of business networks and library networks; it may even be part of political networks, such as when it throws the weight of its needs or ideals behind good causes.

These two examples illustrate how the daily struggles within actual organizations can be understood as the product of the coexistence of many different social groups, with different characteristics and expectations. They also illustrate how diffuse power has become within organizations: because most modern organizations are not simple hierarchies, any one individual can only attain significant power to the extent that he participates in several groups simultaneously and appears to share the ideals of all of these different groups at the same time.

3.3.2 Small-group examples

The five archetypes can also be used to help understand the nature of much smaller types of organizations, such as marriage, the family, and slavery. Each of these is now briefly discussed.

Marriage

The historical "ideal marriage" concept in Western society (for example, the 1950s image of marriage in the US) is a bilateral monopoly in which each marriage partner is "supposed" to be the monopoly supplier of particular services (primarily sex and reproductive services) to the other. Note that this image is fully sustainable by the Love Principle: both partners are, by design, both powerful towards each other and weak at the same time. It is thus an arrangement that one would expect to engender love.

In equal marriages, each member can deny the other access to services, yet is also exposed to power from the other in that the available alternatives to obtaining services from the spouse are either illegal or at least carry a heavy social stigma. In the idealized view of marriage, this bilateral monopoly leads to a continuous stream of reciprocity within the marriage, where both partners work towards their mutual benefit. These relations are strengthened by an entire system of outside reinforcement, including the ritual of the wedding, the legal institutions surrounding marriage, and the social norms surrounding marriage that are passed on within families and communities.

Recalling the five archetypal groups, one can categorize marriage as a tiny reciprocal group that derives its meaning and structure from larger groups. It is within the power structures of larger groups that partners interact in a marriage, which allows the meaning of marriage to shift over time and place. In places or eras where the ideals held by the larger groups within which marriage functions relate mainly to "the solidarity of men" (as opposed to women), for example, one should expect the power relations inside a marriage to be highly unequal, and for marriage to be more like a small hierarchy than a reciprocal relationship. In places or eras where the groups that set the wider context are made up of male and female citizens united by a jointly held abstraction such as "our nation," one should expect the power relations inside a marriage to reflect that wider reality and thus to be more equal, making marriage more like a small reciprocal group.

Drawing on the understanding of love from Chapter 2, we can slightly extend this conceptualization of marriage. While both men and women adhere to the norms of marriage mainly due to the enforcement mechanisms provided by the wider groups in which it exists, there are still raw differences in power between the two genders. Men's superior physical force, together with their still-superior social power compared to women in most present-day societies, implies that notwithstanding national ideals of equality, women are on average at a power disadvantage compared to their men at any given instant of time.

Yet men do not, as a rule, treat their wives as slaves in modern societies. Is there any reason for this other than their blind adherence to ideals of equality, or fear of societal retribution? First, a wife who finds such ideals appealing and views her marriage as not adhering to them could make life quite uncomfortable for her husband. She could resist by biting or scratching, sabotaging him, and refusing to cooperate more than minimally. She could also run away and appeal to the social norms in the society at large for protection. In Western societies she indeed derives some power from this outside option to flee from her husband without the rest of society catching her and sending her back.

Second, even in countries where national ideals of equality between the sexes have not yet been embedded, both sexes pass through cycles of relatively higher and lower power in their everyday lives (e.g., due to sickness, sleeping, or experiencing personal and professional successes or failures). Because of this, despite men's greater average strength, partners within any given marriage take turns over time being more powerful than the other, and hence take turns perceiving the other from a position of weakness. This dynamic helps to sustain their mutual love, and hence underpins the reciprocal nature of marriage in the longer term.

There are many as-yet unresolved questions regarding the heterogeneity of views and emotions within marriage, and within groups more broadly. For example, the standard neuroscientific finding that men tend more towards abstraction and women tend more towards emotion would suggest that for men, the reciprocal relation they have is more with the idea of marriage, and that for women the reciprocal relation is more with their actual partner, complete with his emotions. The scientific examination of such hypotheses is left for future work.

The family

In a parent–child relationship, parents have power over their children during a limited period of time. Parents in hunter-gatherer societies have almost absolute control over their very young children, because the children have no alternative care provider, but as they grow children gradually become more capable and start to take on responsibilities of their own. The flow of goods and services thereby changes over time from one-directional (from parent to child) during early childhood to two-directional in early adulthood. When the child is a mature adult and the parent close to death, the flow of goods changes again to one-directional (from child to parent). The balance of power changes in the same ways.

The peculiar aspect of the parent–child relationship is that the child is not aware in the early years of the eventual reversal of the power relations later on, and hence feels himself to be under the complete control of the parent, which leads to very strong affective bonds. As detailed in Chapter 2, the parent likewise is partially under the control of the child, with the expectation of gradually losing more and more power over time.

Many aspects of the child–parent relation vary across cultures and across time. As Keith (1991) details, in the ancient Roman culture, the (male) head of the family had near absolute power over all female members of his family of all ages. In modern Western culture, power over children is constrained by regulation, and formally ends when children become adults, at around eighteen years of age.

The role of children in family production has similarly changed from being full contributors to the family income at an early age – such as during the Middle Ages, when everyone worked on the land as soon as they were able to – to being a drain on family income in the modern era, where children by and large make no contribution to the family income and instead are legally obliged to attend school and learn what "society" wants children to learn. Many social and legal institutions (also including, for example, inheritance law and alimony regulations) affect the parent–child relationship, often directly influencing the power structure of the relationship. As with marriage, the actual child–parent relation cannot be understood outside of a wider "group power" context.

Slavery

In ancient Rome, circa AD 50, rich Roman men could buy slaves at a market. Their power over these slaves was absolute: the master could simply dictate access to the labor time and the sexual services of the slave. Slaves had no right to complain or refuse any request; their children would automatically be born into slavery too. For the slave, the only realistic alternatives to this complete domination were to run away or to earn so much money on the side that he could buy freedom from the master. The main reward a slave could hope for in his life was to be set free by his master. Freed slaves became full members of Roman society, and could even become emperors (Emperor Trajanus, for example, was a freed slave).

What upheld the slave system in ancient Rome was the system of solidarity amongst free male Romans to aid each other whenever their slaves ran away or misbehaved. This solidarity was enshrined in Roman law, with specialized slave catchers who could be hired for a fee. In light of the group-type taxonomy above, the archetypal master–slave relation is a small hierarchy that is sanctioned and made possible because of the power of an overarching group.

Slavery has almost died out in modern times, but remnants survive in some agricultural communities where individuals are almost entirely at the mercy of the owner of their land. The main point again is that these relations are derivative of the wider "power equilibrium" in the societies in which they emerge, rather than being a function of the actual individual traits of the slave and master involved, or related to any list of current possessions.

3.3.3 The emergence of the nation state from the interaction of social groups

We can now reinterpret many of the gradual historical changes considered previously as changes in social dynamics due to interactions between different types of social groups. Hunter-gatherer societies were small circles of reciprocity. Early agricultural kingdoms were combinations of small hierarchies and circles of reciprocity. The elites in these kingdoms formed circles of reciprocity (often along family lines) that kept control of strict hierarchies that were used to extract resources from farmers. Farming in those days was a particularly easy target for hierarchies because land cannot run away, and hence farmers can be credibly threatened with eviction or death. Such threats were made more effective by the fact that farmers at that time hardly interacted outside their own group, meaning that their alternative paths to subsistence were scarce.

Larger kingdoms only emerged after a long period of strife amongst smaller kingdoms, each vying for the creation of a large hierarchy under its control, until eventually large regions came to be dominated by one elite. This happened most clearly in China, where seven earlier kingdoms were joined into one region by the first emperor.[8] That empire developed bureaucratic hierarchies to support itself, which themselves were led by small circles of reciprocity (where those circles were based on membership in a particular family – in the case of the emperor – or class). In Western Europe, the gradual agglomeration of smaller entities led to what we now think of as France, England, Germany, Spain, and the other modern nation states. This process involved hundreds of years of warfare wherein people leading hierarchies of various sizes from within small circles of reciprocity tried to increase the amount of territory controlled by their particular hierarchy.

The eventual social organization that prevailed in the evolutionary struggle for social supremacy was the nation state, which is a large circle of reciprocity. The ideals of the nation state are disseminated via schools whose curricula are strongly influenced by specialized hierarchical entities (ministries of education), and its ideals are upheld by courts that are seen by members of the nation state to be empowered by the "wishes of the nation." The nation state is run by legions of small hierarchies (its bureaucratic departments) and defended by a state-organized army that is run internally as a hierarchy, even though

---

[8] These seven kingdoms were the Qin, Chu, Yan, Qi, Wei, Zhao, and Han, which became united under the Qin dynasty around 220 BC; see p. 33 of Killion (2006).

its members are also part of the large circle of reciprocity that defines the nation state.[9]

The nation state "reciprocates" towards its citizens via providing an organized police force that keeps the internal peace, social insurance programs, and inputs that facilitate the creation of networks (e.g., infrastructure). The Western nation state's leadership is organized via elections, which can be interpreted as rituals in which aspiring leaders-to-be must appeal for the sympathy of the citizens. This normally involves would-be leaders trying desperately to be seen to have only the best interests of the nation as a whole at heart, thereby proving their loyalty to the shared ideal that forms the centerpiece of the circle of reciprocity. The nation state is indeed a marvel of social organization, with its basic building blocks the five archetypal social groups.

The move from local reciprocal groups within which individuals work and live to more anonymous interactions that operate via more central authorities is well-documented in the rise of the Italian city states of the fifteenth century. Padgett and Mclean (2011) analyze the emergence of anonymous business relations during the rise of the Italian city of Florence, which introduced many "capitalist inventions" now taken for granted, including double-entry bookkeeping, bills of exchange, partnership contracts, and commercial courts. Those inventions quite explicitly drew upon the mediation of the central city authorities and displaced the economic function of the loyalty present within smaller groups.

However, this transition was not a radical jump, but happened organically. Indeed, group loyalties were very important for generating the initial trust needed to enter more anonymous business relations. Mainly drawing on the 1427 tax census by the authorities of that city, Padgett and Mclean (2011) note (p. 2) how important existing social groups were for the emergence of new forms of businesses: "New business transactions did not displace the oligarchic social networks of the time, we argue; rather, they built on and formalized these relationships into markets." These authors also note that the central authority of the city itself was made up of a patchwork of smaller interest groups, i.e., those same merchants who were experimenting with the more

---

[9] Military coups take place when pressure from the hierarchy conflicts with and overpowers pressure from the circle of reciprocity, in terms of the self-interest and idealism of the soldiers.

anonymous forms of business interactions. Hence the move within Florence from small reciprocal groups to a larger reciprocal group within which economic relations are organized via more formal institutions (in regard to bookkeeping, contracts, and courts) was a gradual one. People essentially outgrew their smaller groups, rather than experiencing a revolutionary jump from one to the other.

I here refer to Frijters and Foster (2013) for additional examples of how more historical developments can be interpreted within the framework of the five group archetypes, including the internal dynamics of the French Revolution of the late eighteenth century, the Russian Revolution of the early twentieth century, and the more recent "War on Terror" in the early twenty-first century.[10]

3.3.4 Multiple group identities

People can be, and invariably are, members of several groups at the same time. Each can be a source of their identity. For example, a person can be a mother (i.e., a member of a nuclear family, a very small circle of reciprocity), a coach at the local football club (a member of a circle of reciprocity), a company CEO (the top of a hierarchy), a Canadian (a member of a large circle of reciprocity), a scientist (a member of another large circle of reciprocity), and a consumer (a member of a network). Nowadays, people often have far more identities than in previous eras, including virtual identities.

[10] In that follow-up book we discuss the history of social organization at much greater length, with a major focus on the gradual move towards democratic nation states. The stylized story of development is a transition from small reciprocal groups to larger reciprocal groups. An important element of that story in Europe was the idealism of the social classes that experienced high levels of social interaction ("contact classes") during the period in which kingdoms still dominated Western Europe. The idealization of the ancient Greek democratic states held in the hearts of merchants and other contact makers during the Renaissance is viewed as a crucial influence on the direction taken by the contact classes as their economic power gradually overtook the political dominance of European kings and nobility. The gradual strengthening of those democratic ideals as industrialization emerged, along with an associated belief that other forms of society could actually work, was pivotal in helping to embolden the contact classes enough to overthrow old regimes, or at least challenge them sufficiently to become included in new shared power structures. The fact that many early revolutionaries paid with their lives for this challenge demands a theoretical framework that recognizes non-greed motives.

The existence of multiple identities brings with it the possibility that someone who behaves openly selfishly in one (say, hierarchical) role can also be part of a reciprocal group where he pays lip service to, and in fact materially furthers, some common goal. Selfish behavior in one group and a willingness to play along with ideals in another reciprocal group are not mutually exclusive at all. An example demonstrating this lack of mutual exclusion is shown in the dynamics of the emergence of the Magna Carta in England in 1215, which was put forward by a coalition of purely selfish barons who individually were leaders of parasitical hierarchies, but who as a group won the acquiescence of King John of England to an agreement built around the ideal of sharing power. This was a significant step in England's social evolution towards its modern form.

This example not only illuminates how one person can be an advocate of hierarchy in one group and of reciprocity in another. It also illustrates a more general point, well understood by economists but poorly understood by many others because it goes against all common intuition: purely selfish actions can lead to good outcomes at the aggregate level. The notion that "we" should not trust selfish people to do good things fits in perfectly with the ideologies of the circles of reciprocity to which all of us patriots belong, but it ignores evidence that many "good" historical decisions were taken for selfish reasons.

3.3.5 The genesis of groups

New groups are established all the time, and most quickly disappear again. New companies are established because the initiator wants some benefit out of them, and the majority go bankrupt. Regional identities come and go throughout history. Many of these identities are based on little more than a modicum of shared history and a large dose of propaganda by a local ruler who promotes the idea of a regional identity in order to be able to tap into group loyalties when making war on someone else. New identities thus often arise out of economic or political entrepreneurship. Less often, new identities merely rise from the ashes of older identities, such as the re-emergence of a Welsh identity that is primarily led by the regional state bureaucracy of the region of Wales. Thanks to this resurrection, teaching the Welsh language – something that was nearly extinct fifty years ago – is now compulsory in Wales.

Small circles of reciprocity often emerge from shared interests, sustained mutual material ideals, mutual dependence (e.g., when each of two individuals or existing groups holds some power over the other's needs) or even simply from labeling. The psychologist Jane Elliott demonstrated this quite dramatically by a well-known experiment in Iowa in 1968 in which she divided her classroom into "the brown eyes" and "the blue eyes." Within days, the two groups had established strong identities, had adopted various stories about the inferiority of the other group, and were actively discriminating against each other, showing that virtually any means of distinguishing individuals has the potential to spawn a reciprocal group.

In the process of creating new large circles of reciprocity, such as those surrounding religions and "isms," books and stories can play an organizing role. Stories containing ideas that reach and appeal to millions of people can potentially unite them. Each idealistic story contained in a book, pamphlet, painting, sculpture, blog, or any other means of disseminating stories, is a potential core element of a new circle of reciprocity.

3.3.6 *External validation I: The presumption of reciprocity*

The core underlying assumption behind the emergence and functioning of circles of reciprocity is the same as that which underpins the Love Principle: individuals are endowed with an automatic presumption of reciprocity towards the unknown. When they are put under stress or desperately want something, they unconsciously presume that the object of their desire is reciprocal, and they will therefore sacrifice towards it and start to adopt it as part of their self-image in an unconscious effort to make a bargain with the object and thereby obtain the good they desire.

Despite the historical and psychological evidence presented so far in favor of this underlying assumption, one can wonder whether the assumption is truly predictive of how modern humans behave. Recent experiments (Frijters and Baron 2012) explicitly test whether reciprocity towards an abstraction would be observed in the laboratory. The experimental design used in Frijters and Baron (2012) involved about 500 student subjects playing rounds of simple games via which they could earn "products." At the end of each round, subjects were told that the value (price) of each product they had earned so far would be determined by "Theoi, the market maker." They were told that it was unknown how Theoi reached his decisions, but they were given the option to "contribute" a fraction of their winnings in that round to Theoi. In each case, the actual price was determined entirely at random and independently the contribution of the participants, making "Theoi" simply a labeled source of unknown uncertainty from the perspective of the participants. Variations of the game included the possibility of priming, where the contribution was 10 percent unless the participants changed it; the labeling of the uncertainty, using the word "weather" instead of "Theoi"; the possibility of sharing information amongst participants; and variations in the degree of variation of the price over time.

Results showed that the average participant contributed nearly half of his winnings to Theoi in the first round, and that this percentage declined to about 25 percent after ten periods but stayed stable thereafter. This finding was unaffected by priming, indicating that individuals would manually increase the contribution when primed to give 10 percent. It was also unaffected by sharing information. Using the word "weather" decreased contributions by about one-quarter, showing that labeling matters and that an entity that a modern person can reasonably expect not to be reciprocal (the weather) is indeed presumed by fewer to be reciprocal. The big change in contributions was found in relation to the level of uncertainty. When uncertainty was set at zero in particular experiments ("Theoi" always made exactly the same choice), then contributions shrank to no more than about 5 percent of total winnings after a couple of rounds, with the vast majority of participants no longer contributing anything to Theoi after ten rounds. Interestingly, contribution levels were not dependent on whether individuals were members of any organized religion.

Frijters and Baron (2012) thus found in their 500 subjects a strong presumption of reciprocity towards an unknown force that was perceived to be able to influence something they cared about, and around which there was sufficient uncertainty to allow a belief of reciprocity to maintain itself for long periods, and this presumption appeared unrelated to religious devotion. These findings can be seen as consistent with an in-built human ability, and even tendency, to enter into reciprocal relations with abstract entities such as "Theoi." The authors further surmise that this ability had a strong evolutionary benefit in the sense of catalyzing stronger group bonding on the basis of a shared abstraction.

3.3.7 External validation II: Individual versus group decision making

A direct and nontrivial implication of the assumption that individuals presume reciprocity towards an unknown follows when one links this notion to the fact that group ideals themselves gradually evolve in the direction of conformity with the interests of their members. Individual members of a small group, operating independently and sacrificing towards the current group norms, are going to be more constrained by the social norms of the group than will be all individuals in the whole group when acting together. This is because the group as a whole can redefine its social norms towards what is truly in the best interests of its members, whereas the individual acting alone cannot.[11]

As a result, it should be true that when one presents entire small groups with a situation in which everyone's collective interests would be better served by being less reciprocal and altruistic than warranted under the "usual" social norm in the group, then the entire group should behave more selfishly and be quicker to adjust its behavior in this direction than its individual members, acting alone.

Sutter (2009) argues that the recent experimental literature on collective choices shows exactly this (p. 2248):

In contrast to individual decision making under group membership, team decision making requires several subjects to reach a joint decision, where there is typically no internal conflict in terms of payoffs among team members. The literature on team decision making has captured a lot of interest in recent years, because many economic decisions are made by teams, such as families, company boards, management teams, committees, or central bank boards. Cooper and Kagel (2005) provide a thorough survey of the relevant literature, documenting that team decisions are typically closer to standard game theoretic predictions than individual decisions are. For

---

[11] This corollary does not hold well for large groups, where it is logistically impossible to include all members together in a given process of collaboratively reviewing information and making a decision. Yet, even then, the argument applies that at the level of representatives it is possible to advocate and adopt new social norms that individuals themselves cannot advocate.

example, teams send and accept smaller transfers in the ultimatum game (Bornstein and Yaniv 1998), send or return smaller amounts in the trust game (Cox 2002, Kugler, Bornstein, Kocher, and Sutter 2007), and are more selfish in dictator games (Wolfgang, Rocher, and Sutter 2009). Teams exit the centipede game at earlier stages (Bornstein, Kugler, and Ziegelmeyer 2004), and they outperform individuals in beauty-contest games because they converge more quickly to the equilibrium (Kocher and Sutter 2005). Concerning nonstrategic tasks, teams take more rational decisions in intellective tasks, such as the Wason selection task (Maciejovsky and Budescu 2007), they are more forward-looking in a noninteractive common-pool-resource game (Gillet, Schram, and Sonnesmans 2009), and they achieve a higher payoff/risk ratio in a portfolio selection task (Rockenbach, Sadrieh, and Mathauschek 2007). Charness, Karni, and Levin (2007) also show that teams violate the principles of Bayesian updating less often than individuals do. Summarizing the evidence, teams can be considered more "rational players" (Bornstein and Yaniv 1998) in a broad variety of strategic and nonstrategic tasks.

While variations in individual behavior away from rationality may not be fully in line with group ideals, Sutter also finds that individuals will change their behavior towards what is in the interests of a particular group if they are reminded of their membership in that group (in an experimental setting, group identification can be achieved by telling individuals that what they will earn through their choices will also be paid to other people in their group). Indeed, Sutter (2009) finds that individuals primed in this way behave almost identically to how the whole group would decide collectively to behave – underscoring the fact that reminding people of their group identities aligns their behavior more with the interests of a whole group.

3.4 Examples of the rise and application of group power

In Chapter 2 we looked at power and desire from the perspective of the person being manipulated. Having not yet built up an understanding of groups, however, the explanations in that chapter mainly ignored the question of where power originates and what its limits are. To illuminate these areas, I now examine the other side of manipulation: power from the view of the manipulator, who has some knowledge about the genesis and limits of that power.

Put yourself into the position of a manipulator who wishes to influence the actions of an individual or of a whole group of individuals.

Examples one can think of include an employer wishing to get an individual to do a job for him; a king trying to get people to pay taxes; a wife trying to get her husband to stop snoring; or even an abstract entity, such as "the legal system," that wishes an individual to comply with safety belt laws, or a religion trying to get a group to adhere to particular norms.

How can one get an individual to comply with the desired behavior? The general economic rule is that one must make the individual believe that compliance is going to be better for him than the available alternatives in a material sense: the material reward associated with compliance must be higher than the material reward associated with noncompliance. In most cases, this means one must offer a credible reward for compliance or a credible punishment for noncompliance. From what we now know of love, another strategy is to influence the individual to identify with the desired behavior: to make him believe that the desired behavior fits with his existing loyalties.

Let us examine this more closely by looking at various instruments of power and how they can be applied towards compliance.

3.4.1 Instruments of power: Violence

The most direct instrument of power is violence. The threat of violence can provoke a strong degree of fear in the individual who is to be manipulated. Individuals have been found to go to great lengths to avoid violence to their persons. In terms of manipulating people in the short run, the fear induced by the threat of violence is perhaps the quickest and surest means of manipulation. As briefly mentioned in Chapter 2, it appears that the presence of fear actively reduces the strength of all other emotions in the brain, virtually constricting an individual to think of nothing but the element being feared, as noted by many neuroscientists (e.g., Debiec and Ledoux 2004).

What does one need in order to be able to credibly threaten someone else with violence? The answer to this question depends on the time frame involved. A short-term threat merely requires that one has more directly available physical power than the person being threatened. A long-term threat requires that there is no realistic escape route for the threatened person, either in terms of becoming more powerful themselves over time or in terms of trying to flee the whole situation.

If one can make a credible short-term threat but not a long-term threat, then there is the obvious danger of revenge. The main situations in which short-term violence would be advisable are thus those in which the possibility of revenge is not likely, either because the threatened object will be dead or because it will have no clear target upon which to enact revenge, which will be the case, for example, when the violence is applied anonymously.

Long-term threats of violence require a whole apparatus aligned on the side of the manipulator. Not only must one be able to muster physical violence at any point in time in the future, but one furthermore needs to reduce the appeal of all of the other options available, so that compliance with the threat remains more appealing to the individual than any long-run alternative, even if violence were to be applied. This is one reason why long-term threats of violence are seen mainly in large groups of individuals, where the threat is not really made by one individual against another, but more by a whole stable system against individuals.

Perhaps the most important historical examples of a long-term threat of physical violence have been those associated with denying access to basic production factors such as land and water, and with the denial of sexual access. Restricted access to land and water has generated amongst the most bitter conflicts known to man, because access rights often decide who gets to live and who does not: being denied access is essentially equivalent to being physically punished. Enforcing access to land and water also does not require constant monitoring or a constant threat of direct violence: in order to prevent unauthorized access on a continual basis, such as for the maintenance of a village or family, all one needs is the occasional availability of physical force. Land and water cannot be easily taken away and stored in great quantities, making the denial of access to them a particularly effective form of physical threat that can be used to force compliant behavior, such as tax payment from individuals.

Access to sex is another important means of control in many societies, and can be thought of as carrying an implicit threat of physical violence to an individual, since no sexual access implies no reproduction. One extreme case is that of the Ottoman Empire where the ruler kept a "harem" of women who would be given as rewards to loyal servants (Inalcik 2000). Less extreme cases include societies in which marriages are arranged between young women and richer men, effectively denying access to poor young men, who are thereby given an incentive to do whatever it takes to attain wealth and status. The internal tensions that such arrangements create are quite formidable, and are thus one of the main characterizing elements of a culture.

Historical examples of the direct use of violence to gain control over more resources are abundant. Tribes have successfully killed rival tribes for territory, such as during the Roman invasion of Gaul that included the wholesale extermination of many tribes who consequently played no further part in history and whose territories were given to the conquering soldiers. Kings have successfully managed to overpower the armies of other kings to increase their territory, such as William the Conqueror who successfully put his family on the throne of England in 1066 and whose family, the Plantagenets, remained on that throne for centuries. The earliest tax collectors in Europe were little more than fully armored knights coming to demand payments from frightened peasants. Religions have been physically wiped out by the adherents of rival religions who thereby implanted themselves onto a new population, such as the native South American religions that were wiped out by the Spanish Inquisition. Given numerous such examples, there is nothing unexpected or irrational about the use of violence in historic times to satisfy the material and social wants of those who wield it.

The main modern example of a persistent apparatus of violence is the coercive power of the nation state. In modern times, states are the main vehicles through which organized violence occurs, as the states themselves have made all other forms of violence essentially illegal. Apart from state-sponsored violence, the only other violence observed in our Western societies usually involves unplanned short-run goals, such as a brawl in a pub, or a fight between spouses, or the activities of illegal groups who have not yet been successfully repressed by the state, such as criminal gangs.

The importance of expectations

We can here briefly delve into the question of the role of expectations and the actual use of power by posing the question of who actually commits the acts of violence and why they would consent to do so.

In modern societies, actual violence is performed by individual police officers and soldiers. As implied in Chapter 2, the reason that they do not refuse orders is either because they are so indoctrinated that they truly think this is what they should do, or because they fear the consequences of disobedience. Why would they fear disobedience? Their fear of disobedience is essentially the fear that other policemen or soldiers will punish them if they do not comply. Those policemen and soldiers in turn fear retribution by others if they do not comply. The train goes on and on, implying that it is a "circle of self-fulfilling expectations" that enforces any particular set of rules. Note that if there are a few individuals within such a circle who, either out of habit or out of loyalty[12] towards their duty, will indeed mete out punishment to those they are supposed to punish, then the rest will indeed face credible threats and will comply. Such habits and loyalties are created over time, again implying that systems of punishment will take time to build up.

Frijters and Tieman (1999) build an explicit game-theoretical mathematical model of how central authorities could arise from local interactions between agents. A more detailed version of their model appears in Chapter 6, but their main argument is that one can see central authorities as being no more than a particular "program" that enforces itself upon others. A system of central authority starts via the conscious decision of a small group of individuals who can perfectly observe each other and who can thus decide mutually to adopt the action that is best for all. These individuals can also enforce this decision upon all those connected to this core group who can be credibly threatened with even more violence than anyone else threatening them. This core-group "program" then copies itself, in the sense that anyone outside the core group is simply forced to communicate the program to all of their neighbors, which includes the commitment to report any deviation they observe by any of their neighbors. What ultimately enforces the quite complex punishment schemes needed in this model is the expectation on the part of group members that a fixed percentage of individuals will simply follow orders without any calculation (which one can call love or habit; the two have the same effect in that model). Frijters and Tieman (1999) then show that one can get one or more central authorities to emerge in a large population, depending on

---

[12] One can think of two different kinds of loyalty. One is deliberate, conditional loyalty that arises because someone believes it in their best interests to be loyal. The other is loyalty out of a true attachment. The latter is in essence the same as love and reflects what loyalty means when used in this book. The former is not really pure loyalty, in the sense that it is dependent on a continuous calculus and would hence change as soon as there is a benefit to being disloyal.

whether there is some "home advantage" in terms of threats of violence. If there is no home advantage, then only one central authority remains in their model. With a home advantage, understood as the superior ability to apply force close by relative to far away, then several central authorities can remain, all unable to threaten the borders of their neighbors sufficiently to grow further.[13]

The rise of power is all about creating expectations. In that sense, legal systems, education systems, social norms, and so forth are all expectation-creation devices. This is often not their only role, but they all actively create expectations about who should actually punish whom under which circumstances.

Though one could attempt to analyze any power as a sustained set of expectations, it is often not very useful to envisage power in this way, because it is simply too difficult to solve models with many agents influencing one another's expectations simultaneously. Such a view merely allows us to interpret many of the arguments made in other literatures using language with which mainstream economists are somewhat familiar.

3.4.2 Instruments of power: Material rewards

Another direct way to get individuals to comply with a demand is to offer a reward in the form of material goods, services, or the means to get these (specifically, money or information), via a simple quid-pro-quo transaction. The wage–work contract that forms the core of the labor market in modern economies is an obvious example, as is any interaction of simple exchange.

---

[13] Though the Frijters and Tieman (1999) model shows that one can formalize many of the power arguments given above, their attempt also shows the inherent drawbacks of using the formal expectation-based game-theoretical apparatus. In order to gain analytical results, one must reduce the number of factors one examines to no more than a handful, and overlay a large number of auxiliary assumptions as well (such as the precise nature of the interaction, the timing of information, the size of groups, the spacing of individuals, the military technology, etc.). One thus gets a very precise answer to a very specialized question that will no more than vaguely resemble the real-life processes one is trying to capture. Conversely, this means that one should interpret the various "small" stories in this chapter and indeed in this book as a mosaic of models whose connection is that they include an important role for various recurring themes.

What does one need in order to be able to credibly offer material rewards and reasonably expect to achieve compliance? Apart from having something to offer, which one can broadly term as "wealth," the main thing one needs is some system of outside monitoring of both the offered reward and the outcome. Unlike in the case of violence, where the person who makes the threat of violence can also be the person who oversees compliance and actually performs the violence if there is no compliance, merely offering material rewards in return for something else is not a closed system. Something else is required in order to ensure that the reward is actually given in return for the compliance: without some outside authority, one can renege on promises. In other words, the power of having material goods on offer to others is derivative of some other power that oversees transactions based on wealth. This is not true with violence, where there is no reason to lie about what one wants in return for no violence, though there can be an incentive to exaggerate the threat of violence.

History has seen various forms of "overseeing powers" relevant to the situation of an offered reward-for-service. The cheapest "enforcement" mechanism is trust between individuals, where avoiding the internal psychic pain of cheating on a deal is worth more to both sides than the direct material benefit of cheating. That form of blind trust is itself a social norm and derivative of group processes. Trust is particularly useful when the stakes are low, such as when a person buys something in the supermarket. When the stakes are very high, one modern solution is to have a highly specialized legal system in which individuals have the right of redress if they can prove they upheld their side of a bargain but the other party did not. In that case, the power of wealth exists only if the power of violence exists to back it up, implying that the real power of wealth lies in our expectations regarding the intended actions of those who wield the violence to be applied in case a contract is violated.

Even in our modern societies, many transactions are not covered by the legal system, either because the transaction is too small to bother with the expense of setting up legal contracts, or because it is too costly for the outside enforcer to observe what is going on. A good example of enforcement mechanisms that evolve to suit transactions outside the reach of the formal legal system is the reputation mechanisms employed on the internet (e.g., on eBay), where individuals are rated by their former trading partners in regard to their reliability. These ratings are available for all potential future buyers to see, creating a tangible reputational cost of cheating on any given trading partner.

Reputations that develop because of repeated interactions are not a blind form of trust, but rather a form of trust that develops on the basis of calculated self-interest within networks or other large groups. Within networks, this trust is essentially an embryonic emotive group relation emerging from purely self-interested interaction and is thereby a first step towards the transformation from a network to a circle of reciprocity. More will be said on this important link between economic interactions and group dynamics in the next chapter.

The wage–work contract as a specific example

Perhaps surprisingly, one important example of where the legal system cannot realistically uphold a bargain is the wage–work contract. Many wage–work contracts take the form of hiring individuals for at least a year, or sometimes even for life, to do work that is not perfectly spelled out. In case of conflict, proving that a worker has reneged on such a contract is often very difficult. Except for very particular cases when it is fairly easy to judge how much labor time someone has devoted to a very specific job, such as when one rewards an individual for felling a number of trees, it is almost impossible for an employer to prove that an employee has reneged on a promise to provide labor time towards a particular objective. How can you legally prove that someone is a bad teacher because they "have not put in the effort?" How does one ascertain whether a judge is too lazy to think about proper sentencing, and instead makes decisions whimsically? The worker involved can nearly always claim to have worked hard but to simply have nothing to show for it. The presumption of innocence then leads courts to overturn dismissals made on the grounds of incompetency.

A more realistic punishment available to the employer is not to withhold the wage, but rather to reassign the worker to a different job associated with less pleasant conditions. Another possible punishment is to get rid of the employee after the stipulated period, and to withhold positive reference letters in the future. The real power of the employer is often in his ability to affect the reputation of the worker, and thus the worker's ability to hold on to his current job or to find a future job. A favorable reputation is obviously more important to a young worker with a whole working life ahead of him, than to an old person who is about to retire anyway. Such threats are furthermore only useful when workers have spent a long time investing in particular skills. That prior investment is then threatened by a poor reputation.

The power of reputation does not arise in a vacuum, however. Reputation can only exist if outside employers can observe things about the work history of a potential employee. References only have value if others ask for them and trust them, requiring that potential new employers must be able to find previous employers and that the giver of references must himself have some interest in giving truthful answers, i.e., in his own reputation as a reputable employer. The existence of these various connective aspects requires a fairly stable surrounding, where employers are around for long enough to care about their reputations and are willing to be contacted. Only in stable environments is it possible for future employers to determine what a potential employee is likely to have done in the preceding years, because only then is an employee unable to hide his lack of good references.

On reflection, therefore, the modern wage–work contract is only enforceable in the medium term if a fairly stable system is in place. It relies on various social norms (the convention of reference letters, general beliefs about how individuals spend their lives before they apply for jobs, and so on) and is only indirectly backed up by the threat of violence (i.e., once fired, the employee cannot return to the job). Many of these aspects are both crucial to the ability of the employer to use material rewards, and also not in the power of any individual employer or employee. They arise out of a whole system rather than from the individual decision of any employer. This is why it should not be surprising that the modern wage–work contract is a fairly new invention. The mechanisms of enforcement have been in place for no longer than about a hundred years, and the general population before that time did not generally make particularly long-term educational investments, meaning that the historical relations between employers and employees were of a far different kind than what we observe today. In previous centuries, the employee either had no escape and was thus essentially in slavery or some form of bondage, or was involved in fairly direct, short-term quid-pro-quo labor transactions where direct enforcement of compliance was feasible. An example of the latter is the case of sailors shipped off to some trading post far away: any misbehaving employee could be physically punished along the way.

The universal requirement of an outside social system
of enforcement

The main difficulty in analyzing power at the individual level should already be clear from the above example. The limited degree of power an employer has over his employees only exists within a specific set of social norms, a legal system, and predictable habits of behavior. The same actions taken by the same employer in a different time or culture would not necessarily have the desired effect of producing motivated employees. This creates a high degree of interdependence amongst the powers of various institutions, making it very hard in practice to say which individual wields what amount of power at any particular time.

The concept of trade is known in every society, along with many different enforcement mechanisms. The Australian Aborigines, for example, traded with adjacent "bands" (groups of thirty to fifty members) of other Aborigines. On particular days of the year, there would be a truce between bands who would then trade various items: food, weapons, and raw materials, and also women. Trading women was deemed necessary in order to sustain healthy bands, because marrying within small groups for sustained periods leads to genetic weaknesses. One can imagine the tensions between the various bands of otherwise hostile individuals when trading under such a temporary truce. Elaborate social rules applied to behavior during these truces, and successful transactions essentially relied upon band members feeling constrained by their wish to adhere to these norms of social behavior deemed respectable within their band (e.g., that no revenge for past wrongs was to be taken on the particular trading days). Also, a fairly direct and credible threat of violence applied in case of a reneging on instantaneous bargains, such that reneging on one side of the bargain would almost surely lead to mutual violence.

Another example of a cultural institution backing up agreed-upon transactions is that of royal weddings in medieval Europe. Kings looking for a military or economic alliance with other kings (essentially, a direct trade in the political arena, resulting in mutual benefit) would marry each other's sisters or other relatives, such that each had something to lose from a future reneging. The transactions in this case were backed up by the co-opting of family loyalties. We have already seen previously that this is a recurring theme: transactions and institutions are often backed up by a pre-existing loyalty towards something else. This is logical if one reflects on the fact that problems of determining credibility (trustworthiness) are likely to be solved ultimately via falling back on some form of existing loyalty. This phenomenon makes the problem of building organizations an evolutionary problem: the material one can use to build new organizations largely consists of the loyalties already in place, which were often created by existing organizations.

3.4.3 Instruments of power: Group membership

One social need that a manipulator can often exploit is group membership. A manipulator can in various ways threaten to take group membership away from an individual, or else can try to manipulate the content of group membership such that an individual wishes to comply. This works most directly due to the significant material benefits that accrue to individual group members.[14]

Membership in a group can be bluntly denied in those cases where membership is defined physically and the manipulator ultimately has recourse to some threat of violence in order to control entry. Obvious examples are pubs, dance halls, clubs, political parties, and so forth, to which entry can be denied if there is noncompliance with some particular code of conduct. The reward for compliance in this case is not directly handed out by the manipulator, but rather the manipulator can deny access to the rewards generated by others (specifically, the rewards that come with group membership). Yet again, co-optation is very appealing to the manipulator: it is often much easier to deny

---

[14] Within the economics and general social science literature, the idea that group membership bestows advantages is often associated with the term "social capital." The sociologist Bourdieu (1986, cited in Mattessich 2009, p. 50) thus defines social capital as "an attribute of an individual in a social context. One can acquire social capital through purposeful actions and can transform social capital into conventional economic gains. The ability to do so, however, depends on the nature of the social obligations, connections, and networks available to you." Similarly, the economist Sobel (2002) (p. 139) defines it as "circumstances in which individuals can use membership in groups and networks to secure benefits."

In this book, I will use the term "social capital" to capture other phenomena, such as trust and other social norms. However, the above definition of social capital corresponds closely to the idea of group membership, and captures the same basic argument that group membership brings economic advantages that can be pursued or withheld.

physical access to an existing complicated set of social group rewards than it would be to organize them from scratch.

Groups that themselves provide access to lucrative opportunities, such as groups of medical professionals or lawyers, can demand both explicit and implicit forms of compliance depending on how group membership is organized. Explicit forms of compliance can include the attainment of particular forms of education deemed necessary for entry, such as a medical degree in the case of various medical professions. Implicit forms of compliance can include cooperative behavior with other group members, such as when group membership requires "gentlemanly behavior" and access depends upon having senior group members speaking up on your behalf.

A general feature of groups with internally regulated access to lucrative opportunities is that they can exist for a very long time and thus can give rise to their own habits and social norms. They can themselves be seen in this sense as long-term manipulators, particularly if access is restricted to those whose ancestors made the "proper choice," such as when group membership is defined by bloodline, giving group members an incentive to make particular marriage choices in order to ensure opportunities for their progeny.

Where, instead of relying on formalized, internally regulated access, a group's existence relies upon its members themselves controlling access – such as in the case of professions (such as economics PhDs or barristers) – the degree of discretionary power of any individual group member over others is very limited. The power of the whole group over its members may be quite large, but making specific decisions requires the gathering of support from a sizeable fraction of the group, which takes time and essentially involves evaluating competing proposals.

Groups of friends and colleagues within large organizations are in the peculiar situation that access to the group is not controlled by themselves, but by an employer who can potentially be very distant from the group in question. The main point to make about this situation is that the employer can co-opt the group's own loyalties in order to demand some form of payment for continued access to the group, rather like a club can charge entry. Put in pure economic terms, an employer who finds himself in the situation that a group of his employees are good friends can lower the wages of all of them and still expect to retain them, because for any employee to leave the organization would mean leaving his friends (i.e., relinquishing the benefits of group membership).

In historical times, controlling access to group membership was relatively simple, and was therefore frequently used if more sophisticated means of control were not available. Banishment from a community was historically quite a normal form of punishment for delinquent behavior, particularly when the manipulating group, such as the community itself, lacked the capability to track down an individual in order to punish him for noncompliance. In tribal societies, banishment was often the most severe form of punishment open to a tribe, but even the Romans used banishment as a form of punishment. Today, the means of tracking individuals have improved so much that physical banishment is hardly used at all in Western societies.

Finally, one should note that the content of group identity itself is subject to subtle outside manipulation, albeit only in the long term. This form of control arises from the fact that social norms are decided within groups by means of the slow adoption of new forms of behavior. Individuals within the group experiment with new social norms but make sure they do not sway too much outside of the existing social norm until the rest of the group has also changed their norm in the same direction. Both the process of experimentation itself, and the speed with which other group members take up the changed behavior, are open to outside manipulation by someone with access to lines of communication with many group members. The outsider can simply suggest various aspects of group identity in the hope of these becoming adopted via sustained exposure. This is more likely to succeed if the manipulator is capable of having his preferred vision communicated effectively to the group. If that degree of information monopoly is not available, more subtle means include offering individual group members the opportunity to experiment with alternative behaviors. One can even lie outright as to how many are already adopting the changed modes of behavior, in the hope that the lie spurs so many group members to change their behavior that the lie becomes true.

It should be clear that these forms of manipulation are risky and difficult if attempted by an individual or small subgroup. One of the risks in trying to manipulate group identity is that the manipulated group as a whole may become aware that someone is trying to manipulate them; another risk is that experimenters will start to experiment in a direction undesired by the manipulator.

3.4.4 Instruments of power: Institutions

In the short run, the social norms and habits of individuals are given, and any manipulator is best advised to keep the degree to which he overtly demands changes in social norms to a minimum. However, in the long run a manipulator can directly influence social norms and habits by setting up institutions. Institutions that embody and create social norms include the education system, the legal system, and physical control systems (e.g., the police and the army), but also sustained modes of behavior, such as table manners, or a continuously expounded belief that group X is "god's favored group."

Education systems

As already discussed in Chapter 2, the education system directly rewards and punishes new generations, leading them into compliance. This does not only include compliance with acquiring productive skills, but also compliance with a set of behaviors deemed important. It is obviously much easier to enforce compliance with social norms if the social norms one is trying to enforce are shared with the parents and peers of the children within the education system, since the parents and peers have some additional power over the individual child. In the case that the education system rewards entirely different social norms than those promulgated by the children's families and communities, it is much harder for the education system to get its way, and the levels of physical violence and material rewards needed to produce compliance become larger.

The central role of education in socialization is a standard argument outside economics. Gradstein and Justman (2002) summarize the accepted wisdom in sociology and political science about the role of education thus (p. 1192):

The economic benefits of education as a socializing force are realized in various ways. Instilling civic virtues from an early age, through education, can reduce the cost of enforcing desirable social norms. Relatedly, when society is divided along ethnic or religious lines, uniform schooling in a common culture can lessen the potential for redistributional conflict among distinct social groups. The present paper focuses on a third benefit of common socialization: the role of state schooling in reducing transaction costs by shrinking the 'social distance' between individuals in the economy.

Another way to frame these points is to say that education engenders a common identity, with associated advantages of joint expectations and social norms that reduce the costs of interaction and the potential for conflict.[15]

History is full of examples of education systems expressly set up to change the social norms of populations. Influencing institutions is still a common method of influence today, witnessed for example by the "information programs" surrounding passive smoking, or the direct control of the state over the curricula that schoolchildren are taught in many countries.

Historically speaking, some attempts at particular forms of socialization via education have succeeded, and others have failed. A prime example of a successful attempt is what occurred in France in the early nineteenth century. At that time, every region in France had its own language, including Dutch in the far north, Basque and Catalan in areas near Spain, and German near Alsace. What the French bureaucracy did was to set up a single education system for the whole of France (as well as a single army). Thus, whatever the region in which one was born, one was taught in the same language and one was also told about "being French," with the literary and historical training that accompanied this identity. While there were regional factions with separate identities who actively opposed this "indoctrination," the French central bureaucracy was successful in exporting the language of Paris to all of the other regions of France and, indeed, in creating a self-enforcing national identity amongst its inhabitants. It is true that even to this day, there are remnants of Catalan and Basque culture within France, but these are not the serious threats to its national identity that they were 150 years ago.

Part of the reason for the success of the central regime in this case was that the territories of France already had mixed identities in the sense of having been part of "France" (in addition to having other regional

---

[15] These points have of course been recognized amongst economists, but have simply not been incorporated into mainstream thinking. Bowles (1998) for instance argues (p. 101) that "Gintis and I ... suggest that schooling may raise earnings through its contribution to the acquisition of such personality traits as a lower rate of time preference, a lower disutility of effort, or a cooperative relationship to authority figures, which are relevant to the work situation but which are not measured on the existing cognitive measures." Yet, in the same article (p. 102) he laments that economists still "premise that policies and constitutions do not affect preferences."

identities) for over 500 years. Hence, the Basque area of France had already participated on the side of Paris during the Napoleonic wars (1790–1815), and had been taught from the French translation of the Bible for centuries. Its success was also partly due to the mixing of individuals within the French state: in principle, anyone from any region was seen to have a chance to "make it" within the French system. The French *Grandes Ecoles*, whose graduates became the elite, admitted students from all over the French Empire, meaning that it was quite possible for those outside the core French region around Paris to rise to the top. Napoleon himself, a Corsican by birth, was of course a prime example of this.

Another successful example of educational indoctrination is given by the conversion of the Albanian population to Islam by the Ottoman Empire. The Ottoman Empire existed from 1281 until the end of World War I and was centered around modern-day Turkey, but at its height also included the Middle East, parts of North Africa, and large areas in southeastern Europe. The empire was established by a tribe of Oghuz Turks in western Anatolia, with the ruling sultans from the Osmanli dynasty. It was often referred to as "the Porte," partially in reference to the greeting ceremonies for foreign ambassadors held at the palace gate, and partially in reference to the Ottoman Empire's position as a gateway between Asia and Europe (Inalcik 2000, Imber 2002).

For many centuries, the Ottomans ruled what is now Albania. When they first conquered Albania, they realized that the conquered population was not going to convert to Islam if simply asked politely. Instead, the Ottomans took away the young male babies of the elite in Albania, raised them in specialized schools in the center of the Ottoman Empire (Turkey), and then sent many of them back to positions of power within the conquered territory. Because the babies were taken away at a very young age, there was no overwriting of existing social norms required, and they were easily raised as Muslims, versed in the ways of the Ottomans. Once sent back, they found themselves in charge of an area that was mainly Christian but where they still perceived strong family ties. Hence, in the main they married, raised their own children as Muslims, and influenced many of their family members to be "proper Ottomans."

The ability of the Ottomans to remove children from the influence of their prior culture was of course backed up by a tremendous degree of superior physical force. The basic trick of influencing social norms by re-educating children has been repeated many times in history, with examples from places as diverse as China and Australia. Nowadays, such policies would be regarded as cultural genocide, and they are rarely seen on the international political stage. However, one remnant of the same principle that survives today is in the form of boarding schools, where parents wishing their children to grow up in a culture very different from their own can deliberately send them.

Ingredients for the successful use of institutional power

What goes for the education system goes for other institutions, such as an army, a tax collection system, a state-sponsored religion, and so on. Some such institutions have been spectacularly successful at socialization, and others have failed. The general rule regarding success is the same: the less the new social norm desired by the manipulating institution differs from any pre-existing social norm, and the more the institution can reward compliance and punish noncompliance, the more successful the conversion to the new social norm will be.

These observations suggest that building institutions is a long-term strategy that is likely to take several generations before being completely successful. Unless one has the ability to use extreme violence, any newly introduced institution will only slowly change the individuals going through it, while the rest of the population will keep adhering to previous social norms, often including those associated with a whole array of other identities based on ethnic, religious, and family bonds. Even something as comprehensive and invasive as an education system will not ensnare all members of a new generation and will encounter children whose parents fiercely adhere to other norms.

When a would-be manipulator's hold on power is weak, a second-best way of getting populations to accept new norms is to become a patron of existing educational institutions, such as existing religious temples and schools. Spencer (1969) (p. 45) thus says of the southern Indian King Rajaraja (around AD 1000) that "[i]n order to understand the importance to Rajaraja of patronage to the Tanjore temple, we must recognize that such patronage, far from representing the self-glorification of a despotic ruler, was in fact a method adopted by an ambitious ruler to enhance his very uncertain power." Spencer (1969) documents a similar survival motive for the marriage between secular and religious power in many cases of religious patronage in India:

becoming a patron of the independent religious education systems was a reasonably "cheap" way of mimicking the usefulness of outright socialization via forced education.

Further limitations of institutions arise from the fact that large institutions are usually not controlled by a single conscious entity. The degree to which pressure towards new norms can be exerted within a large institution depends not just on the individuals working in the institution and their subgroup identities, but on the whole group that backs up the power of the institution. Within a modern national education system, for example, the civil servants controlling the curriculum may have different incentives than the political elite of the day. School principals may disagree with the ministry's curriculum, and may in various ways escape it. Individual teachers may have their own ideas as to what to teach. Parents and communities will also have their own ideas, and can in various ways also influence what is taught. Even the students can influence the content of their education, not just in terms of the subjects they choose but also in terms of self-help groups and activities they organize themselves. The reality of any large institution is therefore that power is wielded by many subgroups simultaneously that might have competing agendas. In this sense, it is seldom the case that a single decision maker can truly "decide" what an institution is going to do unless that single decision maker is backed up by a large group of like-minded individuals all prepared to help implement his intentions.

While influence through institutions is therefore not an easy or short-term proposition, it can deliver lasting benefits. As a good example of the long-term gain flowing from an adopted social norm, consider tax compliance (Torgler et al. 2009). As noted in the Preview, the basic observation in the large literature on tax compliance is that it makes no sense at the individual level, from a simple material-maximizing point of view, to pay all of one's taxes: the chance of being found to have cheated is very small, and the punishment when found out is not great (usually, the individual is forced to pay the outstanding taxes in addition to a relatively modest fine). Hence from a pure material cost-benefit point of view, tax evasion should be far more prevalent than it is. In this light, while high levels of tax compliance are extremely beneficial to our societies, they also appear to reflect a form of individual meekness. Yet historically speaking, taxes were bitterly resisted, and violent uprisings have been associated with the introduction of many new taxes. How can these two observations be reconciled?

The standard answer lies in the powerful influence of gradually changing social norms. Modern populations comply out of habit, which includes ignorance of the low probability of being caught and of the low levels of punishment, as well as an internalized social norm that one "should" pay taxes. Yet at the time that taxes were introduced, there was no recourse to these social norms, and payment had to be enforced at the point of a sword. Modern economies that can rely on helpful social norms thus have an immense advantage over economies where tax morale still lacks the backing of social norms.

3.4.5 Instruments of power: Stories

At first glance, telling stories to someone in the hope of eliciting particular behavior seems like a fairly weak attempt at influence. Yet, stories can be very powerful instruments of power.

One reason why stories can be so powerful is that they have a rationale of their own: embedded within them are causal implications about how the world works and what the individual or his group should do in various circumstances. Simply by casting reality in a particular way, adherents to a particular story will habitually act in the way the story suggests. One might say that stories provide mental heuristics for how to react to particular circumstances, and that individuals apply these heuristics because of the great degree of effort involved in coming up with different, perhaps more suitable, heuristics.

The power of the story

The most compelling example I can give of the power of a story is the case of the self-destruction of the Xhosa kingdom of Transkei, a coastal kingdom roughly in the middle of South Africa, in the nineteenth century (as retold by Canetti 1984). In 1856, a Xhosa man believed himself to have received instructions from dead ancestors to have all the cattle in the kingdom slaughtered. In his vision, he was promised that the dead spirits would gather and drive away the advancing British Army, as well as filling the *kraals* (cattle yards) with new cattle. Virtually the entire kingdom followed the implication of this vision, and indeed proceeded to kill all the cattle in the hope of enlisting the help of the dead against the British Army. Colonial representatives of the British

Empire and church priests argued in vain against this self-destruction. By early 1857, food ran out and approximately two-thirds of the entire population perished, including the king and much of the kingdom's elite.

The example shows many things, but for my purposes the key points are: (1) the king was powerful enough, and commanded enough absolute loyalty, for the ordinary person to follow his command despite the words of intelligent outsiders; (2) a mere set of words that no one else can verify (i.e., a retold vision) but that can be reconciled with accepted beliefs and modes of storytelling can be believed; and (3) once established within the upper echelon of power, a set of theories about how the world works can assume a life of its own.

Less striking but probably more relevant for today is the power of stories that frighten an audience and offer a particular course of action as the solution to the depicted problem. Stories of the "fires of hell" are probably the best-known stories that frighten believers into compliance, without there necessarily being any other enforcement. Some social scientists have gone so far as to say that governments only exist because they manage to frighten their populations, and hence would break down if "we" could rid ourselves of irrational fears of diseases, terrorism, natural disasters, and so forth. This position seems too extreme, both in that fear is not the only element of control, and because our fears are in fact sometimes warranted. More fundamentally, this position supposes that governments belong to a different group from their populations, while they are in fact both part of a single large reciprocal group. Most importantly perhaps, several real risks have diminished over time, at least partly due to organized measures taken by governments. By and large, government health programs have been successful at radically reducing childhood diseases; food agencies have ensured fewer cases of food poisoning; driving regulations and seat belts have reduced the number of serious road accidents; dikes do prevent flooding; and so on. While it would be naïve to think that politicians do not use the power of fear to their advantage, it would be equally naïve to say that they rule only on the basis of unwarranted fears.

Stories in action

Stories come in a wide variety of forms, and can include histories, poems, songs, plays, fairy tales, political ideologies, and scientific disciplines. The individual "decision" to adopt a story is a complex one, and depends on whether the individual who is exposed to the story already agrees with its explicit messages, its implicit social norms, and the state of the world that would come about if the advice in the story were followed through by others. For example, the decision to adopt a story suggesting that a rival group is "made up of monstrous individuals who cannibalize their own children and should be eradicated" will depend upon whether the individual thinks his whole group will adopt the story, the degree to which he already has grievances about the other group, the amount of personal and group gain he expects from eradication, the strength of his prior belief in the likelihood of cannibalism, and so on.

Also, those used to casting everything in religious terms will, mainly out of habit, only be prone to take up a new story if it involves religious sensitivities. Those used to thinking about the economic system in terms of perfect markets and their imperfections will have trouble understanding any economic problem, and hence adhering to a story about an economic problem that is not molded in such terms.

Science itself also follows accepted modes of storytelling. The ideals of debate and scientific inquiry are predicated upon group norms in which members are supposed to be logical and consistent in their thoughts and actions. To the degree that this ideal holds, individual members of the scientific professions can be persuaded by stories that follow the group's beliefs about what constitutes a rational, consistent, and convincing argument. Stories with superior predictive and didactic properties will hence appeal to these groups because of their adherence to existing shared group ideals of rationality, consistency, and being open to logical persuasion.

It will hardly ever be the case that an individual is fed only one story. Rather, many different stories about many aspects of life are offered to us continuously. The number of dangers the Western media reports as something "we should do something about" run into the thousands per day, of which only a small fraction become taken up by any sizeable group. There is furthermore no guarantee that the stories individuals adopt make sense when combined together. Unless an individual has an iron wish to be internally consistent, he may well adopt one story as a heuristic for one aspect of his life, and another story completely inconsistent with the first as a heuristic for other aspects of his life. It is not abnormal, for example, to find unions vehemently denying that monetary incentives provided at work change their members' performance, but they are also amongst the first groups to protest if their employers suggest lowering their wages.

How do stories become embedded? The more often a story is repeated and the more individuals it is repeated to, the more plausible it sounds to people and the more likely it will be adopted. Adoption is therefore a function not only of people's prior beliefs and the extent to which they will gain from following the story, but of the amount of resources invested into dissemination.[16] Galbraith (1984) (p. 24) calls this instrument of power a form of "conditioned power," distinct from "compensatory power" that is applied through consciously perceived rewards and punishments. He says of conditioned power that

neither those exercising it nor those subject to it need always be aware that it is being exerted. The acceptance of authority, the submission to the will of others, becomes the higher preference of those submitting. This preference can be deliberately cultivated – by persuasion or education. This is explicit conditioning. Or it can be dictated by the culture itself; the submission is considered to be normal, proper, or traditionally correct. This is implicit conditioning. No sharp line divides one from the other; explicit conditioning shades by degrees into implicit.

In Galbraith's 1984 classification structure, institutions such as education would mainly be viewed as providing "explicit conditioning," while stories would be viewed as a means of "implicit conditioning."

3.4.6 Power as a product of groups

At the individual level, a change in the behavior of individual A towards the wishes of individual B can only be ensured if individual A inherently wants to please the other (resulting from love), if individual B can offer something valuable (i.e., some form of wealth), if individual

---

[16] Hirschman and Vaughan (1983) and Bowles (1998) expound at length on the ability of repeated stories to create values and habits of behavior. Bowles (1998) emphasizes how the framing of issues by societal participants subtly changes the way other individuals view reality, thereby slowly changing their habits of thought. Hirschman and Vaughan (1983) provide quotations and passages from Edmund Burke, Alexis de Tocqueville, Karl Marx, John Stuart Mill, and Frederick Hayek to support their claim that market interactions, laws, and commonly repeated storylines influence people via what they value and habitually think.

B can threaten individual A with sufficient personal destruction (i.e., violence or denial of access to groups), or if individual B is able to convince individual A that it is in his own best interests to comply without any reward or threat (i.e., through the use of stories). These individual instruments of power can be approximately summarized as love, wealth, violence, and communication. To the person facing these instruments, they will appear variously as physical power, mental power, and social power, a taxonomy introduced in Chapter 2. Each instrument's force depends on whole groups and on the technologies available to whole groups. In this sense, all sources of power are derivative of and/or heavily constrained by groups.

Having more love at one's disposal greatly increases one's power because love taps into group power. If one is backed by devoted supporters, one's threat of violence against anyone whose behavior one wishes to influence becomes more credible. To fill this role, love does not have to be tied to a single individual but can be tied to the idea of an individual, such as "the monarch," or even to an abstract ideal such as "our country." A direct threat made by the leader of such a large group against another such leader is really the threat of a whole group against another whole group.

Great wealth, including intangible wealth such as physical beauty or transferable reputation, is by definition not something that exists outside of groups. Outside of the notion of a group-defended property right, material wealth is limited to whatever an individual can keep a personal guard upon (which is not much if he does not have the active cooperation of others). Hence the ability to offer and obtain significant material rewards is usually confined to those situations where group sanctioning plays a role.

Physical power is also related to group power. Not only do groups have various rules as to who can threaten others with what types of physical power within the group (for example, in modern countries any threat of violence by ordinary members of "the public" is illegal), but the very means of violence available depend upon group institutions. Access to modern weaponry and knowledge of how to use it are functions of group organizations such as the army, a market for weapons, internet sites with explanations about the use of weapons, and so on. Thus both the constraints on the use of violence and the actual means of violence are heavily determined by the resources and ethics of the whole group.

Communication is certainly possible at the one-to-one level without the help or knowledge of any group, but in practice, manipulative communication often requires the resources and acquiescence of whole groups. Acquiescence is drawn from official rules as to who can communicate what to others (for example, certain topics such as defamation, military secrets, or sex are not allowed to be discussed via certain avenues or in certain contexts) as well as from the degree to which the message is in accordance with the existing ideals of the group: depending on the degree of accord, individual group members' behavior can amplify or reduce the dissemination of the intended message. Group resources are used when communication occurs along group channels, such as via the media, shared information resources like the internet, and so on.

Hence all of the sources of power brought to bear by one individual against another are heavily tainted and modified by the norms and resources of groups. The use of power is so group-dependent that it is hardly of any use to think of power as a quantity of which individuals have given measures, because that construct presumes that any subgroup could use its "share" of power in any way it sees fit without the opinions and actions of the others mattering. A more useful way of viewing power, if one wishes to explain aggregate outcomes, is to see power as an outcome of group processes. The power-related choices of individuals are, in this light, mainly attempts to acquire and use the power of whole groups in pursuit of certain outcomes.

3.5 The evolution of distinct group types to solve distinct economic problems

The discussions above show how most human organizations and applications of power can be understood as springing from the combined influence of a very small set of archetypal human groups. Yet so far, while networks are a natural outgrowth of economic trade, the origin of the emotive groups (i.e., circles of reciprocity and hierarchies) has been unexplained. What is it about these particular constellations of individuals that enables them to survive for long periods of time?

Chapters 1 and 2 of this book underscored the central role of self-interest both in driving people towards direct domination and in leading them to love. Given that the motives associated with the individual love response and simple greed are fundamentally identical –

i.e., to get what we want – it seems reasonable that the satisfaction of self-interest is also what should be required in order to sustain different group types. The group types that have proven to be stable over time, which not by accident also involve love and greed, must therefore have a comparative advantage in delivering individual benefits. They must solve frequently recurring economic problems in a way that other competing, unobserved but hypothetically possible group types, apparently cannot do as well. What are these problems that distinct groups are good at solving?

3.5.1 Small circles of reciprocity

A large economic management literature exists that has tried to argue the benefits of hierarchies and "teams," where "team" is the word used in that literature for what is here called a small circle of reciprocity. The benefits of small reciprocal groups arise from the joint production made possible by group cohesion.[17] That group cohesion in no small part derives from full monitoring: as already noted, a key aspect of small reciprocal groups is the shared mental score sheets as to how much each group member has contributed to and taken from the group as a whole. This is an efficient means of organizing production in the case that the activities of the group members are highly complementary, meaning where the group as a whole can attain better outcomes than individuals on their own. The small reciprocal group is therefore an efficient solution to organizing highly complementary activities requiring a limited number of individuals.

It is not hard to see where the complementarities lie in the case of hunter-gatherers. No individual alone can produce procreation,

---

[17] Alesina and Ferrara (2005) review the large literature on the production of public goods and the homogeneity of the communities that produce them (p. 763): "Fragmented societies are often more prone to poor policy management and pose more politico-economic challenges than homogenous ones; it is easy to find rather voluminous evidence on this point." Yet, they also find that "ethnic diversity can be beneficial (or at least less detrimental) at higher levels of development." I agree with this latter statement as it ties in with the argument in this chapter that the more-advanced countries are all typified by a strong large circle of reciprocity oriented around the nation state. Within such a large circle, the homogeneity of smaller communities matters much less, and some advantages of diversity, such as a greater degree of experimentation with production methods, become more evident.

defense, knowledge, or insurance in meaningful amounts. Modern teams can similarly be built around goals that require cooperation of team members, each of whom is better off if he cooperates than if he works against others.

The main price of making a small reciprocal group work is the effort involved in generating and maintaining group cohesion. This effort foremost includes the constant monitoring of team members. That effort goes up quadratically with the number of group members, as each individual in the group keeps tabs on everyone else. This is also what limits the size of small circles of reciprocity: the effort of keeping tabs on every group member simply becomes insurmountable when groups become too large, at which point groups more profitably disband into smaller groups. Other costs of maintaining cohesion include the effort involved in maintaining the joint social norms of the group: these norms must be codified, kept consistent across group members, taught to each member of the next generation, and enforced. Further costs include the effort of maintaining a story about the history and place of the group in the wider world.

3.5.2 Small hierarchies

Hierarchies, both small and large, can do away with many of these costs. Mainly, there is no need for everyone to monitor everyone else. As long as everyone in the hierarchy keeps tabs on those directly below him, the whole group can function towards a common goal without further monitoring of others. This greatly simplifies communication and speeds up decision-making processes. Maintaining group cohesion inside the hierarchy is also far less of a problem, precisely because a hierarchy cannot stand alone from other groups and is typically led by a small reciprocal group (such as an extended family, a palace guard, or a cabinet): it is only inside the controlling small circle that one needs to make the effort to maintain full information about the members of that circle. Within the hierarchy, control is maintained by making credible threats, offering explicitly understood rewards, and preventing those lower down from forming new groups to rise up against the hierarchy. Inside modern nation states, where the required enforcement mechanisms lie outside of the hierarchy itself (e.g., property rights and contract law), hierarchies can operate efficiently with minimum costs of monitoring and cohesion.

Another advantage of hierarchies, and probably the core economic reason why they arose in the first instance, is that they allow those at the top far more resources and prestige than those at the bottom. They are hence potential vehicles for the satisfaction of individual ambition. The reason that kingdoms are so new to humanity is probably not that our ancestors never wanted to be almighty, but rather that kingdoms could not arise and be sustained on the back of the meager surplus generated by simple hunter-gatherer life. It took several thousands of years of agriculture, with associated increases in the size of villages and the gradual emergence of small elites that tax the rest of the population, before such a lofty position as a kingship came within reach. Levi-Strauss (1944) highlights this keystone in the evolution of the hierarchy, pointing as an example to the early development of writing as merely a means by which a small elite could suppress and tax the peasants.

The view that private for-profit organizations best resemble hierarchies is also common in economic debates. Williamson (1991), for example, explicitly makes this point. Some sociologists, such as Podolny and Page (1998), in a similar vein, interpret the importance of principal–agent relations in the mainstream economic description of relations inside firms as reflecting the presumption of a hierarchical relation between an owner and a worker (or a manager and an employee). While Williamson (1991) and Podolny and Page (1998) both recognize that firms are not merely hierarchies, they do view a hierarchical structure as a core feature of the internal organization of large, for-profit enterprises.

The main disadvantage of a hierarchy is in regard to the innate difficulty it faces in engendering loyalty. Those lower in the pecking order, however much they are told the opposite, will feel jealous of the higher-ups and frustrated at their relatively lower station in life. They will seek solace in circles of reciprocity (small and large), and even in smaller hierarchies within which they can try to obtain some greater benefits for themselves. The main threat to the stability of a large hierarchy is hence the problem of how to prevent the breakup of the group. Ultimately, maintaining cohesion in the long term appears possible only when the hierarchy operates inside a large reciprocal group. Ackerman (1996) observes the inability of hierarchical for-profit firms to engender great loyalty. He even argues that this is the prime reason why, even in fully developed market economies, many private organizations that supply some community benefit (such as research funding, private schools, private universities, or private hospitals) are explicitly non-profit: it is that label itself that attracts others in society to donate to them and to trust them.

3.5.3 Large hierarchies

Small hierarchies are efficient ways of achieving faster decision making and slicing off, for the leaders, a greater piece of the pie. Yet the natural outgrowth of individual greed is to set up as large a hierarchy as possible and to try to get to the top of it. The countervailing force is that of the individual ambitions of everyone else, who will shop around exploring other hierarchies and continuously form smaller groups around their own wishes. As a rule of thumb, one should thus see hierarchies "tried on for size" in every situation where individuals can get away with it, which is when potentially more efficient other types of groups are either not allowed or are actually not more efficient.

Large hierarchies in particular are most naturally suited to activities requiring the joining of very many different specialized activities, such as for example a modern space program that involves many smaller teams, or activities that are strongly substitutable, such as large cadres of infantry or crop harvesters. Large hierarchies enjoy returns to scale when it comes to generating and maintaining the know-how of complicated tasks, such as building a car, and when it comes to interacting with many others in a predictable and repeated pattern, such as the schooling system. As a means of enforcing a general standard on a large population, such as, say, a national curriculum that all children in a country have to follow, a large hierarchy is really the only type of organization that can do it.

Large hierarchies have even more problems with internal cohesion than small hierarchies. Not only will the lower-downs want to salvage some self-esteem by forming circles of reciprocity, but the larger a hierarchy, the more scope for the emergence of separate smaller hierarchies within the large hierarchy simply because of imperfect monitoring. Here one can think of a large army whose ambitious local commanders turn their units into their private armies, a frequent occurrence in ancient Rome. One can also imagine large ministries within which smaller departments may start to be run as local kingdoms, not necessarily in keeping with the purpose of the organization as a whole. This is indeed a recurring problem in modern bureaucracies.[18]

The limits to the growth of a hierarchy are mainly given by the internal and external competition it faces. Royal courts that gain surplus from farmers face the threat of other royal courts, which means the size of the hierarchy is determined by the competing forces of the incidental military victories of one over the other versus the internal breakup into smaller entities. Similarly, ministries compete for tax revenue with other ministries and are also subject to processes of amalgamation and internal breakup. Private enterprises face competition from other private enterprises, and furthermore face the problem that their employees can more easily vote with their feet. For a large private enterprise to survive for any length of time, it must therefore either have some clear rent for which no other enterprise can compete, such as a patent or the rights to mine somewhere, or else succeed in co-opting outside groups to monitor it.

The task of holding a large hierarchy together and operating without too many inefficiencies requires that it operate within a large, overarching group with a sufficient degree of loyalty to something else that the constituent individuals will spend time monitoring the various parts of the organization. Such outside monitoring is possible within a large circle of reciprocity, but is much harder within a pure for-profit environment. While government departments might thus easily remain stable for centuries, rejuvenated from time to time by enthusiastic patriots, the average longevity of a multinational business (such as listed on the Fortune 500) is less than fifty years. Simply put, most hierarchies fall apart.[19]

3.5.4 Large circles of reciprocity

Large circles of reciprocity seem the most efficient solution for generating mass loyalty, which in turn allows for very complex societies in

---

[18] This dynamic is one of the reasons for advocating the rotation of high-level bureaucrats and politicians within and between organizational units.

[19] There are some very long-lived firms, such as Swedish mining firms (Stora, founded in 1288) and German breweries (Weihenstphan, founded in 1040) that trace back to the early Middle Ages, but they are relatively small and the list of old companies is dominated by family businesses. The musings at www.businessweek.com/chapter/degeus.htm provide a typical example of speculation in the business world as to the low longevity of corporations.

which a huge number of activities are coordinated at many different layers of decision making by a huge number of smaller groups.

Just as large hierarchies can grow out of smaller ones, so too can large circles of reciprocity grow out of smaller ones. Some religions started with a small band of followers (e.g., the apostles) that brought the faith to many others, and ethnic identities must have begun with some smaller group propagating an articulated form of "group similarity."

Large circles of reciprocity also seem capable of arising out of business networks or even out of large hierarchies. A good example of the latter is the nation states in Europe, whose historical roots lie in fairly hierarchical royal courts that transformed into focal points of large circles.

Unlike with any of the other three emotive groups, it would seem unlikely that this group type arose out of some conscious knowledge of humanity's ability to form and ultimately benefit from such a group. It would seem more likely that the success of large circles of reciprocity in creating mass loyalty came as a surprise. I imagine for example that wealthy Romans around AD 150 would have experienced something of a shock when they witnessed the growth of Christianity amongst their slaves and the proletariat.

The weakness of a large circle of reciprocity is that it needs supporting institutions to maintain itself and to prevent an internal takeover by hierarchies. Without educational institutions that teach the next generation (and new immigrants) about the shared group ideals, that next generation would be enticed by other groups and other stories. Also, usurpation by a smaller hierarchical group that adopts the language of the reciprocal group but in reality only looks out for its own interest is a constant danger for a large circle of reciprocity.

This weakness mainly arises because, unlike in small reciprocal groups, mutual monitoring is quite weak in a large reciprocal group. Because the relation is one between a group abstraction and the individual, the maintenance of the reciprocal relation at the core is almost entirely a matter of perception, not reality. As long as individuals can be kept in a state wherein they believe the group abstraction is reciprocal, individuals will not actually have much incentive or proclivity to monitor the actions of group leaders. This weak monitoring helps to extend the life of a large circle, but comes at the cost that the degree of internal erosion may become enormous.

For abstractions that have some degree of visibility, such as nation states, the illusion of reciprocity cannot be kept up forever without some real reciprocal benefits to individual members, which limits the degree to which leaders can look out only for themselves. For abstractions that never become visible, such as deities, the illusion of reciprocity can be kept up forever and the means of keeping leaders in check has to come from other sources, such as the monitoring of nation states or the military threat of other groups.

3.6 Individual traits and the evolution of group types

We know from anthropology that humans evolved from primates who lived in small hunter-gatherer groups for eons. This means that large groups will have been unknown to humans until relatively recently. This makes it unlikely that much of our basic psychology has emerged because it is useful in large groups. Rather, a basic psychology is likely to have evolved in line with our needs while operating in small reciprocal hunter-gatherer groups, and this psychology more or less "accidentally" happened to be amenable to supporting life inside larger groups. This raises the question of whether there are any special coping mechanisms that social evolution has delivered to help us operate within the newer types of groups.

The realization that the groups in which we live now are by and large "abnormal" from an evolutionary point of view also begs the question of whether there is anything inevitable about the group types we see now. There is really no reason to expect that the major group types we see now are the only group types with which human societies have experimented. There has been and undoubtedly still is a continuous experimentation with quite different group types, based around quite different principles than reciprocity and authority. It would thus appear to be the case that we now see a few dominant group types because they solve the most recurring problems in the most efficient way and are, probably quite unexpectedly, capable of functioning without too much internal strife.

3.6.1 Embedding individual habits of mind in support of large groups

Modern education in many ways prepares children for life inside hierarchies and large circles of reciprocity. The internal mental life of group members is particular to the group, and takes years of education for group members to acquire. Nations are the main agents that socialize individuals to possess mental habits that prepare them for life in the nation state and in other group types they are likely to encounter, even if many group members are not explicitly aware of this process.

For example, national school systems typically focus on teaching self-discipline. The discipline that children are taught early on is not just useful in making sure that they are quiet in the classroom and ready to absorb the knowledge teachers bestow on them. It also, probably far more importantly, equips them with a habit of following orders without too much questioning. This habit is very useful to a society comprising many hierarchies, both small and large. There was probably a co-evolution of educational institutions that prepared children better and better for life within certain group types, together with an economy that increasingly valued individuals with the ability to function well in those group types. In the end, the education systems that we observe today are likely due to a combination of demand from parents and businesses, moral conviction on the side of education authorities, and trial-and-error in building schooling habits.

Yet there is more to learning how to be part of groups than merely becoming disciplined. Morality and moral conventions also have to be learned: group morality is specific, and has changed over time. In previous centuries, for example, large reciprocal groups often defined themselves with reference to their ethnic heritage, wherein the expected reciprocity was between members sharing the same "blood." More modern nation states have more abstract concepts with which people are reciprocal, such as "the American way of life." That shift in morality, which is very useful in societies that see a lot of migration, also must be imprinted on the next generation.

There are many subtleties involved in group life, beyond the mere hierarchy/reciprocity distinction, where mental preparation plays a role. Consider the case where one wishes people to adhere to the notion that all humans have innate value and should be respected. At face value this is a universal ideal that can be propagated as one of the abstractions people can have a relation with. Yet, things are more difficult because in reality this kind of ideal is inconsistent with other ideals, such as self-preservation when under threat. Internal consistency then requires that in order for the group to be justified in killing or punishing a particular individual or group, one needs some artifice with which to

declare that individual or group outside of the realm of "human." One
needs to call the enemy "beasts," "inhuman," or in some other way to
make it clear to one's own group that the "normal" rules of the group
do not apply to members of the enemy. Such a moral detour takes time
to embed within a population, and is thus part of what needs to be
communicated during the formative years.

Simpler forms of group life, such as when a group is more openly
oriented towards the welfare of its current members, come with less
need to teach complicated emotional and intellectual detours. If one's
moral code dictates that only, say, those with Aztec blood matter,
then no complicated dehumanization is necessary in order to sanc-
tion killing and robbing anyone who is clearly not an Aztec. Only in
more inclusive moral systems, such as the major world religions and
most modern nation states, does one need complicated mechanisms to
"undo" the moral directions that are normally taught to the population. One of the reasons to have more complicated moral systems is
that they allow for more complicated and fluid notions of "us," which
in turn makes it possible to absorb immigrants and people of different
faiths.

The social norms around which groups define themselves are constantly changing and do not even appear identical in hindsight, from
the point of view of long-term history. The great modern increase in
nation states that have inclusive moralities is quite new, and directly
conflicts with the ethnic self-identification of most earlier moral systems. Jointly, the changing moral and education structures we have
seen through time make it unlikely that humans were somehow "programmed" towards life within large groups with particular forms of
morality.

3.7 Relation with existing theories of group formation and power

The problem of how to conceptualize groups and power is one of the
central concerns of social science. Accordingly, there are hundreds of
classifications, theories, and propositions on the matter. Given that a
complete discussion of all of these is beyond the scope of this book, I
will confine the discussion here to some of the more prominent current
theories.

3.7.1 Psychological theories of groups

Within psychology, there are two important and closely related theories of groups. The first is categorization theory, and the second is social identity theory.

Categorization theory was already encountered in Chapter 2. The work by Tajfel (Tajfel 1969, Tajfel et al. 1971, Tajfel 1982) shows that individuals will display behavior that is favorable towards other individuals who share a characteristic with them and unfavorable behavior towards individuals with other characteristics, even if the characteristic in question is merely the invention of some outside observer. The mere labeling of sets of individuals alone appears to evoke some degree of identification with the members of each defined group. The underlying neuroscientific basis of this theory is the fact that humans automatically categorize almost everything they see into abstract groups (Harnad 2005). The mental habit of categorization is a necessary trait to make sense of an avalanche of information, and to some degree also applies to how we perceive ourselves: this person belongs to my group, that person does not belong, that person might belong, and so on.

Categorization theory in turn is heavily used in social identity theory. Tajfel (1982) (p. 67) conceptualizes social identity as arising from "the individual's knowledge that he belongs to certain groups together with some emotional and value significance to him of this membership." The short-hand version of this definition is that social identity is the sum of the groups into which individuals self-categorize.

The theory of group archetypes offered above in many ways fits in well with social identity theory. As with social identity theory, the proposed archetypal-group theory also contains the idea that people can be part of many groups at the same time. Furthermore, the high degree of identification seen in psychological experiments is an underlying reason for my argument that group members share common abstract (rather than materially observable) identities. The extreme ease with which new groups can be formed in the lab also fits my contention that group formation is itself an opportunistic and fluid phenomenon: individuals can easily establish new groups and join existing ones to which they do not yet belong, and will do so if it is in their best material interests. The findings of Tajfel (1982) and Jane Elliott in her 1968 experiment (Swan 2007) that group members use stories about ideal behavior and group identity to justify their behavior and to enforce expected behavior of others also fit in seamlessly with my depiction of the internal workings of both reciprocal and hierarchical groups, including the use of stories as providing behavioral heuristics.

The contention that individuals are in their own minds personally attached to group abstractions, and have reciprocal relations with these abstractions, is another feature shared between existing theories and archetypal-group theory. Miller, Smith, and Mackie (2004) state (p. 222) in relation to "intergroup emotion theory," which can be seen as a somewhat stronger version of social identity theory: "when individuals categorize themselves as members of a group, they regard themselves as relatively interchangeable exemplars of the group rather than as unique individuals." While I would not go as far as to say that people necessarily see themselves as completely interchangeable, even inside strongly reciprocal groups, I do appeal to the same idea when talking about members of reciprocal groups as sharing a similar abstraction of what the group is all about, and in that sense, indeed sharing the same identity.

The tensions between categorization/social identity theory and my proposed archetypal-group theory are in two areas: the degree to which previous group identities can be abandoned, and the nature of internal group structures.

Through the lens of categorization theory, one might surmise that groups are very non-cohesive in terms of identity and that group power should thus be brittle – much more brittle than groups must be in order to be sustained in my framework. The main observations to make on this point are that the experiments in support of categorization theory focus on dividing up some fairly weak existing group into two or more new groups; and that the experimenters effectively operate outside the institutions that continuously impact upon real-life group members, which maintain internal cohesion in most real-world groups of consequence.

The existing groups that categorization theorists have tried to break up are truly weak: a class of schoolchildren, or a prison population. Understandably, categorization theorists have not tried to take an existing army platoon, divide it into two subgroups based on meaningless labels, and see how long it takes for members of the two subgroups to start killing each other. Not only are initial group ties in categorization-theory experiments weak, but the pressure applied to overcome any existing strong ties is also weak. It is understandable from the research-ethics point of view that one would not want to scar experimental participants, but it does mean that categorization theory is not particularly informative about the strength of existing group ties in groups with active institutions that continuously reinforce cohesion.

Categorization theory is also fairly silent about internal group structures: it does not lead one to think in terms of reciprocal versus hierarchical groups, nor does it have much to say against that dichotomy. In terms of experimental design, categorization theorists must use small groups, not large groups, and also by design the experimenter himself holds a hierarchical position. Applying the power of the hierarchy that reflects the relation between participants and experimenter is what makes experiments possible. Thus, by the very nature of what labs can and cannot do, the most immediate group structure on which the experiment is run is a small reciprocal group dominated by an outside hierarchy.

In sum, categorization theory fits in well with archetypal-group theory. Where categorization theory is lacking is mainly in descriptive or prescriptive power. From the observation that almost anything can be the basis of a group, one does not learn much about how groups form in reality, whether different kinds might exist, and if so, what kinds might be more or less stable. Categorization theory is in this light somewhat like a nuts-and-bolts theory: it helps in either reaffirming or negating more high-level theories of groups, but itself can only support a mechanism for group formation occurring at the "micro" level. To use a flowery metaphor, categorization theory provides a story of leaves, but not of trees or forests. It is helpful to eliminate candidate theories of groups that possess odd-looking leaves, but a description of the leaves alone cannot yield a description of the aggregate economic or historical phenomena that we observe in the forest.

3.7.2 Sociological theories of groups and power

Class theory
Probably the most influential theory of groups in sociology is that of class. Originally attributed to nineteenth-century and early twentieth-century thinkers such as Karl Marx and Max Weber, the basic idea here is that modern societies are roughly stratified into layers that relate

to each other hierarchically. There is thus minimally an upper class, a middle class, and a lower class. Some recent users of class theory distinguish amongst more than three groups, such as Gilbert (2010), who suggests the existence of six groups: the capitalist class, the upper middle class, the middle class, the working class, the working poor, and the underclass. Scholars have estimated the percentage of the population in each of these classes, and have described some of the more important characteristics of individuals within these classes.

Class membership within this tradition is not just due to wealth, but is also a function of habits, political opinions, religion, and ethnic ancestry. Authors in this tradition explicitly recognize that these classes are in reality not mutually exclusive and perfect descriptions of how people see themselves, but nevertheless adopt them in order to shed more light on the political dynamics within a country. Roughly speaking, a class is a layer of society with more or less similar material interests. To some degree, classes are hence groups which "should" band together in political discussions about issues such as taxation, welfare, and rights.

While the notion of class is quite unpopular in mainstream economic writings, and also rare in modern psychology, the idea of class is still part of sociology, though even there there is plenty of criticism. Dogan (2004) thus claims that the importance of class has reduced in group formation, with culture and religion increasingly the basis of group identities. Yet even Dogan (2004) still appeals to class theories when he discusses the French elite. The idea of class is also still very much part of popular culture: whenever commentators use words like "the elite" or "middle-class families," they implicitly appeal to the class-like idea that people with similar attributes and material interests are part of a group with an implicit joint agenda.

Archetypal-group theory strongly disagrees with some of the central tenets of class theory, but does share some important traits. One area where I disagree with class theory is in the descriptions of groups. Individuals in my story know that they are part of a given group and would also be able to tell an outsider about the group ideals and norms of expected behavior. The groups in my theory are therefore somewhat easy to observe. By contrast, the idea of social class lacks that self-awareness and visibility. An individual might not even be aware that he is being pigeon-holed into a particular class, nor agree with the supposed political views associated with it.

Class theory is also an almost "too grand" depiction of groups, in that it would lead one to think of group conflict inside organizations as occurring between the larger classes in society. Within archetypal-group theory, organizations themselves actively engage in group formation, and house many different groups that compete with each other on the basis of all kinds of identifying elements. The large automobile factory is thus not just a place where there are bosses and workers representing a capitalist class and the working class. It also houses engineers, designers, secretaries, Christians, canteen personnel, and so on. These other groups are not necessarily tied to obvious group labels such as "culture" or "religion," but rather are associated with education, local self-interest, location, and job title. In many important ways, these groups are more important in determining the behavior of individuals inside the automobile factory than is their supposed "class."

The theory of class is also a somewhat poor theory of how groups form and change. It allows for only a very limited appreciation of how groups can co-opt other groups, how groups try to manipulate the stories told by other groups about what is valuable and what is not, and how coalitions of individuals from many different groups come together on the basis of common language and ideals. In short, it lacks psychological and descriptive detail.

Perhaps most importantly, class theory does not recognize that there are groups with the explicit ability to transcend class. The most important group in my story is the major reciprocal group formed around a nation-state abstraction. Such reciprocal groups embed an ideal of equality and a joint belief amongst all members, poor or rich, that they belong together and owe some allegiance to that ideal. While in class-based theory there is usually some elite that is taken to be in charge of the main vehicles of power, within my story there is no such clear elite: the power and functioning of the nation state arise from its members' joint adherence to shared ideals. Class-based theories, somewhat out of necessity, instead must belittle "nationalism" as an instrument of power wielded by the ruling class in order to subjugate the working class.

Yet nationalism is stronger than an elite. No small elite can break away from the nation-state ideal without incurring the wrath of many others. This means that even the most powerful subgroup is most likely to try to further its ends by influencing the central ideals and stories internal to the nation-state abstraction. A modern elite is thus not in absolute control, and instead is constrained by the dominant nation-state abstraction. This provides a particular view of subgroup political power within nation states: subgroups vie for control of the "nation-state story," rather than for overt dominion over other subgroups. Apart from the nation-state abstraction, religious, ethnic, and even political philosophies too can transcend class.

What is perhaps the most important drawback of class theory is its notion that the groups at the bottom form a cohesive group called a "working class" or an "underclass." Within the broader context of groups being formed on the basis of shared interests, it becomes quite possible that especially those at the bottom of the wealth ladder form groups on bases other than wealth. For example, the poor can more fervently belong to groups that increase their self-esteem and sense of belonging to a powerful and more respected larger group. Since self-respect is harder to achieve if one explicitly acknowledges one's underprivileged position in the material hierarchy, I would expect the poor to be loathe to band together as a group of "losers," and instead to become more fervent members of religious groups, patriotic groups, and other larger reciprocal groups.

In this regard, the main predictive failure of much of class theory is to underestimate the appeal of the nation-state identity to individuals at the bottom of society. Witness, for example, the astonishment of the socialist leaders in Western Europe at the enthusiasm with which workers were prepared to kill workers from other countries in the trenches of the Great War (Simmel 1964, Stern 1995). In large part, their nationalism allowed individuals at the bottom of society to be closer to and less in competition with richer and more powerful individuals. Individuals' wish to be closer "in the abstract" to individuals above them is a common observation of social commentators. Take for example the following observation from Adam Smith's *Theory of Moral Sentiments* (Smith 1759) (p. 53):

This disposition to admire, and almost to worship, the rich and the powerful, and to despise, or, at least, to neglect persons of poor and mean condition, though necessary both to establish and to maintain the distinction of ranks and the order of society, is, at the same time, the great and most universal cause of the corruption of our moral sentiments. That wealth and greatness are often regarded with the respect and admiration which are due only to wisdom and virtue; and that the contempt, of which vice and folly are the only proper objects, is often most unjustly bestowed upon poverty and weakness, has been the complaint of moralists in all ages.

In short, there is little solidarity at the bottom because no one wants to be there, and that lack of solidarity at the bottom makes the use of labels such as "lower class" somewhat misleading.

Yet, like class theorists, I agree that it is useful to think in terms of a small number of groups. Class-based theory creates a few groups with which to think about political reality, which in turn has proven to be extraordinarily successful in terms of helping populations talk about politics. The simplicity of having just a few groups based on something that is not too hard to observe means many observers can use it and can relate to it. That applicability is something that more "micro" stories of groups lack, which is also why one should expect few political commentators to start using the language of categorization theorists.

Yet, the basis of reduction is very different between class theory and archetypal-group theory. While class theory abstracts from the thousands of smaller groups it observes in reality and tries to settle upon a small set of "most important groups" that typify a modern society, I prefer to categorize those thousands of groups into a few archetypes of which there are mainly impure instances in reality (i.e., most real-life groups include aspects of multiple group archetypes). While it is quite possible in my theory that in practice, wealth position might become a major defining feature of large political groups, I essentially treat this as an empirical question: in some places and times, the notion of class warfare may indeed be a good simple description of what happens in politics, but in other times and places it may not. The main "big groups" that I have found of most use in describing current reality are the nation-state bureaucracy, the government, business, and voters.

Other sociological theories of groups

Apart from the central notion of class in much of sociological writing, several major tenets of sociological thought are represented in the story of this chapter. Weber's notion of the nation state as the victor of an evolutionary struggle is adopted almost wholesale. Perhaps most importantly, the notion that power is mainly a group phenomenon is widespread in sociology. For example, Cook and Emerson (1978) and Yamagishi, Gillmore, and Cook (1988) study the relation between power and group formation using computer simulations and historical examples. They explicitly argue that power cannot be meaningfully studied as a one-on-one relation and only makes sense as a "social structural phenomenon." These authors also argue that trade networks, which they call exchange processes, innately carry an element of political power in them, although these authors do allow for power to exist apart from trade networks. The next chapter will delve into this issue in more depth, and by and large will adhere to this line of thought.

In broad agreement with the conception that reciprocal groups make use of group stories about ancestry, purpose, and the group's place in the world, Bar-Tal (1989) notes (p. 324) that "beliefs … cannot be studied on an individual's level. Individuals who live in groups hold common beliefs which define their reality, not only as persons, but also as group members. This reality becomes especially important when group members become aware that they share it." Most tellingly, Bar-Tal invokes the idea that amending the group story to the detriment of the contribution, or even the group membership, of a subgroup is a necessary prelude to the persecution of that group. Bar-Tal (1989) had in mind the German Jews in the 1930s, who were "de-legitimized" by alterations to the preceding story of German nationhood. This observation fits in perfectly with the idea that large reciprocal groups are defined and maintained by common stories that may evolve through time.

Also in broad agreement with the story of large reciprocal groups, Canetti (1984) (pp. 169–179) makes telling observations with regard to the relation between individuals and the countries to which they belong. He notes, for example (pp. 170–171), the importance of "crowd symbols" with which each individual in a country can identify, including flags, pictures on coins, images from history, and important symbols of national prowess (such as sports teams).

In line with Bar-Tal (1989), Canetti (1984) argues that individuals are not consciously aware of the many ways in which they identify with their country, but that there is such a thing as a national identity and a reciprocal relation between the individual and the country as a whole. The existence of such a common identity means that injuries to the esteem of that identity can explain why whole countries can go looking for vengeance. The main example Canetti (1984) had in mind is the persecution of Jews in Germany during the 1925–1945 period, which he contends was an attempt to regain Germany's national pride following the humiliation it suffered after World War I. This kind of reasoning is very close to that adhered to in this chapter. Where this chapter advances beyond Canetti (1984) is in detailing group archetypes and linking individual actions within and outside groups with individual incentives.

3.7.3 Classic economic theories of groups and power

There are four prominent theories of groups and power in economics that I review here: interest-group theory, expectations/game theory, the Akerlof/Kranton identity models, and modern behavioral experimental economics.

Interest-group theory and political rent-seeking

Perhaps the most prominent story of groups in economics is offered by the contributors to interest-group theory. This includes the private interest-group theory model of Stigler (1971), the Chicago school model of political competition by Becker (1983), and the rent-seeking theory by Buchanan, Tollison, and Tullock (1980). These basic models and the approach they represent are still dominant within mainstream theories of politics: about half of the twenty-five most popular introductory textbooks in economics, as identified by Lopus and Paringer (2011), discuss the rent-seeking model of political processes (including, e.g., Dolan 2010 and Taylor and Weerapana 2010), while the other popular textbooks (e.g., Mankiw 2009) do not discuss groups at all and only provide a simplified description of political processes that implicitly treats voters as rational and atomistic, such as the median-voter model wherein individuals have immutable wishes and the resulting policy is that favored by the majority.[20]

The common element in the various representations of interest-group theory is the notion that political pressure groups form on the

---

[20] O'Sullivan, Sheffrin, and Perez (2010) is one of the few main textbooks that explicitly discusses the tensions between the "public choice" description of political decision making, wherein voters are treated as rational with immutable tastes (though not truly rational, for then the voters would not turn up to vote), and the interest-group depiction of politics wherein opinions can be swayed by lobbying (which is labeled as the "alternative" to the median-voter model).

basis of material self-interest. Stigler (1971) thus viewed economic regulation as the regulation of groups with particular material interests. Becker (1983) viewed political competition as occurring between groups with different material interests. Buchanan et al. (1980) saw the whole of society as being made up of competition between rent-seeking individuals and groups of individuals with common rent-seeking objectives.

Interest-group theory in many ways is very reminiscent of class theory. Both view material incentives as the prime reason to form groups and act collectively. This basic idea is also present in work in game theory, most notably the models of Olsen (1982), who saw the decline of nations as the effect that rent-seeking groups had on total output, where only upheavals akin to revolutions could help the majority shake off an overload of established rent-seekers.

While I am sympathetic to interest-group theory's basic assumptions regarding how politics and group formation arise, this theory differs from the archetypal-group theory in important ways. Mainly, as with class theory, a depiction of groups as being solely oriented around material self-interest simply does not do justice to groups that form around non-material interests, or to the degree to which ideals arise even within groups initially set up for purely materialistic purposes. Also as in class theory, the depiction of the behaviors engendered by groups is very much a black box: there is no role for ideals, language, rituals, and so on. There is also no real detail as to whom the groups are trying to influence, or how. The issue of how political influence actually works is not itself described in terms of group processes, meaning that groups exist as vehicles for joint political action, but that individual voters and politicians somehow exist outside of groups.

Perhaps most importantly, interest-group theory offers no story for what the rules of the political game actually are, and why they are adhered to. Such rules of the political game are simply assumed in formal models within this tradition, but this of course begs the question of what in actuality has led to the adoption and maintenance of the political rules of the game. It is self-evident that neither political culture nor constitutions arise in a vacuum or are unchanging, so in this sense interest-group theory is incomplete. It offers no actual theory of power, since ultimate power is simply assumed to rest on the side of the rules of the game, and groups can only attain local power by combining material resources ("money is power").

Due to its lack of detailed descriptions of groups, the mainstream story of interest groups does not include any overt clashes with the archetypal-group theory presented in this chapter. There is little with which interest-group theorists can actually disagree, since I too explicitly acknowledge that material interests are a powerful reason for new group formation. I too would, for example, describe unions as groups with members that share similar material motives, and lobby groups as coalitions of individuals and organizations aligned to further their common material interests. Indeed, the description of society as being made up of many different competing groups, some of which slowly dissolve and others of which arise due to shared interests (material or otherwise), is similar in spirit to the Olsen (1982) setup and the entire school of thought around political rent-seeking.

Where I would differ with Olsen (1982) is in his pessimism regarding the inevitable decline of civilizations due to rent-seeking. Within my theory, rent-seeking was with us at every stage, and to a large extent was responsible for the rise of civilizations. The implicit depiction of Olsen (1982) that civilization arose separate from rent-seeking and somehow is merely victim to it is an idealized notion of the rise of civilization that I do not share. Similar nuances can be highlighted in regard to all other specific rent-seeking models, but in their essential assumptions about how interest groups form and what they roughly do, there is no serious disagreement.

Social norms and identity

A more recent strand of group-related theories in economics is the model of peers and social norms in the works of Akerlof and Kranton (2000) and the many papers following on in that mold (such as the study on taboos by Fershtman, Gnezy, and Hoffman [2011]; see also the studies cited therein). Akerlof and Kranton (2000) set up a world in which there are already a few groups, typified by an "identity" and associated with a set of norms. The examples they have in mind include local groups prevalent at schools ("jocks" and "nerds"), groups at work, and small social groups, including "gangs." They study the circumstances in which one would choose to become part of one group rather than another, typically arguing that one chooses the group that fits one best in terms of *ex ante* characteristics. Nevertheless, they allow for dysfunctional behavior of groups, wherein members are drawn into behavior that is not in their material best interests (such as a life of drugs and vandalism).

As with interest-group theories, this "identity model" has few points of disagreement with the archetypal-group theory presented in this chapter. The main difference is the implicit orientation of the latter. My objective is to try to come up with rules of thumb about groups, power, and group formation that extend but ultimately fit into standard economics. In the Akerlof and Kranton world, groups are mainly given exogenously, and the research interest is in regard to local decision making around which group to join. While I do not fundamentally disagree with their model, it misses the point that the whole political constellation under which we live, i.e., in a country with representative institutions, is itself a large group within which there are many other large groups. The Akerlof and Kranton (2000) setup is silent about the whole issue of large-group power and cannot describe how groups relate to the wider economy.

The Akerlof and Kranton (2000) setup is also rather limited in its description of what a group is, how it works internally, how individuals in their own minds relate to groups, and what the mechanisms are for becoming more attached to group norms. Such things are neither considered nor taken as important. In short, the Akerlof and Kranton (2000) setup, and its many subsequent models, do not lend themselves to upscaling, and as such it is hard to see how their framework can survive in the long run within wider economic thought.

Expectations/game theory

Game theory provides a language in which to describe almost any phenomenon, including groups and power. The main way in which game theorists seem to have thought about groups is as coalitions that form via a rational cost-benefit analysis, while power is either seen as somewhat derivative of existing wealth (or wealth-creating capacity) or else as some advantage in the processing of information.

An early example of a game theorist who tried to formalize the notion of power was Harsanyi (1962), who, building on the work by Dahl (1957), thought of power as the ability of person A to get person B to do something person B did not otherwise want to do. Harsanyi (1962) effectively modeled this situation as one of resources available for manipulation, as well as the opportunity costs of both actors in "obtaining or avoiding power." In essence therefore, Harsanyi (1962) treated power as something that could be bought with resources, such that one could fruitfully think of power as something an agent had a certain amount of relative to another, effectively equating power with wealth (all else equal). Jordan (2006) similarly sees power as both leading from and resulting in greater individual wealth.

Several more recent game theorists propagate variations on this individualistic and materialistic theme, whereby power is mainly relevant in a one-on-one bargaining situation (Binmore 2007). Gomez, Gonzalez-Aranguena, Manuel, Owen, and del Pozo (2003) relate power to the "centrality" of an individual or subgroup, by which they roughly mean the degree to which the payoff of whole groups depend on the contribution of that individual or subgroup. The more pivotal a person is to others, the greater his "power" in the sense of being able to threaten worse things. Wiese (2009) is one of several authors who relate power to a person's "Shapley value," which is a measure of the marginal contribution that individual makes within different coalitions.

Groups in this literature are usually conflated with coalitions. Ray (2007) thus reviews the game-theoretic literature on power and coalition formation, focusing in particular on how some exogenous notion of "power" gives rise to the formation of particular coalitions of powerful individuals that appropriate as much as possible for themselves to the detriment of the less powerful (see, e.g., Piccione and Rubenstein 2007 or Acemoglu and Egorov 2008).

What is mainly lacking in the game-theoretical literature is a more realistic treatise on power relations inside modern societies. I cannot find any explicit treatise in the game-theory literature about elections as a ritualized means of transferring power from one small group to another, nor even a description of "handovers" of representative power as an institutionalized means of realigning expectations about whose orders should be followed on what. Indeed, the whole notion of realigning expectations of authority, which is really what any transfer of power is about, is simply absent from this literature.

As a result of missing the wider picture of actual power relations in modern society, the game-theoretical analysis of power and groups lacks a sense of realism about what game theory can do in this realm. This implicitly invites authors in this field to construct models that lack any obvious purpose. For instance, Piccione and Razin (2009) in a recent piece try to work out the group structure of society that results when one starts from a given allocation of individual power and a certain constellation of wishes and informational constraints. This not only presupposes that power can be meaningfully seen as separate from groups (i.e., that an individual has a certain fixed amount of power in any group), but also presupposes that all individuals know about everyone else's power, know the value everyone else would have in any coalition, and have the ability to instantaneously switch coalitions when an opportunity is spotted. This is not merely highly unlike any actual situation or even long-run tendency, but more importantly fails to acknowledge the basic point that groups and power constellations can only be fruitfully seen as growing out of previous power structures and groups.

Hence, while I agree with this literature that groups in the long run are also economic coalitions and that power at the one-on-one level can be seen as a set of expectations about the consequences of ignoring or following through on requests, this literature has so far not offered particularly useful tools for generating insights on power or groups at an aggregate level.

It would therefore seem better to treat game theory as an *ex post* language rather than a first-principles tool, in the sense that I advocate looking for game-theoretical models of groups and power *after* formulating theories of groups and power by means of historical study or interdisciplinary theorizing. This is exactly what two of the models in Chapter 6 aim to do. The second model in Chapter 6 generates a game-theoretical description of the group archetypes, while the third model uses evolutionary game theory to describe the possible evolution of smaller entities into states. These are very much descriptive models, as they are too detailed to be useful in either measuring or predicting power and group dynamics.

Behavioral experimental economics
Within the experimental branch of the relatively young field of behavioral economics, many of the core arguments in this chapter on groups have already been made and some of their implications have been tested in the laboratory. I review some of the most important ideas and results from this subfield here.

The importance of groups and the social norms within those groups for cooperation, as well as the role of punishment in enforcing cooperation, is succinctly summarized thus by Bernhard, Fehr, and Fischbacher (2006) (p. 217):

Social norms are standards of behavior that are based on widely shared beliefs about how individual group members ought to behave in a given situation. Social norms affect almost every aspect of human life, and humans are probably unique among all species in the extent to which they regulate social affairs with social norms. There are norms of fairness, cooperation, politeness, honesty, and subordination; norms regarding gender relations, race relations, parent–child relations, and so on. Many people often obey social norms voluntarily because their individual goals are in line with the behavior normatively prescribed. The situation where all group members' interests align with the prevailing norms in a society, however, is indeed rare. The threat of punishment thus generally plays a crucial role in enforcing adherence to norms. Some social norms in modern societies take the form of legal rules that the police and the courts enforce. But even today, private third parties, i.e., individuals whom the violation does not affect economically, often enforce norms by imposing informal sanctions. In fact, the existence of private third-party sanctions can be viewed as a hallmark of social norms because if only the victims of norm violations were willing to punish, the scope for norm enforcement, and thus for norms in regulating social life, would be quite limited. Another important aspect of social norms is that they are group specific. There are no norms without social groups – social norms emerge through interactions in groups, they apply to interactions within groups, and group members enforce them.

These observations mirror my focus on reciprocity within groups; on the role of punishment in upholding social norms; and on the important point that many individuals in a group might not, out of their own accord, be sufficiently idealistic to conform to group norms without the threat of punishment. Many side results in the behavioral literature also fit well with archetypal-group theory, such as for example the widely cited argument by Frey and Meier (2004) that paying people for things they used to do for charity (such as donating blood or cleaning public spaces) can lead to a reduction in these activities. Within the language of this book, such a crowding-out effect occurs because paying for such activities implies leaving a reciprocal relation and entering into a hierarchical or network relation, which can easily be seen as an attempt at domination of the volunteer.

Bolton and Ockenfels (2000), as well as Frey and Meier (2004) and Benabou and Tirole (2006), similarly comment upon the central role of reciprocity within groups. Chen and Li (2009) is a typical example of a recent study that finds that individuals behave much more cooperatively and altruistically towards individuals of the same group than towards members of out-groups. Yet, while reciprocity is a recognized trait in many circumstances, all authors mentioned above agree that individuals are often not reciprocal and behave as if they are maximizing their own wealth without regard for others. It is thus a recognized challenge to find a single story that rationalizes and predicts the occurrence of reciprocity in some circumstances, and the dominance of greed in other circumstances.

Also, despite the strong overlap of the description and results about how groups operate internally and in relation to other groups, the authors in the behavioral experimental literature have remained agnostic about the notion that there are different types of groups, and generally silent on the role and origin of group power. As a result, the literature mainly offers a huge number of unreconciled facts pertaining to the precise circumstances that produce or affect interactions, information, and framing, coupled with many small theories that extend the mainstream model of human decision making in one particular dimension.

A typical complaint about the lack of an overall framework in this field is provided by Rubinstein (2005), who drily writes the following about the tendency of some behavioral economists to update the mainstream model incrementally in order to fit a particular anomaly (p. 247):

Rabin goes out of his way to beat, if I may use his own phrase, the "dead parrot" of full rationality. Of course there are many facts that are hard to reconcile with full rationality. But the psychology and economics literature has replaced a dead parrot with one that is equally dead ... A major drawback of the behavioural economics models is that they lack both the elegance and generality that characterise the literature of General Equilibrium and Game Theory.

Fudenberg (2006) (p. 694) goes one step further when he advocates that behavioral economics "devote more attention to the foundations of its models, and develop unified explanations for a wider range of phenomena." There is hence a recognized challenge in experimental economics to embed some of the main points of that literature into a more general theory of human behavior without losing the main insights of the mainstream view.

3.8 Conclusions

This chapter has discussed notions of groups and power. It has intro-duced a small number of archetypal groups characterized respectively by reciprocity, hierarchical relations, and emotional anonymity. It has reaffirmed that power is a group phenomenon, illustrated the various instruments of power wielded by groups, and re-interpreted both the functioning of modern society and historical processes as group pro-cesses. The story in this chapter is in line with the needs of the overall story of mainstream economics. It is a workable, descriptive, and causal story of groups and group power.

3.8.1 The group archetypes

Perhaps most importantly from a mainstream economics perspective, archetypal groups are easy to spot: it is easy in any particular circum-stance to say which groups are present and what types of groups they are. The five archetypal groups I suggest are very distinct in nature, and their defining characteristics (emotional bonds, lines of hierarchy, and degrees of anonymity) are easy for an outside observer to see. This means that they can potentially be used as a basis upon which to build and calibrate useful models of the world.

Traditional relations that have already surfaced in mainstream economics writings have quite natural counterparts in the archetypal-group story. Perfect markets, for example, require large anonymous networks within which the rules of transactions are backed up by the power of a large reciprocal group. Similarly, a firm made up of owners and workers is a hierarchical group, also reliant on the enforcement mechanisms provided by a large reciprocal group, where many of the workers are also members of smaller circles of reciprocity that partially define how they see themselves. Hence, the fundamental group archetypes quite naturally incorporate and extend the main types of groups that economists already use in their thinking.

Economists are also often concerned with predicting behavior, and this is another area in which the story presented here is helpful. I will show more directly in later chapters how the proposed archetypal-group theory assists in making predictions about both individual and group behavior. Briefly, once one knows what kind of group is important for an individual in a particular context, then one can safely surmise things about him that are not otherwise obvious.

For example, in large reciprocal groups, like the science of economics itself, there is no individual in charge and no one member will claim to be "above" the ideals of that group. This means that you can confidently predict that members of that group will willingly debase themselves towards the group ideals, particularly when being observed by other economists, and will expect anyone else in that group to debase themselves in like fashion (and will greatly distrust any supposed group member who does not). This is not only a descriptive statement about the behavior one will find within such a group, but it is also a causal statement about the behavior one should display in order to achieve the goal of being accepted as part of this group. This reverses the meaning of the usual economic prescript that there is "no accounting for tastes." This prescript is usually interpreted to say that people have different fixed tastes about which there is no point arguing. I would say by contrast that people (even economists) adjust their tastes to suit their groups, and that if they were to argue about them with other members of a given group, then they would no longer be considered part of that group.

3.8.2 A summary of power

To think of society in terms of overlapping archetypal groups provides a more tractable framework for talking about power than any framework provided by an individual-level understanding of power. It enabled me in this chapter to illustrate the importance of violence, fear, habits, stories, group access, and other instruments of individual and group power. Background information from psychology, as well as many historical and current examples of the deliberate use of power aimed at changing the behavior and ideals of other groups, can be understood within this framework. Education programs, conscription armies, local translations of holy books, wars against joint enemies, inclusive cultures, and so forth can all be re-interpreted as instruments of indoctrination and assimilation into various groups.

I claim that individual power hardly exists: nearly all examples of power are group-based, and the individual application of power is almost invariably mediated by group norms. Hence, from a practical point of view, mainstream economics should refrain from trying to describe or predict individual power, and should exclusively deal with power as a group property.

To integrate this group perspective of power into the mainstream economics view requires the mental ability to have a dual perspective, in the sense of being able to switch from the usual individual-level reasoning to a group perspective when dealing with the sources and application of power. In the final main chapter of this book, I return to the question of what kind of mental heuristics can be applied to achieve this ability, as well as providing examples of what insights one gains from the exercise beyond existing practice. However, before we can turn to that overview, we need a clearer picture of the link between economic processes and group politics.

4 | Networks and markets

In this chapter I consider trade networks, the last of the "black boxes" within mainstream economics to be examined and incorporated explicitly into an aggregate view of our socioeconomic system. Trade networks were introduced in Chapter 3 as one of the five group archetypes, and moreover as the only one featuring the peculiar characteristic of being divorced from ideals and other emotional relations between group members. Market economies rely heavily on such anonymous networks, and this chapter is devoted to exploring their role in more detail.[1]

Considering the range of phenomena that can be explained by adding theories about love, power, and groups to basic greed, why do we need networks as well? The major element that the story in this book still lacks is a link between economics and politics. Most importantly, nothing in the story so far would make the emergence of democracy and nation states "inevitable." Also, many economic phenomena not yet discussed would remain mysterious, were we not to explicitly consider the role of networks. For example, this book has not yet provided a reason why one should observe growth cycles, it has not explained the observation of output collapses upon the breakdown of communist control mechanisms, and it has given no hint about the roles of money and financial institutions in our socioeconomic system. In short, the story so far has ignored many important questions of economics, mainly surrounding the link between the economy and politics. Networks provide the missing puzzle piece and will enable me to address these questions.

In the first part of this chapter, the basic arguments for the importance of networks to the economy are set out, and the nature of

---

[1] For ease of exposition, the word "network" in this chapter (and throughout the book) refers mainly to a trade network.

networks themselves is analyzed in fine detail. Drawing on human experience after the fall of the Soviet Union, I present a baseline theory of how networks operate and why they are so crucial to the economy.[2] This theory is then fleshed out to form a theory of economic growth that is grounded in the functioning of networks, with implications for how different political and economic scenarios are likely to catalyze or hinder the operations of networks, and hence the growth of an economy. Several other real-world examples centering on growth and business cycles are then reviewed, to show how this theory of networks can help to illuminate the causes and consequences of real-world events. Finally, the view in this chapter is compared with some of the major existing economic theories of networks, including social network theory and matching.

4.1 Power and market economics: The role of continuous contact makers

Merchants, bankers, doctors, craftsmen of all sorts, scientists, teachers, shopkeepers, manufacturers, and especially "businessmen" are examples of what I will call "contact makers." They generally reside in cities and sometimes oversee great amounts of capital. The unifying characteristic of contact makers is that there is change over time in the people they work for and work with. Merchants trade with many different people over time, and continuously search for new people with whom to trade; bankers are forever looking for more people to lend money to, and to borrow money from; doctors are continually losing old patients and finding new ones; craftsmen sell their wares to a changing set of consumers and obtain their inputs from changing suppliers, depending on all sorts of factors (seasons, tastes, trade routes, etc.); scientists continually interact with other scientists, and regularly meet new ones at conferences and seminars, in order to advance their knowledge.

A contact maker is in principle restlessly searching for better opportunities that he can exploit. He searches for better connections to trade

---

[2] Several models in Chapter 6 provide some guidance about how one might mathematically formalize some of these arguments, drawing on Frijters, Bezemer, and Dulleck (2003), Bezemer, Dulleck, and Frijters (2004), and Antic and Frijters (2012). It bears repeating that I view such mathematical exercises as "proofs of possibility," but not as "proofs of being right."

with; for better colleagues to work with; for better employees to replace those who retire; for suppliers of better goods; for better informants about the quality of other persons and goods; and so on.

4.1.1 Contact makers in action

Continuously making new contacts is not a natural activity for every economic agent. Medieval European peasants, for example, forever worked the same fields and hardly ever made new contacts, bar with their direct rulers (Elias 1939). Some modern laborers likewise have hardly any need to change or refresh their contacts with any great frequency. The distinction between those who are contact makers and those who are not cannot be drawn with a sharp line, but those who often make new contacts are important to distinguish conceptually from those who make them infrequently.

The best common-sense argument I can offer that points to the importance of contact makers for the operation of modern economies is that we observe so many economic activities that require contact making. Virtually every job requires some contact formation, and a vast array of modern economic activities are, at their core, nothing more than recombinations of individuals, tasks, and goods. Most of the work of sales departments is to find customers for existing goods: the task of the sales department (or of a retail shop) is not to produce a new good, but to combine people with goods. Similarly, the activities of advertisement departments are all about combining people with goods, not creating new goods. Many activities of managers inside organizations revolve around connecting individuals with tasks. Meetings are often all about assigning certain persons to certain tasks. If all of these activities were very simple, we would not have sales departments, meetings, advertisement departments, or managers: instead, the economy would allocate all of the resources they use towards producing more goods.

The everyday activities of continuous contact makers are key to the advancement of a modern economy. The businessman recognizes a new technology, then sets his technicians to work on making it, and then combines laborers, capital, and advertising to make and sell a product based on the new technology. Managers inside organizations create more productive matches between individuals and departments. Scientists, both in commercial enterprises and in universities, try to think up better ways of doing things, and other contact makers then eventually begin to apply them. Implementing better technologies requires millions of small rearrangements among workers, technicians, suppliers, and consumers. The traditional notion that a single brilliant inventor comes up with a new idea, and that his invention somehow automatically gets translated into better technologies everywhere, rarely corresponds to reality. Generations of inventors are often required to get some new principle to yield something useful.[3] A process of trial and error, involving countless interacting agents, is required in order to discover how to use new inventions in our daily lives. In their continuous restless search for better productive connections, the contact makers in an economy serve as society's agents of technological change.

4.1.2 Contacts, networks, and specialization

A contact maker with many contacts is able implicitly to rely on their diversity, and to focus his own productive efforts on what he is best at.[4]

All of the productive activities in which the contact maker and any "unit" he controls do not possess a comparative advantage can be outsourced to others in his network of contacts. An economy where every agent has many contacts with many others allows each individual agent to concentrate productive efforts wherever that agent's comparative advantage lies. By contrast, an economy where everyone has only very few contacts leads to limited specialization. Simply due to the existence of comparative advantage, a greater degree of specialization leads to higher individual productivity.[5] Conversely, those agents

---

[3] Jared Diamond (Diamond 1997) provides many examples of this. More than a hundred years lay between the first steam engine and any useful steam machinery, far too long to be able to consider the steam engine as the willed result of one brilliant individual. The economist Joseph Schumpeter (Schumpeter 1934) made a similar point and thus distinguished between various technologies in his Mark I and Mark II theories of entrepreneurship.

[4] Modern economics contains many studies that examine the role of networks and contacts (also termed "links") in making exchange possible, and hence in enabling the economy to reap the benefits of comparative advantage and increasing returns to scale (Krugman 1991, Audretsch and Stephan 1996, Goyal 2005, Duffy, Ganster, Shaw, Johnson, and Milan 2006, Meier and O'Toole 2007).

[5] The observation that specialization is critical to an agent's productivity has a long history, and is shared by several different fields. Within economics, the most

without contacts have to produce everything they want themselves: they are autarkic. It should be clear that one million autarkic persons, each individually and in isolation growing food, making machines, making clothes, etc., would be almost infinitely poorer than a million persons who have each specialized by producing the one thing they are comparatively best at producing. This points to the strong economic importance of dense sets of contacts.

Conceptualizing a "network" as the sum of the contacts of an individual economic agent, the arguments above imply that we can gauge the importance of specialization in a given economy by measuring that economy's total amount of networks. Specialization in turn is commonly recognized as central to economic productivity and growth. Add this to the contention above that technological change is gradually brought to society directly through the activities of contact makers, and the natural conclusion is that the strength of an economy, both at a point in time and over time, is at least partly a function of the density of its networks.

Long-term economic growth in this context is supported by reduced costs of contact making and more contacts per individual, leading to more efficient specialization. Williamson (2011) documents some of this dynamic in his analysis of the growth spurt of Western economies from the early nineteenth century until the middle of the twentieth century. His main argument is that the globalization of Western economies, featuring strongly increased levels of bilateral trade, was directly responsible for the growth divergence between those economies and the ones left behind, such as those of India and the Ottoman Empire. Williamson (2011) explicitly recognizes that increased trade ties brought increased commodity specialization because someone who can trade with many others can focus on his own comparative advantage.

Williamson (2011) further notes the importance of the "resource curse" in hindering the development of many poor countries.[6] The

---

prominent observers of this fact are Adam Smith (Smith 1776) (commenting on the far greater individual productivity of a worker within a pin factory than that same worker as a pin-craftsman without a factory) and David Ricardo (Ricardo 1817). In sociology, Emile Durkheim (Durkheim 1893) stands out as having remarked on the importance of specialization for economic activity.

[6] Williamson uses the term "Dutch disease," named after the economically debilitating effect of natural gas revenues in the Netherlands, but the basic idea is the same as with a resource curse.

argument is that natural resource extraction, such as mining, crowds out other sectors in an economy because of the higher exchange rate due to easy exports. Export revenues also increase the price of intermediate goods within the country, piling further difficulties onto the non-resource sectors. I would add to this that natural resource extraction also leads to more parasitical political systems, which in turn hinder the future development of a normal manufacturing and service economy. A key question taken up further in this chapter is why political systems should become more parasitical in this situation.

4.1.3 Examples and characteristics of contacts

So far contacts have been described as trade relations. This views a contact between parties A and B as the expectation of party A that B would buy product X at some price P. A two-way contact is where B expects to be able to buy X from A at price P. There are then equivalent contacts whereby party A expects to be able to buy some Y from party C at some other price. The more contacts party A then has, both in terms of parties B he can sell to and parties C he can buy from, the more he can specialize in what he is best at.

At its core, a contact is thus a set of expectations involving the knowledge of what the two parties can supply and what they want, such as when a baker has a set of customers coming to buy bread for a known price each morning. The two-way contact between the baker and his customers thus allows the baker to bake fresh bread every day, while the expectation that the baker will bake bread leads customers to go to the bakery.

Yet, there are many different types of contacts reflecting different types of trade, and they bear on different aspects of the economic system. Contacts can differ in terms of their scope, their intensity, their timing, and their interdependency.

Some contacts have very limited scope, such as when a potato farmer sells only potatoes to his customers and nothing else. By the same token, that potato farmer will usually buy only a car from a car salesman, and only pesticides from a chemical supplier. Each contact between the potato farmer and one of his clients or suppliers will be limited to a single precise good. If the potato farmer were to produce something else, he would have to find new customers and probably a new chemical supplier as well. Other contacts have much wider scope, such as the contacts of customers with supermarkets, along which a much larger set of goods is traded.

Some contacts are intense, in that a large proportion of the time of one of the parties is oriented towards producing what that single other party wants. A contact can also last for a very long time or be very short-term. As an example of the former, consider a local police officer who supplies his services to the local police force. More often than not, he has no one else to whom he can sell those particular services. Moreover, it takes years to become a police officer, and hence the contact between the police officer and the local police force requires a large amount of both current and future time expenditure by that police officer. As a result, the police force itself must be very stable and predictable if this contact is to eventuate. If it were not, then no one would have confidence enough to invest so much time in becoming a police officer. Specialized institutions further assist in stabilizing the relation between the officer and the force. Yet, a baker supplies services to a whole myriad of customers via contacts that can be very short-lived, and therefore is much less dependent on the whims of any one of them, meaning there is less use for institutions that guarantee the stability of the bakery market.

Another aspect of the intensity of a given contact is the likelihood that exchange will actually take place along it. Some contacts do not involve 100 percent confidence that a supplier–customer trade will take place, but rather involve an estimate of probability. A contact can still be said to exist in the presence of a reasonable expectation that, for example, there is a 1 percent chance that a particular customer will buy from a particular supplier over some window of time. Such probabilistic contacts are clearly important for bakeries, where some customers, such as passing tourists, have a low chance of purchasing bread from any particular bakery. In such a case, each individual contact is made quickly and cheaply and is likely to be one-off. Yet, a baker can still treat the whole population of tourists as an entity that is somewhat predictable and that yields a steady level of demand for bakery services. In this sense, a baker has an "aggregate" contact with "the tourists" which rests on many individual contacts along which actual trade only takes place with a low likelihood. We might conceptualize the aggregate contact as "fractionalized" into many constituent contacts, each bringing a low probability of trade.

The idea that a given aggregate contact is fractionalized in this way brings uncertainty. How is the baker to know that his aggregate contact with "the tourists" will remain in the future, i.e., that tourists will keep coming and will not buy their bread elsewhere? A baker may lose contacts without knowing it, at least initially. In the long run, a baker can infer from his realized trades how his aggregate contact with the tourists has changed, but this takes time and involves a one-sided risk. If on a given day far more tourists show up than he anticipated, the baker will sell 100 percent of his goods at the prior announced price and no more, independent of exactly how many tourists do show up. Yet when no tourist shows up on a given day, a large amount of his goods will have to be written off. The baker's very need to form these expectations on the basis of essentially no information about each individual constituent contact thereby creates the possibility of a disconnect between expectations and outcomes, which in general does not lead to symmetric economic consequences for him. If his expectations of trades are higher than actual trades, then the loss will be greater than the additional profits made given an equal-sized error in the opposite direction. Fractionalized contacts coupled with some degree of previous investment (having baked the goods that morning and set up shop in a particular location) and sluggish production (being unable to bake more immediately in order to meet higher observed demand) thereby give rise to a direct loss from greater uncertainty.

The timing element of contacts is another important feature. Some contacts, such as those that arise in online shopping, are formed instantaneously and immediately yield actual exchange. In the case of other contacts, actual trades can take place many years after the initial formation of the contact. This occurs in the example of the policeman, who makes investments for years under the expectation that he will one day be hired by the police force as a policeman. Many other professional groups require years of apprenticeship before the expectation on one or both sides of a labor contact is realized in an actual exchange of work for wages. For many specialized forms of production, such as medical services or aviation engineering, prospective suppliers of the good or service will first have to obtain specialized qualifications and only later will go on to make trade contacts. The investments in earning the qualifications therefore take place under an expectation that future contacts will exist, making those investments highly dependent on a stable environment. Again here, the potential loss of expecting more demand than there will actually be is greater than the potential benefits of an unanticipated boom in demand. For this reason, members of highly specialized professional groups will naturally be politically supportive of a stable environment. Members of these groups are essentially dependent on a de-personalized "economic system" for their future livelihoods, and face the ever-present possibility of being a victim of unforeseen changes.

Timing matters even for simpler contacts. Returning to the example of the baker, he is actually capable of producing many different types of bread and cakes, but different bakery products require different inputs and cater for different types of clients. It takes time for a baker to learn that previous products are not as popular as they once were, and to start making new products. As a result of that redirection, some previous suppliers and previous customers (those who supported the production of previous products) will lose their contacts with the baker, and for both sides of those contacts, replacements will need to be found. It costs the baker time to find new suppliers and customers, and it also costs his previous customers and suppliers time to find alternative trading partners. Most importantly, "going back" is not easy: whole lines of inputs can be axed as "demand" dries up, meaning that customers who ask for defunct products will be turned away. Because at least some old contacts will not want the new products, and because of the time it takes to replace old contacts, technological advancement (i.e., redirecting production towards new products) almost inevitably involves a costly severing of previous contacts.

There is finally an aspect of interdependency for a given contact. Some contacts are purely bilateral, in the sense that no one else would be immediately affected if the contact were to cease. Such contacts would be easily found in primitive societies where individuals trade the direct results of their production, such as when subsistence farmers trade produce with each other. On the other extreme, some contacts are interdependent in the sense that one contact has no staying power without many other contacts being in existence at the same time. The long-term contact between a tobacco wholesaler and a tobacco retail shop, for example, is itself only meaningful if the wholesaler has contacts with tobacco importers; the tobacco importers have contacts with tobacco farmers; the tobacco farmers have contacts with input suppliers; and the tobacco retailer has contacts with tobacco users. Should one of the contacts in this supply chain fall away, then the other contacts too will quickly mean nothing in terms of exchange. As in the case of fractionalized contacts or those requiring long-term investments, the presence of contacts that rely on many others (i.e., those with high interconnectivity) increases the importance of a stable environment, and from the point of view of each individual, increases his dependence on forces over which he has no control.

Contacts and recessions

These characteristics highlight the importance of contacts in understanding the difficulties that economies experience during recessions. Uncertainty and contraction in one part of the economy will lead to severed contacts elsewhere, and that severing will not immediately be clear to all concerned, yet will lead to unsold inventory, insolvency, and uncertainty as to how to redirect productive capacity. It should also be clear that in the presence of greater connectivity, it is harder to redirect capacity: whole new chains of suppliers and customers have to be established, involving clear fixed costs, in order for production to resume.

Within an economy featuring fractionalized contacts, long-term investments in advance of exchange taking place, and high interconnectivity of contacts, it starts to make sense to talk of involuntary unemployment and aggregate demand. Workers who previously operated in the midst of a set of contacts in which they produced something highly specific, requiring years of previous learning, may find that the demand for what they were producing has ceased to exist. This in turn leads to the breakup of their labor contract and the supply chain underlying it, making it very hard to resurrect that exact same chain again. Such workers find themselves stranded. Unable to set up new chains and re-train into something else overnight, they could still produce something, but more primitive production involving less interconnected contacts would occur at the expense of trying to find a new, higher-productivity link to more interconnected contacts. It may be optimal to search for a replacement "real job" rather than to be involved in a job requiring little interconnectivity of contacts or investments in advance of trade. This is then the phenomenon of involuntary unemployment.

Aggregate demand, through this lens, is essentially about the extent to which customers and suppliers honor the expectations embedded in their existing contacts – i.e., to consume and produce as one is antic-ipated to do. It is not merely the sheer volume of "spending plans" that is important in measuring aggregate demand. What matters also is whether that spending will take place within the network of existing contacts, or instead involve new contacts. The breakup of old contacts implies the breakup of additional, interconnected contacts, potentially leading to overall losses even if the sheer volume of "demand" stays the same.

As a stylized simple example, imagine that all individuals one year decide to not buy anything at bakeries, but to buy more meat at butch-ers. At the end of that year, butchers as a group will end up somewhat better off, but all the bakers and their supply chains will have gone bankrupt and a substantial negative impact on the whole economy will have been felt due to the lost investments in bakeries. Were this spending shift to continue into the future, the bakers would eventually all become butchers. The economy would recover, but it would take many years and a major recession in the meantime, even if initially there were no change in the sheer volume of "spending plans." This stylized example illustrates how both the volume and the predictability of "aggregate demand," via the nature of the contacts on which it rests, are important in attaining a high level of economic activity.

4.1.4 Measuring the size of the "contact-making sector"

How much of a modern economy is involved in contact making, ver-sus being involved in the actual production of goods that can be directly consumed? In the idealized perfect market economy, zero resources would be allocated to making contacts, as there are no costs to obtaining information.

A reasonable guess of the size of the contact-making sector comes from studies where scientists measure how individuals spend their time: we can simply count the number of hours that economic agents spend looking for information and exchanging information. (While not identical activities, making contacts and searching for information are closely linked.) The best-known such studies are now somewhat old, but they are suggestive: Machlup (1962) and Porat (1977) both reviewed official US statistics regarding how workers spend their time. Machlup estimates that 29 percent of the total value of all activities (i.e., time) in the US consists of the search and dissemination of information.

Porat puts this figure close to 50 percent. Focusing only on the "official information seeking" done at work, such as browsing through libraries and consulting co-workers, Robinson (2010) estimates that the average worker spends some 14.2 percent of his time on these narrow forms of information seeking.

In his Nobel Prize lecture, Joseph Stiglitz advocated an "economics of information,"[7] and enumerated many sectors of the economy that he would classify as almost completely concerned with the type of information seeking that is here called contact making. For example, he interprets much of our expenditure on education as an attempt by individuals to signal their innate worth (rather than to create additional abilities), which in turn improves the ease with which they can make profitable contacts. Stiglitz also counts activities in the world of pricing, advertising, and reputation as investments in information, exactly of the type that increase the amount of contacts individuals have through which to improve or extend their trading opportunities.

These statistics and arguments are easy to contest on various grounds. For example, Machlup (1962) and Porat (1977) include the time spent on meetings and conferences in their estimates of the share of time spent on searching for and disseminating information. I would count these as contact making activities, but one could reasonably object to this categorization, claiming that meetings are not about information exchange or reviewing who does what (which is a form of contact formation) but rather about creating a team spirit – i.e., reinforcing the ideals of a group. That objection would mean that the statistics quoted in Machlup (1962) and Porat (1977) are too high. As an example in the other direction, is a salesman of used cars nothing more than someone who makes intermediate contacts between the first-hand owners and the second-hand owners, or does the salesman somehow also add value to the cars by cleaning and/or servicing? Machlup (1962) and Porat (1977) appear to count the activities of the second-hand car salesman as directly productive, rather than as contact making. While it is unclear exactly what percentage of the revenue of a used-car salesman should count as contact formation, it is surely more than 0 percent, which would mean that the Machlup (1962) and Porat (1977) estimates are too low.

---

[7] www.nobelprize.org/nobel_prizes/economics/laureates/2001/stiglitz-lecture.pdf

Such measurement uncertainties arise perennially in empirical research, and they illustrate the messiness of trying to match large-scale abstractions to exact numbers in the real world. Nevertheless, the estimates of Machlup (1962) and Porat (1977), as well as the whole literature on information economics championed by Stiglitz, give support for theories in which contact formation is a central component of the economy. Whatever the relevant number is, it is substantial, and not the 0 percent that it should be under idealized perfect-market conditions.

As a side note, national statistical agencies are more prone to measuring countable objects (e.g., buildings, goods, flows of money) rather than how labor time is actually spent, or the density or frequency of use of fluid relations between individuals. This focus on the tangible is entirely rational on the part of statistical agencies. It is already difficult enough to measure the stocks and flows of goods and services, let alone trying to measure the much more intangible idea of "contact making." I must therefore proceed without the backing of much statistical information, and will instead rely mainly upon common-sense observations about how time is spent and examples from the literature.

4.1.5 Networks and politics

I have argued that contact and network formation underpins both productivity and growth in modern economies, through diffusing technological change and catalyzing specialization. The reason that this chapter focuses on networks, rather than on technological change or specialization, is that it is the networks – not the technological change or specialization that they bring – that carry political externalities. Contact makers can use their trade networks for political influence. When needed, trade networks can transform into military organizations that organize the production and sales of arms, or that gather support and intelligence in order to fight a war. Less dramatically, trade networks provide a means of coordination with others of similar views.

To bring out the main political dynamics of an economy in which there is continuous contact formation and destruction, let us consider three figures representing isolated phases of such a stylized economy. The first figure represents an initial period with existing contacts between economic agents, but prior to the dynamic activity of contact makers. The second figure represents a period of contact-making activities, and the third figure represents the "out-come" period, after these activities have taken place. (Naturally, in any real-world economy, all phases depicted are occurring simultaneously in myriad different markets.)

Figures 4.1, 4.2, and 4.3 should be read as follows. Figure 4.1 shows an initial situation where there is an existing network of con-tacts, represented as lines between individual economic agents, which are represented as points. Each contact consists of a trade relation, which is in essence nothing more than a line of communication that can be used to trade labor time, land, and/or capital. Via these con-tacts, trade and production occurs. The more contacts are present in the economy, the more specialized and hence the more productive the economy.

Figure 4.2 represents the dynamic activities of contact makers. This figure represents contact makers' continual attempts to find more pro-ductive combinations with other partners, which necessarily involves severing unproductive relations. The severing of unproductive relations is depicted by a cross through an existing contact, and the making of a new contact is depicted by a dotted line. The making of new contacts is greatly dependent on the speed with which one can recognize oppor-tunities and capitalize on them. This speed itself, in the real world, is highly dependent upon the presence of various institutions and search engines: for example, the presence of the internet makes it much easier to find a buyer for a second-hand good today than it was fifty years ago. Later in this chapter, descriptions of how the underlying factors behind the speed of contact making have changed over time will give us an "ultimate reason" for the actual changes we have observed in people's political and material cultures.

Figure 4.3 shows the result of the contact making of the second period. We see that the total number of contacts has gone up, i.e., the figures together depict a period of expansion, which is in reality not always the case. We see in Figure 4.3 that there are many net gainers in terms of numbers of contacts, because of the search activities of the second period. These net gainers are enclosed in stars. There are also some, though fewer, who lose on net from these activities; the dots depicting these losing agents are surrounded by circles.

These figures illustrate many key aspects of the politics of contact making, and simultaneously show the fortitude of the entire system and the reason why independent contact making has been frustrated

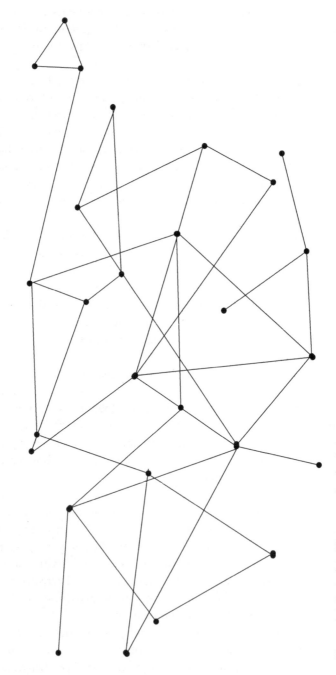

Figure 4.1 Period 1: The network of existing contacts

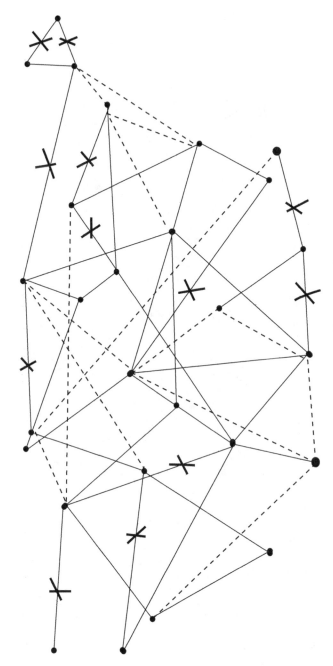

Figure 4.2 Period 2: A period of network growth, accompanied by creative destruction

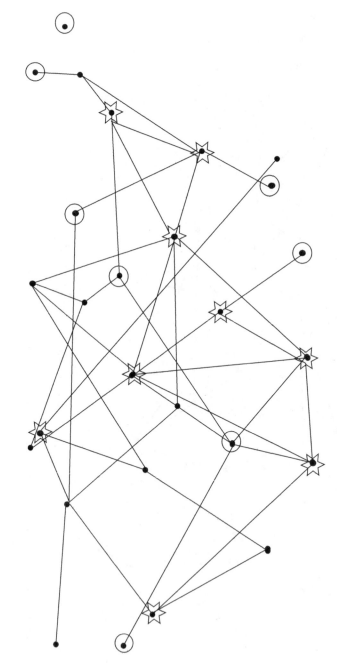

Figure 4.3 Period 3: The new network, complete with winners and losers

by so many bureaucracies and rulers in the past and today. The key observations to make are as follows.

- Change in the whole network implies changes in the organizing opportunities of all agents, including those in power. In the dynamic process of contact making, new alliances are made and old ones disappear; some agents become able to tap new sources of information, and others lose sources of information. From the point of view of someone in power trying to control everything, this process represents a nightmare. Some of his "spies" will become useless because their contacts will be severed, or because they are no longer in the middle of activities. A ruler desperate to keep control will hence outlaw or otherwise stem contact-making activities. A bureaucracy with the same aim of retaining power will also align itself against contact-making activities. Note that this will prevent new opportunities from being taken, and will entail a slowdown in overall economic growth.
- Change in the whole network implies the emergence of net losers. These agents lose not directly because of their own actions, but as the by-product of the optimizing actions of others. They lose because one of their customers or suppliers finds a better match with someone else. Changing to that better match may be in the best interests of the agent breaking away, but it is certainly not in the best interests of the one left behind. Those in power in a society do not always wish losers to emerge. If the loser happens to be the dictator's son, for example, it is clear that the change in the network will be met by heavy political opposition. Any individual, family, community, industry, or indeed country suffering such unwanted losses will probably try to appeal to politicians for protection. One obvious means through which a ruling group can obtain resources is thus to demand some form of payment for the service of preventing such activities. A bureaucracy can, for example, directly outlaw the severing of certain contacts. This prevents losses to a special interest group, which itself can compensate the bureaucracy through providing political support, while it also hinders overall growth. This type of activity by ruling groups (including bureaucracies) is the essence of negative political interference with the market system.

These first two observations form the heart of my explanation for the slowdown of growth and the stifling of activity during the Soviet era, as well as for the economic slowdown that occurred in medieval China when the Chinese bureaucracy increased control (Maddison 2007) and, generally, for the economic worries of many current developing countries.

- Contact makers have power independent of any ruling group. This is precisely because of the fluidity of their network: their contact-making activities, even though guided by a self-interested search for productive opportunities, lead to a dynamic network of contacts available to the contact-making group as a whole. Such a network can be used for purposes other than economic ones, including political or military purposes. The very processes that bring a region economic growth hence lead naturally to the emergence of an independent, powerful group: the contact makers themselves. Any ruler who directly precedes the emergence of these strong contact-making groups faces a direct trade-off: he can frustrate or outlaw the contact makers' activities, at the cost of tax revenue and with potential strife, or he can encourage them, which entails gaining temporarily higher tax revenues but losing power in the longer term. This is my main interpretation of the power dynamics in late-medieval Europe, as well as in many nation states today (Dulleck and Frijters 2004). It also forms the heart of the argument for why and how a resource curse leads to a parasitical regime: revenues that are more easily controlled and that do not depend on shifting networks do not force politicians to tolerate constantly shifting coalitions of contact makers. Politicians can simply take over the resource industry, or dominate its revenues by contracts, and suppress more fluid economic sectors that threaten their power.
- The relative size of the contact-making group is in constant flux. The total number of contacts of each agent changes over time, as does the number and composition of the possible coalitions each agent can form. As a group, contact makers would have extreme difficulty in maintaining a strong sense of hierarchy: their own productive characteristics simply change too fast to be able to say that person A is the "top contact maker," person B is the "second-tier contact maker," and so forth. As a result of this, the contact-making group as a whole is more likely to evolve into a single reciprocal group than into a hierarchy, when and if it becomes the framework for a new emotive group. Yet, due to the inherent dispassionate self-interest that underpins the activities of the group of contact makers,

the common ideal binding this nascent reciprocal group together would have to be very indiscriminate, such as the "joint humanity" or "rights" of the contact makers.

- Contact makers can benefit from state-sponsored activities that increase the speed of contact making. There are many simple examples of what a nation state and its bureaucracy can do to assist contact makers. The rule of law makes contact making simpler and more rewarding. Education systems that raise the aggregate level of skills and provide signals on the skills of different agents greatly facilitate the emergence and recognition of productive advances. The maintenance of roads and other communication systems directly increases the speed of contact making. All of these institutions have a strong public-goods aspect to them: that is, many people benefit from them once they are established, even if not everyone paid for their formation, because no one can easily be excluded from enjoying the benefits they provide. Standard economics teaches that public goods such as these will be provided in socially efficient quantities only by an institution like the state, which has the power to coerce many agents into paying for them, as well as the unique resources required to organize their production. The same argument holds for defense, waterworks, and many other public goods. This means that the group of contact makers as a whole derives great benefits from the public goods provided by the modern state, and therefore would not want to do away with the state. The interests of the contact makers are served by a state devoid of the parasitical aspects that characterize dominant greed-oriented hierarchies, such as a ruling family or a set of stagnant ruling hierarchies (such as a powerful nobility).

Combining this point with the previous one generates my explanation for why contact makers generally advocate democracy and human rights. This observation yields predictions for the future of democracy in various countries whose groups of contact makers are increasing in size and importance.

- The entire process stands or falls by the continuous arrival of new opportunities. By new opportunities, I mean such things as the opportunity to combine together people who were previously working with others; the opportunity to incorporate new technologies where they were not used before; opportunities to trade with new partners; and opportunities for making goods and services that had not before existed. Without the continuous arrival of new opportunities, the process of contact making, leading to technological advancement and increasing specialization, breaks down. This observation can be formed into a powerful predictive tool regarding cultural changes in various technological scenarios. For example, should a society ever run out of new opportunities, then the need to allow contact makers to do their job in order to sustain economic growth falls away. Restraining the control of any ruling group or bureaucracy in that scenario would therefore not be as necessary from the perspective of a benevolent social planner. A less extreme example is that of a bureaucracy that wishes to prevent certain forms of technological progress, such as the proliferation of military technology. A strategy to accomplish this is to disrupt all forms of independent contact making in certain circumstances. As long as new opportunities keep arising, however, the perennial search for growth due to the competition between countries should dissuade any single country from pursuing the disruption of contact-making activities as a long-term strategy.

Many elements of the economic process of contact making are subject to political choices, not only within a given political system but also between different systems. Contact making requires the existence and self-interested efforts of many individuals with something to gain from seeking new opportunities. Because the number of opportunities that present themselves continuously within an economy is at present simply far beyond the span of control of any bureaucracy, we should naturally expect that a capitalist economy will perform far better than a communist one or an autocratic one. Neither a king and his court nor a central bureaucracy would be remotely able to observe, recognize, and exploit the millions of new opportunities that arise constantly and require quick action. As an example, what bureaucracy would be able to react within a day to the hundreds of thousands of laborers who become ill during a day? In the absence of decentralized decision makers *with something to gain* from reacting, there would very likely be no reaction to such occurrences at all, meaning that all the work that depended upon input from these sick individuals would be stalled. Only if a laborer were sick for a very long time would a central agency be able to adapt. Whenever production consists of integrated processes, an inability to react quickly to millions of inevitable small mishaps like this would by itself greatly cost the entire economy, and would prevent many opportunities for improvement from ever being exploited. Any economic policy that does not accommodate the perennial need for real-time flexibility leads to less aggregate economic wealth than one that does.

A corollary of this need for flexibility is that individuals must be able to "pull out" of previous interactions in favor of those that are better suited to them. This implies that any rigidity that prevents the breakup of existing contacts mechanically reduces the takeup rate of new opportunities, and thereby hinders long-term economic growth. Such rigidities – which often fall under the sphere of influence of ruling parties – can take the form of lifelong contracts, prohibitions on producing in various ways, and production monopolies held by small groups.

4.1.6 The role of formal and informal contacts

Contact making is faster when information is cheap and reliable. What types of information exchange characterize an economy with plentiful cheap and reliable information?

Many long-term contacts arise through informal information exchange, particularly when the type of contact sought is very specific and intense. Informal contacts can be useful in such cases because they typically bring detailed information about the parties involved, including details about psychological compatibility, trustworthiness, and so on. An uncle who knows how well you would fit into a particular organization; a mother who knows which partners are well-suited for you; and many other people contribute to the informal market and thereby catalyze the contact-making process. In developing economies, the exchange of information via such informal contacts is a common feature of many different markets.

An informal contact is characterized by the presence of some type of emotional tie between the people sharing information, which provides an incentive to disclose honestly the sensitive and often unverifiable information that is potentially important to those who are trading. In terms of group archetypes, two agents with an informal contact belong to a reciprocal group as well as to a trading network. Informal networks are therefore best understood as a combination of (potentially very weak) reciprocal groups and pure information networks. Most reciprocal groups are thus also informal networks as well, although they do not always function this way because individuals who share membership in a given large circle of reciprocity may nevertheless have no direct emotional tie at all, and thus would not trust each other to reveal sensitive information.

A formal market, by contrast, consists of emotion-free networks. Such a market is well-suited to making relatively standardized contacts at high speed. In modern economies, featuring high levels of special-ization and therefore functional formal markets at fine levels of detail, formal market institutions to a large extent have substituted for the previous informal means of information exchange and hence contact making. Frijters et al. (2003) and Bezemer et al. (2004) argue that modern economies are on a long-term trend towards institutional for-mal search arrangements rather than informal search arrangements simply because the former are more efficient. In a market economy, for example, one no longer asks one's uncle for a particular job, but rather one applies for a hundred jobs online per day. One no longer asks an informed aunt about the best fish on the market, but looks instead for the consumer-group label. One no longer invests in prop-erty via a friend, but rather joins with a hundred others using the same banker who invests on behalf of the large group. One no longer asks a befriended scholar whether a particular young person has decent skills, but instead accepts the diplomas earned by that person as reli-able indicators of his skills. Informal social ties gradually lose their economic meaning as economies develop, and are replaced by more formal, standardized means of contact making.

This observation puts into proper perspective the complaint that capitalism destroys social ties. It indeed does destroy part of their pre-vious usefulness, simply because their productive roles are taken over by more efficient anonymous institutions. The power of many recipro-cal groups thus reduces, and with it the emotional bonds within these groups also reduce. Contact making hence has more implications for the socioeconomic system than merely catalyzing a long-run increase in specialization and the advent of democratic political systems.[8]

---

[8] Frijters et al. (2003) and Bezemer et al. (2004) also draw wider economic impli-cations from the creation and destruction of contacts. For example, downward economic cycles can be understood as the simultaneous severing of unproductive contacts and the upgrading of human technology. (This also fits the observation

4.2 Case study: The Eastern European economic transition

I now turn to a first real-world example of the place of networks in our socioeconomic system. My analysis of this case study is largely based on Bezemer, Dulleck, and Frijters (2003), and Frijters et al. (2003); the model used in the latter paper appears in Chapter 6 of this book.

The output collapse during the Eastern European transition at the start of the 1990s resulted from one of the biggest economic experiments of that era. In a space of less than one year, more than 350 million people went from a centrally controlled economic system to a more or less market-based economy of varying degrees. This transition was accompanied by high hopes of fast growth because the "forces of capitalism" had been "set free." The subsequently miserable and unpredicted outcomes present a strong challenge to the traditional view of a market economy.

The economic experience of the transition countries is best illustrated by the national accounts data shown in Figure 4.4.

This figure shows declines in aggregate production in all countries that experienced a transition. The data series depicted are not uncontested, which is not surprising given how many abstractions they are intended to measure. Objections can be raised against the method of measuring the size of the economy, which changed over the period in question from net material product to gross domestic product, and from administrative to market prices. One can also object to the accuracy of these measures during the period. One may furthermore argue

that training intensities are higher during recessions.) The reason why firms and other organizations are observed to coordinate on their contact destruction is twofold. On the one hand, there is the fact that if everyone else is trying to replace their unproductive contacts, then it makes more sense to replace one's own unproductive contacts at that time as well rather than to make new ones because new ones will not last as long in recessions (the technological upgrading from replacing contacts lasts, whereas additional suppliers and consumers are more likely during a recession than a boom to sever their contacts). The second reason is a type of "Saturday night effect" whereby it pays for everyone on the market to search for better technologies at the same time, simply because there are more others doing the same thing and hence more potential new contacts with whom to cooperate. As a second example, there may be economic benefits in managing transitions rather than letting transitions happen in a laissez-faire "big bang" fashion. The reason is that when new contacts take time to set up, there is a large initial loss of output associated with a wave of contact severing. This issue will be revisited later in the chapter.

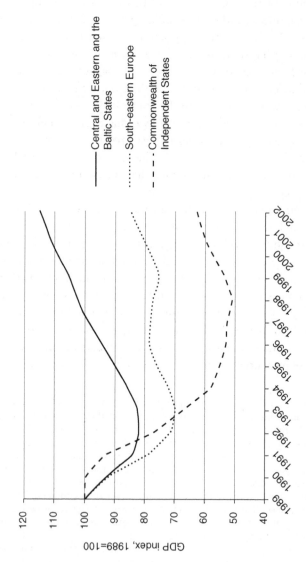

Figure 4.4 The Eastern European economic collapse in terms of GDP trajectories in transition regions, 1989–2002

that not all of the decline in physical output represented a decline in welfare, because part of socialist production was characterized by negative value-added at market prices (Gaddy and Ickes 2002). These are valuable points, and imply that we should not take the figure on its own as proof of anything.

However, studies using alternative output measures, using consumption rather than production data, and using individuals' responses to survey questions asking when life was better in a material sense also indicate that the fall in output amounted to a true collapse (Gavrilenkov and Koen 1995). More than half of the former population of the USSR was involved in producing their own food in 1999. Energy consumption fell by an amount comparable to the decline in observed income. The combined evidence regarding trends in production, income, welfare, and poverty makes it very likely that a true economic meltdown indeed occurred.

Campos and Coricelli (2002) review the many factors discussed in the literature as possibly having contributed to the output fall. These factors are often country-specific. One factor is the institutional difficulty in setting up new enterprises and effectively privatizing old ones (Swaan and Lissowaska 1992, Lieberman and Nellis 1995, Bornstein 1999). Another factor is the fall in demand due to monetary stabilization policies (Rosati 1994). Blanchard (1997) finds these factors insufficient as a general explanation because many countries were not institutionally constrained, and many sectors were not strongly affected by monetary policies. The output fall in East Germany that occurred after it was joined with West Germany was particularly instructive, as East Germany inherited overnight the property-rights structure of West Germany.

Another thought is that the output fall was due to new opportunities in multiple sectors that by their nature involved capital depreciation and labor reallocation on a large scale. Campos and Coricelli (2002), however, point out that returns to capital actually fell, that foreign investment was low, that "old firms" accounted for much of the observed new growth, and that there was little labor reallocation between sectors during this period. Campos and Coricelli (2002) hence dismiss this sectoral reallocation explanation, for which they use the term "creative destruction." (In contrast, I use the term "creative destruction" to describe contact formation and severing processes that mainly occur within sectors and firms.)[9]

The explanation of Bezemer et al. (2003), more fully expounded in the formal model reproduced in Chapter 6, is best illustrated by the following set of figures.

In the initial situation, depicted in Figure 4.5, there is a coordinating ministry depicted as a very large center circle, that organizes processes for many other productive units. This coordinating ministry is a primary source of information and trade for many organizations, which is reflected in the figure in the many lines of contact with the central hub. Such a hub-and-spoke system is itself a quite efficient way to organize information because it means information only needs to be gathered once by a central agency. Yet, precisely that efficiency makes it more fragile: take away the central hub and all the individual units are without connections.

In this initial situation, individual agents are constrained in making new contacts, as they are simply forbidden to change output relations. This is a reflection of the real world: individual firms trying to change suppliers or clients were indeed prevented from doing so under the old Soviet regime, and are still hindered from doing so in countries that remain communist today. The economic coordination in the socialist system is based on the enforcement of business contacts, and rules out or hinders the unilateral destruction of old contacts by individual firms.

Perhaps less obvious is the fact that it is in the interests of each individual firm in such a system to prevent the breaking up of other firms' contacts (which I term "creative destruction") when those other firms are connected to them: each individual firm would want other firms that are clients and suppliers to them not to be able to break their ties with the firm. Firms in socialist systems can then individually lobby the coordinating ministry to prevent their suppliers and clients from breaking up with them, and this indeed seems to have been done (Nove 1987, Braguinsky and Yavlinsky 2000). So-called *tolkachi* in the old Soviet Union were essentially envoys sent by firms to prevent

---

[9] Schumpeter's (1934) notion of creative destruction is broader still, since the term as used in this book is less driven by single unique individuals and more by millions of small advancements. I hence borrow the term with the caveat that it is used here to capture only part of the mental world of Schumpeter.

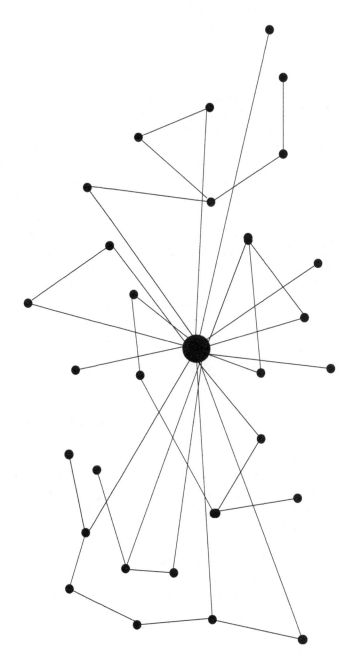

Figure 4.5 Before a cold-turkey market liberalization

other firms from severing ties with them. At the aggregate level this then prevents technological upgrading.

Why does this system eventually fail? The essence of the problem is that the "span of control" of the central ministry is simply not large enough to mimic the infinite number of small advances required for technological progress. Could a central bureaucracy write a plan for every shoe shop in every little village that specifies what to do in case one employee gets sick? Could a central bureaucracy observe and act upon a business opportunity that is only available for a couple of hours, perhaps because a consumer happens to be traveling instead of stationary? Could a central bureaucracy ever react instantaneously to all of the opportunities that open up when a new technological discovery is made (say, the personal computer) for which there are potentially millions of purposes, but none known with any certainty in advance? Surely not. The lack of technological progress due to this rigidity has been similarly discussed in the literature on command economies (Gros and Steinherr 1995, Aslund 2002). In a market economy by contrast, millions of small contact makers, in their search for profit, eventually try out every possibility. Unhindered contact makers eventually hit upon better technologies, and will incorporate them everywhere they can find a marketable use for them. The political cost of this economic boon is a dynamic, uncontrollable network that forms a power separate from the governing group.

Two things occur during the cold-turkey transition depicted in Figure 4.6. First, the central control apparatus is dismantled. This dismantling can take the form of mass privatization, or an implosion of the center, or, as in the Soviet case, the deliberate abandonment of the control principle by the ruling hierarchy itself. Second, there is a scramble to make different contacts by the firms that are suddenly no longer prevented from doing so. This sudden scramble results in some firms and other organizations finding new links with more productive partners, while many former trading ties are severed.

Figure 4.7 shows the net result of these activities. In spite of the scramble to find new contacts, the sudden removal of the control apparatus leads to a large decrease in the total amount of contacts. The individual-level reason why this aggregate reduction in contacts leads to an output fall is that some agents no longer have any trading ties with others. This means that they have no means of specializing in what they are best at, and must instead rely on self-sufficient production.

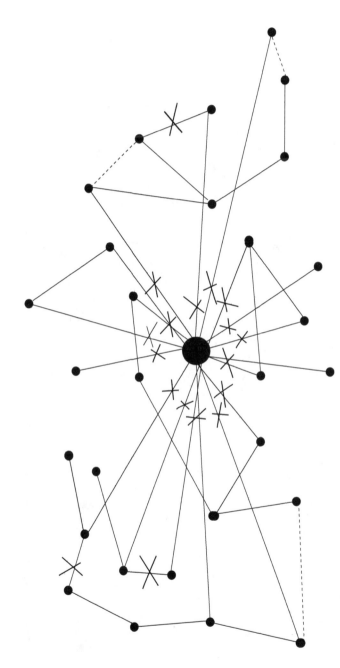

Figure 4.6 At the point of political collapse

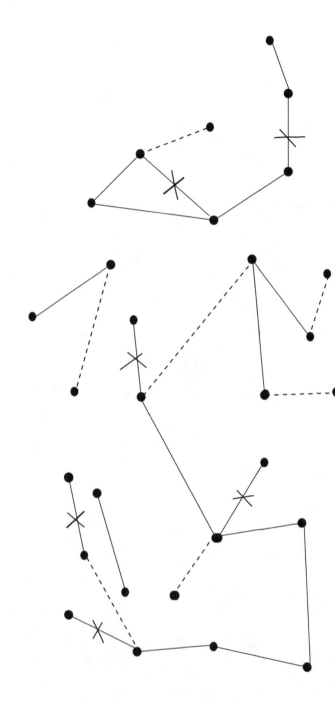

Figure 4.7 The immediate aftermath of the transition

This reasoning is entirely consistent with one of the best-documented fallouts of the economic transition: the migration of the economy towards self-sufficiency after the Soviet collapse. This process was aptly termed "primitivization" by Hedlund and Sundstrom (1996), commenting on the Russian economy. Primitivization included an increase in bartering, home production, and the "kiosk economy," which was observed throughout the former Soviet Union (Seabright 2000). In the extreme, people and households may retreat into near-autarky by producing their own food – as many households in Russia indeed did (Caskie 2000). Bezemer (2001) estimates that in the mid-1990s, two-thirds of the Russian population were involved in household food production.

This observed primitivization is at odds with mainstream reasoning about market economies, in which information costs nothing. In the mainstream view, finding contacts takes milliseconds and any severed contact can be instantly replaced by another. Adjustment is immediate. In my model of slowly accumulated and expanding contacts, such processes take much more time. This revised model fits many real-world observations, including not only household food production after the collapse of the communist planning system, but also physics professors driving taxis in Moscow and East German firms collapsing despite an abundance of capital and borrowing opportunities. The failure of the perfect market model to predict an output fall after the transition is perhaps the best indication that there is something for economists to learn from the transition experience.

We see the process of creative destruction continue in Figure 4.7: old ties continue to be broken in the search for better ones. There is also a gradual increase in the number of new ties that are made, which do not require the breaking up of old ties. These are the agents who are looking for more suppliers and clients in order to take advantage of their full productive capacity, but not for new technologies that would require them to break with old contacts. Figure 4.8 then presents a final picture of incumbent recovery. More ties are being made than broken, while agents in aggregate now have "better" ties, and hence technologies, than before the transition.

Bezemer et al. (2003) discuss at length various alternative explanations for the economic breakdown. Many leading candidates can be discounted almost out of hand (see Blanchard 1997). One leading example is the notion that property rights and other market institutions

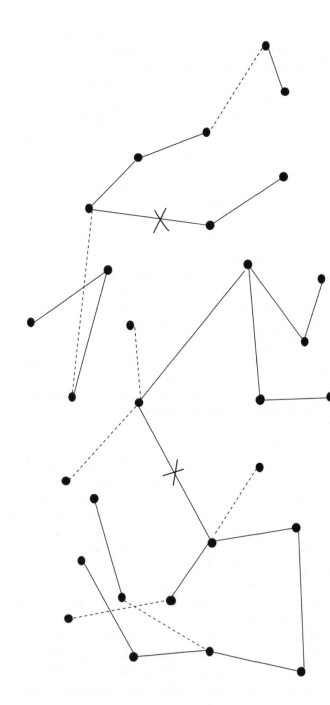

Figure 4.8 The continuing aftermath of the transition

were badly established. This is simply not true for several transition regions whose output collapsed, such as East Germany, Poland, and Chechnya. It is also not the case that the output collapse was only an effect of political corruption: again, plenty of transition countries had reasonably well-functioning political systems (e.g., Poland, East Germany, and Hungary) yet nevertheless experienced large output falls. Many economists predicted high growth levels for these countries at the outset of the transition, which only materialized years later.

The challenges to reform were also far more intricate and complicated than I have so far sketched. In particular, I have not talked above about the many and various ways in which the existing system was interlocked. For example, most organizations in the Soviet system had loans and debts on one another's books, which meant that most of them were immediately bankrupt once the center collapsed. Also, many organizations had both productive and social roles, such as when they combined a factory, a child care center, and a health clinic. Such community organizations are not easily disbanded into smaller bits. Additionally, local bureaucrats could extort funds in many ways from activities in their territory, such as through charging money for permits or nominating particular people as co-workers. To reform such an interlocking system is a nightmare. It is therefore far easier to point to mechanisms explaining the collapse of the economy than to say what should have been done, although I return below to this latter question.

4.2.1 Car manufacturing in Central Europe

A real-life illustration of the argument above is provided in Meyer (2000), who analyzes the automotive industry in Central Europe.

Prior to 1989, nine independent manufacturers in Central Europe (amongst them Wartburg and Trabant in East Germany, Skoda in Czechoslovakia, and Dacia in Romania) were producing some 3.2 million cars annually, primarily for the CoMEcon (Council for Mutual Economic Assistance) market. Soon after 1989, all major producers of passenger cars in Central Europe either formed joint ventures with, or were taken over by, Western partners.

The most successful case was that of the Czech car manufacturer Skoda, which was taken over by the Volkswagen Group. While the change in ownership brought an increase in foreign direct investment (FDI) into Skoda as well as direct assistance in technological innovation, the main benefits of the change came through new business links. Skoda pressured its local partners to link up with Western partners, while VW urged its global suppliers to acquire or to form joint ventures with local Czech firms. Approximately fifty multinational automotive suppliers did so, amongst them Lucas Group (providing brake systems) and Rockwell (providing sun roofs) from Britain, and the German Siemens/Sommer-Allibert (providing part of the chassis). It is mainly via the new networks created around Skoda and its subsidiaries that those companies were able to adopt new technologies, change their production methods, and learn how to produce goods for the international market.

The Skoda–VW collaboration highlights the contrast between those local enterprises that benefitted from the contact replacement process after the Soviet fall, and those that did not. As Meyer (2000) notes (p. 141), "great opportunities emerged for local suppliers to become global suppliers through the VW group," but "[o]ther Czech suppliers who did not succeed in securing contracts … struggled for survival… " There were gains for firms that became Skoda–VW suppliers, and losses for those Czech suppliers who lost their old contacts.

4.2.2 Political fallout from the transition

The great reduction in network density that resulted from the economic transition reduced the power of the groups in charge, leaving the possibility for others, such as criminals and their networks, to fill the power vacuum. The failure of socialist idealism furthermore meant that the previous ideological motivation and justification for the bureaucracy fell away, leaving the path open for other ideologies and their supporters (i.e., true believers loyal to a cause) to take over the role of ultimate motivator for the bureaucracy. The other loyalties around which new large reciprocal groups could form most naturally included regional loyalties, and regional nationalists indeed quickly took over in many areas, leading to the physical breakup of the Soviet Union into smaller countries.

The retreat of the socialist true believers spelled the end of the large circle of reciprocity defined around socialism, and as such marked a major loss of political power for the Soviet hierarchy. In various regions of the old Soviet Union, incumbent politicians who had enjoyed privileged positions within this hierarchy therefore naturally tried to hinder the reforms and prevent the arrival of a modern economy. For example, Dulleck and Frijters (2004) point in particular to Ukraine and some of the "Stans," such as Uzbekistan, which went into reverse gear politically. In those countries, the political elites prevented the rise of a more modern political system, effectively setting back the political clock to before the mid-1800s. The question of why some countries went into reverse and others did not can be answered by considering the direct effects of existing loyalties and alternative sources of income. Specifically, there were strong tribal loyalties that could be used as the foundation for an autocracy in some of the "Stans." There were also more opportunities, within the countries that were observed to go into reverse, for obtaining taxes from sectors whose productivity is not heavily reliant upon frequent contact making, such as natural resource extraction (e.g., oil and gas).

4.2.3 Comparisons with China

The model above implies the existence of an optimal speed of transition, and suggests the option of actively freezing some sectors (or regions) of a transitioning economy while allowing other sectors to engage in contact making and contact breaking.

This is a stylized description of what was done in China. The Chinese bureaucracy allowed the rearrangement of existing productive relations in some coastal regions in the 1980s and 1990s, while freezing production relations for many inland industries. They also allowed farmers to produce surplus food for anyone but only if they kept honoring their commitments to the "plan." The resulting "dual price" system allowed the emergence of new networks alongside existing ones in the agricultural sector.

Only in the 1990s did the Chinese authorities allow the breakup of most state companies, and only recently have controls on internal migration been loosened (Meng, Manning, Li, and Effendi 2010). These restrictions in all likelihood prevented significant unemployment and large-scale idleness of existing workers and machinery in the early years of the Chinese economic reforms. The idea behind this active management was to stall the inevitable breakup of the old state firms until the modern developing sector was large enough to absorb the laborers released from the state sector – i.e., until contacts could be made quickly enough that workers could find something productive to do.

Why did the Russians adopt a cold-turkey approach, rather than, like the Chinese, following a gradual road to reforms? Apart from the political difficulties of maintaining the cohesion of a control apparatus during slow reforms in Russia, a key practical difficulty was that the Soviet Union was far more centralized than China by the time reforms were begun. China in the 1950s initially copied the geographical concentration model of the Soviets (Teiwes and Sun 1999). Yet, at the end of the 1950s, the Chinese leadership decided to shift away from that model and in one "Great Leap" stimulate the development of more decentralized industries all over China simultaneously. This policy proved to be disastrous (Greene 1965): decentralization involved shipping modern machinery to smaller companies and farmers all over the country, who had no idea what to do with the new equipment but who were nevertheless supposed to, almost overnight, become modern manufacturers. The ensuing agricultural disaster cost tens of millions of lives.

While China's decentralization hence came at a tremendous cost and was quite unsuccessful when it was introduced, it did place China into a different position than the Soviet Union at the dawn of economic transition. The Soviets found themselves with far more heavily concentrated industries compared to the Chinese – for example, most Soviet steel production was in a handful of places in 1990, while the Chinese had spread their steel facilities around after the 1960s. The same goes for other industries, and even for political power. For this reason, it was not so difficult for China to siphon off a region and experiment there with different systems. Regions were no longer highly economically integrated, and there were few clear impediments to such a course of action. The Soviets, by contrast, did not have that option, and were furthermore naturally mindful that the complete chaos following the disbanding of national industries under the Great Leap Forward policies had resulted in an unmitigated human catastrophe. The output collapse of the former Soviet Union was the Eastern European echo of China's Great Leap, being similarly caused by a breakdown in central coordination, and being followed by a similar level of economic misery as was the Great Leap, although with less loss of life.

4.2.4 What should have been done?

Even with the benefit of hindsight, the dilemmas faced by the Soviet communist leadership in the years leading up to 1990 were formidable. The leaders presided over a failing economic system that they wanted to reform, yet each aspect of the system connected heavily with others, making any small reform to one part dependent on simultaneous reform elsewhere. In addition to the deeply interlocked features of the economy and parasitical local bureaucrats, there was also the fact that all kinds of experiments with private ownership had been undertaken over the decades and had not shown a path to full reform. Individual incentives had been tried out in agriculture for example, within state-organized farms (*sovkhosi*) in which there was very little role for private incentives and within community-organized collective farms (*kolkhosi*) in which there was some room for private production. These experiments had some success, but were invariably limited due to the interdependent nature of the entire supply chain. Given these and many other nuances I have not mentioned, one can really only provide a best guess as to what should have been done. It is simply not realistic to expect to understand the Soviet system better than the leaders at the time, who spent their whole lives living in it and analyzing it.

A centerpiece of the problem was the degree of perceived legitimacy of the overarching circle of reciprocity. Since the communist planning system had become a recognized drag on the economy in many regions of the USSR, the ability of the socialist ideal to cement the country's central institutions was already severely weakened. Hence, the leadership's open abandonment of the socialist circle of reciprocity would invite a role for other large reciprocal circles, notably nationalism. This in turn would lead to the separation of regions as well as a loss of control for the economic ministries, leading to a collapse in the whole economic network. This dynamic indeed occurred, and quickly eroded any potential for an orderly path to reform.

Worse, the logic of the socialist ideal itself presented an obstacle to reform. Truly experimenting with the economic system in any major way would generate winners and losers, and those industries and regions that would stand to lose would actively lobby the center, appealing to the ideal that each should receive according to his need. The winners naturally would urge the center to keep experimenting.

Facing the potential for such severe internal conflicts, it is not clear how the USSR could have maintained its socialist ideology while in reality moving towards a market economy.

What then should have been done by Gorbachev and the other communist leaders thinking about reform after 1985?

The key considerations I wish to highlight are: (i) new business links can only form slowly, so from an economic perspective, the pace of change had to be slow; (ii) the political power of the central elite was already uncertain, and any overt abandonment of the organizing ideology only weakened it further; and finally, (iii) actual power lay in the hands of the bureaucratic elite and local party bosses, so any change had to be supported by them.

If one reflects on the last point, then the first solid rule of the transition towards a market economy should have been to hand over true ownership of most of the means of production to local party bosses, bureaucrats, and directors of companies. One of the major mistakes in the transition was to wait until far too late before finally doing this via the privatizations of the early 1990s, by which time the output crash had already happened.

Giving control over property earlier to those who already had de facto political control would have been unpopular, but it would have given powerful local groups incentives to invest and innovate. This mistake was not repeated in China, where growth was accompanied by the phenomenon of *xiahai*, wherein many bureaucrats or families of bureaucrats turned into entrepreneurs (Li 1998). This intertwining between bureaucracy and firm ownership helped the Chinese economy in many ways, through giving bureaucrats incentives to provide local public goods and devise useful legislation.

The ideal political path in the case of the USSR was to maintain the socialist ideology as long as possible, but gradually let it transition into a new ideology that included a legitimate role for private enterprise. In this regard, it was a mistake by the Soviet leadership to allow *glasnost*, which entailed political openness and encouraged debate, because one of the first things that then happened was that the legitimacy of the socialist ideal was further eroded and competing circles of reciprocity grew in strength.[10] In addition to focusing on a redefinition of

---

[10] With the same reasoning in mind, I would advocate for smaller Eastern European countries, such as Croatia and Romania, that they foremost adopt a national project to aim for, such as entry into the EU. Such a national ideal can serve

socialism such that it became compatible with private enterprise, the Soviets would have benefitted from recognizing that nationalism was an inevitable eventual driver in the dominant circle of reciprocity. This made it even more imperative to give local bosses an interest in local business, which itself depended on trade between sectors and regions of the Soviet bloc, hence providing a countervailing economic incentive for people to keep the state together even in the face of growing regional nationalism.

Additionally, the command economy structure should first have been loosened in the economic and political heartland of Russia, such as the area around St. Petersburg. This area was densely populated, politically stable, and relatively prosperous, and had been entrepreneurial in historical times. In the heartland, there is far less danger that small regions will break away, because they would fear a reaction from the central government. The circle of reciprocity of Russian nationalism would thus have shielded the heartland area from political instability. It is in the heartland that local bureaucrats should have been allowed to export for profit, experiment with small firms, rewrite regulations, and so on. Once growth generation under the new system had been established in the heartland, independence would have then seemed less appealing for regions more loosely associated with Russia, such as Ukraine and Belarus.

Finally, it would have been beneficial to recognize that the Soviet Union was in grave danger of falling prey to a natural resource curse. In many ways, the high dependence on exported natural resources was already a major problem for the Soviet hierarchy in the late 1980s. In order to prevent a natural resource curse, it would have been preferable for the USSR to out-source some of its most lucrative resource-based industries to international agencies and companies. One might envision a deal between the USSR, a major oil company, and, say, the World Bank, whereby the proceeds of oil sales would have been deposited into a "USSR fund" at the World Bank that paid out annuities to the Soviet state. By having the majority of the funds invested in world stock markets, far less revenue would have flowed into the USSR. This may

as a focal point for reforms and a means of overcoming smaller-level interests. The basic advice that means of production have to be divided over those with the power on the ground, i.e., those leading hierarchies or representing cohesive circles of reciprocity, remains the same for smaller countries too.

sound like a bad thing when one is close to bankruptcy, but it would have increased the incentives for all actors to export other types of goods. Companies would face a lower exchange rate and politicians would have less reason to fight others over the existing revenue stream from resources, and would be more prone to promoting new potential income streams.

In such a way, the detrimental effects of a high exchange rate and political parasitism associated with large natural resource sales might have been reduced. Once the Soviet economy was large enough that oil revenues had become a minor element, the outsourcing construction could have been dismantled. Similarly, once the entrepreneurial element in the economy had taken strong enough root, the socialist ideology of the past could have been quietly packed away. Whether or not this course of action was politically feasible at the time is hard to tell. Quite probably not, in which case the question is whether something close to it was feasible.

4.3 Implications for economic theories of long-term growth

In this section, I use the network view of market economies developed above to draw out some implications for current theories of growth. These arguments are mainly based on Frijters et al. (2009) and Antic and Frijters (2012).[11]

The societal role of networks, as argued above, is to make exchange possible and hence to enable the economy to reap the benefits of comparative advantage and increasing returns to scale – implying a direct connection of networks to economic productivity as technology advances. Despite a plethora of microeconomic models and empirical studies of networks (Krugman 1991, Audretsch and Stephan 1996, Rauch 2001, Goyal 2005, Duffy et al. 2006, Meier and O'Toole 2007), there are nonetheless, to my knowledge, few explicit models of how the creation and destruction of business networks are related to either long-term growth or short-term cycles.

---

[11] Ricardo (1817) and Durkheim (1893) envisaged an economy as growing because larger tasks became more and more disaggregated into smaller tasks, which per the arguments above is directly related to the matching up of production factors. This reasoning is also featured in the modern macro-models of Matsuyama (1999), and is still prevalent in the literature on creative destruction and innovation (Antic and Frijters 2012).

One can map the value of networks into a standard production function for the aggregate economy, by interpreting contacts as an input that unites other production factors, including those involved in organizing input purchases and selling eventual outputs. This general function can be thought of as analogous to that of human capital: due to limits to human understanding and information-gathering, there is economic value in the specific knowledge of how to combine other production factors, and in knowing the preferences and comparative advantages of consumers and suppliers.[12] The problem of exchange arising from transaction costs can be seen as necessitating another production factor, just as the time involved in information acquisition and absorption necessitates a role for human capital.

Previous economic studies have suggested business links as an important and previously overlooked missing production factor. Baumol (2002), Acs and Audretsch (2003), and Frijters et al. (2003) all suggest that entrepreneurial links are the missing factor in production function models required to explain cross-country differences in economic performance. The paper by Bezemer et al. (2003) focuses on the political differences between socialism and capitalism. Audretsch and Keilbach (2004) (p. 951) present an explicit production function with an institutional factor called "entrepreneurial capital," which is defined as "factors conducive to the creation of new business links." However, the role of links in production itself is not modeled or expanded upon by these authors.

Yet, despite the absence of links as direct production factors in the economic literature, they do figure prominently in an indirect manner. For example, economists have recently been contemplating the economic importance of institutions and governance. In the recent survey by Dixit (2009) (p. 5), he defines these concepts as follows:

By economic governance I mean the structure and functioning of the legal and social institutions that support economic activity and economic transactions by protecting property rights, enforcing contracts, and taking collective action to provide physical and organizational infrastructure.

Dixit (2009) (p. 5) furthermore writes "economic governance is important because markets, and economic activity ... cannot function

---

[12] The implicit definition of human capital that I suggest here (which will be discussed more fully below) is not the only one present in the literature.

well in its absence." Likewise, trust is an informal institution that is being increasingly studied by economists. Glaeser, Laibson, Scheinkman, and Soutter (2000), for example, construct measures of trust and find that these are correlated with economic performance.

The underlying question in such explorations is how these institutions affect the real economy. Institutional concepts such as trust and other institutions that facilitate economic activity do not have a direct effect on the standard production factors, such as capital and labor. Yet they do affect business contacts – more precisely, they make the formation of business contacts easier and cheaper, and it is through this channel that they could wield an influence on the economy. A production function that includes business contacts therefore helps to reconcile these booming areas of research (Dixit 2009 suggests that there were over 33,000 papers on EconLit targeting these questions at the end of 2008) with theories of economic growth.

In short, networks have the potential to unify many arguments in macro-economics surrounding institutions and growth. Frijters et al. (2009) show how one can add business links to an otherwise standard discussion of production factors, and how this allows a reinterpretation of other concepts (such as institutions and social capital) as having an effect on the whole economy via their effect on the costs of making and breaking links. The main reasoning in Frijters et al. (2009) is repeated below.

4.3.1 Sources of long-term growth

In the long run, how much you consume as a country must be linked to how much you produce. Economic growth in the long run is thus linked inextricably to how productive a country is. One can summarize all the things believed to affect the long-run wealth of a country by means of a comprehensive list of production factors. The basic production factors mentioned in most textbooks are natural resources, labor, and capital. I add the links between these three production factors created by entrepreneurs. The sources of long-term growth are then these production factors themselves, plus anything believed to lead a country to possess high amounts of these basic production factors.

I make distinctions amongst the following long-run sources of economic growth:

- Basic production factors. Natural resources, labor time, physical capital, and human capital.

- Facilitating factors I. Trade links (contacts).
- Facilitating factors II. Institutional capital and social capital.

Each of these factors will be considered, but at the most aggregate level, the economy is seen as consisting of a small set of factors that actually produce things of consumption value, with a potentially large number of layers of additional production factors. Some of those additional production factors, such as contacts, have the fairly direct role of enhancing the ease with which the basic factors can find each other in their most productive combinations, and the ease with which the actual output of those combinations can reach the persons willing to pay the most for them. Others have a role that is very indirect, such as when trust affects "sold production" through its effect on the cost of making contacts. Economists so far have considered models where those intermediate roles are either performed automatically, as if by some costless market magic (such as the Swan–Solow model and its many modern derivatives), or else invoke a single additional production factor. I advocate a change from this mindset. A more useful way of looking at the economy is to realize that there is not just one additional coordinating production factor, but rather whole layers of additional factors.

Natural resources

Having more natural resources makes a country richer in the short run because it can sell or lease them on the world market. Natural resources are essentially fixed: either there is, or there is not, a lot of oil, minerals, sunshine, land, and other natural resources in a given country. Resources clearly have economic advantages: in centuries gone by, people from a given country would invade other countries to acquire resource-rich territories, although this is much less frequent today.[13]

While natural resources are a source of wealth, they are also widely cited as a drag on long-run growth. This is first and foremost because having many natural resources can lead to unhelpful internal fights over the virtually immediate wealth that they bring. A classic example of this

---

[13] Frijters and Foster (2013) theorize about the ultimate reasons for the reduction in the prevalence of wars as a means of gaining wealth. The essential reason favored is that growth is more easily achieved in the modern era via the accumulation of other production factors, and that the current political equilibrium has empowered more individuals who stand to lose from wars.

is Nigeria, which is rich in oil but equally encumbered with political fighting over oil revenues. This fighting is believed to have made it impossible to get other businesses going, and as a result Nigeria has seen no economic growth for the past twenty years (something Lane and Tornell 1996 too attribute to political infighting over resources, which they call a "voracity effect"). Even if political problems do not arise as a result of the presence of natural resources, rich natural resources make it harder for a country to compete in other markets because the robust natural resource sector drives up the prices of other production inputs: it simply outbids other sectors for good workers, entrepreneurs, and materials. By definition, the comparative advantage of the country that possesses abundant natural resources lies in exporting those resources, rather than in producing other goods and services. Since the natural resource sector is not believed to lead to inventions or practices that are extensively used in other sectors of the economy, this can also slow down growth indirectly. This is another aspect of the "Dutch disease" discussed previously.

Labor
The size of a population is fixed at any moment in time, but can be somewhat manipulated by government. One can increase the stock of labor in an economy either by increasing the population or by getting the existing population to spend more time at work.

The raw number of people can be increased through increases in life expectancy, higher birth rates, higher immigration, and lower emigration. Each of these factors is to some extent subject to government policy: governments can improve life expectancy by having good public health systems; they can promote higher birth rates by giving monetary incentives for having children; they can increase immigration by lowering the barriers to foreigners or actively promoting their country amongst potential immigrants; and they can decrease emigration by making it harder to leave the country.

The amount of time that individuals spend in formal work, which by definition is made up of taxable activities, can be manipulated by changing the individual incentives to work or the degree to which work is seen as a desirable social norm. Individual material incentives to work depend on the amount of resources one can get from not working, for instance by drawing on government welfare benefits, and the degree to which formal work is taxed more than other activities, i.e., marginal taxation.

Perhaps more importantly, work can be stimulated by stigmatizing non-work and glorifying work. Stigmatization is relatively easy for a government or a large group to achieve as it "merely" entails the propagation of a social norm that formal work is morally uplifting and desirable. One might call such a social norm a work ethic. Apart from telling and retelling stories about the value of work, outright stigmatization of those without formal jobs is also quite feasible, for instance by forcing those who do not work into demeaning situations and activities whose primary purpose is to shame them for not working.

Shaming individuals for their lack of a formal job can be done by forcing individuals to beg regularly for handouts, or forcing them to spend their welfare payments on particular goods, which implies a lack of trust in their own ability to judge what is good for them. Another popular method of shaming those out of work is to make state support contingent upon their undertaking activities that signal their subservience to the work ethic, such as checking that they respond to official job advertisements, rather than letting those out of work decide themselves whether and how to search for work. This may be done solely for its shaming effect, and despite the fact that searching for jobs informally might well in reality be a more successful way to find jobs. For example, Frijters, Shields, and Wheatley-Price (2005) found that many individuals from ethnic minorities in the UK found their jobs informally, which in turn implies that forcing them to use official channels would not improve their odds of finding jobs but would merely force them to acknowledge the social norm that having a job is desirable.

Physical capital

Physical capital includes machines, buildings, roads, harbors, airports, and so forth. The catch-all term "technology" can be understood as referring to the quality of physical capital, so that better technology implies more productive physical capital. The main way in which one acquires more and better physical capital is through investment, which can be undertaken either by the private sector or by the government sector. The government can stimulate the stock of physical capital either by investing itself (i.e., by building more roads, buildings, and so on) or by creating circumstances conducive to private-sector investments.

The circumstances that encourage private-sector investments mainly relate to the availability of many profitable opportunities and the ability of private entrepreneurs to keep the profits they make by taking those opportunities. Higher taxes on investments (relative to the alternative countries where one could invest) and few profitable opportunities discourage investment by the private sector.

Human capital

A working definition of human capital is "knowledge regarding the optimal use of other production factors," measured at the level of the individual. A person with more human capital than someone else can individually attain a higher productivity with the same amount of basic production factors (i.e., resources, time, and physical capital). Examples of human capital include the knowledge of how to work a machine, when to plant particular crops, how to use a computer, and how to work successfully with other people. This latter skill includes subsetting social skills such as being punctual, knowing what to say in order to reduce conflicts, and adhering to important social codes (e.g., regarding dress and body language).

Human capital can be increased by spending time learning how to do things, which is generally done through education, experience, and training. At the aggregate level, human capital investments consist of time investments by teachers, parents, children, and the government bureaucracy into increasing the level of knowledge of the current and incipient generations. Greater human capital also leads to innovations in that people invent ways to get more production out of the same amount of basic resources.

Societies can increase human capital most easily by expanding education. Virtually all attempts in the last 150 years by large countries to achieve faster economic growth have been accompanied by a vast expansion of the education system. Well-known historical examples are given by Japan in the 1880s, the Soviet Union in the 1920s, and South Korea after World War II. We can see the same basic plan being applied in the modern day by the Chinese government: the average years of education completed by new cohorts of Chinese have almost doubled in the last twenty years, as part of a major push towards greater economic prosperity (Meng et al. 2010). Education in India is similarly starting to expand. Greater investments in education have been a well-recognized part of the essential recipe for achieving growth in a developing country.

Just as new technology implies an improvement in the quality of physical capital beyond previous bounds, so too can there be technological breakthroughs in human capital. For example, new ways to work together in teams, new management practices, and new accounting practices can be created and then taught to new generations. Generating this new technology requires investments.

To some extent, labeling the output of modern education as a form of capital is a slight misnomer. The problem is not so much that human capital, unlike physical capital, cannot be seen, bundled up, sold, and transferred across individuals. The bigger problem is that by thinking of human capital as a quantity that is additive, one is effectively pretending that human capital is only about producing more of what is already being produced, rather than about inventing and producing something new.

In reality, general education (giving rise to what is referred to as general, rather than specific, human capital) readies individuals for many different tasks. Growth in the overall economy is then not only the result of applying a known production process to make a fixed amount of output using fewer resources, although there is some of that, but also results from the increasing specialization of production and the continued development of more products, both of which rely on creativity. It takes creativity to work out how to craft and then contribute to a more sophisticated production process that involves inputs from more specialized agents, and creativity to think up new products and how to make them. Human capital is in large part about the ability to quickly adopt production processes that do not yet exist and that differ from what other people in the economy do. The flexibility to be creative, rather than the possession of fixed stores of knowledge that many others also already have, is therefore a better way to conceptualize any given individual's human capital in terms of its ultimate economic value.

Finally, it is important to point out that the concept of human capital presupposes that there is a cost to gathering and absorbing information: without such a cost, complete education would occur instantaneously.

Human capital only captures information about how to get the most out of different possible combinations of resources, time, and physical capital. For many users of this term, it also captures knowledge of how to interact with other people, which in turn would mean it reduces the cost of interacting with others. Yet it does not contain the knowledge of what all others in an economy are able to do and willing to provide. That knowledge and the ability to act on that knowledge form the heart of trade relations, and will require another factor of production to capture.

Trade links

Entrepreneurs and other organizers create "jobs," which can be understood as bundles of individual producers that are matched up, following a given production process, with certain amounts of basic production factors. These jobs are organized into larger production units, such as firms, in which there is an alignment between the inputs and outputs of many jobs: some workers produce inputs for others within the firm, and final outputs are sold to outside consumers. The bundling of producers to inputs at the micro-level, and the alignment of production processes within the firm, can be viewed as creating "links," or contacts, between the basic production factors of labor time, resources, human capital, and physical capital.

Examples of this type of link formation include combining a set of workers with some buildings, some machines, some input suppliers, and some customers to create a beer factory and distribution system. No individual worker, machine, customer, or supplier on his own would have produced or consumed beer. Only the combination of specific factors creates the production and consumption of beer, and then only after everyone's specific roles in the process are made clear. Entrepreneurs can also decide to invest in technological breakthroughs by directing certain production factors (specifically, inventors and capital) towards the goal of discovering new technologies. These entrepreneurial activities also can be described as creating particular links between existing production factors.

As with human capital, to conceptualize links themselves as a separate production factor is a way of capturing the importance of something more complex, which in this case is the problem of organizing the basic production factors into production processes for many different products and aligning these processes with one another. The whole system of exchange can be viewed as an enormous array of links between the basic production factors. A complete market is then no more than a fully linked set of individuals.

How can a government facilitate the building of more and better links? Entrepreneurs must face incentives to build better links, which can be assisted through the passage of patent laws, contract laws, and other forms of property rights protection. Cheap information must be available about potential new production methods, and the government can either produce and disseminate this information or assist in its production or dissemination. Finally, a legal system, which is clearly in the direct purview of government, is needed to back up the contractual arrangements that entrepreneurs enter into with suppliers, workers, and customers. This line of thought is crucial in the upcoming discussion about further facilitating production factors.

At a more abstract level, trade links are essentially a layer of activities that enhance the "final" productivity of the basic production factors. There are several such layers, but links form a very important one because the other "facilitating" factors – institutional and social capital – mainly facilitate the formation of links, and only indirectly facilitate the formation of basic production factors.

The distinction between human capital and trade links should now be clearer. Human capital is about knowing what to do when the most basic production factors (natural resources, labor time, and physical capital) are available. Trade links create the knowledge and expectations that bring together particular combinations of more basic production factors, and thereby capture the process of exchange. One can make a theoretical distinction between the bringing together of the production factors and the trading of the ultimate output, but these two roles are here collapsed into one because, at an abstract level, the activity in question is similar.

Institutional capital

Institutional capital describes the degree to which the institutions in a given economy reduce the cost of creating and/or maintaining links and basic production factors. Both formal and informal institutions can be seen as the lubricants of an economy, allowing the smooth operation of other activities without too much costly friction.

Formal institutions include all organizations that are designed to resolve conflicts as cheaply as possible. This includes parliament, the legal system, the police, and other organizations aimed at conflict resolution. These formal institutions help prevent and resolve conflicts between people, businesses, and, in the case of parliament, whole groups in society. Formal institutions also include institutions designed to make it cheaper to build links between production factors, both domestically and abroad. Such institutions include those involved with money and the financial sector, such as central banks; and regulatory institutions such as the bodies that regulate particular industries, and those that regulate competition. These organizations oversee the smooth running of markets and promote the use of money as a means of exchange and a store of value. Formal institutions that reduce the cost of creating human capital include schools, universities, and laws setting compulsory learning and national curriculum standards that support these institutions.

There are also informal institutions that are neither enshrined in law nor otherwise formalized, yet also reduce the costs of conflict and/or aid production. Good examples are social norms surrounding tax compliance and adherence to the rule of law. The more that individuals voluntarily adhere to the law and pay taxes, the cheaper it is for a government to collect taxes and to force the law upon the few remaining individuals who defy it. When there are no social norms regarding tax compliance and adherence to laws, then a government has to invest many more resources in order to collect taxes and enforce laws. Informal institutions that support the development of human capital include social beliefs regarding the use and efficacy of what is taught in schools. If what is taught in schools is seen as a form of unwanted indoctrination, then communities will resist this by encouraging their children to disrupt the education process.[14] The lack of social norms regarding

---

[14] A good example is the education riots in South Africa in the 1980s, in which the black youth effectively rebelled against the state school system that was perceived to be a form of white-led indoctrination (Gann and Duignan 1991, Smith-Mckoy 2001).

A more subtle example of the disconnect between formal institutions and social norms is given by Muslim education authorities in India. Chaudhary and Rubin (2011) argue that in areas where Muslim authorities were stronger, these local authorities encouraged the local Muslim population to attend Muslim schools whose primary objective was more oriented towards the legitimization of the local rulers rather than towards literacy. Chaudhary and Rubin (2011) argue that this created a geographical pattern in social norms that explains why, even today, areas with larger populations of Muslims have lower levels of literacy amongst Muslims than do areas in which Muslims are the minority. Controlling for a wide variety of other possible explanations, including the socioeconomic development of the whole district, they indeed find that Muslim literacy rates in 1911 and 1921 were higher in areas with fewer Muslims.

taxation, the rule of law, and the value of education are real problems for developing countries that attempt to emulate rich countries by simply adopting their formal institutions.

Both formal and informal institutions can make it much cheaper to acquire capital, to produce, and to trade. In an abstract sense, institutions mainly work by making link formation cheaper. For instance, without the rule of law, an entrepreneur considering investing in a new business would fear that someone else might simply steal the fruits of his investments. The entrepreneur would have to engage in costly enforcement mechanisms before undertaking the investment. Good laws make it possible for trading partners to make promises to one another that are credible on both sides of the transaction, as when employers hire workers by offering contracts that say, in essence, "if you work for me, I will pay you in the future and I will not fire you without good reason." Without such laws, workers would be suspicious; they would want to be paid upfront, and would not have an incentive to get to know the business out of fear that the employer would not keep his word about job security. Free contracting in general is thus a pillar of being able to run profitable businesses, as it allows the easy formation of ever-improving links, meaning that more capital is quickly directed towards more useful ends. Free contracting in turn requires institutions, such as good laws and their enforcement.

Social capital I: Trust

Social capital is a rather fuzzy term that captures the importance of social cohesion for the operation of an economy. Through the lens of this book, one can think of both particular habits useful in an economy and of the sheer strength of group relations.

The most important example of useful habits is the notion of trust. If people generally trust other people, then trade becomes cheaper in the sense that building the links required for trade is cheaper. A good example in a modern economy of a situation of high trust can be witnessed in any supermarket. Normally, people trust that the supermarket is not selling products past their sell-by date, and that they will not be charged something different at the counter than what is advertised in the aisles. If people did not trust these aspects of the situation, then they would put more time into checking for themselves whether the products on the shelves are still fresh and into keeping track of the prices.

With trust, people can just toss products into their trolleys, go to the checkout counter, and pay the total amount that is asked of them.

Similarly, supermarkets implicitly trust their customers not to switch bar codes on the products or to cheat in other ways. Supermarkets do check on their customers, for example by searching bags in order to dissuade shoplifting, but not nearly as much as they would have to check them if they mistrusted every customer. In this way, a high degree of trust between each supermarket and their customers allows both parties to spend very little effort on monitoring the other, which is good for both sides. More generally, trust reduces the cost of doing business in all aspects of an economy: it reduces the cost of making links.

How can one create the habit of trust? This question has not yet been clearly answered. In some ways, laws and law enforcement uphold a social norm that it is important to trust and be trustworthy, but they do not explain where the norm came from or how it increased. What some social scientists have argued (Putnam 1993, Gulati 1995, Jackson, Rodriguez-Barraquer, and Tan 2012) is that individuals might start out with very little trust towards people they do not know, but that frequent interactions with many others over time created trust both across and within larger communities. Hence, centuries of ever-increasing interaction within and between villages, provinces, and countries eventually led to a high degree of trust between people and organizations hailing from diverse walks of life. Putnam thus relates trust to the development of what he calls "horizontal networks of association," but that I would simply call trade networks. In this sense, trust, like other forms of social capital, is a by-product of economic interactions that is adopted by individuals and gradually becomes solidified in laws and norms. This implies that it might be possible to stimulate the growth of trust by making interaction between people and regions cheaper through government intervention aimed at lowering the barriers to interaction.

Social capital II: Nontrust

"Social capital" is also sometimes used to describe the strength of group relations, and in particular informal networks amongst people, such as sports clubs, debating societies, and links between members of families and communities. Through the lens of this book, these are small reciprocal groups. The social cohesion that is believed to result from more and stronger reciprocal groups within an overall larger circle is believed to catalyze development, as it becomes cheaper to trade when building links is cheaper. As briefly discussed above, economic development itself involves the gradual replacement of informal links by formal links. However, even in modern societies today, reciprocal groups and their informal networks retain some degree of economic importance.

How does one help small reciprocal groups thrive? As one might expect based on Chapter 3, more homogeneous communities appear to have more and stronger social networks. People who share the same language, the same beliefs, and similar education are more likely to build groups with each other than people who cannot understand each other, believe different things, and have different knowledge. The government, through education policy and in other ways, can therefore affect social capital by promoting a degree of similarity across people. As an example, Australia actively does this by testing new citizens and by forcing all schools in a given state to comply with the same standard curriculum.

4.4 Out-of-sample evidence

This chapter so far has presented a theory of contacts and networks mainly based on the experience of the collapse of the Soviet Union, and has recast the standard production-factor explanation of long-term growth in light of this theory of networks. I now ask whether the theory of networks presented above also fits evidence on business cycles, which it was not originally designed to fit.

There are several elements of past and current recessions that become clearer once one allows an economic role for business links. As mentioned before, being unemployed can be viewed simply as having relatively few links. This then does not mean someone who is unemployed cannot produce anything, but rather that his ability to specialize in producing something is not actually being used in any formal organizations, because he is unlinked. He is hence less productive, rather than totally unproductive. He faces the dilemma of whether to spend time on low-productivity activities, such as working as a gardener or a cleaner, or alternatively to continue searching for more productive "jobs," i.e., to invest in link formation while unemployed. The concept of "links" thus provides a natural lens through which to make sense of both involuntary unemployment and "underemployment."

Links also help in understanding what is actually being destroyed when homeowners lose their houses, or when banks go bankrupt. It is not physical capital or human capital that is destroyed as a result of these processes. Rather, individuals who lose their houses and have to relocate, effectively lose their local links. They lose their local employment opportunities as well as their informal links that helped them make more formal trade links, implying that the cost of making trade links goes up, which in turn means they are more likely to be unlinked for a longer time. Similarly, a bank that goes bankrupt effectively creates a severing of the links between creditors and debtors. The role of banks in investment is as intermediaries, implying that a bundle of links become severed when any one bank goes bankrupt. Major economy-wide bankruptcy thereby produces a reduction in the overall degree of economic coordination, which should be expected to have negative effects for as long as it takes for economic agents to find new links.

This interpretation is somewhat related to the standard discourse regarding aggregate demand being "too low" during recessions. A destruction of contacts can certainly be thought of as a reduction in aggregate demand, in that those with fewer contacts enjoy fewer opportunities to sell their wares than they anticipated. Yet, the converse does not quite hold: an increase in the demand for goods does not automatically translate into the appearance of new contacts that soak up the production factors left idle by the breakup of previous contacts. An increase in aggregate demand can initially mean an intensification of existing contacts, and would only slowly lead to new connections for idle production factors as the expanding sectors build up production capacity.

4.4.1 Business links and the Great Depression

One of the main reasons for the misery during the Great Depression of the 1930s was the long time it took for workers who became unemployed to find new jobs. Implicitly, theories of the Great Depression that see unemployment as involuntary therefore appeal to some difficulty in forming links. Authors such as Summers (1986), for example, explicitly relate the Great Depression in the US to a problem of exchange. Other authors are less explicit but still take Summers' view. A review of conflicting theories about the severity of the Great Depression by White (1990) mentions a number of theories that implicitly rely on some notion of the problem of exchange, and the loss of business links. Descriptions of the Great Depression in terms of business links include explanations that rely on the importance of bankruptcies, which have no role in market-clearing theories because bankruptcies merely "free up" production factors that should immediately be taken up again and re-used in production. Any theory that relies on bankruptcies as part of its explanation thus implicitly appeals to a difficulty in "re-matching" the production factors involved in the bankruptcy. In short, the Great Depression fits the theory of networks in this chapter, but the literature has not yet explicitly called for a network production factor as the immediate factor that declined during the Depression.

In this light, the theories that rely on some conception of business links include Keynesian explanations that center around demand factors creating bankruptcies; monetarist explanations that point to money creation or price interference as factors that led to bankruptcies; Austrian theories that rely on the over-expansion of credit before the Depression as a factor explaining bankruptcies; and theories of banking that contend that the Great Depression was caused by the collapse of several agricultural banks, which in turn spawned a great many bankruptcies and loan defaults. While explicit mention in these theories of "links" or "business networks" is generally absent, they all appeal to the difficulties of re-matching the production factors left idle by bankruptcies.

4.4.2 Business links and the Indonesian downturn

The Indonesian downturn of 1997 was part of the Asian crisis, which is widely believed to have been initiated by a financial crisis. I am unaware of any analysis of this crisis that examines the production factors involved in the downturn, yet there are plentiful statements by business leaders and others testifying to the extensive disestablishment of business links. A good example is the *Jakarta Times* article (Koning 1998), which reported the following:

Currently entrepreneurial skills are near paralyzed by an undervalued rupiah, very high domestic interest rates (both for US dollars and rupiah) for very limited liquidity, a high level of debt aggravated by unhedged dollar borrowings, and an economy in which vital supplies of raw materials and intermediate goods are diminishing or disappearing. To compound this all, the local distribution network for many goods is also crumbling.

Of all the potential explanations mentioned in this list, only the last one can be seen as a potential production factor, since the others are either price reports or mere re-statements of the fact that the economy was collapsing. An editorial in the *Jakarta Times* on November 12th, 1997 carried the same basic message: small and medium-sized firms were going bankrupt due to collapsing networks.

In his analysis of the Asian crisis, Phelps (1999) argues that one of the causes of the crisis was the intervention of government in the corporate sector, and that this induced business links to be created that were based on over-optimism. This, coupled with the fact that bankruptcy regulations and other institutions were insufficiently strong to support a capitalist system, resulted in the large decline in output that many Asian economies experienced following 1997. Hence, collapsing networks seem likely to be involved in the Indonesian downturn.

4.4.3 Business links and the global financial crisis of 2008–2011

The global financial crisis of 2008–2011 began with bankruptcies of several major United States banks and financial institutions, such as Lehman Brothers. Following the spread of panic, the unwinding of large volumes of debt in the US and in Europe was accompanied by a marked slowdown in economic activity, including persistent double-digit unemployment rates in some regions.

Apart from the ability of networks to explain the persistence of high involuntary unemployment, there are also specific predictions particular to the theory of links and networks that one can look for in this financial crisis. For example, because links are the means of matching and coordination between parts of a given supply and demand chain, the severing of a link in one part of the chain implies likely destruction in other parts of the chain in close proximity, or in other words, a cascade of network destruction. Koopman, Lucas, and Schwaab (2010) show that defaults in US industries were indeed clustered.

There are thus many aspects of historical and more recent recessions that make more sense if one allows for a specific production factor that captures the problem of exchange.

4.5 Modern democracy and networking

Using the theory of networks discussed in this chapter and the theory of groups from Chapter 3, I now want to make a number of obser-vations on democracy within modern Western states. There are many different forms of democracy in the world, so I will focus on the main characteristics they share.

4.5.1 Temporary rulers

The most important thing about democracy as depicted in political science is that the subgroup in control is periodically changed in a peaceful manner. Those in control at any given time are therefore only in temporary control. This restriction on control obviously can only be enforced if those in control are not in complete control, i.e., when there is within the government bureaucracy some loyalty to demo-cratic ideals (including periodic power changes) that is stronger than the loyalty to whatever subgroup is in control at a given moment. Such idealism, which is characteristic of a large circle of reciprocity, prevents the subgroup in control from simply rewriting existing laws in order to allow them to stay in power forever. Democracy simply could not work without nationalism or some other form of overarching ideology whose true believers serve to counterbalance the temporary power of those currently in charge.

There are many advantages to a society of allowing only tempo-rary control by any given subgroup. The main advantage is that the ephemeral nature of the control prevents others' loyalties to any par-ticular group or person holding the reins temporarily from becoming too great. This is firstly because the control wielded by the controlling subgroup does not last as long as the nationalism enforced by the state system (through education, the army, state media, and so on), which in a stable democracy is essentially continuous. Thus the subgroup in temporary control lacks the time to fully bind the state bureaucracy and other key parts of the population to them. The second reason why a population's loyalty to those in power in democracies does not become overly strong is that the mere possibility that the subgroup currently in charge will be replaced by another group severely diminishes the degree to which the present controlling subgroup is deemed unassailable. The perceived vulnerability of the group in charge is directly related to the degree to which they are respected and loved by the rest of the population, including the bureaucracy. The mere belief that the subgroup in charge can be replaced reduces that subgroup's authority, and thus diminishes the degree to which that subgroup's members attract people's loyalties. This latter observation is important in explaining how countries that have been dominated by a single party for decades on end could still be called democratic, and indeed could experience changes of government after many years. Mexico, whose main legislative assembly was dominated by a single party from 1917 to 1997, is a good example. Sweden, dominated by the social democrats from 1950 to 1990, is another. Each eventually experienced an almost seamless handover to another political party, despite the generations-long continuous rule by one party.

This second mechanism also shows the importance of state propaganda. If a state issues propaganda that exults its democratic values, even though its actual leaders have rigged previous elections and do not intend ever to relinquish power, then there is the inherent danger that people will believe the propaganda, direct their loyalties accordingly, and eventually force the current leaders from power. This is a stylized version of precisely what is argued to have happened in Mexico in the 1980s, and in Serbia in 2000. A dictatorial subgroup intending to keep power forever should thus not engage in democratic propaganda. This was the "mistake" made by the Serbian leader Slobodan Milošević. He allowed the state to disseminate democratic propaganda, and his population came to believe in it to the extent that they forced him out of office when he was seen to be rigging elections. His own people then handed him to the international war crimes court in The Hague.

4.5.2 *Majority rulers*

A second important observation to make about democracy is that the ruling subgroup is virtually always part of the "broad majority group." To put this statement in statistical terms: if the ruling subgroup were in fact a "random draw" from the general population, then the US should have had at least one female president by now; most European nations should have had someone with different skin color as a leader by now; some Muslim group should have been substantively in charge of India by now (not only in the role of president, which in that country is a ceremonial role now and then filled by a Muslim); some non-Muslim group should have been in charge of Indonesia by now; and so on. None of these events has occurred. It is plain that democracy in practice means one male member of the majority being periodically exchanged for another male member of the majority as ruler. What makes the changeover relevant at all is that the successive ruling subgroups are not part of the same small subgroup: they are part of different small subgroups (e.g., political parties) within the majority group that principally carries and identifies itself with the large circle of reciprocity of the nation state. This is an important observation, because it invalidates common myths that democracy automatically means that very diverse groups are all part of government. It also implies that the broad majority in a given dictatorship need not fear losing complete control to a minority group in the event that the society moves to a democratic system.

4.5.3 Other observations on democracy

I may add to the advantages cited above the usual arguments in favor of democracy that are found in the literature. These include the ability of new political issues to be signaled by the emergence of a new minority party, after which such issues are usually taken up by a majority party that simply adopts the issue into its agenda. An example of this is the case of the immigration reforms enforced in Europe over the period 1990–2010. Migrants from outside the European Union now face citizenship tests, compulsory national curricula, and greater barriers to family reunification. Reforms like these were initially suggested by so-called "far-right" parties – e.g., those led by Jean-Marie Le Pen in France, Pim Fortuyn in the Netherlands, and others. Their suggestions about immigration are now official government policies, despite the fact that none of the parties initially bringing the suggestions have made it into power, because their stated immigration agendas have simply been absorbed by the mainstream parties.

The tendency of the electorate to remain loyal to particular parties yet agree with the policies of other parties should not come as a surprise, given the theory of groups discussed in Chapter 3. While the leaders of smaller groups may advocate policies that the majority would agree with, they remain the leaders of smaller groups, and hence are not serious candidates for election by the majority. Only individuals seen to be vying for the sympathies of the entire reciprocal group can be seen as serious candidate leaders. In the cases of Le Pen and Fortuyn, the mere fact that they were seen to be advocating minority opinions made them suspect in the eyes of the majority, and thus a focal point for resistance. To appreciate this requires an understanding of loyalty to groups or ideologies.

4.5.4 The role of networks in democracy

From the point of view of networks, democracy is the logical form of politics to accompany an economy dominated by constantly changing network relations. The inability of any subgroup to truly dominate others protects the vested interests of the existing contact makers, while the indiscriminate ideology (e.g., "human rights," "fairness," and "freedom") fits in with the non-hierarchical yet non-emotive nature of networks, and more generally with the fluidity of the underlying balance of power between individuals and subgroups in a society dominated by contact makers. Democracy virtually guarantees that contact makers' interests are served, and carries little risk that the state will be taken over by some smaller subgroup who would then suppress networking activities.

I furthermore contend that democracy originally emerged for these essentially economic reasons, and that the ideologies with which we now associate it came into play historically in a second stage, only after the economic rationale. While ideology is a more emotive aspect of democracy than anything to do with networks or markets, the supposed superior morality of democracy due to the one-man-one-vote principle is not an innate advantage of democracy that will forever protect it against demise. Rather, our dominant current morality simply holds that principle to be an argument in favor of democracy. That principle was not part of the historical operation or introduction of democracy (Acemoglu and Robinson 2001). Historically speaking, democracy has been more about the efficient deployment of the power of the contact-making majority, rather than about true power sharing with the powerless.

For example, the citizens of Athens had a form of democracy, but it was by no means a one-man-one-vote situation. Neither slaves, nor women, nor the poor had any say in anything. It was men with contacts and position amongst whom the one-man-one-vote principle applied. Exactly the same can be said of nineteenth-century American and European democracy: it was only amongst the recognized, well-to-do men that the one-man-one-vote principle applied. Then too, women by and large had no say, and neither did anyone in financial distress (obtaining welfare carried with it a loss of the right to vote).

To contend that the current form of democracy in the West ultimately depends on a one-man-one-vote ideology ignores the far more important role of networking in maintaining democracy.[15] The reversal of the political process towards embracing "participation for all" is not in fact as unthinkable as it may seem: various economic (and other) advantages of democracy would remain even if the franchise were again to be restricted.

Even today, there are restrictions on who can vote. For instance, in virtually no country can illegal immigrants or those in prison vote. In some countries, one must pre-register to vote and one must be a citizen, adding more barriers. A system of pre-registering, coupled with taxation based on the resulting registration list, is then an obvious method of excluding some people. The distance to polling stations and the ease with which citizens who are abroad can vote are further subtleties making it harder for some to vote than for others. These subtleties reflect the power balance between various citizens, and barriers to voting can be further increased or reduced without great cost.

It is thus quite easy for a powerful group to restrict the vote to a smaller group. Indeed, one may ask why restrictions are not more prevalent than they are. For example, why are those on welfare still allowed to vote in every Western country, despite their almost non-existent economic power and organizing potential? The answer is because of the existence of democratic ideals. Whereas economic exchange may have been the first mover in bringing us democracy, ideals do play a role in sustaining democracy in the form we recognize. This implies that we should examine the determinants of the underlying idealism in modern states if we wish to predict what will happen to democracy as we know it. Through the lens of this book, the ultimate determinant of this idealism is that contact makers' interests are served

---

[15] In a similar vein, McCloskey (2006) argues on the basis of her historical study of the rise of merchants and capitalists in Holland and Britain that the "virtues" associated with more modern countries arose as a by-product of their economic activities. Though McCloskey does not formally theorize about networks, she explicitly recognizes that to be trusting and honest, and even to have some basic sympathy, makes for good business and thus will arise from the "capitalist system."

by human rights ideals. Hence, the origins of modern state ideals are economic, meaning that we need to keep our market economies rich in contact makers if we wish to retain democracy.

Developments within the Communist Party in China are instructive about how democratic adoption might proceed in China as a result of its expanding economic networks. In 2011, the Chinese Communist Party, which rules the country at present, had a membership of about 7 percent of the Chinese population. About one-sixth of its members were female, while half of the overall population was female; some 50 percent of Communist Party members are high school graduates, which was several times more than the percentage of high school graduates in the overall population of adults. More highly educated men were thus heavily overrepresented. The Communist Party has only recently decided to admit individuals of sufficient wealth or other economic achievements.

At the same time, the internal structure of the Party is becoming more democratic, with more and more decisions being taken by representatives of the members. Through the Party's structure itself, there is thus a creeping increase in participation of (mainly) wealthy and educated men in the political process, and these new additions (mainly) belong to the contact-making groups in Chinese society. A clear historical analogy can be drawn with the early Anglo-Saxon democratic system, which began as a club restricted to men of standing. From the point of view of percentages of the total population having some political say, Chinese democracy in 2011 was roughly where much of Western democracy was in the late nineteenth century. This implies that ignoring all other points of difference between Europe and China and assuming no major upheavals, we should expect Communist Party members to usher in the gradual emergence of Chinese democracy, with a fully modern democratic state developing there within the next thirty to forty years. The growth of the entrepreneurial sector in China might translate itself into a Western-style democracy more quickly if every Chinese person were accepted as a member of the Communist Party, with subparties holding elections for the leadership of the Communist Party. What this would require is a redefinition of the word "communist" to be interpreted as "nationalist" or "communal."

4.6 Relation with existing theories of networks

There are three broad strands of economic literature that can be compared to the story of networks presented in this chapter. The first is the large literature on search frictions between different actors, mainly oriented around labor markets, which give rise to non-ignorable issues of matching, bargaining, and intermediary institutions. The second is the development-economics literature on network formation across generations and localities, which include discussions of different types of networks and different types of supporting institutions. The third is the relatively new field of social network analysis that completely abstracts from individual agents, focusing entirely on measurable relations such as trade flows or hyperlinks between large entities, such as countries and firms.

4.6.1 Search and matching

Petrongolo and Pissarides (2001) discuss the early literature on the matching required between two market parties, often labeled as "workers" and "jobs." This is a literature containing formal models and stylized representations, but nevertheless at its heart is the notion that buyers and sellers of a good need to meet, and that there are non-negligible search frictions between them, necessitating that both sides search for one another. In these models, institutions that facilitate search affect final outcomes by means of improving the "matching function" that maps the effort of each search party to the likelihood of becoming matched. Different models explore different situations, such as allowing market parties to pre-commit to a price before they match (called "wage-posting") or allowing market parties to keep searching while they negotiate with a current trade partner they have already found. The emphasis in this literature is usually on the efficiency of the whole market and the role of these frictions in market fluctuations, since shocks to productivity or resource availability take time to work through a system with frictions.

These matching models have in more recent years been augmented with exceptionally stylized models of network formation (Jackson and Wolinsky 1996, Goyal 2005, Gilles, Lazarova, and Ruys 2011) in

which there is a complete description of the search environment, leading to predictions about the types of networks that would develop in
those environments. These models try to represent every aspect of the
formation of the network, which requires authors to make detailed
assumptions about who knows what at which stages of the network
formation process; who expects what at which stages; how the information set of each agent changes with each addition to the network;
and so on.

One recurring argument in these theoretical models is that when
individuals have some reasonable information about the costs and benefits of further augmentation to the network, the network will start to
look like a star – i.e., every person will link with a central person –
because that is the cheapest way to form an indirect connection to all
other parties. Gilles et al. (2011) thus argue that a central "hierarchy"
brings stability to a network. Many internet platforms indeed have
that kind of setup: individuals looking for a bilateral match will con-
gregate at the same central place, rather like a physical marketplace,
because the remaining search frictions are vastly reduced in that central
place. The group running the internet platform then fills the role of a
small hierarchy that sets the rules of engagement for everyone in that
network.

Another argument that arises in this literature is that the uncertain
nature of the search environment can augment or reduce the occurrence
of particular social norms (see the many examples in Cohendet, Llerena, Stahn, and Umbhauer 1998). As Bowles (1998) (p. 75) observes,
"Markets and other economic institutions do more than allocate goods
and services: they also influence the evolution of values, tastes, and per-
sonalities." Importantly, interactions that are repeated and through
which there is some learning amongst individuals who are connected
indirectly, i.e., through mutual contacts who know both matched parties, give rise to importance being placed on having a reputation for
being cooperative and truthful.

There is real-world evidence on this point. On the basis of models
and experiments with Indian villagers, Jackson et al. (2012) comment
that in a situation where many individuals interact with others somewhat similar to themselves, there is a higher chance of some mutual
connection being able to spot deviant behavior – which in turn leads
to the emergence of loose reciprocal groups, in which there are cooperative social norms that stipulate that individuals do not cheat each other.

This is an important observation, because it ties a contact-making economy directly to the endogenous emergence of social norms about being dependable and honest.

A direct modern example of this is the emerging practice on the internet of rating one's interactions with other people, such as when one writes publicly accessible feedback about whether or not someone has paid his bills on time or delivered purchased goods without mishap. This in turn gives rise to variability in the reputations of firms and individuals. People who, for example, do not pay their bills on the internet thereby quickly get "black-balled" by the people with whom they have done business, and will find it harder to find more trading partners in the future. This endogenous emergence of social norms can also be viewed as the emergence of an embryonic large reciprocal group.

The story in this chapter naturally complements this literature. The formal models in Chapter 6 in fact appeal directly to the idea of a matching function when modeling the formation of links. What the theory in this chapter adds to this existing literature is a more extended and directed appreciation of links. Not only are links between workers and jobs important, but jobs themselves are essentially conceived of as bundles of links between more basic production factors, outside clients, and input suppliers. Networks of links are also seen as important in political processes and tied in with the dynamics within and between groups. As such, the theory in this chapter generalizes the importance of search frictions and matching models.

This generalization comes with the costs and benefits of any simplification. In order to keep the discussion and models tractable, the wide variety of contracting situations and asymmetric information scenarios is reduced to a simpler story relating to a single additional factor of production. Just as "human capital" captures a wide array of different types of knowledge that can be used in many different situations, so too do networks – a single additive factor of production – capture at one stroke the myriad detailed observations regarding search frictions and matching environments.

The benefit of this reduction in complexity is that it becomes easier to interpret phenomena further up and down the hierarchy of production factors, and easier to build a fuller picture of society that accommodates not only economics but also politics. It becomes easier, for example, to talk about the role of institutions and the internet in contributing towards reductions in the cost of generating links. In terms of politics, informal networks within small groups can be seen as vying for the same economic role as their formal cousins, leading to the prediction that the recent vast increase in the ease of making formal contacts will undermine the cohesion of more informal groups.

4.6.2 Social network theory and development economics

In social network theory, the main question revolves around the role played by ties within groups in the operation of the economy. The focus is often on small villages or migrant communities.

One recent example relates to the role played by migrant communities in New York in terms of enforcing norms amongst their members when they become taxi drivers (Jackson and Schneider 2011). The basic hypothesis is that a person from a migrant community is punished by other community members if he is not sufficiently careful with the taxis he drives that are owned by members of that community. Jackson and Schneider (2011) indeed find that "social connections" within migrant communities act like an enforcement device for the social norm of being careful with the possessions of other community members. Similar examples from within the recent economics literature detail the role of migrant networks in the labor market (Frijters et al. 2005, Jarvis and Lee 2008, Pellizzari 2010); the role of social ties in lending within a group (Cassar, Crowley, and Wydick 2007, Banerjee, Duflo, Glennerster, and Kinnan 2010); and the importance of friendship networks in work environments (Mas and Moretti 2009).

These studies generally underscore the argument that group homogeneity is an important determinant of successful group coordination, because groups of more similar people can enforce social norms more stringently. Cassar et al. (2007) thus find that "social homogeneity" is an important determinant of whether participants in their experiments in Armenia and South Africa pay back loans to others in the community. Jarvis and Lee (2008), editing a collection of studies on historical migrant communities, find that a common way for merchants to ensure that they were not defrauded by the people who ran their ships or took out loans with them was to share the riskiest parts of their business with people from within their own groups. This general point was found to be valid for Portuguese Jews in Amsterdam in the seventeenth century, for Balkan merchants in the Ottoman port of Odessa, for immigrant communities in nineteenth-century Antwerp, and for many other migrant communities.

While somewhat related to the network theory discussed in this chapter, such findings are particularly redolent of the theory of groups presented in Chapter 3. Members of immigrant groups bound to ideals of reciprocity amongst members, when faced with the need to manage economic risk, would naturally lean on their existing group structure to do so. As a by-product, the group itself would thereby become more important to its members and hence enjoy greater cohesion.

Another aspect of this literature on social networks is the flexible, multi-faceted nature of groups and the connections between group members. Groups can function as banks, employers, religious communities, marriage markets, job search centers, child care centers, shops, and even police forces. The great variety of things that groups can do for their members has led to a proliferation of labels for different types of networks.

The networks discussed in this chapter would mainly be classified as trade networks in the social network theory literature, although as a general intermediate production factor, the concept of links also includes information networks and political networks. The main difference between my theory of networks and the existing social network theory literature is that the former explicitly relates networks to emotive groups. What others term "social networks," "social cohesion," and "migrant networks" are simply called "groups" in this book. The ties between members of emotive groups (mainly the reciprocal groups) will often coincide with what others call "social networks" or "informal networks," but in principle there need be nothing informal about those ties. What makes a tie formal or informal is a function of the relative position of a group within the larger set of groups in the society of which they are a part. Ties between members of a nation state, for example, can be entirely formalized: such ties are clearly observable via taxation, welfare, and other government programs. Ties within a family are usually informal, because they are only partially monitored by the nation state (though ties between members of a royal family could still be called "formal"). Hence, the phrase "informal networks" from the perspective of this book merely indicates the position of the subgroup within the wider set of groups present. Ties amongst members of a small group with a somewhat different loyalty to the dominant group would thus be called informal ties, but only because that small group is not dominant.

In my proposed theory, trade and information networks exist outside of emotive groups, but only because they are explicitly allowed by those groups to exist. It is by the grace of formal and informal institutions, themselves backed up by group loyalties, that interactions in open markets such as the internet, job centers, and other contact-making devices operate. While not immediately consisting of emotive social ties, the links between buyers and sellers on eBay are links that only materialize because of the underlying enforcement mechanisms of nation states.

Perhaps the biggest addition to social network theory in this chapter is the idea that networks start out as purely non-emotive, for-profit sets of contacts between members of different groups, but can rearrange themselves to gain political influence on the basis of mutual interests when the need arises. This idea is very prevalent in the early sociological literature. Elias (1939) explicitly discusses the rise of networks of merchants and capitalists in medieval Europe, including their transformation into political pressure groups that managed to get increased representation in parliaments and the like. More recent thinkers too have observed the same connection between trade and information networks and political power. Grewal (2008) explicitly talks about "network power," by which he means an as-yet unnamed power that is gradually emerging from the interactions of people across national borders. He argues that increases in international trade and in the exchange of information and political ideas will almost inevitably give rise to a new "in-group" of well-connected individuals who see themselves as the embryonic elite of a new world order.

I am personally skeptical about the ability of international networks to break the stranglehold of nation states. To me, modern international trade and information flows are permitted by the grace of nation states, and only because individual nations perceive themselves to benefit from them. Yet, the notion that link formation originally motivated by profit can gradually produce political entities is perfectly in line with my story. The transformation of trade networks into new large reciprocal groups was argued in Chapter 3 to have been a core element in the historical move from mercantilism to democracy in the period 1500–1848, as well as a key aspect of the American War of Independence.

4.6.3 *Social network analysis*

Rauch (2010) and Maoz (2011) review the field of social network analysis ("SNA") and "network theory," which has its origins in data on bilateral relations between large entities, such as countries or large firms. Scholars in this field assemble information on bilateral characteristics, such as trade flows, language similarities, characteristics of the legal system, the size of migrant communities, historical conflicts, the frequency of common hyperlinks, and ownership over sub-entities, and then translate this information into a network matrix illustrating the strength of each bilateral link present within a whole set of entities. Moreover, these entities (countries and firms) are themselves seen as networks of smaller units with particular patterns of concentration and information flow.

Though this literature is mainly statistical in nature, and mainly concerned with empirical questions about network concentration and the speed of diffusion of ideas and shocks within the network, there is an explicit appreciation by authors in this field that networks have a political component. For example, the main question in Maoz's analysis is the explanation of friendly or unfriendly relations between nations: war or peace is conceived as a function of network ties and characteristics of each bilateral relation.

Also, completely in line with what has been argued in this chapter, network analysts such as Wellman (1983) view political outcomes largely as the result of the characteristics of networks. Though Wellman (1983) is less strident than I in his wish to link the characteristics of economic networks to individual incentives and existing group loyalties, he and other network analysts also accept the central argument that there is an inevitability to the eventual political influence of trade and information networks.

Conceptualizing the world economy as a seething mass of interconnected networks that affect each other, in which the underlying entities are usually networks themselves, is a view fairly in accord with that presented in this book. The empirical orientation of this literature towards questions about what is going to happen next, through posing testable questions about which hypotheses are formulated, is also appealing.

The main critique to be made of SNA is that it does not itself entail causal story-lines about how the bilateral characteristics (trade, language, history, and so forth) came about. Statistical relations between the measured entities are explained using causal story-lines from social science disciplines, but SNA itself lacks an endogenous causal story of the formation or destruction of these constituent characteristics. As a result, while SNA is a useful tool for trying to measure visible networks, such as trade relations, its lack of stories of causation at the individual level and its requirement instead of strong abstractive capacity on the part of its intended audience (i.e., policy makers and economic practitioners) means that it must rely on an implicitly shared belief about individual causation stories via which to interpret its results. SNA should therefore not be seen as a full alternative theory of social networks, but rather as a statistical and analytical tool that in itself is neither in agreement nor in disagreement with the story of social life presented in this book.

4.7 Conclusions

This chapter considered the role of network formation and destruction in market economies, drawing particular attention to the politics of networks and the aspects of changing networks that are relevant to economic growth.

The theory of networks was shown to be useful in describing socio-economic realities as well as important political realities. One key element in this description was the alignment of the self-interest of dynamic contact makers with democratic procedures. Several specific causal relations were then suggested on this basis that would not be considered trivially true within mainstream economics. For example, the story in this chapter predicts that in an economy where the main economic activities require constant networking and where many individuals are involved in network formation, there will be strong support amongst the economic elite for something like democracy. However, in an economy where the main economic activities require no significant degree of contact formation (such as oil sales, extractive mining, or subsistence agriculture), the economic elite is much less likely to see democracy as in its interests, and more parasitic types of political arrangements are expected to emerge or to be maintained. This line of thought is not only useful in describing the links between economics and politics within current developing and developed countries. It is also predictive of the dynamics one should expect if, for example, networking activities become much more difficult due to government interference, or much less important due to the advent of technologies that negate the need for constant networking. It is thus a causal line of thought that can be used to think through the ultimate political consequences of new technologies and regulations.

PART III

Implications and examples

5 | *The aggregate view*

In this chapter, the separate views on love, groups, power, and networks presented in the previous chapters are brought together to paint a simplified picture of our socioeconomic system, using the existing mainstream economics view as a foundation. I have already begun to tackle this integrative endeavor at points in some previous chapters – for example, when the notion of group power was integrated into existing economic views of our political system, and when the interpretation of the role of trade networks was integrated into standard growth theory. This chapter takes the task of integration as its primary objective and builds on all of the prior work presented in the book.

The first part of this chapter begins by drawing out the interplay between the central notion of greed in mainstream economics, and the reality of group power that arises within the different group archetypes. Then, the entire socioeconomic system is re-interpreted as arising from an interplay between greed and love, treating trade networks and groups as the instruments and catalysts of these two forces.

The second part of the chapter sets up a new policy heuristic that extends the stylized policy heuristic offered by mainstream economics.

5.1 Markets, groups, and power

5.1.1 The symbiosis of the private sector, the public sector, and the nation state

The fact that a perfect market economy will create a positive outcome for the group, because of individual greed, explains why most modern economies feature a large private sector where organizations are allowed to operate for profit. In order to make organizations compete on low-cost production, a well-functioning, market-supporting bureaucracy actively closes down all other ways to compete, such as killing competitors, stealing their technologies, organizing all the sellers in a market in order to get a higher price (collusion), and so forth.

In modern economies operating within nation states, the private sector comprises 50–80 percent of the whole economy,[1] and it is the sector most associated with new products, trade, imports, and more generally with wealth creation. It is where the greatest individual fortunes are made. The other large sector in the economy, the state sector, is mainly concerned with spending the wealth created by the private sector. By this I do not mean that state spending is somehow taking away resources that would otherwise go into more wealth creation. Quite the opposite is often true. Not only does the state help to optimize resource allocation by closing down forms of competition between competitors other than price competition, but it actively helps create the inputs necessary for the private sector to operate.

Public education, for example, is a necessary ingredient in the skill development of the next generation. (In other ways, of course, education also perpetuates the ideals and cohesion of the large circle of reciprocity that is the nation state.) A state-financed army exists in part to protect the wealth of the country. The police, courts, and legal system, all funded by the state, exist in part to ensure that private parties can make agreements with each other (contracts) that are ultimately enforced by the state. However, the greatest degree of individual freedom to boss other people around is to be found in the private sector, precisely because within the large circle of reciprocity that is the nation state, private hierarchical companies are correctly seen as having the overall beneficial role of wealth creation.

The potential gains to be had in the private sector entice those individuals most motivated by greed to work within that sector and thus stay out of the state sector. This is an important factor in the relative stability of the nation state: the corrupting effect of greed at the top of the state's bureaucratic hierarchy is not as powerful, because the innately greediest individuals are not at the top of the state sector.

---

[1] See Ischinger (2008); also see p. 110 of Pierson (1996).

5.1.2 Tensions between inherent greed and circles of reciprocity, including the nation state

Although the private sector is where greed is least constrained, greed also operates inside every organization, including the nation state. Within large companies and within ministries, managers and workers continuously look to expand their spheres of influence. Within companies, departments try to expand the number of duties they have mainly because heads of departments want to be more powerful. Within ministries, people in a given unit will continuously think up good reasons why they should also control other areas and why more people should be hired into their unit. Labor unions naturally seek expansion in order for union bosses to have more individual prestige and in order for the group as a whole to be more powerful. Within each smaller group, such as a team, there is a more or less explicit undercurrent of constant jockeying for resources, higher-paid positions, and influence. This rat-race involves deliberate disinformation of others – the less others know, the harder it is for them to stop self-serving decisions – and involves constantly shifting coalitions of individuals looking for individual and group gain.

More generally, any large organization (and particularly, any large hierarchical organization) will, because of greed, gradually tend to take over all other smaller organizations. It is only the fact that these other organizations are trying to do the same that leads to an equilibrium of forces. So, what prevents the single most powerful organization, which is the bureaucracy of the nation state, from taking over all other organizations? What prevents modern countries from becoming dictatorships? To answer this question we need to consider some of the main natural sources of tension between the private sector and the state.

5.1.3 The private sector versus state ideals

The relationship between the private sector and the nation state is naturally strained, because it goes against the ideals of a large circle of reciprocity to allow some individuals within that circle to have disproportionate personal power and wealth. In addition, the state sector houses the military might of the whole group and is more directly invested with the power of the whole group. The key reason that the state sector does not crush the private sector through regulations or by outright seizure of private organizations is that the private sector is believed to be the wealth creator within the nation state. The private sector is in fact protected by the overall wish of the entire population to be part of a wealthy nation state. This wish is of course partially a function of greed: the wish of people to belong to a successful country. The notion that the private sector "safeguards" economic growth has been explicitly understood and accepted by the rulers of most countries in centuries gone by, and it is almost universally accepted in circles of power today. Most people living in modern countries also adhere to this notion, supporting the claim that it is the perceived self-interest of the members of the nation state that allows the private sector to exist.

Another natural strain between the private sector and the nation state arises when we consider the natural ideology of private-sector entrepreneurs, compared to that of the nation state, in regard to the weakest members of society. The private sector, unsurprisingly, almost invariably advocates work and talent as the reasons for success. Hence, successful people in the private sector will not naturally see everyone in the nation state as innately equal. The private sector will in fact be the source of the harshest proposals as to how to deal with society's poor. Conversely, the bureaucracy of the nation state will be the strongest carrier of the ideals of the nation state, and will therefore be naturally protective of the poor in society. Related to this, the private sector will naturally see taxes as a form of parasitism that is to be reduced.

5.1.4 The private sector and political power

A subtle interrelation between the nation state and the private sector emerges if we consider support for representative democracy. The first parliaments and other forms of representative democracy in Europe resulted from the actions of a group of rich and greedy men, who – as a result of their mutual distrust – pushed the initial elites of Europe into accepting these new power-balancing institutions. This dynamic persists today. As a group of rich individuals, private entrepreneurs and managers of large private organizations still naturally distrust each other, and will therefore generally support systems of rotating power sharing in order to prevent any amongst them from enslaving the others. Hence the private sector is naturally in favor of democracy, although it is not necessarily in favor of sharing the right to vote with everyone in a country: the early ideals of equality that entered political debates in the eighteenth century were exclusively applied to well-to-do men. Neither women nor the poor – neither of whom were contenders for power in the eighteenth century – were allowed to vote in the new parliaments until more than a hundred years later, when the mass patriotism exhibited during World War I bound the European elites to enshrine into law the legal equality of everyone within a country.[2]

Given the private sector's natural support for power sharing, an important question arises: can a king or existing land-based nobility somehow keep the private sector out of political power, and therefore unable to further its power-sharing objective? The main reason that this was and is a practical impossibility is that the merchants, industrialists, and service providers who form the backbone of the private sector are all networkers. They continuously search for new clients and new suppliers, and that search is a pivotal ingredient in their success. To enable this continuous search, private-sector workers participate in large and shifting networks of information and trade. As soon as people form lines of communication about their joint economic interests, they will naturally use these lines to share information about other joint interests when the need arises. These networks are therefore highly efficient potential means of organizing armies, supplies, media activities, and other political activities. Hence, an automatic potential for political power arises from the networking activities of the modern private sector, which those in power cannot effectively quarantine. The gradual increase in trade and networks that occurred throughout Europe starting in the early Middle Ages is, in this sense, the proximate cause for the changes thereafter in European political organization. This gradual increase in networking itself is one reflection of the trend towards greater specialization, which itself requires networks and also engenders more networks.

Not all private economic activities require the same flexibility in their associated networks. While bankers, doctors, and teachers will almost inevitably continuously interact with new lenders, borrowers, patients, and students, the same is not necessarily true of mining and agriculture, to pick two important private-sector industries. It is quite possible for representatives of a mining company to interact with only a

---

[2] For a discussion of this dynamic in the case of the UK, see Pugh (1978).

few suppliers and clients, particularly if the clients are overseas. Similarly, local farmers can in principle spend their whole lives working on their fields while being supplied by and supplying to only one single organization, such as a large landholder. Containing the networks of mining and agriculture is hence far easier, making mining and agriculture more natural "prey" for hierarchical political organizations that want to extract surplus from these economic activities without facing significant pressure towards the creation of power-sharing institutions. Unsurprisingly, therefore, economies based mainly on large-scale agriculture and mining-for-export in principle allow for far more hierarchical and parasitic political systems than economies based on private-sector activities requiring more fluid networking. Many of the most corrupt political regimes observable in 2012 were found in predominantly agricultural societies (such as Pakistan) and in mining and other resource-extraction economies (such as Nigeria, which has oil, or Congo, which has diamonds and other minerals).[3] Indeed, the recent war in resource-rich Congo was partially the result of the private armies of the surrounding countries fighting over who would be paid off by the foreign mining companies.

5.1.5 The balance of power between personal greed and the nation state

The bureaucracy of the nation state, the private sector, democracy, greed, and economic wealth creation are a very unusual set of bedfellows. It is the greed of competing large circles of reciprocity (competing

---

[3] Pp. 628–629 of Caselli and Cunningham (2009) cites the widespread poverty in resource-rich African nations to support the hypothesis that resource richness per se is a curse (see also Collier 2007); empirical work documents the association of resource richness with poverty (Hussain, Chaudhry, and Malik 2009). My explanation for the association of resource abundance with poverty is roughly in line with the view made popular by economists that resource abundance is bad for growth because it discourages the development of industry (see p. 494 of Matsen and Torvik 2005 for a succinct review of this position). The key difference between this common "Dutch disease" explanation and mine is that in my story a primary role is played by the networks and political tendencies, rather than the learning-by-doing, arising naturally within the industrial sector. If it were only about learning-by-doing or some other form of human capital, then each individual firm could be contained and isolated. It is the networking that makes or breaks the possibility of containment.

nation states) that protects the private sector from being regulated out of existence. It is that same private sector, also mainly driven by greed, that is the main natural protector of the ideal of democracy within the nation state and the main advocate of those roles of the state bureaucracy that are instrumental in creating greater future wealth (such as education, internal stability, and so forth). If one of these bedfellows were taken out of the equation, then the balance between the private sector and the state bureaucracy would fall apart. If, for instance, all nation states were to unite into one single nation state, then the motivation to keep amassing more wealth in order to be wealthier than other countries would fall away. That in turn would remove a powerful source of protection for the private sector. What would result is a gradual shift within the state sector towards expanding its sphere of influence (because of its own greed) until the private sector is effectively neutered by being completely brought under the control of the state. The lack of a functioning private sector would then take away the motivation to support democracy.

5.2 The main game: Love and greed

The "main game" of social life is a perennial struggle between love and greed, whereby our greed leads us forever to seek power and other advantages within every social organization of which we are a member, but where ties of love are forever formed as a result of the existence and application of power. Whatever actions are taken by someone with a greedy motive, they are nearly always labeled for public consumption in terms of the particular ideals of reciprocal groups, precisely in order not to raise the ire of the true believers. Hence, even purely profit-motivated salesmen will nevertheless speak of "your interests" and their "corporate responsibility" as a sign of their ultimate subservience to the implicit group (the society as a whole, or at least one portion of it).

Within the modern economy, there are various perennial competitions between greed and love. Greed causes us to try to find loopholes in any tax code. The representatives of the ideals of the whole group will perennially try to close down these loopholes. The fact that these "tax regulators" often will get personal benefits from closing down tax loopholes because of the internal organization of tax institutions does not diminish the overall assessment that they are, in a way, working against greed. Indeed, free competition between individuals motivated by greed in a sense enables a kind of triumph of love over greed, in that (as explained earlier) it can give rise to group benefits that none of the greedy individuals themselves were aiming for. Free competition catalyzes the triumph of love because it is love that underpins the benevolent regulation needed to constrain the competing greedy individuals and their hierarchical vehicles (i.e., private-sector firms).

What goes for the whole economy also goes within households, within firms, and within the international arena. Within the household, self-interest and the interests of the whole household lock horns continuously: the question of whether household members will actively subjugate themselves towards the common interest underpins a great many domestic tensions. The various subunits within a firm are partially kept together by group identities, and there is a near-automatic emergence of the concept of "the welfare of the members of the firm," where these subgroup identities and overall ideals are often in competition with the naked self-interest of the subunits and individual people within the firm. In the international arena, new ideals emerge all the time as individuals and groups strive towards common goals, such as "preservation of the world environment," "world peace," "tax harmonization," "free trade," and so on. Such international ideals perennially come up against the individual self-interest of countries, companies, or even lobby groups themselves that promote these goals.

The only institutions and organizations that survive in the long run are those that, to an adequate degree, serve the economic interests of the subgroups supporting them. Institutions and organizations that do not deliver in this sense are simply susceptible to internal breakup or to being taken over by other, more successful groups. Yet it is not the case that institutions or organizations must be in the material interest of each individual they contain: in some cases, the group cohesion that benefits the whole group may well be diametrically opposed to individual self-interest (as in the case of perfect competition, where the individual competitor perennially wishes the constraints imposed would apply only to others and not to him). It is in that regard that love, as the glue that upholds the ideals of the group, works against individual greed but towards the group's interest.

5.2.1 Illustration in international trade

A good example of the tension between love and greed can be seen in the politics of international trade. In general, having low trade barriers (such as tariffs, quotas, trade taxes, and so forth) allows for greater specialization across borders and is therefore overall wealth-increasing for both sides. Yet, within each country, producers of anything specific have an incentive to argue against allowing overseas competitors into their markets because they can demand higher prices when there is less competition. Thus, invariably, specific industries and unions will lobby for trade protection in the media and amongst politicians. The amorphous mass of consumers and other producers who would stand to gain from fewer trade barriers is not so well-organized, and is also often quite ignorant of their own best interests.

Who argues the case of consumers? Their case is argued by economists and high-level advisors and civil servants within the bureaucracy of the nation state who see themselves, and are seen, as "the custodians" of the economic welfare of their country. The members of this group all point to the benefit to the group as a whole of having lower trade barriers. Arguing against the interests of the few and for the interests of the group is precisely what much of the work of Adam Smith was about at the end of the eighteenth century.[4]

In the world recession of 2009, the concerted bureaucratic and political elites of the world agreed not to increase trade barriers significantly and to effectively sabotage the efforts of individual industries to maintain or push through more trade barriers. The overall lack of major trade barriers, both within and between countries, that has resulted is a clear "victory" of the general interest (love) over the private interest of the few (greed). It has been carried not by popular opinion, which is almost invariably susceptible to the idea that trade barriers are somehow in "our" favor, but by the shared beliefs amongst those

---

[4] As stated by Wood (1984) (p. 221), "[Smith] argued in the *Moral Sentiments* that, in general, the interest of the group was to be preferred to that of the individual"; as subsequently quoted from *The Wealth of Nations*, Smith (1776) (p. 193) further argued that "those exertions of the natural liberty of a few individuals, which might endanger the security of the whole society, are, and ought to be, restrained by the laws of all governments; of the most free, as well as the most despotical." Contrary to his modern-day reputation, Adam Smith's writings argue that individual greed is not the only phenomenon required in order to attain the social good; see Muller (1995) (p. 2 and ensuing).

in control as to what would benefit the group as a whole. It is the loss of face within that group that prevents opportunistic politicians, economists, and civil servants from successfully representing industry interests.

5.2.2 Illustration in leadership

A corollary of the fact that greed has been gradually institutionally contained by love is that there is not really anyone in charge in this world. Power is exceptionally diffuse, being shared by the members of whole groups rather than residing in the hands of a few. Even presidents of powerful countries are far less powerful than they seem.

Consider the supposed power of the President of the United States. For one, the information that the president hears is heavily filtered by several layers of bureaucrats. This is for good reason: there are millions of decisions taken every day within the bureaucracy of the US, ranging from the color of the toilet paper in schools, to the appointment of directors of local forest departments, to what type of airplane to buy for this or that military campaign. No single individual can possibly be on top of all of those decisions, and hence there is a filtering system that determines what information the president has access to. Second, the president is surrounded by thousands of staff members, each with independent wishes and agendas, of most of which the president will be entirely ignorant. No single individual has thousands of friends, and hence the vast majority of presidential appointees are in fact selected by other people. A president is furthermore constrained by his oath to the welfare of the whole country, and more generally by the fact that his power is merely borrowed from the whole nation and is conditional on his appearing to do the right thing. If a president is not seen to behave "normally," then there are all kinds of procedures in place for the people around him to make him politically impotent.

The president must therefore keep convincing those around him that he is sane and is still working towards the goals recognized as valid by those around him. Moreover, there is almost nothing a president gets to truly decide without the active support of many around him: without the support of the United States Congress, very little legislation can be decided upon by the president alone; without active support from his staff, the legislation would not be written in the way he intended, nor would it reach the right ears first. Finally, what are seen to be "executive decisions" are not in fact unrefusable directives at all: legislation is frequently sabotaged by those supposed to implement it, or is simply ignored, misunderstood, or misplaced. It takes the active and willing cooperation of many others to interpret, explain, and enforce any regulation.

What goes for the US President goes for any supposed leader of any large circle of reciprocity: the leader's powers are conditional on the goodwill of many others, and are therefore heavily contained. This means that grand changes to nation states or the world as a whole require mobilizing the support of millions of individuals. In this sense, the individual psychology of this or that leader has become virtually irrelevant in determining outcomes.[5] Rather, it really only makes sense in the modern world to talk about the interests of whole groups, where greed and love are organizing strategies channeling the urges, fears, and hopes of these groups.

5.2.3 Which is stronger, love or greed?

Love and greed both heavily color many of our actions, and there is no easy way to determine which one is stronger. If I had to choose, I would say that in the short run love is the most powerful, in that most socially relevant short-term decisions are labeled as idealistic and any clear group-related choice between greed and love would be won by love. There are not many who lay down their lives for their greed, but quite a few who die for love.

However, in the medium run, greed always wins. Anything that does not strongly take greed into account or tries to co-opt greed will eventually be overtaken by it, because the very greedy will exploit it, and those who are merely a bit greedy will nevertheless follow in order not to be left behind. Hence any welfare policy will eventually become dominated by self-interest; any tax loophole will get massively exploited; any set of "peaceful farmers" will get raped and pillaged if the greedy can reasonably get away with doing so; any gullible person will eventually get ripped off by those searching for him; any great human need will find someone pretending to satisfy it; and so forth. Any obvious route to material gain will eventually get adopted by everyone, and

---

[5] This is not as clearly the case in hierarchies that continue to survive today, such as those in Zimbabwe or North Korea.

anything (such as socialism) that solely relies on love will not survive for long.

Yet, judging from historical trajectories, in the long run it appears that love is winning out, at least at the level of nations. The general thrust of history has been towards institutions in which greed is recognized, but more and more contained by and subjugated to the ideals of the whole group. Even power that is initially brought to bear for the sole purpose of domination and personal gain will, over time, attract loyalty. Even greedy, powerful individuals will eventually adopt ideals in a sense that "undoes them," in that they become bound by the ideals that they are relying upon for their further power. Thus the ruthless set of warlords who took over England in the eleventh century eventually adopted the ideals of being kings "for the benefit of the English" in order to have even more power, which in turn ultimately enslaved future kings to be somewhat beholden to these ideals.

In my view, the grand story of history is therefore that love dominates our short-term decisions, that greed wins in the medium run and had a period of dominating the post-hunter-gatherer world, and that greed has been increasingly co-opted by love over the past five hundred to a thousand years and, perhaps only temporarily, has been subjugated by love in the modern developed world.

Yet, love is clearly not on a universal victory march. An important part of the makeup of the nation state (in particular, the independent private sector, and even democracy itself) is dependent upon material competition with other entities, which occurs because of greed. It is not clear that greed would not once again dominate our social institutions if that competition were to come to an end.

Love is not that different from greed in terms of its ultimate source. Although their behavioral implications and the internal emotional experiences that they engender are quite different, both are attempts – one by our conscious mind, and the other by our unconscious mind – to satisfy our basic needs. Hence, if one had to select a single motivator for human behavior, I would still advocate that greed be selected. Assuming that people only pursue their own direct material interests in any situation, one would often make poor behavioral predictions in the short run, and one would have no idea about how to operate within any existing group, but one's behavioral predictions would be more right than wrong in the medium term. It is only if one wishes to understand why people say what they say, and which short-run constraints on behavior are also long-run constraints, that one must understand love as a distinct human strategy.

5.3 A heuristic for reading dynamic social situations

The story in this book would not be complete without a recipe for how to apply it to uncover the truth in situations not specifically addressed thus far. In this section, I walk through that recipe. First, I explain a heuristic grounded in the book's story for analyzing a multifaceted, dynamic social issue, and then I revisit the stylized problems presented in the Introduction to show what additional insights we gain from applying this heuristic.

The heuristic requires thinking through the answers to the following four questions, in the context of the issue one wishes to illuminate: (1) "where have I seen this problem before?"; (2) "who benefits from what?"; (3) "which big groups are involved?," and (4) "who faces which powers?" The first two of these steps are standard elements in mainstream economic analyses of a problem. The latter two incorporate an awareness of the importance of love.

- *Where have I seen this problem before?* This is an exercise in broad pattern recognition, and brings context to a problem. It involves comparing the problem with a large database of scenarios from history and from imagination, and selecting the instances that most resemble the current one.[6] Drawing analogies illuminates what happened in similar situations in human history, what humans are capable of in such situations, and what the main elements of the current problem are likely to be. This process involves an iterative interaction between the mental model built up by such analogies and the application of steps (2) through (4) in the heuristic: the model built up determines the boundaries of the problem and thus points out the groups and incentives to analyze. This first step is therefore a continuous activity that goes on in the background throughout the application of the heuristic to a situation.

---

[6] A brand of this technique was a significant element in the toolkit of Arthur Conan Doyle's Sherlock Holmes character. Quoting directly from *A Study in Scarlet* (Conan Doyle 1887) (p. 25): "There is a strong family resemblance about misdeeds, and if you have all the details of a thousand at your finger ends, it is odd if you can't unravel the thousand and first."

- *Who benefits from what ("qui bono")?* This is the core question of standard economics, and its answer tells you who has the material incentive to do what: who will support what outcome, who is a likely source of disinformation, and what various players would do – based on their (greedy) material motives – if a situation were to change. It is thus both a question and a useful guide for the outline of any solution. A solution that aligns individuals' personal material incentives with desired group outcomes is nearly always the ideal to strive for, for any solution that runs significantly against people's material interests and hence requires sustained idealistic fervor is almost bound to fail.
- *Which big groups are involved?* This is a question of both power and loyalty at the aggregate level, and its answer illuminates the main forces involved in any situation, telling you first of all which group's material benefits are really at stake. An analysis of the relative power of the groups involved will illuminate which groups are in charge of the given situation. The answer to this question also plays an important role in identifying possible solutions, because almost any solution will rely to some degree on people's loyalties to their groups. A common mistake is to look at a situation only from the point of view of one of the groups involved.
- *Who faces which powers?* The answer to this question tells you about ideals, and therefore about the frames and language in which any situation is understood by different players. If you find that a particular person acknowledges no power other than his own, then any possible solution cannot rely on that person worshipping anything but himself. If you deduce that members of a group submit only to the internal ideals of that group, then you will know it makes no sense to appeal to other groups' ideals in order to change their behavior. Thinking about this question helps develop a solution consistent with the rule of thumb that individuals naturally worship the main power they acknowledge in their world, and that that power is the source of their ideals and language. In short, addressing this question illuminates the makeup and cohesion of both actual and potential groups.

To illustrate the usefulness of the heuristic comprised of these four questions, I now revisit the examples in the Introduction, demonstrating how our understanding improves with the application of this heuristic in place of the standard economics approach by itself. I will take the standard economics approach to mean the application of the first two questions in the heuristic; the benefit offered by this book is mainly embodied in the addition of the last two questions.

5.3.1 International trade

Should policy makers hinder international trade or assist it? To focus this question, let us take a topical example of a policy issue directly in this area: the case of banana quotas for Australia.

Australia produces bananas on its east coast. This industry is made up of over 2,000 small businesses (growers), and generates a usual annual total revenue in excess of 200 million Australian dollars. In the decade 2000–2010, this industry successfully lobbied the Australian government to ban the import of foreign bananas, including bananas from the Philippines and the United States. This ban greatly increased the retail price of bananas faced by Australian consumers and also increased the profits of the Australian banana industry. This ban has been the cause of a long-running investigation by the World Trade Organization, which was asked to assess the ban's legitimacy.

The first question we now ask, following the heuristic proposed above, is "Where have I seen this problem before?" The answer is that the imposition of banana import restrictions is a textbook example of a supply restriction. From standard economic history and theory, obeying the request of the domestic industry will bring about a reduction in the supply of foreign bananas, which in turn will increase the price domestic firms can fetch. The economic importance of the supply restriction depends on the ability of the remaining (domestic) suppliers to increase supply in response to the higher price. The less Australian land is suitable for growing bananas, and the longer it takes for domestic supply to expand in response to the higher prices (for instance, due to the time it takes for banana plants to grow), the higher the monopoly rents that accrue to present domestic producers from hindering foreign imports.

The second question is "Who benefits?" The beneficiaries in this case are the domestic banana growers. The losers include both Australian consumers and foreign banana growers. The ban creates a net loss to Australian welfare as a whole, because there are profitable gains from trade between Australian consumers and foreign banana growers that are not realized when the ban is in place. It is thus no wonder that economists in Australia are by and large opposed to the banana import ban (Gallagher 2011).

The third question in the heuristic, and the first point at which we depart from what is deemed relevant in standard economic analysis, is "Which groups are involved?" The banana growers, the state bureaucracy, the foreign banana growers, and the Australian consumers are the four major groups involved. Each has quite predictable material goals and associated opinions on this issue. It will also be clear that the group of banana growers was the first mover in this policy issue, as it is that group in the first instance that actively and successfully lobbied the Australian government for protection. The most powerful player involved here is the Australian government and its bureaucracy. Both the domestic growers and the foreign growers face that power directly. The domestic banana growers face the power of the Australian government quite plainly: it is that government that decides whether or not to grant it protection. This means that the government is the group that is lobbied.

The fourth and final question is "Who faces which powers?" The individual banana growers only to a limited degree face the power of other banana growers as they are mainly competitors and geographically spread out. It is only in relation to protection that they face the power of their whole group and it is thus to that degree that their group is cohesive. On the other side, the bureaucrats involved in the protection face the power of the whole government machinery, meaning that they will insist upon the language and ideals of that bureaucracy. The politicians face the power of the voters and, only indirectly, the influence of the banana growers via that lobby's ability to sway public opinion. As such it is towards the consumers (voters) that the eventual decisions need to be explained, and it is a political judgment as to whether or not there are more votes to be lost being seen to go against the banana growers and thus forgo their support in election campaigns than there are to be gained by keeping prices lower and adhering to open competition. Yet, because the government is the group that is lobbied, it is the government's ideals that shape the language that the request for protection takes – in this case, the approach of the domestic lobbyists is to appeal to what is beneficial for Australia as a whole.

How can the banana industry argue that its protection benefits everyone rather than just themselves? In this case, it did so by appealing to the notion that the sensitivity (or purity) of the Australian ecosystem necessitates quarantine. The industry focused on the threat that foreign bananas pose to the domestic ecosystem and local banana production, in the form of banana plant diseases. The language of a potential "bio-threat" was adopted and propagated further by the Australian government bureaucracy. In 2009, a special unit within the government bureaucracy in Canberra, called Biosecurity Australia, released an "Import Risk Analysis" of allowing foreign bananas onto the Australian market. This report took almost five years to complete, and the bottom line of the report was that Filipino growers would have to adopt very expensive new methods in order to make absolutely certain that foreign bananas would not bring any diseases into Australia before they would be allowed into the market. The long delay in writing the report, and the insistence on absolute certainty, have been highly effective in keeping foreign bananas out of Australia during the first decade of the 2000s. In 2011, a "bio-threat" was still the official reason for maintaining the banana import ban, which was associated that year with a domestic banana price that soared well above 400 percent of the international price.

What are the objective merits of the bio-threat argument? Its objective merits are in fact highly dubious. Bananas are grown both in gardens and in the wild in Australia, as well as on commercial plantations, and the feared banana diseases mentioned in the government's report are well and truly present in Australia already. As a result, the transportation of bananas within Australia *already* risks spreading these diseases to "unspoiled" areas, which means that it is absurd to ask that foreign bananas to be 100 percent safe when domestic bananas transported around Australia are already not 100 percent safe. This also implies that a direct import of foreign bananas into parts of Australia where almost no bananas are grown domestically, such as Western Australia or Victoria, would pose no greater threat than the shipment to those areas of Australian-grown bananas, which may well already carry diseases. Yet such region-specific importing is not allowed, even though it would involve a lower total amount of transportation of, and hence risk from the spread of, bananas with potential diseases.

Additionally, even if it were the case that banana imports would result in more Australian banana plants eventually suffering from diseases specific to banana plants, this would only mean that Australia would then be on a par with banana growers elsewhere who have battled these diseases for a long time. Fear of this scenario amounts to a lack of belief in the power of technology to fight such diseases successfully, despite the clear evidence provided by robust banana sales worldwide that we are successfully coping with these diseases. Finally, of course, from standard economics one can argue that Australia has no comparative advantage in banana production, and that from an efficiency perspective it should therefore not have a banana industry in the first place, making it irrelevant whether or not banana diseases are imported.

In summary, what can we learn about this international trade example from applying the four-part heuristic? From standard economics, we would arrive at the conclusion that import hindrance in the case of bananas in Australia is the result of a well-organized small lobby that serves its own interests at the expense of the consumer and foreign competitors. With the additional insights offered by the story in this book, we can make better sense of how this political game is played. In order not to be rejected out of hand, the banana lobby must phrase its request for protection to the Australian government in terms of the well-being of the whole of Australia, for which the "bio-threat" argument fits the bill. Even if the bio-threat notion is but a meager fig-leaf that crumbles on closer objective inspection, it is an essential one in order that the protection request not be seen to run against the interests of the general Australian population. This makes perfect sense in light of the story in this book, whereby smaller groups that need something from the overarching circle of reciprocity that is the nation state must appeal to that circle's ideals. Any other example of requests to hinder foreign trade in a modern Western country will feature some other "reason" that appeals to some benefit to the country as a whole, rather than just the interests of a small group.

Using the four-part heuristic, I come to almost exactly the same final opinion regarding international trade as does standard economics, merely adding additional insights about the particulars of why and how the political lobbying takes place.

5.3.2 Competition regulation

Should monopoly formation be frustrated? To examine this question, let us again take a specific example: the case of the merger of two US companies, General Electric and Honeywell. This case came before the

European Commissioner for Competition, who at the time was the economist Mario Monti, in 2001.

General Electric and Honeywell were both active in the market for aircraft components, including engines and electronic systems. Their proposed merger was approved by the US competition authorities, but refused by the European authorities, whose press release on the issue began with the following statement:[7]

> The merger between GE and Honeywell, as it was notified, would have severely reduced competition in the aerospace industry and resulted ultimately in higher prices for customers, particularly airlines. However, there were ways of eliminating these concerns and allowing the merger to proceed. I regret that the companies were not able to agree on a solution that would have met the Commission's competition concerns ... The combination of the two companies' activities would have resulted in the creation of dominant positions in the markets for the supply of avionics, non-avionics and corporate jet engines, as well as to the strengthening of GE's existing dominant positions in jet engines for large commercial and large regional jets.

Applying the first two questions in the four-part heuristic, one would surmise that the merger is desired by the firms due to a combination of returns-to-scale (implying potential cost reduction from upscaling operations) and the potential for increased market power, which should both result in higher profits for the firms. Not only would the companies involved benefit from the merger, but so would the country in which their operations are located, as long as most of their production feeds the export market. The losers from the merger would be some of the industry's workers who lose their jobs as part of the cost savings brought about by upscaling, as well as domestic and foreign consumers who would face higher prices. The groups involved are the companies in question, the government bureaucracies of the EU and the US, and consumers. Finally, the powers faced by the first-moving groups, GE and Honeywell, are mainly those embodied in the state bureaucracies. At the individual level, the employees of the companies face the power of their organizations, while the regulators face the power of the rest of the European Commission as well as of the outside monitoring groups.

[7] http://europa.eu/rapid/press-release_IP-01-939_en.htm

Whether or not this particular merger really would have led to monopoly rents is an open question. GE and Honeywell argued in their submissions to the Competition Commission that their merger would stimulate innovation (a "good" thing from the point of view of the welfare-promotion ideals of the EU), while the European Commissioner argued that it would lead to higher prices for existing products (a "bad" thing from that point of view). Many nuances in economic theory were used to defend both positions. For example, since the aviation industry is already highly concentrated, with only a few large airplane manufacturers that buy aviation engines (primarily Boeing and Airbus), it is unclear whether or not the more efficient solution is to have many, instead of few, suppliers of engines and electronic systems. Because there are only a few "downstream" clients, the incentives for innovation could actually be higher if there were also only a few "upstream" suppliers of parts, who would be motivated by the potential to gain a slice of the overall profits of the whole aviation industry. While the European Commissioner recognized the potential validity of such arguments, he argued that the main effect of the merger would be on market concentration rather than in the form of a shift in optimal investment incentives.

I am no expert on the aviation industry, and therefore I cannot credibly say who was right and who was wrong in this case. The point is instead that, as with trade restrictions, the way the actual political struggle played out – in this case and in others – only makes sense in light of a wider understanding of groups and power than is provided by mainstream economics. Specifically, the power and ideals of the nation-state bureaucracy dictated the way in which the companies involved stated their case. Whatever the true merits of their case, the arguments they brought were couched in terms of how their intended actions would benefit the welfare of the countries from which they sought permission.

An understanding of power and ideals is also needed to comprehend why the scenario of companies vying for the permission of a commission arose at all. The existence of competition authorities in the first place derived from the ideals of nation states in regard to furthering the well-being of their citizens, while the power of those authorities derives from the fact that they are seen to represent the interests of larger groups – namely, the European nation states. Economic thought also frequently plays a role in helping the representatives of the group as a whole (the EU, in the case of GE and Honeywell) to recognize the trade-offs operating in any particular case.

The ideals held by the group of economists also to some extent act like a control on the power of the independent regulator in question. The independent commissioners deciding on such competition cases are often economists themselves, with friends and colleagues in the profession, and they will often return to academic positions after they have been regulators (Coen and Thatcher 2005), giving them an incentive to abide by the ideals of economics. The very fact that I am discussing this case right here in this book is itself a form of *ex post* monitoring, which involves at least some implicit comment on whether or not the commissioner did the right thing. It is precisely that implicit "monitoring-group" activity, which in part defines their profession, that makes economists candidates for such positions of power in the first place.

The view at which this book arrives regarding competition regulation is thus very close to the standard mainstream view in terms of the merits of any individual case. What is added is an understanding of who the regulators actually are and why they are there, what keeps them honest, where their power comes from, and what language affected parties will use in their appeals to regulators.

5.3.3 Environmental regulation

How can one prevent the pollution of the public space? For this question, let us examine the examples of waste from nuclear power plants and the littering of public city gardens.

Nuclear power plants produce highly toxic waste that remains dangerous to human health for thousands of years. In principle, a private operator has little incentive to care about the effects of his plant's waste (which is very costly to dispose of properly) on human health thousands of years in the future. In a similar way, the littering of public city gardens with plastics and other garbage spreads diseases and is aesthetically displeasing, but is somewhat more convenient for the littering individual than holding on to his garbage until he finds a bin in which to deposit it. In both cases, the person or institution polluting the public space creates a negative externality on others.

The application of the first two questions in the heuristic gives a clear pattern as to who benefits from what: the litterer or polluter benefits in the short run, while it is users of air, water, and land in a given country, and even their far-distant offspring in the case of nuclear waste, who benefit from limiting public littering and the hazardous disposal of nuclear waste. In both cases, the polluting entity does not suffer the full consequences of his pollution, and therefore has an incentive to over-pollute compared to what is socially optimal.

Another important pattern to recognize is that the number of potential polluters in the case of nuclear waste is small, which makes it far easier to control them directly, while by contrast the number of potential polluters of city gardens is huge, which makes them far harder to monitor. It is therefore far easier to set up counterbalancing material incentives for nuclear power plant operators to dispose of their waste in a more socially optimal fashion than it is to offer optimal monetary incentives to all potential litterers. It would simply cost a government too much to monitor all the potential littering activities in public gardens. Monitoring the few nuclear power plants, however, is doable.

From the normal economic arguments associated with problems that feature these patterns, one would conclude that an externality is present in each case that should ideally be internalized by proper cost-pricing. In the case of nuclear waste, this can be done directly for each of the relatively small number of power providers, and indeed is done throughout the world via governments' implementation of tight control over nuclear waste disposal. In the case of public littering, the optimal way to motivate a greedy person would be to have some form of decentralized monitoring coupled with very high fines for littering, such that the expected individual cost of littering reaches the social cost without the need for the government to monitor everyone directly.

The final two questions in the four-part heuristic are required to understand most immediately what form the decentralized monitoring of littering takes, and more fundamentally, why state governments would even care about the health of citizens thousands of years from now.

From a standard economic point of view, in which one discounts the future at some positive rate, what happens thousands of years from now is completely unimportant and irrelevant to anything happening today. It is the imagined continuity of groups down the ages, solidified in social norms of how the current generation should care for the environment and "leave something for future generations," that forms the impetus for group action against nuclear hazards that might eventuate thousands of years from now. Again, the power of the nation state, focused in particular ministries (e.g., the Ministry for the Environment), is borrowed from the large circle of reciprocity making up the nation state under the legitimizing ideal that the ministry is looking out for "us." That "us" in thousands of years' time consists of people whom neither we nor our great-great-grandchildren will ever meet, but that reality is unimportant: what matters is that the power of the nation state is seen by its citizens to derive from their collective strength, which in most Western states is in turn seen to include current citizens and their progeny down through the generations – implicitly also members of the nation state.

Social norms carried by reciprocal groups also come into play in crafting the system of decentralized monitoring needed to limit the littering of city gardens. If potential litterers feel themselves to be part of the group as a whole, then successful appeals can be made to their sense of pride in the public space and to their notion that littering is "not done by people in my group." Importantly, if potential litterers feel that they do not belong to the group as a whole, or at least to the group associated with the public gardens, then a direct appeal to them would be less fruitful. In this case, one can still make appeals to the general public to monitor potential deviants. The generic solutions to the public-littering problem implemented by Western governments throughout the world are indeed to enforce anti-littering social norms, such as by sponsoring initiatives such as Clean-Up Days, and to set high fines for littering.

This book therefore again arrives at a very similar basic position as that of mainstream economists when it comes to how to deal with environmental externalities. Yet, by adding an understanding of groups, we can rationalize why governments are involved in activities whose consequences span thousands of years, and why simple appeals not to foul the public space can be successfully made to citizens. The limits of this type of idealistic appeal, however, are also clearer. One can engender the social norm that littering is bad amongst a community that has a common group identity because the individual costs of not littering are small, and thus are easily borne without too much complaint. Yet appealing to nuclear power plants to just "do the right thing" would be folly, because the costs of proper waste disposal in that case run into millions of dollars.

5.3.4 Voting behavior

An objective economic analysis yields the conclusion that the personal material costs of voting are positive, while the personal material benefits are minuscule. Why then do people bother to vote in elections?

From within mainstream economics, many answers have been offered, but they are uniformly incomplete. If one adopts the line of Faravelli and Walsh (2011) that people vote because they have a "warm glow" of voting for something that they believe in, then the question naturally arises: where else in the economic system should one expect such a "warm glow" to exist and to make a difference to behavior? One could adopt the line of Posner (2002) that even purely greedy people can vote because there is a benefit from being mistaken for an altruist by members of their neighborhood who observe whether or not they have voted. Then, questions arise about the origin of that group of altruists of which one wants to be mistaken as a member, and about what other behaviors are engendered by the desire to be perceived as a member of that group (and, more generally, by the perception of being observed by neighbors). There are many other particular theories proposed by other authors (see the literature cited in Faravelli and Walsh 2011) but they all rely either on some quite spectacular form of self-delusion or on some ad hoc notion related to altruism and groups.

By now the answers to the first two questions in the heuristic should be clear, and they leave us where we began: still unable to rationalize why voters vote. Applying the third and fourth questions in the heuristic, however, an answer to the question emerges. Individuals have ideals and they belong to groups. If the costs of expressing their ideals and their group attachments are relatively small, as they are in the case of voting, then they will indeed turn up to vote for "their candidate" and "their beliefs." Completely in line with this, political scientists find that the more ardent supporters of political parties are more likely to vote (Abramson and Aldrich 1982), that those who feel less part of the dominant groups in society are less likely to vote,[8] and that political campaigns are largely oriented around convincing voters that political parties care about their concerns and represent them.

---

[8] The US Census report for 2008, for example, reported that those in the highest family income bracket (above USD$100,000) were almost twice as likely to vote as those in the poorest families (under USD$20,000): see www.census.gov/hhes/www/socdemo/voting/index.html.

Through the lens of mainstream economics, many of these findings from political science make little sense. Someone who feels less that he belongs to a group will on average have just as much to materially gain or lose from proposed changes in government policies than some other person who feels a stronger sense of belonging. A politician who says he loves his country is merely wasting time on irrelevant and even nonsensical statements. Yet, following the logic of this book as evoked by applying the third and fourth questions of the heuristic, both of these core findings make perfect sense. The person who does not feel himself to be part of a group simply does not feel the need to show allegiance to an internal group identity by voting, while the politician talking about his devotion to the country is trying to sound more patriotic and thus more likely to "do the right thing" for the country as a whole.

5.3.5 Tax-paying behavior

Why do so many people pay their taxes dutifully despite the fact that the odds of being discovered evading taxes, as well as the fines that would be incurred as a result of such a discovery, are so small relative to the average tax liability?

Following a similar line of thought as for voting behavior, one could argue based on the first two questions of the heuristic alone that paying taxes is a form of overt stupidity that will only be undertaken by people not smart enough to see that their material incentives clearly point towards paying far less tax. The policy prescription to further improve tax compliance that follows from answering only the *qui bono* question is to increase monitoring and to increase fines for non-payment of taxes, which is exactly what is argued by Allingham and Sandmo (1972).

By considering the third and fourth questions, however, one can see tax morale in the same light as voting behavior. Once a group is well established and has developed ideals in which paying taxes is considered "normal" and "the right thing to do," the individual group members will require far less in terms of monitoring and fines in order to cause them to comply with tax payment requests. The key ingredients for tax authorities wishing to increase compliance are therefore, first, the establishment of a cohesive group, and second, to promote ideals within that group under which taxation is considered a normal and proper activity for group members. In this light, the centuries of tax revolts and heavy-handed tax collection witnessed in Europe were in fact crucial in producing the high level of voluntary tax compliance we see in modern Western countries. When taxes were originally introduced, such as when the English King Edward III introduced taxes in order to finance a war with France, there was far less identification with the notion of "being English" amongst the taxed population, and compliance was therefore seen as something to be avoided. As a result, the taxes had to be collected at sword-point, were strongly resisted, and resulted in many local revolts (Rogers 1999). Yet, after about a hundred years of such taxes being levied, taxation came to be seen as more normal and was resisted less, partially because there was an increased sense of "Englishness" amongst the taxed. This basic mechanism is well explained and illustrated by Blankson (2007), who reviews the history of taxation in Europe and elsewhere, arguing case-by-case that taxation invariably started as highly involuntary but ended up as something normal and associated with group benefits.

Tax monitoring and instituting fines for noncompliance serve the limited role of providing a clear deterrent to ostentatiously breaking the tax rules, as well as assisting the authorities in being seen to enforce taxation laws by catching the worst offenders. The real key to tax morale, however, is the maintenance of a national identity that incorporates a group ideal of paying taxes to support the nation. Tax morale is thus indirectly stimulated by televised inaugurations, the swearing of allegiance to the flag at schools, national sporting events, celebrated historical occasions, books that detail the joint history and destination of group members, and so on. Paying tax is therefore best seen as a whole-group activity, and as such is only in a very limited way subject to the policies of this or that subgroup in a government ministry. Increased monitoring and punishment make sense when group allegiance is weak, but cannot stand alone, since in the long run it is far more efficient to create a joint national identity in which there is a presumption that the taxed population benefits from its group membership. Once tax morale is very high and group membership is well embedded and internalized, one in fact would want rather to *reduce* the amount of fines and monitoring so as not to alienate those individuals who mistakenly pay too little in taxes due to simple human error.

What is said above for tax morale can also be said for property rights or the rule of law. When such ideas come from the outside, they must be accompanied by tangible, material outside enforcement, and they take time to become internalized by group members, which often involves a change in group affiliations. Yet, once embedded in formal institutions, individual morality, and habits of thought, they become self-sustaining. For example, one does not even have to explain the concepts of rule of law or property rights in formal education anymore: within modern societies, these notions have become so accepted and embedded that parents teach their children from a very early age the morals and rules of thumb with which they are associated. Respecting the property of others, fearing punishment if one were to break the law, and looking down on those who do not toe these lines themselves are all mental habits that most of us are taught at a very early age, and which no longer need to be enforced by any outside power. This represents arguably a highly efficient system solely by virtue of its cost-effectiveness.

This also makes it clear where the limits lie of the power of the kind of group ideal embodied in paying taxes. It can take centuries to truly embed something like a strong tax morale into a population, and the tax morale further must materially "make sense" as a group ideal in order to be sustained. If tax morale were entirely nonsensical from a material perspective, then the natural evolution of groups would give rise to "fitter" groups that went without tax morale but nevertheless managed to deliver the same benefits to their members. That this has not happened is due to the obvious fact that without a strong tax morale, a large group's tax receipts are much lower and its ability to produce public goods is consequently greatly diminished.

The public goods that can be provided with tax revenues must in turn prove themselves in the international competition between nation states and other groups. This means that tax morale is a long-term consequence of the additional fitness that groups can achieve via strong internal cohesion and public-goods provision. This does not preclude the possibility that tax levels in successful groups may overshoot what is socially optimal, but does make it unlikely that the most evolutionary fit form of society is one with almost no taxation.

There is also scope for a joint role for greed and idealism in issues of tax morale. Based on the story in this book, one would think that the more greedy groups, such as hierarchically organized private firms, would be more involved in tax avoidance and tax minimization than smaller reciprocal groups, such as families, and that they are more likely to react to changes in economic incentives. This is indeed the case: as Weichenrieder (1996) and Hanlon, Mills, and Slemrod (2007) argue, the issue of tax minimization is especially relevant for large companies, and they react strongly to changes in material incentives. It should not be surprising to note that churches and other charities, however, also try to minimize taxes by obtaining tax exemptions (see Iannaccone 1998).

5.3.6 Symbolic expenses

Why and when do people pay symbolic expenses?

Mainstream economics has very little to say about symbolic expenses, apart from offering a handful of theories under which they do not in fact exist. Such theories include notably the possibility that people pay symbolic expenses in order to signal something else. Invariably, this implies that they would not pay a symbolic expense if no one else was looking, which clearly would not fit the ubiquitous examples of individual prayer, individual activities such as fasting and being a hermit, or any group sacrifice that no other group watches.

As a result, if we apply only the first two questions of the heuristic, we are simply unable to explain symbolic expenses. Such expenses are paid towards no visible end, by people who only lose materially from making them. In some cases, one could argue that the expense benefits an intermediary, such as a priest or some other representative of a divinity whose livelihood depends in some way on the symbolic expense, but even then the question arises of why the group as a whole undertakes the expense willingly.

If we broaden our perspective by applying the final two questions of the heuristic related to groups and power, symbolic expenses start to make much more sense. Such expenses are attempts by individuals and groups to bargain with the unknown, exactly in line with how love arises in general. Individuals and/or groups believe they face a serious problem related to something they cannot control. They anthropomorphize the uncontrollable phenomenon, and they unconsciously believe that they can obtain favors from this unknown by sacrificing something towards it.

This view has several falsifiable predictions. One is that humans will engage in symbolic sacrifices towards anything that they regard as a problem, and which they do not have other ways of influencing.[9] Life

---

[9] Symbolic sacrifice may also be observed towards phenomena believed to be sources of simple need satisfaction, although this is less of a robust prediction

after death, good weather, luck, and even love itself are all at times desperately desired but uncontrollable good things, towards whose believed ultimate sources humans should be predicted to sacrifice. Moreover, because the belief in the reciprocity of the perceived ultimate power source is held at the unconscious level, a further prediction is that humans would be neither consciously interested in nor knowledgeable about whether the sacrifice actually has any effect in producing the desired good outcome.

When will symbolic expenses be made by a group as a whole? This should happen when the believed relationship with the source of uncertainty is at the group level. Hence, if a "god of rain" has a relationship with the whole group, the symbolic expense will be in the name of, and made by, the whole group. If, on the other hand, the relationship is at the level of the individual, such as when the "god of war" grants individual success in battle or the "god of the afterlife" weighs each soul separately, the symbolic expense is made by the individual.

How widespread is the practice of paying symbolic expenses? Following the story in this book, the amount of symbolic expense should be related to the degree to which the underlying desires and fears of individuals are believed by them to be a function of unknown processes. The less individuals actually understand about their world, therefore, the more symbolic expenses they will be making. It is not easy to say whether our lives have become more or less uncertain over time. On the one hand, as history has progressed, science has delivered more and the more knowledge and reasonable guesses about how things work. On the other, the capacity of any individual to absorb all of that knowledge is limited, and from the perspective of the individual, more knowledge and more people who have it can themselves generate more uncertainty. For example, what is someone with limited mental capacity to make of statements by ministerial bureaucrats that they know how to fix this or that problem? How is someone who lives in a society with hundreds of millions of people and tens of thousands of job specializations to make any sense out of something as grand as "the economy?" It is perfectly conceivable that to the average individual, life has become more uncertain and fuller of threats and unknown processes than ever before, in which case the degree to which symbolic expenses are made will have increased.

in any given case because other sources of satisfying the same need may be available.

While I cannot offer a sure-fire method for deciding whether an expense is symbolic or not, the unconscious bargain that is at the heart of the symbolic expense does offer a heuristic for detecting a symbolic expense. One can ask a person making an expense that is suspected of being symbolic whether he has a rational story in his conscious mind about how the expense is going to lead to a good outcome, or whether he trusts that those who are spending the expense in his name have such a rational story. If the person neither knows nor cares, and blindly trusts that expenses solve problems, then the expense is likely to be symbolic. In the case of a forty-hour fast for example that is done to "help" starving people elsewhere, it is clear that we are looking at a symbolic expense. No individual can provide a strong causal path for how inflicting suffering on oneself in one part of the world is by itself going to help other people living elsewhere. The same expense, monetized, would be more rational (and less symbolic) if it were used to provide goods and services to those in need.

Yet in the case of, say, national spending on reducing educational inequities, who is to say what part is symbolic? Most voters will have little idea about how money spent on something as abstract as "educational inequities" is going to have an effect on something they care about, but this is not to say that they do not trust their national representatives charged with ensuring the expenses are going to be useful. They may well trust in the whole system of government to ensure that expenses indeed have effects. After all, the basic tax-for-services relation between individuals and their country works extraordinarily well in modern Western states. Hence, it might be the case that for a sizeable section of our societies, most group expenses are wholly symbolic, but it might also be the case that they merely *seem* symbolic because of a rational habit of trust in the whole system.

What job does the economist have regarding this question? From the point of view that economists hold the ideal of being the rational advisors to the group as a whole regarding the allocation of resources, it should fall to the economists to redirect symbolic expenses that have no actual effects towards expenses that make more of a difference. In the case that symbolic expenses produce unobservable "feel-good" benefits that cannot be generated any other way, however, it would be the job of economists inside the spending agencies to maximize the degree to which a group obtains these feel-good benefits while minimizing actual costs. One (although not the only) way to do that is to secretly redirect the symbolic expenses towards things that make a difference in some other sphere, while letting the group as a whole believe that the expenses are being directed towards the symbolic activity.

5.3.7 The self-image of economists

What role do economists play in the socioeconomic system, and how sensible are their models and their activities?

From the point of the view of the first two questions of the heuristic, economists should be rent-seekers who individually maximize the degree that they successfully pretend to their ultimate pay-masters (usually, governments) that they are materially useful. The group activities of economists, such as joint education activities, would in that view merely take advantage of increasing returns-to-scale in educational and other reputation-producing activities. Pretences at generating "truth" or "insights into policies and systems" would be either complete cheap talk (i.e., lies), or at best no more than a convenient labeling of economists' activities that an imperfectly informed pay-master is fed.

Addressing the third and fourth questions of the heuristic, a different image emerges of what economists do and are. Economists make up a reciprocal group of people who believe themselves to be more or less equals. Reciprocity is embedded in the notion of the peer review system, and also within smaller reciprocal groups, such as research units and economic departments. Individual economists can "give" to the group in terms of performing a stint as, say, a department head, while they "receive" in the form of emeritus and other honorary positions, and professional awards. Each smaller group can adhere to many ideals, including the notion that economics students should be taught all the basics of "economics." Such an ideal would be a very strange thing for someone who is purely greedy to believe in, since the odds of being monitored on this point are fairly minimal. Other ideals can include social norms regarding how to supervise PhD students, how to handle plagiarism, what to consider as proper research methods, how to behave in seminars, and so on.

From this rich self-image, we would view an economist not as the sole type of benevolent person whom the economic view of man does not fit, but rather as an entirely normal human being who is simply part of a larger reciprocal group. As with other groups, no more than a proportion of economists must truly believe in the group's stated ideals. Even if the majority of individual economists are in reality quite greedy and are actively looking for those activities and subgroup memberships that benefit them materially, the existence of the groups themselves and their associated social norms and self-image strongly constrain the actions of all individual economists. The threat of punishment by the more fervent believers in the group, as well as the semi-formal institutions that carry the group's norms, make each individual economist behave as if he at least somewhat adheres to the group ideals.

It is their group reputation as truth-seeking policy advisors that allows economists to be contracted by outsiders as independent regulators, commentators on public policy, and writers of government reports. What upholds the competent performance of these functions by economists is the internal cohesion of the group as a whole, since it is that cohesion that provides the individual incentive to be at least somewhat honest.

The research activities of economists can now also be better understood. Depending on who reads and uses the output of research activities, one can predict how they are oriented. Research that is only read and judged by other economists is entirely self-referential. As a result, one should expect such research to be oriented towards the more abstract group ideals, and to be unencumbered by any notions of direct applicability. Research directly consumed by other groups has to appeal to the ideals of those other groups, and thus would be predicted to contain stories about how to further their interests.

5.4 Further thoughts on economics

Economics is a broad church that simultaneously looks at micro-phenomena and macro-phenomena, and that struggles with the question of how to judge what useful knowledge is in a situation where there is no "model of everything." Practitioners thus have to somewhat muddle through with implicit heuristics on when any particular economic sub-theory is most relevant. Here I want to add more reflections on the particular problems posed by macroeconomic phenomena and on the question of learning within economics.

5.4.1 Applicability to macroeconomic phenomena, and the production metaphor

Managing aggregate phenomena using the story in this book places special demands on the mental agility of the analyzer. Recognizing what the aggregate problem actually is requires a recognition of abstract patterns that do not obviously relate to group choices. The analyzer must be able to switch perspectives between the pattern recognition phase of the policy heuristic and the later phases of the heuristic that are oriented instead towards thinking through how groups would react to various policies.

For example, when an economist notes that there is upward inflationary pressure and wishes to reduce that pressure, the "solution" to this problem might well be in the form of reducing the available money supply, or increasing the cost of money by increasing interest rates. The background stories about how money supply and interest rates affect the economy themselves involve stories about incentives and group-level reactions to changes, but they involve many groups. Interest rates affect savers differently than they do investors; homeowners differently than renters; young people with study loans differently than pensioners. The mental model that an economist has in mind when thinking about how to reduce inflation is an aggregate model of what the interactions between and amongst all of these various groups would lead to "on average." That mental model might be entirely in terms of concepts such as aggregate investments and housing prices that conjure up no automatic group associations at all. Recognizing patterns in macroeconomic problems therefore requires temporarily suspending the group orientation of the latter parts of the policy heuristic in favor of judging which abstract world is the most accurate stylized view of the problem at hand. Only when thinking in the later stages of analysis about what policies to actually implement would a policy maker need to switch back into "group mode," in order to determine how different individuals and organizations are likely to react, and what they would politically support or oppose.

What holds for inflation and aggregate investment holds for many macroeconomic phenomena. Almost no aggregate measure is the result of the actions of any single group, nor is it trivial to see how one can influence aggregates by encouraging any particular form of group behavior. Important examples of aggregate outcomes that cannot be easily ascribed to the behavior of a single group are things like aggregate output, inflation, or economic growth, which may be influenced via interventions such as fiscal stimulus or printing money. How these aggregate outcomes can best be described and influenced is a nontrivial intellectual problem.

The main contribution of this book to the analysis of aggregate economic outcomes is the discussion of production factors in Chapter 4, and specifically, my illustration of the central role of business networks. I argue that the contacts within business networks are the natural focal point for thinking about recessions, which can be understood as the destruction of part of the network currently in existence in an economy, and/or increases in the price of making new connections. At a macro-level, this view of recessions marries the previous economic concepts of "aggregate demand," now re-formulated as the overall stock of contacts, with the concept of "creative destruction," now re-formulated as the inevitable loss of existing contacts when business partners search for technological improvements. Explaining these previous concepts in terms of stocks and changes of contacts allows for discussions about recessions, technological innovation, and the political system to reflect phenomena that affect the network in an economy. Such phenomena include institutional reductions in the costs of making contacts, and interference by the government to "freeze" contacts during recessions in order to avoid a complete breakdown. This view hence represents a new line of research, with further potential applications for the analysis of financial systems, monetary policy, and questions related to the management of business cycles. The mental model underpinning this view in the short run is almost completely devoid of the element of groups, except insofar as aggregate contacts are fractionalized into individual contacts with members of certain groups, such as "tourists" or "young Australians."

The standard production metaphor is my preferred mental model of the aggregate economy, to be used in the pattern recognition phase of the main decision heuristic. The great value of that metaphor is that it forces its adopter to translate changes in the aggregate output of an economy into changes in a production factor, which itself provides a useful mental discipline, as it requires a serious consideration of many interrelations in the economy. It thus forces one to translate things like "loss of confidence," "export prices," and "competitiveness" into actual changes in production factors, which brings all such notions under a single conceptual umbrella. It is a way of thinking that is easy to explain to students, links in with the biological view of humanity as ultimately dependent on an ecosystem (the only "ultimate" production factors are human time and natural resources), and is also quite prescriptive as to what can be done to influence the aggregate economy. In short, despite the fact that it grossly simplifies a number of key aspects of economic development, the production metaphor fits many stories in our societies and is a useful way for a policy maker to think about the aggregate economy.

There is more to say on this metaphor, and the link between contacts and the financial system in particular, but it will have to wait. The main focus of this book is to introduce the concepts of greed, love, groups, power, and trade networks to the standard economics toolkit. A fuller treatise on the importance of trade networks in driving macroeconomic phenomena is left for future work.

5.4.2 Academic debates and progress in economics

From a long-run perspective, economists have to prove their value as useful policy advisors, company strategists, regulators, and so on. There are other potential candidates for those roles, such as political scientists, psychologists, sociologists, management students, and many others – meaning that there is healthy competition to fill these roles. The fact that economists are chosen to fill them, in the main, implies that there must be a long-run tendency for economists to be guardians and propagators of useful knowledge. The main "knowledge" economists have at the moment that is distinct from other social sciences is the solid conviction that nearly all actors are strongly materially motivated, and as a corollary, that there are particular ways to get that greed to work to the benefit of the group as a whole rather than to its detriment. This core knowledge is propagated in first-year textbooks, codified in mathematical models, and increasingly made known to the broader society. The popular book *Freakonomics* by Steven Levitt and Stephen Dubner (2005), while containing no really new ideas on how the economic system works, uses striking examples to bring the validity of the basic point of economics home to a broad audience.

However, academic journals only quite indirectly depend on the overall reputation of economics and its usefulness (or otherwise) to outsiders. In the main, academic journals and academic papers are self-referential. Journals are judged by how often papers they publish are cited by other journals and other papers. Academics are judged by whether their papers are cited by other academics, and by the reputation of the places where they publish their work. The arbiters of which work is accepted into which journals and publishing houses are peers (i.e., other economic researchers) and editors. Usually, editors are also peers, making the system almost entirely self-feeding.

What the self-referential system of academic debate does on the one hand is to free academic debate from the necessity of speaking the language and sharing the opinions of outsiders. Academic debate can thus generate and employ a more specialized language, and can ignore the everyday demands of practitioners. This is probably a good thing as it allows academic researchers to seek deeper insights into the drivers of economic phenomena in the relative peace and quiet of academia.

On the other hand, the self-referential system of academic debate allows the debates themselves to wander off into their own realms, which are not necessarily grounded in particular policy questions or in line with the interests of the rest of society. Worse, since academics are just as human as the rest of humanity, the self-referential nature of their debate supports the formation of subgroups that try to carve out lucrative and high-status positions. Much as a firm can try to defend itself against outsiders via patents and reputation, so too can subgroups of academics fend off outsiders who want to publish in the same journals or on the same issues by means of subgroup ideals about which only insiders are well-informed, and which would be hard for outsiders to mimic. Worse still, previous investments made by academics give them a potent incentive to become conservative in their views on what a "proper" academic piece should look like, including strong *a priori* views on which conclusions are acceptable and which are not. There is therefore the potential that simple material self-interest will derail academic debates such that they not only lose touch with the ultimate consumers of economic wisdom, or even anything resembling reality, but that they crowd out the development of academic innovations that are more aligned with social interests.

Moreover, as can be said for the contributions of any group that spins stories about how the world works, economists' stories become part of the political landscape and used towards all kinds of ends for which they were not initially devised. Quiggin (2010) argues along these lines that the economic story of efficient markets has been abused in political debates by those who profit from financial market imperfections, in order to protect their own interests. His contention is that these market imperfections have been shoved under the carpet in politically motivated disputes over taxes and regulations, co-opting various famous economists who were more than happy to be the poster-boys for this or that political ideology. While I do not necessarily wish to side with Quiggin, the basic notion that economic ideas themselves become political stories that are used to influence public opinion is something entirely in accord with the story in this book: any group that achieves some standing will be co-opted towards political aims. This is in itself an inevitable result of success, but our scientific social norms then do place a responsibility on economists to be honest about the scope of economic theories and not get swept along by exaggerations of our magnificence.

How then do economists arrive at their more abstract group ideals? The social value of economists as a whole group is still ultimately tied to something wider than the self-referential research activities of the group of economists, and the ideals and set of problems that economics purports to look at will therefore depend ultimately on where their funding streams come from. These funding streams will be directed in modern Western states mainly towards the economic problems faced by the nation state (through organizations such as the National Science Foundation in the US or the Australian Research Council in Australia). This means that the more abstract group ideals of economists will still involve at least some semblance of the language in which nation-state ideals are formulated. Yet, the more layers of abstraction that cloud the connection between actual research and direct scrutiny by representatives of the nation state, and the more that the reading and judging of economic output is conducted by other economists, the less that economic research will be tied to notions of usefulness and the more it will instead be tied to ideals of aesthetics and the preferred self-image of economists as "truth-seekers." Left to its own, the natural direction for research in economics, or in any other academic discipline, is to become entirely idealized, divorced from material needs, and self-referential – in other words, religiously devoted to itself.

One can see the possible tension arising from the above dynamics. Without the impetus of material problems that are experienced by the group as a whole and must be solved, there is a natural drift towards religiosity. This danger would lead one to advocate keeping economists close to real-life problems. Yet, because of the advantages of specialization, the more reflective and thoughtful research will be more removed from the direct problems of every day, as the researcher tries to find commonalities that allow for a more general solution to often-recurring problems rather than just the one under study.

How can one spot the more useful opinions from the more religious ones? From my perspective, this is extraordinarily hard to do. One can follow the same idea as with symbolic expenses, and ask of any position how it is going to lead to some benefit in reality, but the problem in the case of economic thought is that a lot of the benefits of economic thinking derive from a particular mindset, rather than from supposed knowledge. The mindset of the first two parts of the heuristic is, in my experience and opinion, very useful in many cases, but it is a mindset that itself does not come easily. One needs several years of economics education to be able to divorce oneself from the more normal mindset adopted by the rest of society, in which social norms and emotions have a very direct impact on beliefs and behavior. It takes years to be able to look at society as if it were made up of greedy, rational individuals and to recognize the many patterns of information and market imperfections that channel rational greed in different ways. Because that is already such an abstract activity, the study of highly abstract, quasi-religious methods of thought is probably quite helpful in achieving the basic economic mindset.

Even if a theory is entirely nonsensical from the point of view of prediction or description, it is still not automatic that it offers no value. Take as an extended example the basic Samuelson framework of describing economic agents as rationally choosing bundles of goods based on a complete preference map (Samuelson 1983). In Samuelson's model, the act of choosing reveals the underlying preference, pinpointing the choice as the best one that could have been made out of available alternatives (Samuelson 1983). That basic theory, which in turn owes much to Leon Walras and the marginalists of the nineteenth century (see for instance the discussion on this in Daal and Jolink 1993), has been virtually ignored until now in this book but has been used and extended in thousands of academic papers and books. The education of many economics students begins with this theory, exemplified by the assumption that individuals have preferences over every conceivable bundle of goods and in any situation merely enact the relevant preference.

It is easy to criticize the Samuelson framework. For one, neuroscience and cognitive psychology have progressed enough to make it clear that humans are not born with preference maps, that there is no place in the brain that houses preferences, and that there are many reasons to believe that how we make choices will not be constant in different circumstances. Humans appear to be born with reward–punishment systems that themselves evolve over time as individuals learn to like this and loathe that. Humans thus both learn their preferences and are taught their preferences in many areas. The mental traits relevant to choice making, such as patience, rationality, recognition of trade-offs, and the ability to understand notions about resources, must also be learned. Whole cultures differ in terms of how patient or rational their people are. The very notion of an "individual choice" also differs across cultures. Modern education explicitly aims to make children more reflective and rational, implying that in their nascent state, they are not. Hence, one basic criticism to make of the standard preference theory in economics is that it is a very poor descriptive theory of how choices actually arise, and takes for granted a lot about adult humans that in fact has to be taught.

One might then try to defend preference theory by saying that it is a useful predictive tool. Here again, however, evidence suggests otherwise. As Van Praag and Frijters note in their review (Van Praag and Frijters 1999), there has never been a single research paper that has ever measured a whole preference map of any individual. Since preference maps do not actually turn out to exist in people's brains, there is furthermore not much hope of eventually developing some technology that could measure whole preference maps (as discussed in Clark et al. 2008). Hence, as described in Chapter 1 of this book, economists at best simplify the world such that individuals are represented as only wanting a few goods, such as money and leisure, and then measure the trade-offs between them on some aggregate level. The theoretical apparatus of infinite preferences has no direct application in reality except in the vaguest possible sense.

Yet, does this mean that preference theory is entirely useless to practitioners, or that none of it has colored the theories in this book? Absolutely not. The central presumption of Samuelson that preferences are fixed is a strong tenet of this book, but at a far more aggregated notion of what a preference is than Samuelson had in mind. I take materialist motives as more or less immutable and largely not amenable to cultural influences. Within both mainstream economics and the extension to it proposed in this book, people are greedy everywhere and always. I defend this presumption by giving it an evolutionary rationale: a being that was not born or did not stay greedy would surely lose out against a being that was born greedy and, at least to a large degree, remained so.

Furthermore, the essential prescript of Samuelson to distrust what people say and to look more at what they choose is not only adopted, but greatly expanded in my story. I claim that people lie about their motivations because they have good reasons to lie. People want to be seen to adhere to their group ideals and want to think better of themselves, and both of these activities entail a degree of deception. In such circumstances, watching what people actually do when there are serious material consequences is a much cleaner way of ascertaining what they really value than listening to what they say. Yet, unlike Samuelson, I do not take talk to be entirely cheap: ideals and words matter in various ways that Samuelson probably did not foresee.

Basic preference theory also focuses on trade-offs between bundles of goods, which means that it incorporates part of the central policy advice of mainstream economics. By taking an individual and his choices over bundles as the central problem, the Samuelson theory almost automatically forces its user to think of any situation as a choice situation in which there are alternative options that an individual or an organization could select. Hence even the basic framing of the Samuelson model contains useful elements, quite apart from any of its assumptions.

So, while I would argue that the basic Samuelson-type preference theory has poor descriptive value and almost no relevance to what economic practitioners do in its general form, the theory does contain some implicit rules of thumb that are useful. They include the rules of thumb that "aggregated" preferences do not change; that a responsible adult in our culture somewhat rationally makes decisions; and that actions speak louder than words.

The theories within this book themselves give a reason for why one would want to "hide" useful rules of thumb within a formalized world of models: precisely because they take time and effort to learn and require relatively specific abilities, mathematical economic theories require a form of subjugation of the learner. Mathematical and conceptual complexity force the person learning them into a position of weakness, which in turn makes them more likely to adopt the rules of thumb embedded in what is learned. Much like an army sergeant successfully makes a platoon soldier out of the selfish recruit by physical exhaustion, so too does the complexity of economic theory force clever yet ambitious young students to accept the group beliefs inherent in it. It is unlikely that a less-formalized method of learning would equally successfully indoctrinate the smarter and more ambitious students, nor would it appeal to them, as anything that appears too easy would be dismissed as not worthwhile, much like a weak suitor is spurned. In turn, this means it is not really warranted to judge a theory on whether it is applicable but on whether one agrees with the embedded rules of thumb that a student is likely to take away from it, though it is of course well possible that there are even better models and learning methods to achieve the same outcomes than those used at present.

Finally, there is the broad question of how economics should learn: one concept at a time, or by adopting a whole set of interdependent concepts at once.

The combatant nature of academic debate usually means that concepts have to be explained and defended one at a time. I nonetheless take the opposite approach in this book. Love, groups, power, and trade networks together, when added to the mainstream economic view, explain so much more than any of them individually that I believe it is more useful to judge them as a cluster rather than individually.

I also suspect that mainstream economic textbooks have changed so little in recent decades because the case for the usefulness of any single additional concept is weak. It would not be clear, for example, what the concept of "love" in isolation would materially add to mainstream economics, while the potential loss would seem huge because love itself relies on things such as desire, unseen abstractions, and power. If one only imported love and not the other pieces of the story in this book, the fear is that this would constitute an open door to all kinds of loose reasoning about who could be how loyal to what. It is only in the context of power and groups that it becomes clear that only a limited degree of loyalty formation is up for grabs: that the amount of loyalty that can be engendered in a given situation depends entirely on the size and pre-existing cohesion of the relevant group as a whole. Without such an understanding of limits, incorporating the love concept into mainstream economics would lead to more problems than solutions.

The time thus seems ripe in economics to consider whole clusters of ideas rather than to target just one at a time. The key difficulty in considering clusters of ideas is that there is the temptation to invent an entirely new language and to completely get rid of all the main existing ideas. Even if the eventual theory would, from an objective point of view, be better off by the co-invention of a new language, social science cannot learn in that manner. Current practitioners would have to make too large an investment to understand and take up the new theory, which in turn means that new theory could not be taken up by journals, textbooks, or even the general public.

The only way for a completely new theory with an associated new language to establish itself would be to have visibly superior predictive power. But that is an almost impossible task, because there are lock-in effects in measurement. Statistical agencies attempt to measure existing concepts, not the concepts that have as of yet no track record. This means that a new theory would also have to gather its own data, and to compete against the data collected in hundreds of years of data-gathering by thousands of researchers. It should be clear that this is a hopeless task. Hence, even new theories that attempt to introduce clusters of new ideas must, as much as possible, use existing language, appeal to known problems, and show how they relate to the parts of existing thought with which they overlap.

Together, the considerations that knowledge in social science must be evolutionary rather than revolutionary, that the time has come to consider bundles of additional concepts rather than single ones, and that there is value in reductionism, have underpinned the approach taken in this book: to assemble a bundle of interrelated concepts that explain phenomena of recognized importance, and to graft those concepts onto the existing stylized story.

5.5 Conclusions and discussion

Chapter 1 of this book began with the mainstream story of a market economy being made up of greed-oriented individuals who, when engaged in peaceful competition with each other, specialize in what they are individually best at and agree amongst themselves about the most efficient public institutions to support their behavior. The main leaps of faith that this view requires were seen as (i) the presence of some unknown glue that leads individuals to play by the rules of the game; (ii) the absence of a role for group identity or group power; and (iii) the presence of some unknown manner via which all individuals in the market economy had formed an anonymous network with each other, so that each knew everything about everyone else. Each three of these leaps of faith formed the topic of separate ensuing chapters of the book.

Chapter 2 reviewed many empirical instances of individuals forming strong emotional bonds with each other, and also with the inanimate, which led them to be interested in the welfare of others. The simplest theory rationalizing the advent of these bonds of love was that individuals have an innate tendency to expect that what they cannot directly control, but want something from, will be reciprocal. In the case that one individual desperately wants something of another but cannot force the other to provide it, this innate tendency leads the one individual to start to see the other as part of his self-image. In the case that one individual desperately wants something from a non-human entity such as the weather, this innate tendency translates itself into an anthropomorphism of the unknown followed by the same bonding: humans give the unknown a name, imbue the entity with human characteristics, and start to behave towards that entity as if it were reciprocal. This explains the worship of a god of rain, a forest spirit, the world's environment, and an array of other abstractions. Chapter 2 also pointed out the great manipulative potential that lies in the innate human tendency to be reciprocal towards that which cannot be directly controlled; discussed some of the more basic scientific underpinnings of this tendency; and drew out the consequences of this tendency in a variety of circumstances.

Chapter 3 then turned to groups, while also making use of the idea of reciprocity. It began with an empirically guided characterization of five archetypal groups. The first of these is the small reciprocal group, of which the prime evolutionary example is the hunter-gatherer band that has dominated humanity's past; the second is the small hierarchical group, of which perhaps the prime historical example is illustrated in unequal gender relations; the third is the large reciprocal group, such as nation states, mass religions, and mass causes, which have come to currently dominate the group landscape; the fourth is the large hierarchical group, wherein a small reciprocal group has gained authority over a larger population via layers of hierarchy, of which prime modern examples would be a layered bureaucracy or a large private enterprise; and the fifth is the emotion-free anonymous trade network, such as seen in perfect markets, wherein interactions must be sanctioned by some outside provider of rules of the game. Chapter 3 argued that history has seen a slow progression starting with hunter-gatherers who were organized in small reciprocal groups, through the feudal era characterized by large hierarchies but featuring increasingly large networks of merchants and other contact makers, to the current era, where activities in nation states occur within large circles of reciprocity that tolerate other group forms (such as private enterprise) if they are perceived to be in the overall interest of the whole group.

Chapter 4 focused on trade networks, putting them at the heart of markets. It was argued that trade networks were a prime input into the overall production of a society, as larger trade networks allowed for more specialization and lower transaction costs. Several economic institutions were then argued to be essentially about lowering the cost of networking, such as the institution of trust, the institution of rules governing market transactions, the institution of contract law, and so forth. An important unintended effect of trade networks is that they automatically function as embryonic large circles of reciprocity and in that way enable the quick emergence of powerful new group entities. This was precisely what was argued to have happened in the sixteenth to nineteenth centuries in Europe, where the contact makers adopted the ideals that eventually overthrew the monarchies and other large hierarchies that previously dominated Europe.

When we join Homo Economicus with the three main additional elements of love, groups, and trade networks, we arrive at a picture of humanity constantly in the grips of the forces of greed and love, with group formation as the main instrument of those forces. Greed leads individuals to abandon their previous informal ties with family and clans for more anonymous ties with supermarkets, clients, and employers. Greed leads individuals with common material interests to set up new collectives in order to prevent other greedy individuals or groups from dominating them. The collectives then start to lead a life of their own, loved by the weaker ones within them and by those with a strong wish to have a cause. Love is also what underpins friendships and teams, which are crucial components in anything humans do. Greed leads individuals to set up hierarchical groups that serve their private interests. Love continuously erodes the power of any individual leader, in that it supports the genesis of the many small reciprocal groups that develop individual agendas within any large hierarchy.

The interplay between greed and love, both of which use and are used within groups, has led to the incredibly complex mosaic of human relations we witness around us every day. In its simplest form, love provides the constraints by which greed must abide. At the individual level, greedy wishes clash with the demands of love, such as when pursuing our lucrative careers clashes with caring for our children. At the intermediate level greed again clashes with love, such as when the wishes of special interest groups to erect trade barriers are counteracted by the free-trade institutions that the whole reciprocal group has set up to neuter those special interests. At the macro-level greed again clashes with love, such as when the desire of the presently living to use more and more of the earth's resources clashes with the desire of some part of humanity to preserve a world for our children that is worth living in.

In this book, I have thus tried to integrate a more realistic picture of humans as loving and networking group members into the overall framework of standard economics. This depended on an argued choice about what to see as important to add to the existing framework, and what to see as peripheral. This inevitably meant ignoring missing elements whose relevance to generating a complete picture of our societies cannot be doubted, and which simply constitute the next hurdles. Let me briefly foreshadow two such elements.

One important element that is outside of the story of this book and that would seem to be a relevant question is how and why a "regulation of need" has emerged. Modern societies have all kinds of social norms and official institutions that interfere with the expressions of particular needs. Sexuality in particular is something regarding which there are all manner of invasive social norms and legal restrictions. Institutions do not only regulate what one consenting person is allowed to do to another consenting person, but also regulate the self-image aspects of sexual needs by providing moral connotations, such as when some needs are deemed "inappropriate" and when others are deemed "healthy." What goes for sexuality also goes for things like guilt, domination, hope, and other self-reflective needs. For reasons unexplained in this book, our societies have hit upon a very high degree of regulation of our needs, and it is unclear how societies have come to do this, what the relation is between our need regulation and our economies, what the overall costs and benefits are of regulating needs (i.e., what is the optimal need-regulation policy), and what we might expect in the future.

Another missing element is a fuller recognition of the role of self-esteem. While self-esteem has been presented as one of the more basic needs of individuals, which can form a motivation for either love or greed, it has not been presented as a central facet of our lives. This book has only hinted at what might happen to individuals if their self-esteem is put under constant pressure, and how self-esteem leads us to adopt stories that might have nothing to do with the truth but that enhance and protect our self-esteem. I think it likely that many "modern" self-reflective needs that individuals can display, including extreme cleanliness and prudishness, ultimately derive from the pressures put to bear on the self-esteem of individuals when they are subordinates in hierarchical groups. A fuller exploration of this mechanism is left for future work.

The inherent cost of incorporating additional elements into an aggregate view of society is that the story becomes more complicated, and thus demands more of the individual learning it. That cost is almost invariably ignored in any individual academic contribution, but it is crucial when considering the limited time and space that students and practitioners have available to devote towards understanding the socioeconomic system. It is easy to generate complicated theories about any of the many remaining missing elements, of which the above are merely two examples. The greater challenge is to reduce the complexity of whole sets of existing theories offered by social scientists about such remaining elements into simple rules of thumb that can be given a logical place in a coherent aggregate view. That integrative and reductive task has only just begun.

The theories in this book are meant to lead to practical advice, and there are many areas not yet addressed that are worth exploring in the future. In my online writing,[10] I have used the theories in this book to make predictions on schemes to avert or adapt to climate change; the plight of the poor in Western countries; the potential for democratic reforms in the Middle East; the tension between truth and popularity in political debates; economic coordination problems within the Eurozone; and many other areas of socioeconomic debate. I encourage the reader to verify whether these predictions have come true.

Finally, because the overall view presented includes a major role for concepts often viewed in moral terms, such as love, loyalty, social

---

[10] See my archives at http://economics.com.au/?author=18.

norms, authority, and institutions, a question arises regarding the role of morality for an economist.

As noted in the Introduction, the theory advocated in this book is amoral in the sense that morality is itself taken as derivative of the long-run consequences of a balance of power: morality itself is seen as endogenous rather than exogenous to our socioeconomic system. In the long run, love is given to the application of power, so it is simply true that "might becomes right." This naturally does not mean that I personally advocate that one should abide by whatever the presently powerful want for themselves or their countries, but it does mean that in a long-run sense, I see it as inevitable that morality changes over time towards accepting and justifying whatever the powerful do and say. Therefore, if one wants to influence long-run morality, one should be in the business of altering the structure of power in the future. This can be done by various means, including through influencing the costs of making contacts – seen in this book as a crucial long-run component both of the structure of an economy and of its political system.

There is room for personal responsibility in this framework, because individuals and groups have some limited degree of power that they can use to "do their bit" to change the balance of power towards the situation they prefer. Such choices have long-run moral effects when they subtly change the balance of power. One might for instance cynically claim that the advent of representative democracy in modern countries was inevitable given the rise of networks of contact makers, but the actual change from kingdoms to democracies did involve many brave individuals who gave their lives for the ideal of democracy long before it eventuated. The even more cynical response to this observation is that in a large enough population, where ideals of various types are strong enough, one will inevitably observe such fanatics. Yet even this does not negate the important role they play in the actual transition. Individuals and small groups may thus be only pebbles in the avalanche of history, but without all of the pebbles, there would be no avalanche.

More generally, within the story of this book nearly all behavior is both moral and political: any given behavior either strengthens or weakens groups and the adherence to social norms within groups. Economic activity furthermore is itself a system that crucially involves constantly changing group allegiances and constant changes in the relative costs and benefits of setting up and joining different groups. For me, to be a part of group decision making is by itself to take a moral stance: it means choosing the group and the long-run constellation of power that one wants, thereby underscoring or rejecting existing morality.

The implicit moral stance that comes with being involved in group decision making is not restricted to those contexts in which one tries to directly help governments or businesses. Even decision making within an academic discipline is innately moral because disciplines are reciprocal groups that use morality in their own internal operations. To avoid moral choices altogether, and to avoid being in service to any ideal held by anyone else, one would have to go to extreme lengths – refusing to take up space within recognized disciplines, and merely analyzing problems on one's own, without sharing any insights with anyone else. It is only the hermit on top of a mountain mulling over the world who can approach it with a truly amoral position. The rest of us are part of the main game of love and greed, whether we want to be or not.

6 | *Theoretical appendix: Formal models and extensions*

This chapter contains several mathematical models that formalize aspects of the story presented in this book. The first model gives suggestions about how one can include both love and greed in simple models of choice. The second model shows how one can model the interrelations between groups, group power, violence, and social norms. The third model focuses on how the concepts of love and greed can be used in models of many agents to generate the emergence of central authorities. The fourth and final model provides ideas about how one can envisage the relationships between networks, technology, labor time, and business cycles.

The first two models, whose central focus is on love and groups, were generated recently with this book in mind. The third and fourth models were generated years ago for specific projects, and should be seen as stepping stones in the development of the ideas in this book.

6.1 Model 1: Love and greed at the individual level

The object of this model is to formalize how one might conceptualize love in the context of simple choice behavior. Since the object is to capture the basic mechanism, the model abstracts from many of the possibilities covered in the text, such as uncertainty or mistakes. To capture the dynamic-investment aspect of love, whereby investments into love during one stage have repercussions in a later stage, the model includes two time periods. An individual in the first time period has the option of investing in love, which may yield a utility return, and the "cost" of that investment is not only a direct transfer to the love object but also that the lover's identity in the second time period will change. The benefit of loving is the additional consumption that he believes he will receive today in exchange for the investment of his love. This clarifies the trade-off implicit in the potential for love, from the point of view of the loving individual.

Specifically, the startup of a love process in the first period involves a potential inflow of utility in the first period, derived from a real or believed improvement in something the individual cares about (modeled as part of second-period consumption), in exchange for no longer being the same person in the second period and thereby consuming less in the second period than his period-1 self would have wanted.

Think of an individual i who lives for two time periods and faces the following decision utility functions at times $t = 1$ and $t = 2$:

$$U_1 = u_1(y) + \beta(0) \cdot E\{u_2 | y = 0\}$$

$$= f(x_{i1}(y)) + \beta(0) \cdot f(x_{i2})$$

$$U_2 = \beta(y)f(x_{i2} - \tau_{j2}) + (1 - \beta(y))u_2^j$$

$$= \beta(y)f(x_{i2} - \tau_{j2}) + (1 - \beta(y))f(x_{j2} + \tau_{j2})$$

Here, x_{it} denotes some final consumption good that the individual desires; τ_{j2} denotes a direct transfer made by individual i to entity j, the love object, in the second time period; $u_0 = f(.)$ is a nondecreasing concave function with $f(0) = 0$ and $f'(0) = +\infty$, and can be understood as the "greed" part of utility; u_2^j is then the utility of entity j at time 2 where j is the entity potentially loved; U_t denotes the believed welfare an individual derives from period t onwards (i.e., for the rest of his life) when calculated at the end of time period t; and $\beta(y)$ is the fraction of the identity of an individual at time 2 that is still the same as it was at time 1. Conversely, $(1 - \beta(y))$ describes the extent to which the individual at time 2 has adopted the utility of entity j as part of his own identity, which brings with it a direct utility inflow from the loved entity's consumption of the transfer τ_{j2}. Throughout, one should think of x_{it} as believed by the individual to be a function of y. The simplest way to conceive of this is that the individual can buy more x via increased y.

The variable y is an investment of what one can think of as emotional capital that the individual invests into loving someone else. The function $\beta(.)$ is then a translation of this investment into a corresponding utility-relevant identity adjustment. Setting $\beta(0) = 1$ by definition, one can think of the choice $y = 0$ as equivalent to classic greed, under which a person remains completely loyal only to himself in period 2 as well as in period 1. The greater is y, the more an individual cares about something or someone else than himself in period 2. If the chosen value of y is "emotional investment," then $\beta(y)$ can be thought of as the resulting amount of "love" created by that investment. By definition, $\bar{y} > y \geq 0$, $0 < \beta(y) \leq \beta(0) = 1$, and $\beta'(y) < 0$.

Note the peculiar specification here that U_1 depends on $\beta(0)$ and not $\beta(y)$. This reflects the argument that an individual can be completely oblivious of the love-mechanism: an individual in the first period acts as if he will love himself in the second period and not invest anything in the love for others. By the same token, an individual in period 1 calculates his future consumption level as if $y = 0$ in the sense that the individual does not take into account how a higher level of y would influence τ_{j2}. This setup is thus the extreme case in which a person is completely unaware of the impact that y has on future choices.

In this formulation, the individual at time 1 only cares about himself this period and what he views as the "part of him that remains" in period 2, which is reflected in the maximand U_1 as written. He has no care for others – i.e., no potential utility inflow from the consumption enjoyed by others – either now or in the future. Yet, in time 2 the person might well care about more than just himself, which is reflected in the presence of the love object's consumption of the transfer τ_{j2} in U_2. Self 1, who maximizes U_1, takes into account what he believes he will choose in period 2, but only as a constraint.

For simplicity and closer correspondence to standard models of decision making, there are no savings in this model. The individual at time 1 chooses y in order to optimize U_1, while having imperfect foresight about the decisions that he will make at time 2 to maximize U_2.

All that is needed to generate love in this simple framework is to put assumptions on the relations between x_{it} and y. If we for example presume that $x'_{i1}(y) > 0$, and $x''_{i1}(y) < 0$ while x_{i0} is fixed and given, then we get a result by means of solving the solution for each period. In period 1 an individual picks $y = \bar{y}$ as there is no cost to having a higher y but only a believed benefit. In period 2, the optimal solution is to pick the τ_{j2} that solves:

$$\beta(y)f'(x_{i2} - \tau_{j2}) = (1 - \beta(y))f'(x_{j2} + \tau_{j2})$$
$$\rightarrow \tau_{j2} = g(\beta(\bar{y}))$$

In words, there is an implicit nondecreasing function $g(.)$ that describes the optimal transfer in period 2 as a function of the degree of identification with entity j. It can be shown that $g(0) = 0$ and $g'(.) > 0$.

Given this optimal solution at time 1 and 2, the believed utility levels will then be:

$$U_1 = f(x_{i1}(\bar{y})) + f(x_{i2})$$

$$U_2 = \beta(\bar{y})f(x_{i2} - g(\beta(\bar{y}))) + (1 - \beta(\bar{y}))f(x_{j2} + g(\beta(\bar{y})))$$

This thus shows a case whereby the individual "loses his heart" to the maximum degree because he believes it to have current consumption benefits and is completely oblivious to the costs.

The main idea in this stylized model is the notion that the degree of identification of an individual with *himself only* over time is variable, and is subject to emotional investments $(y > 0)$ that are juxtaposed against purely selfish investments (i.e., where $y = 0$). In this simplest of models, an individual is imperfectly aware of everything that goes on: the individual does not know he is in a situation where his unconscious will start investing y, and thus allows it to happen, which can be thought of as unconsciously allowing a certain amount of exposure to the temptation offered by j. In the generic case, choice here will be dynamically inconsistent, in that an individual at each point in time will disagree with the choices that he makes at other points in time.

6.1.1 Stylized extensions

The first extension that would naturally appeal is to vary the degree to which an individual is rational about emotional investments. The baseline case above is the extreme case of complete irrationality. Another extreme case would be where an individual is completely aware of the possibility of changes in his identity, and naïvely believes himself to be able to remain selfish throughout, regardless of his exposure. To depict this latter case, we must make a distinction between what an individual believes and what in fact transpires, as accommodated in the following expressions.

$$U_1 = u_1 + \beta(\alpha y) \cdot E\{u_2 | y^* = \alpha y\}$$

$$= f(x_{i1}) + \beta(\alpha y) \cdot f(x_{i2} - \tau_{j2}^*)$$

$$U_2 = \beta(y)u_2 + (1 - \beta(y))u_2^j$$
$$= \beta(y)f(x_{i2} - \tau_{j2}) + (1 - \beta(y))f(x_{j2} + \tau_{j2})$$

Here, U_2 is as before, but the belief of the individual at period 1 is now that there is a degree of change in his identity. Yet, the belief may not be fully rational in that there is a factor $1 \geq \alpha > 0$ in between the actual level of emotional investment y and the believed level of emotional investment $y^* = \alpha y$. A person with $\alpha = 1$ then behaves as if he is perfectly aware of all the consequences of loving someone. A person with $\alpha = 0$ behaves like the base case scenario above.

The optimal solution can now be found by backward induction. In period 2 an individual chooses the level of transfer $\tau_{j2} = g(\beta(y))$ as above. Yet, there is also a level of believed transfer, which would be $\tau_{j2}^* = g(\beta(\alpha y))$. Given this believed level, the optimal level of y chosen in period 1 in an interior solution has to satisfy

$$y = \arg_y \{x'_{i1}(y)f'(x_{i1})$$
$$= -\alpha\beta'(\alpha y)f(x_{i2} - \tau_{j2}^*) + \alpha\beta'(\alpha y)g'(\beta(\alpha y))f'(x_{i2} - \tau_{j2})\}$$

which generically would imply that $\frac{\partial y}{\partial \alpha} < 0$ though uniqueness here is not guaranteed without further assumptions on $\beta(.)$ and $f(.)$.

This model allows for the extreme of the first case in which individuals will experience far more changes in their identities simply because they are unaware of the changes befalling them. In the main text, I implicitly appealed to the idea that younger individuals are less aware of the mechanism being modeled than are older individuals, who have learned how they "lose their hearts" and are hence more cautious when it comes to emotional investments. I have also appealed to this notion of naïveté when discussing the optimal actions of a manipulator who hides the true intent of his actions in order to engender loyalty in others.

This result also includes an implicit condition that informs us about whether or not a person will be purely greedy. Pure greed will result in the case that $x'_{i1}(0)f'(x_{i1}) < -\alpha\beta'(0)f(x_{i2}) + \alpha\beta'(0)g'(\beta(0))f'(x_{i2})$ because then the optimal level of y is 0. Intuitively, this describes the situation where investing a part of one's personality into love for entity j yields too few benefits currently and/or would cost too much in the future in terms of reduced benefits for the remaining (selfish) part of the individual. If the benefits of love are high enough, then the individual chooses a nonzero level of emotional investment in the first period, forcing that individual into positive transfers to the loved entity in the second period.

Though this model is exceptionally simple, it nevertheless has many immediate implications that are in line with the arguments in the text. Individuals who believe they have less to gain from changing their identities (i.e., those with lower $x'_{i1}(y)$) will invest less in love; individuals with more to lose from changing their identities (i.e., those with higher $f'(\tau_{j2})$) will invest less in love; and individuals who love more easily (i.e., those with higher $\beta'(y)$) will choose lower levels of emotional investments. These direct implications reflect the arguments in the text that more powerful individuals love less easily; that individuals who face more radical demands by the objects of their love (i.e., higher sacrifices) will be more cautious; and that individuals who know they are vulnerable to love (i.e., they are in some sense weak) might well choose rationally to stay away from temptation if they could.

A second extension to this model is in terms of interpretation. x_{it} is presented above as the actual level of final consumption, and the entity towards which investments y were made were reciprocated through the relationship between x_{it} and y. If we exchange the word "actual final consumption" for "believed final consumption," then the model suddenly includes situations in which entity j might not exist at all, and hence in which investments y into that entity, as well as sacrifices τ_{j2} towards that entity, have no actual effect on the utility of any real person besides individual i. Frijters and Baron (2012) show how one can model a believed utility function for an entity j that is reciprocal: a j that cares about the distance between y and x_{it}, and that would thus lead to a believed (but not actual) relation between x_{it} and y.

A third stylized extension is to make the power aspect that has hitherto been implicit in the function $x_{i1}(y)$, more visible. To this end, envision a situation where there are K sources of intermediary consumption goods, c_k. The final consumption good by individual i in period 1, x_{i1}, is itself a function of the levels of each of these intermediary consumption goods c_k, and for each consumption good there is the possibility of investing some love towards an entity j_k. We denote the love investment given to entity j_K as y_K, where the following holds:

$$x_{i1}(y_1, .., y_K) = h(c_1(y_1), .., c_K(y_K))$$

Simple forms of $h(.)$ could be a linear function, a constant elasticity of substitution function, or a Cobb–Douglas function. I will merely assume that the standard Inada conditions apply to $h(.)$. The main point of this extension is to put forward the idea of functions, depicted here as $c_k(y_k)$, that depend on the perceived relative power of entities i and j.

For each consumption good c_k, the entity j_k can be seen as possessing a perceived level of power Pj_k, while for each consumption good, individual i believes himself to have a perceived level of power Pi_k. Power in this model works via an effect on the functions $c_k(y_k)$.

The simplest assumption one can make about power is that the entity with the greatest power can take all of the available consumption goods in that realm (or at least can believe that they are available for the taking). This means that if $Pi_k > Pj_k$, then individual i believes that he can confiscate all of the available c_k, denoted as $\overline{c_k}$, without any emotional investment. Mathematically, this implies that $c_k(0) = \overline{c_k}$ iff $Pi_k > Pj_k$ (where $\overline{c_k}$ depicts the full amount of good k that is available).

If individual i perceives that the amount of power of the other entity is higher than his own, however (i.e., that $Pi_k < Pj_k$), then the Love Principle can be stated mathematically as the presumption that $c_k(0) = 0$ if $Pi_k < Pj_k$ while $c'_k(y_k) > 0$. Summarizing, one can hypothesize that $c_k(y_k) = \overline{c_k} * (Pi_k > Pj_k) + (Pi_k \leq Pj_k) \cdot \beta_k(y_k)$, where $\beta'_k(y_k) > 0$ and $\beta_k(y_k) \leq \overline{c_k}$.

If we now define a kind of aggregate outside entity j such that $y = \sum_k y_k$ and the "cost of love" in future periods is again the inclusion of the term $(1 - \beta(y))f(\tau_{j2})$ in the second-period utility function of individual i, then we get the following solutions to the individual optimization problem:

- For all areas of consumption where $Pi_k > Pj_k$ the individual chooses pure greed, and sets $y_k = 0$.
- The overall level of emotional investment chosen is given by the same formula as before, i.e., $y = \arg_y\{x'_{i1}(y)f'(x_{i1}) = -\alpha\beta'(\alpha y)f(x_{i2} - \tau_{j2}^*) + \alpha\beta'(\alpha y)g'(\beta(\alpha y))f'(x_{i2} - \tau_{j2})\}$.
- For each area k in the set Z for which it holds that $Pi_k \leq Pj_k$, the optimal level of emotional investment y_k^* solves:

$$\frac{\partial c_k}{\partial y_k^*} \frac{\partial h(c_1(y_1^*), .., c_K(y_K^*))}{\partial c_k} = \lambda$$

where λ is a constant and implicitly given by the condition that $y = \sum_{k \in Z} y_k^*(\lambda)$. This solution equation has very simple intuitive properties. The more an individual desires the intermediary good k (where the strength of desire is captured by $\frac{\partial h(.)}{\partial c_k}$), the higher the emotional investment. The less the individual unconsciously believes that the entity with which he is emotionally bargaining is reciprocal (captured by $\frac{\partial c_k}{\partial y_k^*}$), the less is his emotional investment.

Many other assumptions could be made about the precise interaction between these powers, and one could of course invoke more than just two powers to play roles in the consumption profiles. One could also further explore the interpretation of allowing for beliefs rather than realized consumption to affect utility. This extension also shows that even though power itself is mainly an outcome of group processes, it is nonetheless undeniable that at the level of the individual who wants something, power is perceived as simply existing in amounts possessed by himself and outside entities.

The implications of this simple mathematical setup are immediate from the assumptions made, and are in line with the main text. An individual will not love something that he believes has no power over him, in the sense of affecting his consumption; the more he wants something, the more of his love he will invest; an individual can love many different entities at the same time; weak individuals will love more; and individuals who act with great love in one area can be entirely greedy in another. From the perspective of a would-be manipulator, if you want individuals to love an entity, that entity must appear to them to be powerful in the sense of withholding consumption that they desire.

6.1.2 Conclusion and discussion

The model and its extensions above can be further extended to include more time periods, more decisions, more individuals, and more intricate power plays. The framework above should be seen as only one possible way to formalize the arguments on love, identity, and power that are presented in the text. There are many other ways in which these arguments can be modeled, including a more detailed description of the beliefs held by an individual (a route taken by Frijters and Baron 2012), a more intricate model of where power comes from (see, for example, the model presented in the next section), and models whereby whole groups rather than only individuals are the agents of emotional investment.

6.2 Model 2: Stylized groups and group power

In this section of the chapter, I discuss the basic model presented in Frijters and Foster (2010), which details a particular way of envisaging the relationships amongst ideals, groups, and power. Most of this section is a direct copy of the model presented in that paper, which was specifically developed in order to formalize the group-related ideas in this book.

The model starts with individuals who have an innate ability to be idealistic, coupled with a potential for violence towards those who do not behave according to their held ideals. In order for individuals to have an incentive to combine into groups, the economic environment of the model is characterized by uncertainty and the possibility of appropriation. This gives individuals an incentive to pool their resources in order to weather adverse shocks, and an incentive to pool their individual capacities for violence in order to be able to steal the resources of others via threats of violence. The risk-sharing incentive and the appropriation incentive are core features of this model. Groups themselves are associated with social norms regarding behavior, implicit score sheets as to who gets what, and expectations that violence will be directed towards people who violate the group's social norms. Thus, social norms will guide the combined violence potential of the group, which corresponds to how "group power" works in reality.

The model supports in theory several static Nash equilibria corresponding to the archetypal groups outlined in the main text. In an extension, individuals first decide upon their ideals, and then upon their actions, which reduces the possible equilibria.

6.2.1 The model

Throughout the analysis, I assume a fixed population of N individuals divided into $K < N$ mutually exclusive "potential groups," where N_i denotes the number of individuals in a "potential group" to which individual i belongs. Individuals begin by already having something in common with their potential group members, though there is nothing yet that otherwise characterizes the members as a group. In one extension to the original paper, I addressed the possibility of people switching between groups, but that extension is not pursued here.

The utility function of an individual is given by

$$U_i = u_1(y_i) - \sum_{j \in N} v_{ij} - \bar{\beta} \sum_{j \in S_i} v_{ji} - \underline{\beta} \sum_{j \notin S_i} v_{ji}$$

where $u_1(.)$ is a concave subutility function; y_i is disposable income; v_{ij} is the amount of violence individual i directs to individual j; v_{ji} is the amount of violence individual j directs to individual i; S_i denotes the set of individuals to which i belongs; $\bar{\beta}$ is the marginal pain of having violence inflicted upon one by members of one's own group; and $\underline{\beta}$ is the marginal pain of violence inflicted by members of other groups. Throughout, the assumption is made that $\bar{\beta} > \underline{\beta} > 1$, meaning that it is more painful to have violence inflicted than to inflict violence, and that members of one's own group are better able than others to make the violence hurt.

This utility function captures several ideas simultaneously. The first is the notion of trade-offs in the use of violence. Specifically, the use of violence is costly to the person wielding that violence, but even more costly to the person at whom the violence is directed. This immediately means that the credible threat of violence is a very useful means of manipulation: if one can credibly threaten violence, then others wishing to avoid that violence would have an incentive to comply with one's demands. The main point of the model is to illustrate mathematically the mechanism through which groups make these threats self-enforcing and credible.

Another idea incorporated into this utility function is that what ultimately matters to individuals is their disposable income. All of the other aspects, including the group formation, threats of violence, and so on ultimately serve to increase $u_1(y_i)$. In this sense, simple individual greed is the ultimate driver of behavior, although again, loss of own identity will endogenously come about as a by-product of the attempt to increase $u_1(y_i)$.

Ideals do not yet appear directly in this utility function, but are implicit in the following function which determines violence:

$$v_{ij} = \alpha_i f(\tilde{\tau}_{iS_j} - \tau_{ji}) + \gamma_i \alpha_i \sum_{k \in Si \backslash i} f(\tilde{\tau}_{iS_j} - \tau_{jk}) \qquad (6.2.1)$$

$\tilde{\tau}_{iS_j}$ is the ideal tax rate of individual i as applying to the group S_j to which j belongs, meaning that an individual i expects to get a proportion $\tilde{\tau}_{iS_j}$ of the income of each individual j in group S_j (note that this proportion is group-specific). τ_{ji} is the amount of tax actually paid by j to i. α_i, where $0 < \alpha_i < \bar{\alpha}$, is an individually varying parameter that denotes the degree to which group-oriented ideals are important to individual i. $f(x) = 0$ for $x \leq 0$, and $f'(x) > 0$ and $f''(x) = 0$ for $x > 0$. The notation $Si\backslash i$ indicates the set of all individuals within group S_i except for individual i himself. By design, $\tau_{ii} = \tilde{\tau}_{iS_i}$, meaning that an individual complies with his own ideal: we abstract from the possibility of conflicts within an individual.

This violence function captures many ideas at the same time. The main phenomenon captured is a particular mechanism that defines social norms in this context: social norms here relate to how resources should be distributed amongst group members, and what the punishment should be in case individuals fail to distribute resources according to these distributional norms. Distributional norms are captured by the ideal tax rates $\tilde{\tau}_{iS_j}$ that are specific to groups, yet in principle extend to everyone else: the norms within one group do not just apply to how much should be shared within that group, but are also ideals about how much members of that group are owed by others in other groups. Norms about the level of violence that should follow "disobedience" are embedded in the individual parameters α_i and γ_i, where α_i denotes the overall degree to which someone chooses to care about all social norms (whether they apply to him or to others), and γ_i denotes the degree to which i has decided that other members of his group matter to him. In this sense, γ_i serves the role of love in this model and, as with the previous model, it is seen as a choice parameter.

The function $f(.)$ is a physiological violence-response function: it captures the idea that individuals feel compelled to be violent towards others who violate their ideal, which is very much in the line of Reuben and van Winden (2008), Nikiforakis (2010), and other recent experimentalists. The strength of that response depends on α, which as noted above denotes how strongly the individual adheres to the ideal. The first part of the violence equation relates to the violence by i towards j when j pays i less than the ideal; the second part relates to the violence by i towards j when j pays other members of the group to which i belongs less than the ideal. The strength of the second response is related to the choice variable γ_i (where $0 \le \gamma_i \le 1$), which as noted above is an indicator of group cohesion. The latter inequality implies that, regardless of group strength, members maintain a self-preservation response that is at least as strong as their impulse to defend any single other in their group – although the self-preservation response can be dominated by the impulse to defend the entire group.

Disposable income in this simplest framework is generated by transfers between individuals starting from an initial exogenous endowment that itself is uncertain:

$$y_i = (1 - \sum_j \tau_{ij}) Y_{i0} + \sum_j \tau_{ji} Y_{j0}$$

$$\sum_j \tau_{ij} \le 1$$

The elements of the initial vector of endowments Y_0 are drawn independently from a known distribution, with full support between a minimum of $\underline{Y}$ and maximum of $\bar{Y}$.

The choice variables for each individual include α_i (the strength of own adherence to the group's ideals), γ_i (the level of cohesion that individual i displays towards his group S_i), $\tilde{\tau}_{iS_j}$ (ideals that individual i believes define group S_j), and all the τ_{ij} (actual transfers made from individual i to other group members).

The timing and information structure of the static model is as follows:

1. All individuals simultaneously choose the set $\{\alpha_i, \gamma_i, \tilde{\tau}_{iS_j}, \tau_{ij}\}$ in order to maximize expected U_i (where the expectation is over the realizations of Y, and presuming that other individuals will abide by the individual's own chosen ideals), with all elements of the model being common knowledge.
2. Based on the realization of Y_{i0} and the choices of all other players, each individual computes and executes his level of violence.

The assumption that each individual decides $\{\tau_{ij}\}$ under the presumption that others will follow the given individual's chosen ideals is a technical assumption mainly made to keep the model simple, in the sense of ensuring that there is a unique correspondence between all of the initial choices $\{\alpha_i, \gamma_i, \tilde{\tau}_{iS_j}\}$ and the subsequent actions $\{\tau_{ij}\}$. This restricts the coordination problem to step one of the model.[1]

6.2.2 Interim discussion

Before discussing the solution to the static model, it is useful to reflect on the basic components that this model assumes make up the psyche of the individual.

- The idea that individuals care about their level of consumption, via $u_1(.)$, is standard. The assumption that there are no production decisions in the model (Y_{i0} is exogenous) implies that the main motivation for group formation in this model is the insurance motive.

- The parameter γ_i can be interpreted as the degree to which individuals identify with the members of their group and for this reason are violent towards group members who "short-change" the other people within the group. The formulation of violence in Equation 6.2.1 also accommodates the idea of "group punishment," in that the strength of the feelings of the whole group about their ideals directly determines the total extent to which an individual would be punished for violating a "group ideal" (which itself can be represented in the model as a $\tilde{\tau}_{iS_j}$ that is held in common by all members of group j). In the case that an individual outside the group to which i belongs (say, in group g) does not make a transfer to individual m, then the total amount of violence directed towards that person equals $\alpha_i f(\tilde{\tau}_{iS_g})(1 + \sum_{k \in Si \setminus m} \gamma_k)$, with the first component being the violence implemented by individual m himself, and the second component the violence implemented by the other members of m's group.

- The idea that individuals think about others and themselves as belonging to groups of people $S.$, each of which they associate with a single ideal, fits in with the main argument in categorization theory (Turner, Hogg, Oakes, Reicher, and Wetherell 1987) that individuals interpret what they observe by categorizing everything they see into sets (Rosch and Lloyd 1978). The group is itself an abstraction: it only truly exists in the minds of individuals.

---

[1] Without this assumption, step two is indeterminate, which makes it impossible to say how individuals can formulate expectations in step one.

- The constancy of the function $f(.)$ implies that in this model, once a level of baseline "aggressiveness" has been decided upon (via, e.g., prior education or self-training), an individual can no longer help but be aggressive in that predetermined degree towards those who violate his ideas of right and wrong. This corresponds closely to the importance placed on prior violence commitment in assessing the likelihood of future violence, for example as documented in the Historical-Clinical-Risk-Management-20, a best-practice metric for psychiatrists tasked with predicting violence (Andrade 2009). Its evolutionary rationale is most likely to be found in the evolution of whatever preceded the hominids, since the reward and violence parts of our brains precede the hominid additions. One should also note that in a fluid situation where the potential for coordination is very low (leading individuals to make many wrong assumptions about others), one should expect a large degree of violence simply because, if only by accident, many individuals will violate the ideals of many others.

- The model incorporates the notion of narrow obedience in the explicit possibility that $\alpha_i = 0$. In that special case, an individual does not feel adherence to any ideal, and could therefore be forced into compliance by any plausible threat towards him. He would also not be able to credibly threaten anyone else.

- Different aspects of the model relate to different notions of personal choice. First, the eventual distribution of y_i relates to poverty and inequality. As such, a more equal distribution would mean a greater ability of individuals to function in the way deemed normal in their group (since income brings with it the possibility of transferring some of that income to others, thereby satisfying the group's ideals). Second, α_i and y_i relate to the strength with which ideals and group identities are held, and can be interpreted as capturing the degree of aggressiveness and the constraints on the choice to associate with one's group – but with a twist. In this model, these parameters are explicitly related to violence: the more one's beliefs are shared with others, the stronger one's resolve to defend one's beliefs and associations through punishing others who do not abide by one's ideals. This puts constraints on others though. I interpret α_i as the ith individual's degree of aggressiveness, associated both with the positive freedom of i to fight for his ideals and the implications this aggressiveness entails for the reduced choices of others (negative freedom).

Lastly, the combination of the parameters $\{\alpha_i, \gamma_i\}$ and taxes $\tilde{\tau}_{iS_j}$ constitutes a kind of "tax system" facing other individuals, and as such determines the incentive system of others. The very group mechanism itself, as defined by these elements of the model, brings with it a restriction of choice since those who fail to abide by group ideals are punished.

6.2.3 Static solutions

The solution concept is a backward-induction Nash equilibrium in expected utility. The first condition that must hold at the individual level in equilibrium is that no individual is able to improve on his expected utility by changing his choice of $\{\alpha_i, \gamma_i, \tilde{\tau}_{iS_j}, \tau_{ij}\}$ given the choices of all others. Importantly, if the choices of others force i into any violence, then i can improve his utility by changing elements in the subset $\{\alpha_i, \gamma_i, \tilde{\tau}_{iS_j}\}$, because any violence entails a strict loss to the perpetrator. Also, any reduction in τ_{ij} that does not elicit a violent reaction in equilibrium is an improvement for the individual, implying that in any equilibrium either $\tilde{\tau}_{iS_j} = \tau_{ji}$ or $\alpha_i = \tau_{ji} = 0$ for every i and j. To save on notation, $V_i(\tau_{ij}) = (\bar{\beta} \sum_{j \in S_i} v_{ji} + \underline{\beta} \sum_{j \in S_i} v_{ji})$ is used to denote the total level of additional "violence utility" inflicted upon i as a function of τ_{ij}. For any positive τ_{ij}, it must hold in equilibrium that the level of threatened violence utility more than offsets the utility cost of the transfer, i.e., $u_1(y_i + (x - \tau_{ij})Y_{i0}) - V_i(x) \leq u_1(y_i) - V_i(\tau_{ij})$ for any x such that $0 \leq x \leq \tau_{ij}$. Otherwise, the transfer x would constitute an improvement on the original candidate equilibrium.

There are infinitely many Nash equilibria of the static model that solve these conditions: almost any set of transfers can be supported by the appropriate set of beliefs. Usually, in models of economic interactions, the existence of many equilibria is seen as an undesirable outcome, and as such proof of a poorly specified model. In this case, multiple possible equilibria is exactly what is wanted because this allows for many stable configurations of groups starting from the same initial conditions, meaning that the very simple model above is capable of rationalizing many different outcomes. For convenience and to indicate this generality, the model is referred to below as the "Reciprocity-Hierarchy" (RH) model. The task of working out what further conditions would have to apply in order to arrive at any particular subset of outcomes is left for future work.

I will present and discuss five equilibria in particular that correspond to all but one of the stylized group types hypothesized to exist in the main text. It will turn out that the solutions to a more structured dynamic model coincide with these particular static equilibria.

Static solution 1: Local reciprocity

Definition 6.2.1 *A local reciprocity equilibrium to the RH model consists of each group S_i having the sharing rule $\tilde{\tau}_{iS_i} = \frac{1}{N_i}$; $\tilde{\tau}_{iS_j} = 0$ for all $j \notin S_i$; $\alpha_i = \bar{\alpha}$; $\tau_{ji} = \tilde{\tau}_{iS_j}$; and $\gamma_i = 1$.*

Intuitively, this configuration of the model captures the idea of perfect sharing within each group and no transfers between groups, as well as a strong degree of internal enforcement within each group via the high α_i.

Lemma 6.2.2 *A local reciprocity equilibrium to the RH model exists if the following condition is met:*

a) (incentive compatibility within each group)
$$\bar{\beta}(\bar{\alpha} + \bar{\alpha}(N_i - 2)f'(0)) > Y_{j0}u'_1(y_j) \text{ for any } j \in S_i.$$

Incentive compatibility hinges on the marginal point at which each individual j has to decide whether or not to transfer anything to individual i, with the cost of deviating from the ideal being the violent reaction of the individual who is short-changed and the violence of his other group members, which is compared to the benefit of not sharing (i.e., increased consumption). Under the stated condition, everyone within the group rationally complies with what is expected of them by other group members.

It is not hard to see that every other decision that each individual makes cannot be improved upon unilaterally. Increasing any ideal $\tilde{\tau}_{iS_j}$ would mean an individual would automatically engage in costly violence carrying no benefit; and in equilibrium there actually is no violence or mismatch between ideals and actions, and thus α_i can be anything, given the α_j of others.

Several remarks can be made about this equilibrium. The first is that it is within-group socially optimal, in the sense that there is perfect risk-sharing within the group. The second is that the total tax rate faced by each individual is exceptionally high: the marginal taxes on any additional income are $(1 - \frac{1}{N_i})$, which means that in this solution each individual would have very little incentive to create more income.

Naturally, in this model, work incentives are irrelevant because income levels are determined via a process that is entirely outside the control of the individual.

Static solution 2: Anonymous autarky

Definition 6.2.3 *An autarky equilibrium to the RH model consists of* $\tilde{\tau}_{iS_j} = \alpha_i = \tau_{ji} = \gamma_i = 0$ *for all combinations i and j.*

Intuitively, this configuration of the model captures the state of no sharing and no ideals. It is immediate that this is an equilibrium but also that it is not *ex ante* Pareto efficient either within groups or across groups because of the *ex ante* benefit of risk-sharing. Hence, if Pareto efficiency were viewed as another part of any evolutionarily stable situation, then autonomous autarky should not arise.

Static solution 3: Grand reciprocity

Definition 6.2.4 *A grand reciprocity equilibrium to the RH model consists of* $\tilde{\tau}_{iS_j} = \frac{1}{N}$ *for all combinations of i and j;* $\alpha_i = \bar{\alpha}$; $\gamma_i = 1$; *and* $\tau_{ji} = \tilde{\tau}_{iS_j}$.

Intuitively, this configuration of the model captures the notion of a large circle of reciprocity, where each individual gives to the "whole group" and each receives a fair share of the resources of the whole group.

Lemma 6.2.5 *A grand reciprocity equilibrium to the RH model exists if the following condition is met:*

a1) (incentive compatibility between and within each group)
$$\bar{\beta}(\bar{\alpha} + \bar{\alpha}(N_i - 2))f'(0) > Y_{j0}u_1'(y_j) \text{ for any } j \in S_i \text{ and}$$
$$\underline{\beta}(\bar{\alpha} + \bar{\alpha}(N_i - 1))f'(0) > Y_{j0}u_1'(y_j) \text{ for any } j \notin S_i.$$

Again, it is immediate that this is a possible equilibrium as soon as condition a1) is met. It is also immediate that this equilibrium denotes the social welfare optimum of perfect risk-sharing, but where the incentives to create more income (if individuals were able to do so) would be extremely low. By construction, the punishment meted out is related to the size of the group to which each individual belongs. This also gives a reason for why this equilibrium is more easily enforceable if individuals view themselves as part of a single large group, rather than belonging to distinct smaller groups.[2]

Static solution 4: Grand hierarchy
Definition 6.2.6 *A grand hierarchical equilibrium to the RH model consists of the first group (call it $i = 1$, assuming without loss of generality that this group contains individual i) having $\alpha_i = \bar{\alpha}$, $\gamma_i = 1$, and $\tilde{\tau}_{iS_i} = \tilde{\tau}_{iS_j} = \frac{1}{N_i}$ for all i,j. For all other groups, $\alpha_i = 0$, $\gamma_i = 0$, and $\tilde{\tau}_{iS_j} = 0$. For all combinations of i and j, it holds that $\tau_{ji} = \tilde{\tau}_{iS_j}$.*

Intuitively, this configuration of the model captures the idea of exploitation, whereby the members of one dominant group share only amongst themselves and force all individuals in all other groups to give them all their income. This is accompanied by the dominant group having both high internal cohesion (γ_i) and high levels of aggression towards transgressors (α_i). The subordinate groups have low cohesion and low aggression.

Lemma 6.2.7 *A grand hierarchical equilibrium to the RH model exists if the following conditions are met:*

a2) (incentive compatibility within the dominant group)
$$\bar{\beta}(\bar{\alpha} + \bar{\alpha}(N_1 - 2))f'(\tilde{\tau}_{iS_i}) > Y_{j0}u'_1(y_j) \text{ for any } i,j \in S_1.$$
b) (incentive compatibility between groups)
$$\underline{\beta}(\bar{\alpha} + \bar{\alpha}(N_1 - 1))f'(\tilde{\tau}_{iS_i}) > Y_{j0}u'_1(0) \text{ for any } j \notin S_1.$$

The first incentive compatibility constraint is analogous to that required by previous equilibria, and applies within the dominant group. The second constraint captures the incentives facing individuals outside the dominant group. This latter constraint signifies that the violence of the dominant group as a whole has to be sufficient to force any other individual to forgo all consumption. The assumption that α_i and $\tilde{\tau}_{iS_j}$ are both zero for the exploited groups is not strictly speaking necessary, as assuming that $\tilde{\tau}_{iS_j} = 0$ for members of the dominated group is enough to constitute an equilibrium, because that alone will already

---

[2] If some groups are too small to satisfy a1) and others are large enough, then the grand reciprocity equilibrium does not exist, but there is an equilibrium in which the largest coalition consists of only groups large enough to enforce the ideal tax rate.

yield a level of welfare that cannot be improved upon (whereas welfare under any $\tilde{\tau}_{iS_j} > 0$ could be improved upon).

This equilibrium generates some key predictions regarding exploitative situations. In order to maintain exploitation, there must be some solidarity amongst the group doing the exploiting in order to be able to threaten the exploited with violence sufficient that they comply. Also, the exploited must be fairly passive (in terms of having at least $\tilde{\tau}_{iS_j}$ equal to zero, or else $\alpha_i = 0$). While this equilibrium is extreme in the sense that it implies total exploitation of everyone by one dominant group, the underlying logic would remain in only somewhat diluted form if we added features to the model that would make total exploitation infeasible (such as, for example, limited observability of the initial incomes of others[3] or an infinite marginal utility of consumption at zero). What would then be predicted is merely a lower degree of exploitation.

Static solution 5: Local hierarchy

To illustrate one final static example, I will, for pure presentational reasons, presume there to be only one group ($K = 1$), which one should think of as rather small.

Definition 6.2.8 *A local hierarchy equilibrium to the RH model consists of the first $M < N$ individuals in the group having $\alpha_i = \bar{\alpha}$, $\gamma_i = 0$, and $\tilde{\tau}_{iS_i} = \frac{1}{M}$. For the other individuals, $\alpha_i = 0$, $\gamma_i = 1$, and $\tilde{\tau}_{iS_j} = 0$. For $i < M$ and any j it holds that $\tau_{ji} = \frac{1}{M}$. For $i \geq M$ and $j < M$ it holds that $\tau_{ji} = 0$.*

In this case, one part of the group exploits the other part of the group. All the income is consumed by the first M members of the group, a state of affairs that is backed up by aggression on the part of the exploiters. The main difference between this and the grand hierarchy situation is in the parameters γ_i: unlike in the grand hierarchy case, the exploiters now do not form a strong identity ($\gamma_i = 0$) because a strong group identity would force them to be violent towards each other for not transferring

[3] Here I have in mind an equilibrium in which "bosses" spend their time monitoring "workers" at a cost. Workers would then choose not to monitor others because such information is not used by them to determine their actions. In this sense, hierarchy can be seen as a solution to the problem of how to provide incentives to individuals whose actions are poorly observed: hierarchy creates a strong incentive for bosses to monitor, and as such is a logical structure to emerge when monitoring is very difficult but important.

income to the other group members. Again, the subordinate members are passive. One real-world situation I have in mind here is gender relations within a group.

Lemma 6.2.9 *A local hierarchy equilibrium to the RH model exists if the following conditions are met:*

a3) (incentive compatibility within the aggressive subgroup)
   $\bar{\beta}\bar{\alpha}f'(0) > Y_{j0}u'_1(y_j)$, for any $j \leq M$.
b) (incentive compatibility within the nonaggressive subgroup)
   $\bar{\beta}\bar{\alpha}f'(0) > Y_{j0}u'_1(0)$, for any $j > M$.

The condition on aggression is now much stronger than in the grand hierarchy case, in that a single aggressive individual must now be able to threaten a member of the nonaggressive subgroup with sufficient violence to force zero consumption by that latter individual. One would thus generically think of this only arising in small groups (where N is small) and perhaps where some individuals are innately more powerful than others, which could be thought of as heterogeneity in $f(.)$. In the "real world" of local exploitation, such as that of violent men towards women, it is striking how apt the assumption is that violence and the threat of violence are tied to stated ideals: aggressors routinely appeal to perceived norm violation on the part of the victim.[4]

6.2.4 Dynamic solutions

In the static model, there is an infinite number of equilibria, of which five were discussed above that yield group configurations with features typical of social structures we have seen in history and that have been discussed in the main text. One should see these equilibria mainly as descriptive of the internal dynamics of these groups and of how different groups interrelate. There is as yet no reason to suggest that any of these equilibria are "stable" or would "naturally" arise in a dynamic situation. They merely form extremes on a spectrum. It is from reality that one would have to argue for their stability and existence, not from these models.

---

[4] See, for example, Hirschmann (1996), Hearn (1998), and Anderson and Umberson (2001) (p. 367–368) for discussions of how abusive husbands often cite their wives' deficiencies and the man's right to punish them for their deficiencies.

In this subsection, I try to capture more fully what it might mean for individuals to identify with their group, and in the process the number of distinct equilibria is reduced.

I begin with the model above and abstract from the possibility that the highest level of violence a whole group can muster is insufficient to force an individual to comply (i.e., all incentive compatibility constraints for large groups are assumed to be met). I introduce dynamics in terms of the sequential timing of decisions.

In period $t = 1$, an individual must decide upon his α_i, γ_i, and $\tilde{\tau}_{iS_j}$, while in period $t = 2$, the incomes of all individuals are revealed and decisions are made about τ_{ij} that take the choices of period 1 as given. I add to this chronological division a set of additional assumptions that reflect the importance of identity and reciprocity for an individual: specifically, each individual i expects the set $\{\alpha_i, \gamma_i, \tilde{\tau}_{iS_j}\}$ to be the same for all other members of the same identity, and presumes that all others will behave according to that ideal when deciding upon their own transfers. Hence, I presume that the individual decides upon his own set $\{\alpha_i, \gamma_i, \tilde{\tau}_{iS_j}\}$ in period 1 as if all others in the group would choose the same, and in period 2, he acts assuming that others will follow these ideals. This is a particular interpretation of what reciprocity means: an individual chooses how much to expect others to transfer to him $(\tilde{\tau}_{iS_i})$, but does so believing that others will "demand" the same transfer from him. This choice framework therefore implicitly includes an element of blind sacrifice, in the sense that an individual's understanding of another group member is as an abstract but automatically reciprocal entity that asks and rewards at the same levels as those at which the individual himself asks and rewards.

The timing and information structure of the dynamic model are as follows:

$t = 1$ All individuals simultaneously choose the set $\{\alpha_i, \gamma_i, \tilde{\tau}_{iS_j}\}$ in order to maximize expected U_i. Each individual i takes as given that every other individual in group S_i chooses the same $\{\alpha_i, \gamma_i, \tilde{\tau}_{iS_j}\}$.

$t = 2$ Based on the realization of Y_{i0} and the choices $\{\alpha_j, \gamma_j, \tilde{\tau}_{jS_j}\}$ of all other players, each player i decides on the set $\{\tau_{ij}\}$ that maximizes U_i given an expectation that all others will conform to ideal transfers (i.e., expecting that $\tau_{ji} = \tilde{\tau}_{iS_j}$) and given the expected ensuing level of violence in step 3.

$t = 3$ Based on the choices $\{\tau_{..}\}$, each individual computes and executes his level of violence.

The change here, compared to the static model, is that the first stage entails a more stringent identification of the individual with his group, presumed to come from prior choices or contexts (such as upbringing). This means that whereas the static model has an "anything goes" element to it, groups in the dynamic model are more crystallized and oriented around reciprocity towards the group abstraction. One can see this as an assumption that due to an unmodeled evolutionary process, all of the nonreciprocal social norms have been weeded out of the possible set of norms that individuals still entertain.

In order to ascertain the optimal level of transfers, it will be useful to define the anticipated income of individual i as

$$y_i^* = (1 - \sum_j \tau_{ij})Y_{i0} + \sum_j \tilde{\tau}_{iS_j}Y_{j0},$$

which equals the final income of an individual if the behavior of all others accords with the expected ideals.

The main input into a solution is the relation between the decisions τ_{ij} in step two and the set $\{\alpha_i, \gamma_i, \tilde{\tau}_{iS_j}\}$ of step one, which in turn depends on the violence associated with each choice. This is a standard optimal control problem, whose solution follows the following heuristic:

1. An individual i ranks all other individuals j according to $\frac{dV_i(\tilde{\tau}_{jS_j})}{d\tau_{ij}}$. In case of ties (i.e., where more than one j has the same $\frac{dV_i(\tilde{\tau}_{jS_j})}{d\tau_{ij}}$), individuals randomly order the threats.
2. In backward order (from low $\frac{dV_i(\tilde{\tau}_{jS_j})}{d\tau_{ij}}$ to high $\frac{dV_i(\tilde{\tau}_{jS_j})}{d\tau_{ij}}$), an individual chooses, taking their current planned set $\{\tau_{ij}\}$,

$$\tau_{ij} = \begin{cases} \tilde{\tau}_{jS_i} \text{ iff } \sum_{j \neq i} \tilde{\tau}_{jS_i} \leq 1 \text{ and } \forall j, \dfrac{dV_i(\tilde{\tau}_{jS_i})}{d\tau_{ij}} > Y_{i0}u_1'(y_i^*) \\[2ex] 0 \text{ iff } \dfrac{dV_i(\tilde{\tau}_{jS_i})}{d\tau_{ij}} \leq Y_{i0}u_1'(y_i^* + \tilde{\tau}_{jS_i}Y_{i0}) \\[2ex] x \text{ iff } Y_{i0}u_1'(y_i^* + xY_{i0}) = \dfrac{dV_i(\tilde{\tau}_{jS_i})}{d\tau_{ij}} \text{ for an } x \text{ such that } \tilde{\tau}_{jS_i} > x > 0 \end{cases}$$

Intuitively, this plan entails giving in to the biggest threats, accepting the violence ensuing from not giving in to the lowest threats, and potentially accepting an intermediate level of violence from a single intermediate threat.

The dynamic framework within a single group ($K = 1$)

The number of observationally different equilibria (in terms of actual transfers, levels of violence, and utilities) in the dynamic setting where $K = 1$ reduces to one.

Lemma 6.2.10 *In the dynamic RH model there exists only the grand reciprocity equilibrium where there is equal sharing ($\tilde{\tau}_i = \tau_{ij} = \frac{1}{N}$) and where the parameters $\{\alpha, \gamma\}$ have to satisfy $\bar{\beta}(\alpha + \gamma\alpha(N-2))f'(0) \geq Yu'_1(Y)$.*

The condition in Lemma 6.2.10 ensures that there is no possible realization of incomes under which individuals would not comply with the equal sharing rule, which means that the parameters $\{\alpha, \gamma\}$ need not be unique. This equilibrium maximizes expected welfare, and no other sharing rule would also maximize expected welfare.

Local hierarchy is not an equilibrium in this case because of the assumption that the individual expects his group members to have the same parameter set as himself. To imagine within-group exploitation requires an individual to imagine the others in his group believing and/or behaving unlike him.

Dynamic solutions with multiple groups ($K = 2$)

Building on the single-group dynamic model above, I now presume there are two groups of which by design the first one is the largest ($N_1 > N_N$). An equilibrium is again sought in which no individual can improve on his *ex ante* expected welfare. The assumptions on the decision making of each individual in a dynamic setting mean that an individual's decision is the same as the whole group's decision in equilibrium (that is, while a situation can be envisaged in which individuals within groups differ in terms of what they expect other group members to do, this is nevertheless not possible in an equilibrium). In this setting, I offer the following result:

Conjecture 6.2.11 *In the dynamic model with $K = 2$, iff $\underline{\beta}(\bar{\alpha} + \bar{\alpha}(N_1 - 1)) > \bar{\beta}(\bar{\alpha}(N_N - 1))$ then there is only the grand hierarchy equilibrium. Iff $\underline{\beta}(\bar{\alpha} + \bar{\alpha}(N_1 - 1)) < \bar{\beta}(\bar{\alpha}(N_N - 1))$, then any division that satisfies $\sum_{k \neq i} \tilde{\tau}_{iS_k} = 1$ leading to $\tau_{ij} = \tilde{\tau}_{iS_j}$ for all j is an equilibrium supported by $\alpha_s = \bar{\alpha}$, $\gamma_s = 1$ for all S.*

The intuition behind this conjecture is that the threat that can be mustered by the big group against the members of the small group depends on relative numbers and on the ratio $\frac{\bar{\beta}}{\underline{\beta}}$. If that ratio is large, then a slightly smaller group can threaten its own members with a greater degree of violence than that threatened by the bigger group, which makes any division of resources an equilibrium from which no group can individually profitably deviate (because the greater group cannot force the smaller group to hand over their resources). If the ratio $\frac{\bar{\beta}}{\underline{\beta}}$ is small, then the larger group can always credibly threaten more violence, which enables them to usurp all of the resources.

6.2.5 Discussion

In summary, the small reciprocal group, the large reciprocal group, and hierarchical outcomes all are shown here to be able to arise endogenously from a very simple dynamic model of social norms. The model should be seen as a mathematical translation of the main ideas around groups and power explained in the text, rather than an explanation for their "origins." The key ideas in this model are that of the role of social norms as mediators of violence; the role of risk-sharing and appropriation as underlying motives to form groups; the importance of within-group monitoring to sustain cooperative outcomes; and the role of norms about overall aggression and group loyalty in maintaining either a parasitical or a cooperative equilibrium.

Extending this model and proving conjecture 6.2.11 is left for future work.

6.3 Model 3: The operation of central authorities

The bulk of this section was written initially as a paper by myself and Alexander Tieman in 1999 (Frijters and Tieman 1999). After one try, we never offered it to other academic journals because we perceived the topics it covered to be too broad for any journal to be interested in at that time. The part it could play in a wider view was not yet clear, and we let the paper rest. Given that the model in hindsight was an important stepping stone in the development and formalization of some of the main ideas in this book, it is appropriate to reproduce the model here.

The goal of this work is to provide a very detailed account of how one might think about the evolution and operation of a central authority (e.g., a state) in a fully specified micro-model of optimizing agents. Tieman and I describe the circumstances under which such authorities arise, and specify the incentives surrounding every action taken by every agent along the way. The model includes roles for violence, loyalty, limited rationality, and strife between large groups. The endeavor serves more broadly as a proof of concept, illustrating that it is possible to generate detailed micro-models of such macro-phenomena as competing states.

Yet, the endeavor also shows the limitations of any such exercise. Specifically, it appears to be a more or less hopeless task to use micro-models to explain any actual state-level phenomena. The model is useful for replicating a stylized version of behavior one might observe in reality, but proves to be useless in predicting or even accurately describing what goes on in any particular country at any particular time.

The essential obstacle is that in order to pin down the strategic interactions amongst many players who have many different options and that differ in many ways, one's assumptions must be incredibly detailed. One has to specify exactly who can communicate what to whom and when; what types of beliefs are allowed; who can observe the actions of which others; how, by whom, and to whom punishment can be applied; which methods of interaction are allowed and which are impossible; what type of environment is assumed as the *a priori* state; all actual payoffs to all agents of every outcome that any agent might receive; all possibilities of payoff transfers between connected individuals; and so on. The number of specific assumptions required is so vast that although the result we give is indeed a model of macro-level circumstances, it is completely useless as a general theory. The specific assumptions one needs to make in order to solve the model are too unrealistic and restrictive. To be fair, this is a general problem in such micro-models, as one typically cannot allow for many different types of individuals, different types of communication, or different beliefs, due to problems of computational intractability.

Throughout this section, a leading example is used to explain the main concepts. First, the fixed (social, geographic, or product) space in which individuals are situated is described graphically, and all relevant notation is introduced. Second, the possibility of violence is introduced, and the threatening and punishment of players is discussed. Then, individuals' learning processes and payoff structures are addressed, which is followed by a detailed description of the sequence of events during a given time period. Finally, a preliminary result is achieved regarding the formation of central authorities.

6.3.1 The setting

Each of the N (N is large) vertices of the connected finite graph K is the address of one player. Every vertex $s \in K$ is directly connected to a (finite) number of other vertices by the edges of the graph K. No vertex is connected to itself, meaning that the graph K is irreflexive. We assume that all vertices have the same number m (where $0 < m << N$) of edges. The set of vertices directly connected to vertex s is the neighborhood of s. This nonempty set is called V_s. For any set of vertices $R \subset K$, the boundary of R is the set $\partial R = \{\cup_{r \in R} V_r\} \setminus R$. The neighborhood relation is symmetric: if r is a neighbor of s, then s is also a neighbor of r. As a result, there is an edge connecting s and r only if $r \in V_s$ and therefore also $s \in V_r$. Players are referred to by their respective addresses: player s is the player at vertex s, $s = 1, 2, \ldots, N$. A k-clique C_k is a set of k players in K who are all mutual neighbors, meaning that for all $s, r \in C_k$ it holds that $r \in V_s$ and therefore also that $s \in V_r$. A final important element of the initial setup is that players are assumed to have limited knowledge about the graph K. Specifically, each individual only possesses information about the graph structure up to two steps away from their personal location. Each player s thus knows which players are in the set V_s, as well as which are in the sets $V_r \; \forall r \in V_s$. Thus, each player s is able to assess whether the players in V_s are part of a clique.

Objects of choice for all players are actions in the set $\Gamma = \{A, B\}$. This means there are just two possible actions, A and B, which remains the case throughout the analysis. The configuration of the population at time t, describing the action choices of the whole population, is a function $\phi^t : K \rightarrow \Gamma^N$; the action of each player s at time t is described by $\phi^t(s)$. At time $t = 0$, each player is assigned an action at random with probability $\frac{1}{2}$ on each of the actions A and B. Each possible configuration $\phi^0 \in \{A, B\}^N$ therefore has probability $\frac{1}{2^N}$ of being selected as the initial configuration.

For any $R \subset K$ and configuration η, $\eta(R)$ denotes the restriction of η to R. For any set $R \subset K$ of players, $X(R)$ denotes the set of configurations of vertices in R. Let $\phi(-s)$ denote the configuration $\phi(K \setminus \{s\})$, and similarly $\phi(-R)$ denotes the configuration $\phi(K \setminus R)$. For a given configuration ϕ^t and action a, $\phi^t_{s,a}$ denotes the configuration identical to ϕ^t with the exception that player s is using action a.

Finally, for a given configuration ϕ^t and action a, let ϕ^t_a denote the number of players using action a, $a = A, B$, i.e., $\phi^t_a = \sum_{s \in K} I(\phi^t(s) = a)$, where

$$I(\phi^t(s) = a) = \begin{cases} 1 & \text{if } \phi^t(s) = a \\ 0 & \text{otherwise} \end{cases}$$

In analogous fashion, let $\phi^t_a(R)$ be the number of players in the set R playing action a under ϕ^t, i.e., $\phi^t_a(R) = \sum_{s \in R} I(\phi^t(s) = a)$.

6.3.2 Communication, punishment, and externalities

At each round of play $t = 0, 1, 2, \ldots$, each player s signals to each of his neighbors $r \in V_s$ a "conditional strategy" $\psi^t(s, r)$ and associated punishment $v^t(s, r)$. A conditional strategy $\psi^t(s, r) \in \Gamma$ consists of an action that player s would be willing to play, conditional on his neighbors also playing this action. The punishment $v^t(s, r) \geq 0$ is an amount with which player s proposes to threaten to reduce the payoff of player r through punishment if player r does not comply with certain demands of player s, which will be specified below. Each player s is equipped with a maximum punishment potential $\theta(s)$, which is constant over time. The values $\theta(s)$, $s = 1, \ldots, N$, are independent realizations of a random variable θ with distribution Θ, which has its support on a subset of $[0, \theta^{\max}]$. The distribution function of Θ is labeled $f(.)$. In order to be credible, a player cannot threaten any of his neighbors with more than his punishment potential, meaning $v^t(s, r) \leq \theta(s)$, $\forall r \in V_s$, $\forall t$. We assume that violence hurts the person being punished more than it costs the punisher: having an effect of -1 on the payoff of a neighbor through punishment costs the punisher $\frac{1}{c} < 1$, with $c > 1$. With respect to the transfer of knowledge about punishment threats, we assume that any player can see the punishment potential with which each of his neighbors is being threatened at any point in time.

In each round of play $t = 1, 2, \ldots$, with probability $p \in \left(\underline{p}, 1\right)$, $\underline{p} > 0$, each individual receives the opportunity to update his action and conditional strategy, a so-called *learning draw*. All players receiving a learning draw choose an action and a signal to send to their neighbors. With respect to the story in the main text of this book, the absence of a learning draw for a given individual in a given time period is a particular translation of the notion of loyalty, because individuals who do not receive learning draws do not participate in any rethinking of rules: they simply blindly follow them.

In terms of payoff activities, a round consists of a stage game and punishment, where the punishment takes place after the stage game. The total payoff $\Pi\left(s, \phi^t\right)$ to player s at the end of the period t consists of his economic payoff from the stage game $\pi\left(s, \phi^t\right)$ less the costs of the punishment that is administered to him and the costs of punishing others:

$$\Pi\left(s, \phi^t\right) = \pi\left(s, \phi^t\right) - \sum_{r \in V_s} v^t\left(r, s\right) I_{r,s} - \frac{1}{c} \sum_{r \in V_s} v^t\left(s, r\right) I_{s,r},$$

where

$$I_{r,s} = \begin{cases} 1 & \text{when player } s \text{ does not comply with} \\ & \text{the conditions set by player } r \\ 0 & \text{otherwise} \end{cases}$$

The payoff $\pi\left(s, \phi^t\right)$ from the stage game depends on the entire configuration ϕ^t due to both distant and local externalities. An action $\phi^t\left(s\right) = A$ yields a direct payoff $\alpha > 0$ to player s, but it imposes a negative externality $-\lambda < 0$ upon all players $r \in V_s$, and yields an externality μ to all players $r \in K \backslash \{s\}$. An action $\phi^t\left(s\right) = B$ results in a payoff $0 < \beta < \alpha$ to player s, and yields no externalities. Thus we have that

$$\pi\left(s, \phi^t\right) = \begin{cases} \alpha + \left(\phi_A^t - 1\right)\mu - \phi_A^t\left(V_s\right)\lambda, & \text{if } \phi^t\left(s\right) = A, \\ \beta + \phi_A^t\mu - \phi_A^t\left(V_s\right)\lambda, & \text{if } \phi^t\left(s\right) = B \end{cases}$$

Note that the difference in economic payoff from playing either A or B for an individual s is $\alpha - \beta$, since *ceteris paribus* $\left(\phi_A^t | \phi^t\left(s\right) = A\right) = \left(\phi_A^t | \phi^t\left(s\right) = B\right) + 1$. Thus action $\phi^t\left(s\right) = A$ is a dominant action for a player, given $\phi^t\left(-s\right)$. This action affects all players, and in particular hurts the players $r \in V_s$. We assume that players know about the payoff difference $\alpha - \beta$ between the different actions, and also that they have information on the local externalities being administered to them. Specifically, they know by which players these externalities are caused, but do not realize that distant externalities also influence their payoffs. Thus, they observe the payoff effects λ and μ of actions taken by their neighbors, and are able to trace down the exact neighbors generating the externalities. However, they are unable to see which nonneighbors caused the global externality μ to be levied on them.

In each time period, players observe the actions and signals of their neighbors: they know whether each neighbor played A or B, as well as the punishment potential and the conditional strategy to which each of their neighbors has committed. Each player also observes which of his neighbors receives a learning draw that period. Thus, players can infer which of their neighbors do not comply with their conditional strategy while they were handed the learning draw and which of their neighbors do not comply with their conditional strategy because they were not (yet) handed a learning draw. Not only are players unaware of the actions played by those other than their neighbors, but we can even assume that they do not even know about the existence of players other than their neighbors.

We restrict attention to the parameter range in which $\alpha - m\,(\lambda - \mu) < \beta$, that is, the range in which an individual player is better off when no negative externalities are levied upon him than when all of his neighbors levy negative externalities upon him. Outside this range, individuals cannot benefit from cooperating with their nearest neighbors, and no coordination arises. Within this range we focus on two cases. In the first case (henceforth labeled case 1), the total economic payoff is maximized by the configuration with $\phi^t\,(s) = A$, $\forall s$, i.e., the parameters are set such that $\alpha - m\,(\lambda - \mu) < \beta < \alpha + (N-1)\mu - m\lambda$. The second case, labeled case 2, is the one in which the total economic payoff is maximized by the configuration with $\phi^t\,(s) = B$, $\forall s$, i.e., the parameters are set such that $\alpha - m\,(\lambda - \mu) < \alpha + (N-1)\mu - m\lambda < \beta$. In both cases, a player s with $\phi^t\,(s) = A$ is willing to play action B whenever at least some of his neighbors credibly indicate that when he switches action, they will do the same thing. The minimum number of neighbors who would need to switch to action B in order to make it better in terms of individual payoff to agree to a switch is given by the minimum m for which it holds that $\alpha - m\,(\lambda - \mu) < \beta$. Case 2 can be viewed as the standard public goods problem, in which contributing to the public good is a dominated action for the individual, but where the state in which all individuals do contribute yields the highest overall payoff.

Three examples are now presented in order to motivate these cases. The first two examples closely mirror the settings described in Wittfogel (1957).

Example 6.3.1 *Irrigation systems. Suppose that action A represents preventing most of the rainfall upon one's land from flowing to the land of others by channeling it towards the irrigation of one's own patch of land. Take action B to be building an irrigation system that benefits one's neighbors as well as oneself, but where action A increases the payoff of the individual more than action B. Action A will reduce the amount of water available to an individual's neighbors, and the increased relative production of the individual's own land may additionally make them envious, which combined implies a negative local externality of λ. The effects on the rest of the population (that is, those who are not neighbors) of an individual choosing A rather than B may be positive or negative. If the cooperation between neighbors (via action B) reduces the available water for people outside the neighborhood, then one can view this as a positive (distant) externality μ on the rest of the population in case the individual chooses A. An equivalent statement is to say that there is a negative externality on nonneighbors of playing B. Now imagine a group of neighbors who all irrigate their own lands individually, but would all like the others in their neighborhood to start building a large irrigation system that benefits the entire neighborhood. The members of this group of neighbors are better off when they all play action B, and so when they cooperate (i.e., change their actions towards mutual benefit), they will play B. But when all individuals in the population choose B, then the total economic payoff of all N players is suboptimal in case 1 and optimal in case 2.*

Example 6.3.2 *Dikes. Another example is to think of option A for an individual as not building a dike on his section of a river, and option B as building a dike on his section of the river. Building a dike will not increase the direct economic payoff of the individual, because the reduced risk of flooding does not outweigh the cost of the building effort, but it will increase the economic payoff of his nearest neighbors, because they are also likely to benefit somewhat from the reduced risk of flooding in the neighborhood while not having paid any cost* to construct the dike. *Other communities outside the neighborhood will however see their probability of flooding increase if the individual builds a dike, because less superfluous water will be drained at the site of the dike. This can be modeled by thinking of action A as having local negative externalities λ (the neighbors are withheld the reduced risk of flooding) and positive distant externalities (the rest of the population has less risk of flooding under A than under B). The members of this group of neighbors are better off when they all play action B, so when they cooperate, they will play B. Whether it is optimal for the entire population if everyone plays B depends on the strength of the externality.*

Example 6.3.3 *Accessibility of private property. A final example of case 1 is when action A represents restricting the use of one's land by other individuals, while action B is not restricting access. The direct profit to the individual of restricting others' access to his land is that it avoids disrupting his use of the land. Therefore, action A dominates action B from the individual's perspective. Moreover, restricting access allows for specialization of the labor force, and in this way has a positive effect on the payoff of all individuals in the larger population ($\mu > 0$). However, the individual who restricts access creates a direct negative externality (λ) on his neighbors, since they are no longer allowed to use that property for their own productive purposes. Again, a (small) group of neighbors who want to cooperate would all agree to play B, yielding an inferior outcome for the population as a whole when all individuals in the population act in the same way, since the benefits of specialization are lost.*

Intuitively, what will be shown is that in case 1, small coalitions of individuals advocate a set of rules that yield global inefficiencies. However, for coalitions of individuals larger than some substantial minimum size, the effect of the positive distant externalities nullifies the large negative local externalities. Thus, when a coalition grows above this minimum size, it realizes that influencing every group member to play *A* is better than having every group member play *B*, and it thus changes its "rules" accordingly. Large coalitions therefore do not give rise to the global inefficiencies depicted in the above examples of case 1. Cooperation and conditional strategies (rules) will thus arise and change because of economic incentives, while "power" will come to mean the application and coordination of punishment. We now introduce the means for coordination and power.

6.3.3 Introducing an authority

A set of players $R \subset K$ forms a central authority if all players $r \in R$ have agreed voluntarily to join the authority at some time in the past. Different central authorities are disjoint, meaning that players cannot be members of two central authorities at the same time. We denote the union of all central authorities (c.a.s) present on the graph at time t by W^t, i.e., $W^t = \cup_{\text{all c.a.s } R} R$. A central authority is referred to by the set of players R it encompasses. The defining feature of a central authority is that it can communicate directly with all of its members, and it has the added ability to transfer the punishment potential of any consenting individual member to any other member. Hence, whereas an individual $r \in R$ can only punish his neighbors in V_r, a central authority R can direct the combined punishment potential of its members, $\theta (R) = \sum_{r \in R} \theta (r)$, to any of the members $r \in R$ of the central authority or to any of the players on the boundary ∂R of R. The significance of the boundary is that it will be at the boundary that individuals face other individuals outside of the central authority they will end up threatening or being threatened by. For this reason, particular instructions will apply to members on the boundary of, as opposed to members completely within, an authority.

A central authority R advocates a (possibly empty) set of rules to all players in $\cup_{r \in R} V_r = R \cup \partial R$. A set of rules prescribes actions to individual players and contains a punishment scheme for players who do not follow the prescribed action when they could have done so. An empty set of rules is interpreted as the absence of prescribed rules, and therefore as the absence of punishment no matter what a player chooses to do.

We now arrive at a crucial issue. Who or what will decide on the rules of the authority? The following two possible rule-choosing mechanisms are explored below.[5]

1. *Possibility 1.* In each authority, there exists an "honest broker" who, given the combined knowledge of all constituents, computes

---

[5] The social choice literature discusses many other alternative rule-choosing mechanisms (see Pardo and Schneider 1996 for a review).

the expected utility of each possible set of rules, after which the constituents choose one by voting under a Rawlsian veil of ignorance.

2. *Possibility 2.* The group that initially sets up an authority gets to decide what the rules of the authority will be in all subsequent periods that the authority exists.

It is clear that Possibility 1 abstracts from many difficulties: under Possibility 1, there is at least one person available who has no interests of his own to pursue but who will simply calculate optimal rules for a given set of individuals. Following Harsanyi (1985), this means that the chosen set of rules will maximize the combined total expected payoff of the current members. The central authority then makes these rules common knowledge within the authority and to the players on its borders. In this sense, the central authority is no more than a strategy selection device with an information advantage and the ability to transfer punishment potential on its territory.

Possibility 2 is somewhat more realistic, in that those who set up an authority are the ones most likely to reap the future benefits from it. We simplify the decision making amongst the group of individuals who initially set up a central authority by assuming that the rule chosen is that which maximizes the combined payoff of all initial members.

At any time, players can indicate that they want to form or join a central authority. However, they will only do so if this seems profitable for them at the time of joining, independent of the type of mechanism for devising rules. Thus, a group of players will form a new central authority if they foresee profit from doing so and they know that the other potential members of the central authority also foresee this profit for themselves, and so will also join.

The sequence of events in a time period is now specified in detail. Since each player s knows which players in V_s belong to a clique, where a clique consists of players who are all neighbors to everyone in the clique, authorities can assess whether their members are on the border of other authorities. Moreover, since $s \in S$ observes the threats made to all players $r \in V_s$, authority S also knows about the punishment potential with which any other authority might threaten r.

- *Step 1* Players have the opportunity to form a central authority-information. Such an authority can set rules in Step 2, but players only make the final decision about whether to join in Step 3.

- *Step 2* Each central authority S decides upon a set of rules to be adhered to by all players $s \in S \cup \partial S$. It communicates the set of rules to all of these players.
- *Step 3* Learning draws occur. Players s ($s \in S \cup \partial S$ for all c.a.s S) who receive a learning draw simultaneously decide whether to join S or remain in their current situation (i.e., member of another c.a. or nonmember of any c.a.). Players who do not receive a learning draw and are currently not a member of any c.a. cannot join a c.a. Players who do not receive a learning draw, but are members of a c.a. evaluate the rules set by this c.a. against the rules set by any c.a. from which they received a signal in Step 2 (i.e., of which they are a neighbor). Subsequently, each player who has received a learning draw decides whether to remain member of their "current" c.a. or to become member of one of the c.a.s from which they received a signal.

  Once a member of a c.a. a player remains a member of that c.a. at least until Step 3 of the next period.
- *Step 4* Players play an action from Γ.
- *Step 5* Each central authority S observes all information observed by all players $s \in S$. Based on this information, the c.a. decides on administering punishment to the players in $S \cup \partial S$ who did not comply with the rules set in Step 2. It orders individual members $s \in S$ to carry out this punishment, and transfers punishment potential to this end if necessary.

From this sequence of moves and the information structure of the game, we can directly infer the following corollary.

Corollary 6.3.4 *A central authority can only be formed by a subset of players from one clique.*

Proof
Facing the decision of whether or not to participate in a c.a.-in-formation, a player weighs the potential profit from joining against the potential costs of being exploited by others who claim they will join, but do not do so in the end. A c.a.-in-formation can set its rules in Step 2 such that players who choose not to join in Step 3 are punished severely. If the total punishment potential of the c.a. is large enough, this can make not joining in Step 3 harmful. Thus, a necessary condition

for a player to join is that he knows that enough others will join to give the c.a. some sufficient quantity of punishment potential. In a clique, all players know that all other players in the clique face the same decision and will thus also join. Such a necessary common-knowledge information structure is only present within a clique of players.   □

In order to enforce its announced rules, whatever these rules are, a central authority must find an enforcement mechanism. One possible enforcement mechanism is automatically generated when the central authority announces the rules and then compiles a list of individuals to be punished for noncompliance, or for failure to punish when instructed to do so. Because the first player on this list will expect to be punished by the others if he does not comply, he will comply. Hence the first player will comply. Through a repetition (forward induction) of this argument, the second player will comply, and so on. The notion of a list that enforces discipline is similar to the "matrix of discipline" idea of Kuhn (1962). Because individuals cannot coordinate on strategies without forming a central authority, a complete breakdown of the central authority will not occur, and no c.a. can be formed within another one.

An important point is that the rules announced by a c.a. cannot be altered until Step 2 of the next period, which implies that a central authority can credibly precommit on its own rules for one period at a time. One could therefore interpret a period as the length of time it takes for the c.a. to make a decision. Because of the possibility of revising the rules each period, there is a collective time-inconsistency problem in the sense of Asheim (1997).

6.3.4 Basic results

In this section, the (self-confirming) equilibrium of the total model is characterized.

Consider first the circumstances under which a c.a. will form. Corollary 6.3.4 states that we need only consider players in a clique. We now state a sufficient condition on the combined punishment potential of the potential members of a central authority. By $\lfloor . \rfloor$ we denote the entire function, i.e., $\lfloor z \rfloor = \max \{x \in \mathbb{Z} \mid x \leq z\}$.

Theorem 6.3.5 *Consider player $s \in C_k$, with*

$$k \geq \left\lfloor \frac{\alpha - \beta}{\lambda - \mu} \right\rfloor + 2 \ and \ \sum_{r \in C_k \cap V_s \cup \{s\}} \theta\,(r) - \max_{r \in C_k \cap V_s \cup \{s\}} \theta\,(r) > \alpha - \beta.$$

There is a strict positive probability that a central authority will evolve in clique C_k. When

$$k < \left\lfloor \frac{\alpha - \beta}{\lambda - \mu} \right\rfloor + 2 \ or \ \sum_{r \in C_k \cap V_s \cup \{s\}} \theta\,(r) - \max_{r \in C_k \cap V_s \cup \{s\}} \theta\,(r) < \alpha - \beta,$$

the probability of emergence of a central authority in C_k is zero.

Proof. See Frijters and Tieman (1999).

This theorem shows that one needs a sufficient number of mutually connected individuals with similar interests in order to start a central authority. It also shows that a central authority must be powerful enough to be able to punish even its strongest member. For this theorem, it makes no difference whether the rules are devised by an "honest broker" or by the initial group of members, because either mechanism gives rise to the same set of rules in the first period of any central authority. Now we show that the conditions in Theorem 6.3.5 are met when the punishment potentials of different players are random draws from a distribution with positive weight on values above $\frac{\alpha - \beta}{(k-1)}$.

Corollary 6.3.6 *Consider a large population in which a large number of k-cliques with $k \geq \left\lfloor \frac{\alpha - \beta}{\lambda - \mu} \right\rfloor + 2$ are present. Then, when*

$$\int_{\frac{\alpha - \beta}{(k-1)}}^{\theta^{\max}} f\,(\theta)\,d\theta > 0, \tag{6.3.1}$$

almost surely at least one central authority will emerge.

Proof
This condition ensures that in each k-clique there is strict positive probability that $\sum_{r \in C_k} \theta\,(r) - \max_{r \in C_k} \theta\,(r) > \alpha - \beta$ is satisfied and thus that the condition on punishment potential in Theorem 6.3.5 is met. A strong law-of-large-numbers argument guarantees that in a large population with a large number of k-cliques, the condition will almost surely be met.   □

Corollary 6.3.6 implies that heterogeneity across players with respect to punishment potential facilitates the emergence of a central authority. In a population that is homogeneous in punishment potential, a similar strong law-of-large-numbers argument shows that a c.a. will emerge if the homogeneous punishment potential is high enough, i.e., when $\theta(s) = \bar{\theta} > \frac{\alpha-\beta}{(k-1)}$ $\forall s \in K$.

We now address what will happen once one or more central authorities have emerged.

Theorem 6.3.7 *When the conditions of Theorem 6.3.5 are met, then one single central authority, with all players in the population as its members, will be the only stable outcome.*

Proof. See Frijters and Tieman (1999).

Two comments on these results are in order. First, we see that, in equilibrium, punishment will never take place. This implies that the total payoff obtained by any individual in each period simply equals his economic payoff from playing the stage game. Second, although the model is limited to a stage game with two possible actions, we argue that the qualitative results carry over to models incorporating more general stage games. With the inclusion of more action alternatives in the stage game, it is still the case that a c.a. can start only if enough mutually connected and sufficiently strong individuals can all increase their payoffs by forming a c.a. that maximizes their combined utilities (c.a.s with different objectives have less appeal, and thus need more stringent conditions). A c.a. that has begun will still expand further, and the number of c.a.s remaining will still therefore converge to 1. The important changes brought by the inclusion of additional actions have to do with the conditions under which a c.a. starts. The most likely setting in which meaningful changes to these conditions will result is probably when the newly added action alternatives inflict externalities on others.

To illustrate the evolution of play with an honest broker, we consider the two cases introduced previously, where actions A and B are available and differ in terms of the local and distant externalities that they imply. In both cases, in populations without any c.a.s, all players play A. Within the central authorities that arise but that are still small, playing action B will be advocated. In case 2, one c.a. advocating choice B for all members is also the final outcome. In case 1, however, at least one of the authorities will become large enough in the long run to see that the local negative externalities are outweighed by the distant positive externalities of having all its members play A. Consequently, such a large c.a. changes the action it advocates its members to take from B to A. This result is stated in the following corollary.

Corollary 6.3.8 *Suppose a small c.a. has formed and the total economic payoff is maximized by the configuration with $\phi^t(s) = A, \forall s$. Then, the small c.a. will advocate playing B to its members. Only when a c.a. grows sufficiently big will it see the benefits of playing A. Consequently, sufficiently large c.a.s will advocate that their members play A.*

6.3.5 Extensions: Asymmetric punishment and mutations

Two extensions to this basic model are now considered.

Asymmetric punishment

In this section, a slightly altered version of a central authority is considered, in which the ability to punish nonmembers is a fraction $0 < \delta < 1$ of the ability to punish members. This means that punishment potential is asymmetric: it differs according to whether the punishment is implemented between or within central authorities. This asymmetry reflects the argument that it is easier to punish others close to you than it is to punish others who are further away. In this setting, Theorem 6.3.5 and Corollary 6.3.6 still hold. It is only in the case with multiple c.a.s that the implications differ. This is illustrated in the following theorem.

Theorem 6.3.9 *Consider the model with asymmetric punishment potential as described above. Assume that the population is large, that there is a large number of k-cliques in the population with $k \geq \left\lfloor \frac{\alpha-\beta}{\lambda-\mu} \right\rfloor + 2$, and that*

$$\int_{\frac{\alpha-\beta}{(k-1)}}^{\theta^{\max}} f(\theta)\,d\theta > 0.$$

Then, both one single central authority and several central authorities, of which not necessarily all players are members and which have possibly conflicting rules, are possible long-run outcomes of the model.

Proof. See appendix of Frijters and Tieman (1999).

The theorem states that there are several possible outcomes in the limit. The initial configuration of the population, the specific parameter values, and the realizations of the sequences of learning draws will determine which outcome is reached.

Arriving at a situation with multiple c.a.s may yield global inefficiency in which all individuals in all groups are worse off than they would be with a single c.a. since the members in each c.a. do not take account of the effects of their actions on the payoffs to members of other authorities. The possibility that groups of individuals are "locked" into an inefficient equilibrium in which all groups lose out compared to another possible state is analogous to discrimination or conflicts between groups or regions.

Mutations

We now introduce into the model a small probability of mutations, which allows us to identify which of the multiple stationary states sketched in Theorem 6.3.9 is the *stochastically stable state* or *long-run equilibrium*. This is the equilibrium that is played "almost all of the time" when the mutation rate goes to 0 in the limit. This solution concept was developed in Kandori, Mailath, and Rob (1993) and Young (1993), and surveys of this literature are given by Samuelson (1997) and Young (1998). Mutations are usually taken to represent one of three phenomena. First, mutations may represent experimentation by the players aimed at learning about what might happen if they were to be off the equilibrium path. Second, mutations may represent (computational) errors on the part of the individual players in the implementation of an action. Lastly, mutations can represent genetic mutations, to the extent that individuals' actions are "preprogrammed" by their set of genes, given that spontaneous mutations in these genes sometimes occur.

We introduce mutations as follows. At each time t, every player in the population has a small probability $\varepsilon > 0$ of mutating. When mutating, a player joins a randomly selected c.a. to which he is adjacent, with each adjacent c.a. having the same probability of being chosen. If the mutant is not adjacent to any c.a. he does not join any c.a. as a member. On top of joining an arbitrary c.a. a mutant randomly selects an action to play in the stage game. The following theorem states the selection result we obtain when combining mutations with asymmetric punishment potential.

Theorem 6.3.10 *Consider the model with asymmetric punishment potential and mutations. Assume that the population is large, that there is a large number of k-cliques in the population with $k \geq \left\lfloor \frac{\alpha-\beta}{\lambda-\mu} \right\rfloor + 2$, and that*

$$\int_{\frac{\alpha-\beta}{(k-1)}}^{\theta^{\max}} f(\theta)\, d\theta > 0.$$

Then, the only long-run equilibrium of the model is the state in which there is only one c.a. present in the population, of which all players are members.

Proof. See appendix of Frijters and Tieman (1999).

Hence, although multiple equilibria are present in the altered model, introducing a small probability of random mutations serves as a selection device, selecting the stationary state with only one c.a. as the only stochastically stable state.

A typical path to this stochastically stable state may be as follows. From the initial state, the system moves rapidly to a stationary state with multiple central authorities. After some mutations that do not change the power balance between the c.a.s, eventually a mutation does change the power balance and the system moves quickly to a new stationary state with fewer c.a.s remaining. Repeating this procedure in finite time leads to the stochastically stable state being reached.

6.3.6 Discussion

In this model, both groups and loyalty emerge endogenously. Social norms, as with the preceding model about group types, are oriented around material choices and violence. Loyalty to the rules proposed by the central authority is ultimately backed up by an inability of individuals to coordinate into other groups. Loyalty is thus implicitly modeled as something that occurs almost accidentally in large groups, for example as the absence of a learning draw on the part of individuals who would otherwise have profitably recoordinated on something else. One can view this as a kind of failure to pay attention and reconsider whether the action proposed by the central authority is actually optimal.

While the main text of this book proposes far more detailed and intricate mechanisms for the emergence of group loyalty, the translation of love in the model above does correspond to the core argument that only a few true believers are required in order to force the rest of the members of a group into line with prescribed rules. It also reflects the argument in the main text that anything that manages to emerge and be sustained for some amount of time itself generates habits of compliance to whichever behaviors give some solidity to the existing situation.

6.4 Model 4: Politics, social capital, and economic growth

Here I briefly outline a model that examines the relations amongst the search for new technology, the size of the contact network, the politics of creative destruction, and the economy as a whole. It is a model that is designed to be able to capture both the economic transition in Eastern Europe and the slow changes occurring in developing countries.

The model is based on work on transition economies by Bezemer, Dulleck, and Frijters (Frijters et al. 2003, Bezemer, Dulleck, and Frijters 2004, Dulleck and Frijters 2004), and in particular on a recent paper by Antic and Frijters (Antic and Frijters 2012) that looks solely at business cycles. In those papers, a large variety of models is presented, including models that replicate several stylized facts related to the output levels and networks observed in transition and developing economies.

6.4.1 The model

The economy consists of a continuum of representative firms maximizing their profit. Consumption is not explicitly considered, but firms can be viewed as owned by households who provide a fixed endowment of labor to the economy. Households consume all of their income except for a constant share s, as specified below. Firms produce a homogeneous good with unit price. Technology is described by a production function with three inputs: labor, physical capital, and contacts of the firm. Thus, what will be termed "relational capital" (RC_t) is a capital stock, and can be thought of as the number of business contacts. It is an input into the amount of *sold* output y_t.

The key difference between this and the standard definition of output relates to the fact that in this model, market frictions necessitate business contacts. Including RC_t as an input captures the search costs of finding the partnerships that are needed for buying inputs and selling output. Sold output is defined by

$$y_t = y(A_t, L_t - L_t^{rc}, RC_t, K_t) \tag{6.4.1}$$

where y_t is sold production at time t; L_t is the labor force; $L_t - L_t^{rc}$ is net labor input into physical production (blue collar labor); L_t^{rc} is (white collar) labor devoted to the creation of RC_t; A_t is the technology parameter; and K_t is physical capital. $y(.)$ is a constant-returns-to-scale function with the Inada properties of decreasing positive marginal returns to any input and technical complementary between any two inputs.

The economy includes a continuum of such firms with measure 1. This allows the use of $\bar{y}_t$, L_t, K_t, and $\overline{RC}_t$ as respective notations for the total amount of output, labor, and capital stocks in the whole economy. As in standard macroeconomic growth models, the following functional form is assumed for analysis purposes:

$$y_t = y(A_t f(L_t - L_t^{rc}, RC_t), K_t) \tag{6.4.2}$$

where $A_t f(L_t - L_t^{rc}, RC_t)$ is a single composite input. Technology, A_t, is the productivity of the combination of labor and contacts, similar to a labor-augmented (or Harrod-neutral) technology in the standard textbook model. Assumptions on $f(.)$ are implicitly given by the assumptions on $y(.)$.

Firms select levels of L_t and K_t and invest in the stock of RC_t by allocating labor L_t^{rc}. Firms can look for two different types of contacts: an augmentation of their existing contacts, which increases RC_t, and a replacement of some existing contacts, which keeps RC_t constant. A distinction is thus made between D_t^{rc}, the amount of contacts replaced, and N_t^{rc}, the amount of contacts added. Replacing a contact implies destroying an existing contact and creating a new one, as illustrated graphically in the figures in Chapter 4 of the main text. The benefits of replacing a contact will be in terms of superior technology.

Firms select positive levels of D_t^{rc} and N_t^{rc}, and meet in a market for contacts. Firms, and therefore business contacts, are taken to be heterogeneous, leading to search frictions in the matching process. As in most of the search literature (e.g., Pissarides 1990, Petrongolo and Pissarides 2001), this heterogeneity is not explicitly modeled.[6] I capture the effect of this heterogeneity by expressing the costs of searching for contacts in terms of the labor time required to replace or add contacts:

$$\lambda_t L_t^{rc} = \varphi_t D_t^{rc} + N_t^{rc}, \text{ with } \lambda_t > 0, \varphi_t \geq 1 \qquad (6.4.3)$$

where λ_t denotes the conversion rate of labor L_t^{rc} into contacts. In terms of search theory, λ_t can be interpreted as the arrival rate of contacts. I capture the relation between business contacts and social or market networks by positing that λ_t depends positively on both "community social capital" (CSC_t) and market institutions (MI_t).

Because destroying an existing contact results in a direct negative externality (the loss of a contact) on that existing contact, the latter has an incentive to make contact destruction costly. $\varphi_t - 1$ is the cost a firm incurs when breaking an existing contact with another firm, over and above the direct costs of finding a new contact. In completely decentralized economies, firms have no power to raise the cost of breaking contacts with them (despite their desire to do so) and therefore $\varphi_t = 1$: replacing and adding contacts are equally costly for the firm. A higher cost of breaking contacts is assumed to be possible only via the political process. Specifically, if there is some degree of political interference in firms' matching choices, then $\varphi_t \geq 1$. Political interference in matching choices therefore amounts to some degree of centralization of markets. The more an economy is centrally controlled, in this sense, the higher is φ_t.

Contact replacement is inextricably linked to technological progress, captured in A_t. Whenever a firm increases its efficiency by initiating a new production method, producing new products, or changing its internal organization, it will typically make new demands on its

---

[6] This differs from social network models such as Jackson and Wolinsky (1996) or Vega-Redondo (2003), and from the growth model of Routledge and von Amsberg (2003). In those models, the stability and/or trustworthiness of specific links between agents is analyzed. By contrast, I abstract from the specific identities of partners by assuming that these problems are captured implicitly by a matching function.

Implications and examples

input suppliers or output buyers. Since old "transaction partners" were selected specifically in order to match up with old production and sales processes, switching transaction partners will be optimal under new production or sales conditions. As in Schumpeter (1934) and Routledge and von Amsberg (2003), the destruction of old contacts is an inevitable by-product of the creation of new production and sales methods.[7] The replacement of RC_t is therefore termed *creative destruction*, and technological progress is explicitly modeled as depending on the extent of contact replacement D_t^{rc}, following

$$A_t = A_{t-1} + (A_{t-1}^* - A_{t-1})g(\frac{D_{t-1}^{rc}}{L_t}) \tag{6.4.4}$$

where A_t^* denotes the production frontier at time t. The function $1 > g(.) \geq 0$ denotes the technological "catch-up" resulting from the replacement of relational capital per unit of L_t. The lag between D_t^{rc} and A_t reflects the time required for technology takeup. There are decreasing returns in technological investment: $\frac{\partial g(.)}{\partial D_t^{rc}} > 0$, $g(0) = 0$, and $\frac{\partial^2 g(.)}{\partial^2 D_t^{rc}} < 0$. Appendix 1.3 of Frijters et al. (2003) provides micro-arguments for this equation.

Because of the externality generated by contact replacement, the level of RC_t does not only depend on own investment decisions, but also (negatively) on others' contact replacement decisions. This is captured by

$$RC_t = RC_{t-1}e^{-\beta \frac{\bar{D}_t^{rc}}{RC_{t-1}}} + N_t^{rc} \tag{6.4.5}$$

where the term $e^{-\beta \frac{\bar{D}_t^{rc}}{RC_{t-1}}}$ equals the probability of an old contact being destroyed by the creative-destruction decisions of other firms. The parameter β equals the net number of contacts that are destroyed

---

[7] Routledge and von Amsberg (2003) provide a game-theoretic model of social capital, within this model interpreted as directly related to the total sum of contacts in the economy, based on the idea of cooperation in a repeated Prisoner's Dilemma game. To model growth, they too assume that new trading partners are necessary for technological advancement. In their model, faster technological development implies shorter interaction times and hence a destruction of community social capital (CSC_t) in the form of trust. I argue that only relational capital diminishes, through the externality of replacing contacts. Moreover, CSC_t in this model can help to reduce the cost of this externality, in line with much empirical evidence (see for example Miguel 2003, a comment on Routledge and von Amsberg 2003).

when one firm replaces an old contact, thereby destroying his previous partner firm's contact. When that previous partner firm is part of a large value chain of interdependent firms, β is large.

To close the model requires some standard assumptions about the movement of total labor units, the technological frontier, and physical capital formation, as follows:

$$L_t = L$$

$$K_t = (1 - \delta)K_{t-1} + sy_{t-1}$$

$$A_t^* = (1 + a)A_{t-1}^*$$

This makes labor constant and forces capital to abide by the Swan–Solow assumptions of fixed depreciation, a constant savings rate, and exogenous progress along the technological frontier. This specification reflects the assumptions that exogenous savings, no outside investment, and a given technological frontier all apply to the economy.

Finally, the standard assumption is required that firms maximize their discounted stream of profits, equal to $\sum_{t=0}^{\infty}(\frac{1}{1+r_t})^t\{y_t - w_tL - r_tK_t\}$. This goal function is independent of the economic system, which is here modeled entirely via the centralization parameter φ_t. This implies that different economic systems are presumed not to affect the desires of economic agents, but rather to affect the constraints that firms face. For a similar assumption on firm behavior under socialism, see Roberts and Rodriguez (1997).

6.4.2 Discussion

What kind of economic dynamics does this model yield? It turns out that with the assumptions above, one can generate eternal cycles of growth and recessions, as described below.

• Recessions are characterized by collapses in the total amount of networks in an economy (RC_t).
• It is during those recessions that the greatest technological advances are made.
• Recoveries are times in which the disconnected production factors, such as idle workers (who are less productive than they could be if they were employed) and idle capital capacity, find each other.

- Major recessions are periods in which, either because firms were constrained for a very long time in the past, or because of political/financial upheavals, there are unusually large negative shocks to the overall level of networks (connectivity) in the economy.

The interested reader can turn to the works of myself, Dirk Bezemer, Uwe Dulleck, and Nemanja Antic for more details about this model and related references. Solving the model and running simulations of it was nontrivial, and required approximating heuristics as well as significant computer time. In our papers, we re-created an artificial output collapse by looking at an economy that was first characterized by $\varphi_0 = 0$ (no recontacting allowed at all) but that then changed overnight into an economy with perfect recontacting ($\varphi_t = 1$ for all subsequent t). We then were able to find functional form assumptions and parameter choices under which the economy as a whole experienced a massive output collapse (on the order of 50 percent) driven by the collapse in the contact network due to individual firms breaking up with former partners in the search for better ones. By experimenting with the relevant parameters, we also found scenarios under which an economy would be going through various aborted growth cycles wherein the contact classes successively grew and shrank for decades, until they finally grew to such strength that the economy was finally freed of political interference in φ_t and thus hit a long-term state characterized by growth with cycles.

The key element captured by the model here is the role that networks are allowed to have in the economy. Networks are pure investment goods from the point of view of individual firms who make rational decisions about whether or not to search for more contacts. For individual agents, searching for new contacts serves a dual role. The first and most obvious is simply to obtain more contacts with input suppliers and output clients, thereby helping to increase the firm's level of specialization. The second is as a means of updating processes, which in turn requires abandoning former contacts. From the point of view of the whole economy, the externality suffered by the abandoned contacts can become of paramount importance, and can rationalize both very large recessions as reductions in the density of the whole network, and smaller recessions in which for other reasons the connections between trading partners become severed. As noted in the main text, examples of such reasons could include bankruptcies, financial system failures, standard demand shocks, and so forth.

One can envision further externalities to model in this process, with a prime example being those resulting from allowing the whole stock of contacts to reduce costs overall. Dulleck and Frijters (2004) envisaged this type of power-feedback mechanism from networks, wherein both φ_t and λ_t were assumed to depend on the level of overall network activity. Bigger networks implied lower search costs (i.e., higher λ_t) and lower political interference via the reduced ability of the political system to favor incumbent contacts (i.e., lower φ_t). This is a particular parametrization of the central power-network externality discussed in the main text.

6.4.3 Possible extensions

Many extensions and refinements can be introduced within this framework. An important refinement is to develop the micro-level stories one might have in mind as justifications for why bigger networks promote higher aggregate output via increased specialization. Frijters (2005) works out four textbook-style micro-models of the value of networks based on four different mechanisms, each of which relates to the coordination of production in a multigood setting: the depreciation of indivisible intermediaries; economies of scale in information-gathering; comparative advantage; and discount rates in the presence of indivisible intermediaries.

Other extensions allow for more intricate and elaborate factors of production that capture many other aspects of the macro-economy. This approach is already provided conceptually in the main text, but can be further formalized.

In order for the role of collapsing networks in economic downturns to be made visible to the profession, and thereby for the general set of ideas above to truly make an impact on economic decision making, one would need trade networks and the costs of making new connections in the economy to be formally measured. This is a job that is probably too big for any single researcher or even group of researchers, because it involves measurement of many different agents in many different settings over time. The ideal implementors of such a measurement task are large (national or international) statistical agencies. There are many issues that would have to be solved, such as allowing for a variable strength of connections and for the differential value, in terms of added degrees of specialization, that different contacts make possible. However, both networks and connection costs within networks are in principle observable and measurable.

References

Abramson, P. and Aldrich, J. (1982), "The decline of electoral participation in America," *American Political Science Review* 76, 502–521.

Acemoglu, D. and Egorov, G. (2008), "Coalition formation in non-democracies," *Review of Economic Studies* 75(4), 987–1009.

Acemoglu, D. and Robinson, J. (2001), "A theory of political transitions," *American Economic Review* 91(4), 938–963.

Ackerman, S. (1996), "Altruism, nonprofits and economic theory," *Journal of Economic Literature* 34, 701–728.

Acs, Z. and Audretsch, D. (2003), *Handbook of Entrepreneurship Research: An Interdisciplinary Survey and Introduction*, Vol. I of International Handbook Series on Entrepreneurship, Springer, New York.

Akerlof, G. and Kranton, R. (2000), "Economics and identity," *Quarterly Journal of Economics* 105(3), 715–754.

Alchian, A. (1967), "Pricing and society," Technical Report, The Institute of Economic Affairs, Westminster.

Aldrich, J. (1993), "Rational choice and turnout," *American Journal of Political Science* 37(1), 246–278.

Alesina, A. and Ferrara, E. L. (2005), "Ethnic diversity and economic performance," *Journal of Economic Literature* 43, 762–800.

Allingham, M. and Sandmo, A. (1972), "Income tax evasion: a theoretical analysis," *Journal of Public Economics*, 1(3–4), 323–338.

Alston, R., Kearl, J., and Vaughan, M. (1992), "Is there a consensus among economists in the 1990s?," *American Economics Review: Papers and Proceedings* 82(2), 203–209.

An-Nawawi, I. (1997), *An-Nawawi's Forty Hadiths*, Islamic Texts Society, Cambridge. Translated by E. Ibrahim.

Anand, P., Pattanaik, P., and Puppe, C. (2009), *Handbook of Rational and Social Choice*, Oxford University Press.

Anderson, K. L. and Umberson, D. (2001), "Gendering violence: masculinity and power in men's accounts of domestic violence," *Gender and Society* 15(3), 358–380.

397

Andrade, J., ed. (2009), *Handbook of Violence, Risk Assessment and Treatment: New Approaches for Mental Health Professionals*, Springer Publishing, New York.

Andreoni, J. (1989), "Giving with impure altruism: applications to charity and Ricardian equivalence," *The Journal of Political Economy* 97(6), 1447–1458.

Andreoni, J., Erard, B., and Feinstein, J. (1998), "Tax compliance," *Journal of Economic Literature* 36, 818–860.

Antic, N. and Frijters, P. (2012), "Can collapsing business networks explain economic downturns?" Unpublished manuscript.

Aquinas, T. (1935), *Summe der Theologie*, Kröner, Stuttgart.

Arendt, H. (1970), *On Violence*, The Penguin Press, London.

Argyle, M. (1975), *Bodily Communication*, Methuen, London.

Arrow, K. (1963), "Uncertainty and the welfare economics of medical care," *American Economic Review* 53(5), 941–973.

(1974), *The Limits of Organization*, W.W. Norton, New York.

Asheim, G. (1997), "Individual and collective time-inconsistency," *Review of Economic Studies* 64, 427–443.

Aslund, A. (2002), *Building Capitalism: Economic Transition in the Former Soviet Bloc*, Cambridge University Press.

Athens, L. and Ulmer, J. (2003), *Violent Acts and Violentization: Assessing, Applying and Developing Lonnie Athens' Theories*, Elsevier Science Ltd., Oxford.

Audretsch, D. and Keilbach, M. (2004), "Entrepreneurship capital and economic performance," *Regional Studies* 38(8), 949–959.

Audretsch, D. and Stephan, P. (1996), "Company-scientist locational links: the case of biotechnology," *The American Economic Review* 86(3), 641–652.

Ausubel, L., Cramton, P., and Deneckere, R. (2002), "Bargaining with incomplete information," in R. Aumann and S. Hart, eds., *Handbook of Game Theory with Economic Applications*, Vol. III, Elsevier, Amsterdam, chapter 50.

Balcom, D. (2004), *The Greatest Escape: Adventures in the History of Solitude*, iUniverse Inc., Nebraska.

Balk, A. (2008), *Saints and Sinners: An Account of Western Civilization*, Thelema Publications, London.

Banerjee, A., Duflo, E., Glennerster, R., and Kinnan, C. (2010), "The miracle of microfinance? Evidence of a randomized evaluation," Working Paper 278, Bureau of Research and Economic Analysis of Development.

Bar-Tal, D. (1989), *Group Beliefs: A Conception for Analyzing Group Structure, Processes, and Behavior*, Springer-Verlag, New York.

Bartels, L. and Brady, H. (2003), "Economic behaviour in political context," *American Economic Review* 93(2), 156–161.

Baumeister, R., ed. (2001), *Social Psychology and Human Sexuality: Essential Readings*, Sheridan Books, Michigan.

Baumeister, R. and Leary, M. (1995), "The need to belong: desire for interpersonal attachments as a fundamental human motivation," *Psychological Bulletin* 117(3), 497–529.

Baumol, W. (2002), *The Free-market Innovation Machine: Analyzing the Growth Miracle of Capitalism*, Princeton University Press.

Baumol, W. and Blinder, A. (2009), *Microeconomic: Principles and Policy*, eleventh edn., South-Western Cengage Learning, Mason, OH.

Baumol, W., Cave, M., Cramton, P., et al. (2007), "Economists' statement on network neutrality policy," AEI-Brookings Joint Centre for Regulatory Studies.

Becker, G. (1974), "A theory of social interactions," *Journal of Political Economy*, 82(6), 1063–1091.

(1983), "A theory of competition among pressure groups for political influence," *The Quarterly Journal of Economics* 98(3), 371–400.

Benabou, R. and Tirole, J. (2006), "Incentives and prosocial behaviour," *American Economic Review* 96(5), 1652–1678.

Bentham, J. (1954), *Jeremy Bentham's Economic Writings*, Vol. III, critical edition based on printed works and unprinted manuscripts, George Allen & Unwin Ltd., London.

Bereczkei, T. and Csanaky, A. (1996), "Mate choice, marital status, and reproduction in modern society," *Ethology and Sociobiology* 17(1), 17–35.

Bernhard, H., Fehr, E., and Fischbacher, U. (2006), "Group affiliation and altruistic enforcement," *American Economic Review* 96(2), 217–221.

Besse, J. (1910), "Hermits," in C. Herbermann, ed., *The Catholic Encyclopedia*, Vol. VII, Robert Appleton Company, New York.

Bezemer, D. (2001), *Russian Reforms: The Return of the Peasant?*, Nova Science Publishers, New York.

Bezemer, D., Dulleck, U., and Frijters, P. (2003), "Socialism, capitalism, and transition – coordination of economic relations and output performance," Technical Report 0305, University of Vienna.

(2004), "Social capital, creative destruction, and economic growth," Technical Report 0406, University of Vienna.

Binmore, K. (2007), *Does Game Theory Work? The Bargaining Challenge*, MIT Press, Cambridge, MA.

Blais, A. (2000), *To Vote or Not to Vote: The Merits and Limits of Rational Choice Theory*, University of Pittsburgh Press.

Blanchard, O. (1997), *The Economics of Post-Communist Transition*, Clarendon Press, Oxford.

Blanke, O. and Dieguez, S. (2009), "Leaving body and life behind: out-of-body and near-death experience," in S. Laurys and G. Tononi, eds., *The Neurology of Consciousness: Cognitive Neuroscience and Neuropathology*, Academic Press, London, pp. 305–309.

Blankson, S. (2007), *A Brief History of Taxation*, Blankson Enterprises Limited, London.

Blaug, M. (1985), *Economic Theory in Retrospect*, fourth edn., Cambridge University Press.

Bolton, G. and Ockenfels, A. (2000), "ERC: a theory of equity, reciprocity, and competition," *American Economic Review* 90(1), 166–193.

Bond, J. and Coleman, P. (1993), *Ageing in Society: An Introduction to Social Gerontology*, Sage Publications, London.

Bornstein, G., Kugler, T., and Ziegelmeyer, A. (2004), "Individual and group decisions in the centipede game: are groups more 'rational' players?," *Journal of Experimental Social Psychology* 40(5), 599–605.

Bornstein, G. and Yaniv, I. (1998), "Individual and group behavior in the ultimatum game: are groups more 'rational' players?," *Experimental Economics* 1(1), 101–108.

Bornstein, M. (1999), "Framework issues in the privatization strategies of the Czech Republic, Hungary and Poland," *Communist Economics and Economic Transformation* 11, 47–74.

Bourdieu, P. (1986), "The Forms of Capital," in J. G. Richardson, ed., *Handbook of Theory and Research for the Sociology of Education*, Greenwood Press, New York.

Bourquin, S. (1979), "The Zulu military organization and the challenge of 1879," *South African Military History Journal* 4(4). Retrieved from http://samilitaryhistory.org/vol044sb.html on November 1, 2012.

Bowles, S. (1998), "Endogenous preferences: the cultural consequences of markets and other economic institutions," *Journal of Economic Literature* 36, 75–111.

Bowles, S. and Gintis, H. (2003), "The evolutions of strong reciprocity: cooperation in heterogeneous populations," *Theoretical Population Biology* 65, 17–28.

Boyer, D. (2008), "Being human: religion: bound to believe?," *Nature* 445, 1038–1039.

Boyes, W. and Melvin, M. (2011), *Economics*, eighth edn., South-Western Cengage Learning, Mason, OH.

Brady, G. (2003), "International governance of the Internet: an economic analysis," *Economic Affairs* 23(2), 40–44.

Braguinsky, S. and Yavlinsky, G. (2000), *Incentives and Institutions: The Transition to a Market Economy in Russia*, Princeton University Press.

Breiter, H., Gollub, R., Wesskoff, R. et al. (1997), "Acute effects of cocaine on human brain activity and emotion," *Neuron* 19(3), 591–611.

Brewer, M. (1991), "The social self: on being the same and different at the same time," *Personality and Social Psychology Bulletin* 17(5), 475–482.

Brunner, K. and Meckling, W. (1977), "The perception of man and the conception of government," *Journal of Money, Credit and Banking* 9(1), 70–85.

Buchanan, J., Tollison, R., and Tullock, G. (1980), *Toward a Theory of the Rent-Seeking Society*, Texas A&M University. Issue 4 of Texas A&M University Economics Series.

Buddha, S. (30 BC), *Thus Have I Heard: The Long Discourses of the Buddha Dīgha Nikāya*.

Burger, J. (2009), "Replicating Milgram: would people still obey today?," *American Psychologist* 64(1), 1–11.

Burkert, W. (1983), *Homo Necans: The Anthropology of Ancient Greek Sacrificial Ritual and Myth*, University of California Press.

Buss, D. (1989), "Sex differences in human mate preferences: evolutionary hypotheses tested in 37 cultures," *Behavioural and Brain Sciences* 12(1), 1–14.

Byrne, D. (1959), "The effect of a subliminal food stimulus on verbal response," *Journal of Applied Psychology* 43, 249–252.

Cahill, L., Uncapher, M., Kilpatrick, L., Alkire, M., and Turner, J. (2004), "Sex-related hemispheric lateralization of amygdala function in emotionally influenced memory: an fMRI investigation," *Learning and Memory* 11(3), 261.

Campos, N. and Coricelli, F. (2002), "Growth in transition: what we know, what we don't and what we should," *Journal of Economic Literature* 40(3), 793–836.

Canetti, E. (1984), *Crowds and Power*, Farrar, Straus and Giroux, New York.

Caporael, L., Dawes, R., Orbell, J., and van de Kragt, A. (1989), "Selfishness examined: cooperation in the absence of egoistic incentives," *Behavioral and Brain Sciences* 12, 683–699.

Caselli, F. and Cunningham, T. (2009), "Leader behaviour and the natural resource curse," *Oxford Economic Papers* 61(4), 628–650.

Caskie, P. (2000), "Back to basics: household food production in Russia," *Journal of Agricultural Economics* 51(2), 196–209.

Cassar, A., Crowley, L., and Wydick, B. (2007), "The effect of social capital on group loan repayment: evidence from field experiments," *The Economic Journal* 117(517), 85–107.

Chakrabarti, M. (1993), *Gandhian Spiritualism: A Quest for the Essence of Excellence*, Concept Publishing Company, New Delhi.

Chang, H. (2010), *23 Things They Don't Tell You About Capitalism*, Bloomsbury Press, New York.

Charles, A. (1993), *For Good and Evil: The Impact of Taxes on the Course of Civilization*, Madison Books, New York.

Charlesworth, W. (1969), "The role of surprise in cognitive development," in D. Elkind and J. Flavell, eds., *Studies in Cognitive Development*, Oxford University Press, New York, pp. 257–314.

Charness, G., Karni, E., and Levin, D. (2007), "Individual and group decision making under risk: an experimental study of Bayesian updating and violations of first-order stochastic dominance," *Journal of Risk and Uncertainty* 35(2), 129–148.

Chaudhary, L. and Rubin, J. (2011), "Reading, writing and religion: institutions and human capital formation," *Journal of Comparative Economics* 39, 17–33.

Chen, Y. and Li, S. X. (2009), "Group identity and social preferences," *American Economic Review* 99(1), 413–457.

Christian, J. (1970), "Subordination, population density and mammalian evolution," *Science* 168(3927), 84–90.

Clark, A., Diener, E., Georgellis, V., and Lucas, R. (2007), "Lags and leads in life satisfaction: a test of the baseline hypothesis," Technical Report, Centre for Economic Performance. Discussion Paper No. 836.

Clark, A., Frijters, P., and Shields, M. (2008), "A survey of the income happiness gradient," *Journal of Economic Literature* 46(1), 95–144.

Coase, R. (1937), "The nature of the firm," *Economica* 4(16), 386–405.

Coen, D. and Thatcher, M. (2005), "The new governance of markets and non-majoritarian regulators," *Governance: An International Journal of Policy, Administration and Institutions* 18(3), 329–346.

Cohendet, P., Llerena, P., Stahn, H., and Umbhauer, G., eds. (1998), *The Economics of Networks: Interaction and Behaviours*, Springer, Berlin.

Cole, P. (1986), "Children's spontaneous expressive control of facial expression," *Child Development* 57, 1309–1321.

Cole, P., Bruschi, C., and Tamang, B. (2002), "Cultural differences in children's emotional reactions to difficult situations," *Child Development* 73(3), 983–996.

Collier, P. (2007), *The Bottom Billion: Why the Poorest Countries are Failing and What Can be Done About It*, Oxford University Press.

Conan Doyle, A. (1887), *A Study in Scarlet*, Street and Smith Publishers, London.

Cook, K. and Emerson, R. (1978), "Power, equity and commitment in exchange networks," *American Sociological Review* 43, 712–739.

Cooper, D. and Kagel, J. (2005), "Are two heads better than one? Team versus individual play in signaling games," *The American Economic Review* 95(3), 509.

Cox, J. (2002), "Trust, reciprocity, and other-regarding preferences: groups vs. individuals and males vs. females," in R. Zwick and A. Rapoport, eds., *Advances in Experimental Business Research*, Kluwer, New York.

Daal, J. V. and Jolink, A. (1993), *The Equilibrium Economics of Leon Walras*, Routledge, London.

Dahl, R. (1957), "The concept of power," *Behavioural Science* 2(3), 201–215.

(1968), "Power," in D. Sills, ed., *International Encyclopedia of the Social Sciences*, Vol. XII, Free Press, New York, pp. 405–415.

(1986), *A Preface to Economic Democracy*, University of California Press.

Dahrendorf, R. (1968), *Essays in the Theory of Society*, Stanford University Press.

Debiec, J. and Ledoux, J. (2004), "Disruptions of reconsolidation but not consolidation of auditory fear conditioning by noradrenergic blockade in the amygdala," *Neuroscience* 129(2), 267–272.

de Gelder, B. (2006), "Towards the neurobiology of emotional body language," *Nature Review Neuroscience* 7, 242–249.

Diamond, J. (1997), *Guns, Germs, and Steel: The Fates of Human Societies*, W.W. Norton, New York.

Dignam, A. and Galanis, M. (2009), *The Globalization of Corporate Governance*, Ashgate Publishing Limited, Surrey.

Dixit, A. (2003), "Some lessons from transaction-cost politics for less-developed countries," *Economics and Politics* 15(2), 107–133.

(2009), "Governance institutions and economic activity," *American Economic Review* 99(1), 5–24.

Dogan, M. (2004), "From social class and religious identity to status incongruence in post-industrial societies," *Comparative Sociology* 3(2), 163–197.

Dolan, E. (2010), *Introduction to Economics*, fourth edn., BVT Publishing, Readding, CA.

Downs, A. (1957), *An Economic Theory of Democracy*, Harper and Row, New York.

Dreze, J. and de la Vallee Poussin, D. (1971), "A tatonnement process for public goods," *Review of Economic Studies* 38(114), 133–150.

Duffy, M., Ganster, D., Shaw, J., Johnson, J., and Milan, P. (2006), "The social context of undermining behaviour at work," *Organizational Behaviour and Human Decision Processes* 101(1), 105–126.

Dulleck, U. and Frijters, P. (2004), "Why the US and not Brazil? Old elites and the development of a modern economy," Technical Report 0408, Department of Economics, University of Vienna.

Durkheim, E. (1893), *De la Division du Travail Social*, The Free Press, New York. Translated by G. Simpson, 1933.

Durlauf, S., Johnson, P., and Temple, J. (2005), *Growth Econometrics*, North Holland, Amsterdam.

Earnshaw, S. (1997), *Just Postmodernism*, Rodopi, Amsterdam.

Easterly, W. (2007), "Was development assistance a mistake?," *American Economic Review* 97(2), 328–332.

Elias, N. (1939), *The Civilising Process: State Formation and Civilisation*, Vol. II, Basil Blackwell, Oxford.

Fahrbach, S., Morrell, J., and Pfaff, D. (1984), "Oxytocin induction of short-latency maternal behavior in nulliparous, estrogen-primed female rats," *Hormones and Behaviour* 18(3), 267–286.

Fals-Stewart, W. and Lam, W. (2010), "Marital dysfunction," in J. Thomas and M. Hersen, eds., *Handbook of Clinical Psychological Competencies*, Springer, New York.

Faravelli, M. and Walsh, R. (2011), "Smooth politicians and paternalistic voters: a theory of large elections," NBER Working Paper 17397.

Feddersen, T. and Sandroni, A. (2006), "A theory of participation in elections," *American Economic Review* 96(4), 1271–1282.

Fehr, E. and Gachter, S. (2000), "Cooperation and punishment in public goods experiments," *American Economic Review* 90(4), 980–994.

Fershtman, C., Gnezy, U., and Hoffman, M. (2011), "Taboos and identity: considering the unthinkable," *American Economic Journal: Microeconomics* 3(2), 139–164.

Festinger, L. (1957), *A Theory of Cognitive Dissonance*, Stanford University Press.

Foucault, M. (1986), "Disciplinary power and subjection," in S. Lukes, ed., *Power*, Basil Blackwell, Oxford, pp. 229–242.

(2002), *Archaeology of Knowledge*, Routledge, London and New York.

Fox, M. (1971), *Behaviour of Wolves, Dogs and Related Canids*, J. Cape, London.

Freeman, R. (1997), "Working for nothing: the supply of volunteer labor," *Journal of Labor Economics* 15(1), 140–166.

Frey, B. (2003), *Art and Economics: Analysis and Cultural Policy*, second edn., Springer-Verlag, Berlin.

Frey, B. and Meier, S. (2004), "Social comparisons and pro-social behaviour: testing 'conditional cooperation' in a field experiment," *American Economic Review* 94(5), 1717–1722.

Frey, B., Pommerehne, W., Schneider, F., and Gilbert, G. (1984), "Consensus and dissension among economists: an empirical inquiry," *American Economic Review* 74(5), 986–993.

Frijters, P. (2005), "Inside the black-box of social capital: micro-models of the value of contacts." Unpublished manuscript.

Frijters, P. and Baron, J. (2012), "The cult of Theoi: economic uncertainty and religion," *Economic Record* 88, Special Issue, June, 116–136.

Frijters, P., Bezemer, D., and Dulleck, U. (2003), "Contacts, social capital and market institutions – a theory of development," Technical Report 0311, Department of Economics, University of Vienna.

Frijters, P., Dulleck, U., and Torgler, B. (2009), *Introductory Economics for Decision Makers*, second revised edn., Cengage Learning, Australia.

Frijters, P. and Foster, G. (2010), "Reciprocity, hierarchy, and freedom in groups." Unpublished manuscript.

(2013), *Decoding Humanity*, under review.

Frijters, P. and Gregory, R. (2006), "From golden age to golden age: Australia's great leap forward," *The Economic Record* 82(2), 207–225. Issue of *The Economic Record* for the celebration of Prof. Robert Gregory's career.

Frijters, P., Shields, M., and Wheatley-Price, S. (2005), "Job search methods and their success: a comparison of immigrants and natives in the UK," *The Economic Journal* 115(507), 359–376.

Frijters, P. and Tieman, A. (1999), "The role and evolution of central authorities," Technical Report 99–053/1, Tinbergen Institute Discussion Papers.

Fudenberg, D. (2006), "Advancing beyond advances in behavioural economics," *Journal of Economic Literature* 44, 694–711.

Furuboth, E. and Richter, R. (1998), *Institutions and Economic Theory: The Contribution of the New Institutional Economics*, The University of Michigan Press.

Gaddy, C. and Ickes, B. (2002), *Russia's Virtual Economy*, illustrated edn., Brookings Institution Press, Washington DC.

Galbraith, J. (1984), *The Anatomy of Power*, Hamish Hamilton, London.

Gallagher, P. (2011), "A great big (banana) tax," short article retrieved from http://petergallagher.com.au/index.php/site/article/a-great-big-banana-tax1 on November 1, 2012.

Gann, L. and Duignan, P. (1991), *Hope for South Africa?*, Hoover Press, USA.

Gavrilenkov, E. and Koen, V. (1995), "How large was the output collapse in Russia?," Technical Report, IMF. Published in updated form in *Staff Studies for the World Economic Outlook*, September 1995.

Gilbert, D. (2010), *The American Class Structure in an Age of Growing Inequality*, eighth edn., Sage Publications, Thousand Oaks, CA.

Gilbert, P. (2000), *Subordination and Defeat: An Evolutionary Approach to Mood Disorders and their Therapy*, Lawrence Erlbaum, Mahwah, NJ, chapter "Varieties of submissive behavior as forms of social defense: their evolution and role in depression."

Gilboa, I., Postlewaite, A., Samuelson, L., and Schmeidler, D. (2012), "Economic models as analogies," Working paper.

Gilles, R., Lazarova, E. and Ruys, P. (2011), "Economic institutions and stability: a network approach," Discussion paper, Tilburg University, Center for Economic Research.

Gillet, J., Schram, A., and Sonnesmans, J. (2009), "The tragedy of the commons revisited: the importance of group decision-making," *Journal of Public Economics* 93(5–6), 785–797.

Glaeser, E., Laibson, D., Scheinkman, J., and Soutter, C. (2000), "Measuring trust," *Quarterly Journal of Economics* 115(3), 811–846.

Gnepp, J. and Chilamkurti, C. (1988), "Children's use of personality attributions to predict other people's emotional and behavioural reactions," *Child Development* 59(3), 743–754.

Gomez, D., Gonzalez-Aranguena, E., Manuel, C., Owen, G., and del Pozo, M. (2003), "Centrality and power in social networks: a game theoretic approach," *Mathematical Social Sciences* 46(1), 27–54.

Goyal, S. (2005), "Learning in networks," in G. Demange and M. Wooders, eds., *Group Formation in Economics*, Cambridge University Press, pp. 122–168.

Gradstein, M. and Justman, M. (2002), "Education, social cohesion, and economic growth," *American Economic Review* 92(4), 1192–1204.

Greene, F. (1965), *A Curtain of Ignorance: How the American Public Has Been Misinformed About China*, Jonathan Cape, London.

Grewal, D. (2008), *Network Power: The Social Dynamics of Globalization*, Yale University Press.

Gros, D. and Steinherr, A. (1995), *Winds of Change: Economic Transition in Central and Eastern Europe*, Longman, New York and London.

Guicciardini, F. and Moulakis, A. (1998), *Republican Realism in Renaissance Florence: Francesco Guicciardini Discorso di Logrogno*, Rowman and Littlefield, New York.

Gulati, R. (1995), "Does familiarity breed trust? The implications of repeated ties for contractual choice analysis," *Academy of Management Journal* 38, 85–112.

Hanlon, M., Mills, L., and Slemrod, J. (2007), "An empirical examination of corporate tax noncompliance," in A. Auerbach, J. Hines, and J. Slemrod, eds., *Taxing Corporate Income in the 21st Century*, Cambridge University Press.

Harcourt, G. (1982), *The Social Science Imperialists*, Routledge and Kegan Paul, London. Selected essays, G. C. Harcourt. Edited by Prue Kerr.

  (1995), *Capitalism, Socialism, and Post-Keynesianism: Selected Essays of G.C. Harcourt*, Edward Elgar, Aldershot.

Harmatz, M., Well, A., Overtree, C., Kawamura, K., Rosal, M., and Ockene, I. (2000), "Seasonal variation of depression and other moods: a longitudinal approach," *Journal of Biological Rhythms* 15, 344–350.

Harnad, S. (2005), "To cognize is to categorise: cognition is categorization," in H. Cohen and C. Lefebure, eds., *Handbook of Categorization in Cognitive Science*, Elsevier, Amsterdam.

Harsanyi, J. (1962), "Measurement of social power, opportunity cost, and the theory of two-person bargaining games," *Behavioral Sciences* 7, 67–80.

  (1967), "Games with incomplete information played by Bayesian players, I–III," *Management Science* 14(3), 159–182.

  (1977), "Morality and the theory of rational behavior," *Social Research* 44(4), 623–656.

  (1985), "Rule utilitarianism, equality and justice," *Social Philosophy and Policy* 2, 115–127.

Hayek, F. (1979), *The Political Order of a Free People*, University of Chicago Press. *Law, Legislation and Liberty*, Vol. III.

Hearn, J. (1998), *The Violences of Men: How Men Talk About and How Agencies Respond to Men's Violence against Women*, Sage, Thousand Oaks, CA.

Hedlund, E. and Sundstrom, E. (1996), "The Russian economy after systematic change," *Europe-Asia Studies* 48(6), 887–921.

Hirschman, D. and Vaughan, M. (1983), "Food production and income generation in a matrilineal society: rural women in Zomba, Malawi," *Journal of South African Studies* 10(1), 86–99.

Hirschmann, N. (1996), "Domestic violence and the theoretical discourse of freedom," *Frontiers: A Journal of Women Studies* 16(1), 126–151.

Hobbes, T. (1651), *Leviathan*, Cambridge University Press.

Holler, M. (1983), "Tot dem Homo Oeconomicus? Eine Bearbeitung von José Guilherme Merquior, Mort à L'Homo Oeconomicus," *Homo Oeconomicus* 1, 76–79.

Hopfensitz, A. (2009), "The importance of emotions for the effectiveness of social punishment," *The Economic Journal* 119(540), 1534–1559.

Hubbard, R. and O'Brien, A. (2009), *Essentials of Economics*, second edn., Pearson Education, Prentice Hall, New Jersey.

Hume, D. (1740), *Writings on Economics*, University of Wisconsin Press.

Hussain, S., Chaudhry, I., and Malik, S. (2009), "Natural resource abundance and economic growth in Pakistan," *European Journal of Economics, Finance and Administrative Sciences* 15, 189–198.

Iannaccone, L. (1998), "Introduction to the economics of religion," *Journal of Economic Literature* 36(3), 1465–1495.

Iannaccone, L. and Berman, E. (2006), "Religious extremism: the good, the bad, and the deadly," *Public Choice* 128, 109–129.

Imber, C. (2002), *The Ottoman Empire, 1300–1650: The Structure of Power*, Palgrave Macmillan, New York.

Inalcik, H. (2000), *The Ottoman Empire: The Classical Age, 1300–1600*, Orion Publishing Co., United Kingdom.

Insel, T. (1992), "Oxytocin – a neuropeptide for affiliation: evidence from behavioural, receptor autodiographic, and comparative studies," *Psychoneuroendocrinology* 171, 3–35.

Inter-American Commission on Human Rights (1983), *Report on the Human Rights Situation in Suriname*, Technical Report.

Irwin, S., Maguire, C., Martin, G., Martin, R., and Poswa, S. (2004), "The state of justice in Zimbabwe," Technical Report, International Council of Advocates and Barristers.

Ischinger, B. (2008), "Education at a glance: OECD indicators 2008," Technical Report, Organisation for Economic Co-operation and Development, Paris.

Izard, C. (1977), *Human Emotions*, Plenum Press, New York.

   (1992), "Basic emotions, relations among emotion and emotion- cognition relations," *Psychological Review* 99(3), 561–565.

Jackson, C. and Schneider, H. (2011), "Do social connections reduce moral hazard? Evidence from the New York City taxi industry," *American Economic Journal: Applied Economics* 3(3), 244–267.

Jackson, M., Rodriguez-Barraquer, T., and Tan, X. (2012), "Social capital and social quilts: network patterns of favor exchange," *American Economic Review* 102(5), 1857–1897.

Jackson, M. and Wolinsky, A. (1996), "A strategic model of social and economic networks," *Journal of Economic Theory* 71, 44–74.

Jarvis, A. and Lee, W. (2008), *Trade, Migration and Urban Networks in Port Cities, c. 1640–1940*, International Maritime Economic History Association. Originally published by Indiana University.

Jevons, W. (1871), *The Theory of Political Economy*, Hayes Barton Press, London.

Jordan, J. (2006), "Pillage and property," *Journal of Economic Theory*, 131(1), 26–44.

Juslin, P. (2001), *Music and Emotion: Theory and Research*, Oxford University Press, New York.

Kahneman, D. (2003), "A psychological perspective on economics," *American Economic Review* 93(2), 162–168.

(2011), *Thinking, Fast and Slow*, Farrar, Straus and Giroux, New York.

Kandel, E., Schwartz, J., and Jessell, T. (1991), *Principles of Neural Science*, third edn., Elsevier, New York.

(2000), *Principles of Neural Science*, fourth edn., McGraw-Hill, Health Professions Division, New York.

Kandori, M., Mailath, G., and Rob, R. (1993), "Learning, mutation, and long run equilibria in games," *Econometrica* 61, 29–56.

Kasper, W. and Streit, M. (1998), *Institutional Economics: Social Order and Public Policy*, Edward Elgar, Cheltenham.

Kearl, J., Pope, C., Whiting, G., and Wimmer, L. (1979), "A confusion of economists," *American Economic Review* 69, 28–37.

Keenan, J., Nelson, A., O'Connor, M., and Pascual-Leone, A. (2001), "Self-recognition and the right hemisphere," *Nature* 409(6818), 305.

Keith, R. (1991), *Discovering the Roman Family: Studies in Roman Social History*, Oxford University Press, New York.

Kendrick, K., Keverne, E., and Baldwin, B. (1987), "Intracerebroventricular oxytocin stimulates maternal behaviour in the sheep," *Neuroendocrinology* 46, 56–61.

Killion, U. (2006), *A Modern Chinese Journey to the West: Economic Globalization and Dualism*, Nova Science Publishers Inc., New York.

Kirchgassner, G. (1991), "Führt der Homo oeconomicus das Recht in die Irre?, Zur Kritik an der ökonomischen Analyse des Rechts," *Juristenzeitung* 46(3), 104–111.

Klaus, M. (1998), "Mother and infant: early emotional ties," *Pediatrics* 102, 1244.

Klepper, S. and Nagin, D. (2000), "The anatomy of tax evasion," *Journal of Law, Economics, and Organization* 5, 1–24.

Knapp, M., Mark, L., and Hall, J. (1992), *Nonverbal Communication in Human Interaction*, Holf, Rinehart & Winston, New York.

Knight, J., Song, L., and Gunatilaka, R. (2007), "Subjective well-being and its determinants in rural China," Oxford University Department of Economics Discussion Paper Series, No. 334.

Kocher, M. and Sutter, M. (2005), "The decision maker matters: individual versus group behaviour in experimental beauty-contest games," *The Economic Journal* 115(500), 200–223.

Kohut, A., Stokes, B., Gross, E. M., and Speulda, N. (2003), "Global gender gaps: women like their lives better," Technical Report, The Pew Global Attitudes Project.

Kolm, S. (2008), *Reciprocity: An Economics of Social Relations*, Cambridge University Press.

Komter, A. (2005), *Social Solidarity and the Gift*, Cambridge University Press.

   (2010), "The evolutionary origins of human generosity," *Inter- national Sociology* 25(3), 443–464.

Koning, C. (1998), "Companies offer way out of monetary crisis," *Jakarta Times*, February 11.

Koopman, S., Lucas, A., and Schwaab, B. (2010), "Macro, frailty and contagion effects in defaults: lessons from the 2008 credit crisis," Discussion Paper 10–004/2, Tinbergen Institute.

Krings, M., Stone, A., Schmitz, R., Krainitzki, H., Stoneking, M., and Paabo, S. (1997), "Neanderthal DNA sequences and the origin of modern humans," *Cell* 90, 19–30.

Krugman, P. (1991), *Geography and Trade*, reprint/illustrated edn., MIT Press, Cambridge, MA.

Kudoh, T. and Matsumoto, D. (1985), "Cross-cultural examination of the semantic dimensions of body postures," *Journal of Personality and Social Psychology* 48(6), 1440–1446.

Kugler, T., Bornstein, G., Kocher, M., and Sutter, M. (2007), "Trust between individuals and groups: groups are less trusting than individuals but just as trustworthy," *Journal of Economic Psychology* 28(6), 646–657.

Kuhn, T. (1962), *The Structure of Scientific Revolutions*, University of Chicago Press.

Lane, P. and Tornell, A. (1996), "Power, growth and the voracity effect," *Journal of Economic Growth* 1(2), 213–241.

Levi-Strauss, C. (1944), "Reciprocity and hierarchy," *American Anthropologist* 46(2), 266–268.

Levitt, S. and Dubner, S. (2005), *Freakonomics*, Harper Collins, New York.

Lewis, M. and Michalson, L. (1983), *Children's Emotions and Moods: Developmental Theory and Measurement*, Plenum Press, New York.

Lewis, M., Sullivan, M., Stangor, C., and Weiss, M. (1989), "Self development and self-conscious emotion," *Child Development* 60, 146–156.

Li, D. (1998), "Changing incentives of the Chinese bureaucracy," *American Economic Review* 88(2), 393–397.

Lieberman, I. and Nellis, J. (1995), *Russia: Creating Private Enterprises and Efficient Markets*, World Bank, Studies of Economies in Transformation, Washington DC.

Lindquist, N. (1945), "Some notes on development of memory during the first years of life," *ACTA Paediatric* 32, 592–598.

Locke, J. (2002), *John Locke: Essays on the Law of Nature*, Oxford University Press. The Latin text with a Translation, Introduction and Notes; together with transcripts of Locke's shorthand in his Journal for 1676.

Lopus, J. and Paringer, L. (2011), "The principles of economics textbooks: content, coverage, and usage," in K. M. McGoldrick and G. Hoyt, eds., *The International Handbook on Teaching and Learning Economics*, Edward Elgar Publishing, Massachusetts, chapter 28, pp. 296–306.

Lorenz, K. (1959), *Evolution der Organismen*, Fischer, Stuttgart, chapter "Pschologie und Stammesgeschichte."

Lukes, S., ed. (1986), *Power*, Blackwell, Oxford.

Machlup, F. (1962), *Knowledge: Its Creation, Distribution and Economic Significance*, Princeton University Press.

Maciejovsky, B. and Budescu, D. (2007), "Collective induction without cooperation? Learning and knowledge transfer in cooperative groups and competitive auctions," *Journal of Personality and Social Psychology* 92(5), 854–870.

Maclean, P. (1990), *The Triune Brain in Evolution: Role in Paleocerebral Functions*, Plenum Press, New York.

Maddison, A. (2007), "Chinese economic performance in the long run: 960–2030 AD," Technical report, OECD Development Centre Studies, Paris.

Maner, J., Miller, S., Schmidt, N., and Eckel, L. (2009), "Submitting to defeat: social anxiety, dominance threat and decrements in testosterone," *Psychological Science* 19(8), 764–768.

Mankiw, N. (2009), *Principles of Economics*, fifth edn., Cengage Learning, Mason, OH.

Maoz, Z. (2011), *Networks of Nations: The Evolution, Structure and Impact of International Networks, 1816–2001*, Cambridge University Press, New York.

Marazitti, D., Akiskal, H., Rossi, A., and Cassano, B. (1999), "Alteration of the platelet serotonin transporter in romantic love," *Psychological Medicine* 29(3), 741–745.

Mas, A. and Moretti, E. (2009), "Peers at work," *American Economic Review* 99(1), 112–145.

Matsen, E. and Torvik, R. (2005), "Optimal Dutch disease," *Journal of Development Economics* 78, 494–515.

Matsuyama, K. (1999), "Growing through cycles," *Econometrica* 67(2), 335–348.

Mattessich, P. (2009), "Social capital and community building," in R. Phillips and R. Pittman, eds., *An Introduction to Community Development*, Routledge, New York.

Mauss, M. (2002), *The Gift: The Form and Reason for Exchange in Archaic Societies*, reprint edn., Routledge, London. Original written in 1925.

May, E. (1980), *Great Expectations: Marriage and Divorce in Post-Victorian America*, University of Chicago Press.

  (1988), *Homeward Bound: American Families in the Cold War Era*, Basic Books, New York.

McCloskey, D. (2006), *The Bourgeois Virtues: Ethics for the Age of Commerce*, University of Chicago Press.

McConnell, C., Brue, S., and Flynn, S. (2011), *Economics*, nineteenth edn., McGraw-Hill Irwin, New York.

McKenzie, R. (1983), *The Limits of Economic Science*, Kluwer-Nijhoff Publishing, Boston.

McMillan, J. and Rothschild, M. (1994), "Search," in R. Aumann and S. Hart, eds., *Handbook of Game Theory with Economic Applications*, Vol. II, Elsevier, Amsterdam, chapter 27, pp. 905–927.

Mech, D. (2003), *The Wolves: Behavior, Ecology and Conservation*, University of Chicago Press.

Meckling, W. (1976), "Values and the choice of the model of the individual in the social sciences," *Schweizerische Zeitschrift fur Volkswirtschaf* 112, 545–559.

Meer, J. and Rosen, H. (2009), "Altruism and the child cycle of alumni donations," *American Economic Journal: Economic Policy* 1(1), 258–286.

Meeren, H., van Heiknsbergen, C., and de Gelder, B. (2005), "Rapid perceptual integration of facial expression and emotional body language," *Proceedings of the National Academy of Science* 102(45), 16518–16523.

Meier, K. and O'Toole, L. J., Jr. (2007), "Modeling public management," *Public Management Review* 9(4), 503–527.

Meng, X., Manning, A., Li, S., and Effendi, T. (2010), *The Great Migration: Rural-Urban Migration in China and Indonesia*, Edward Elgar, London.

Merquior, J. (1991), "Death to Homo Economicus?," *Critical Review: A Journal of Politics and Society* 5(3), 353–378. Translated with permission from *Archives Européens de Sociologie* 21 (1980), 372–394 by Tony Whit.

Mervin, C. and Frijters, P. (2012), "Is shared misery double misery?" University of Queensland School of Economics Working Paper.

Meyer, K. (2000), "International production networks and enterprise transformation in Central Europe," *Comparative Economic Studies* 42(1), 135–150.

Miguel, E. (2003), "Comment on: social capital and growth," *Journal of Monetary Economics* 50, 195–198.

Milgram, S. (1963), "Behavioral study of obedience," *Journal of Anormal and Social Psychology* 67, 371–378.

Miller, D., Smith, E., and Mackie, D. (2004), "Effects of intergroup contact and political predispositions on prejudice: role of intergroup emotions," *Group Processes and Intergroup Relations* 7(3), 221–237.

Miranda, F., Caballero, R., Gomez, M., and Zamorano, M. (1981), "Obediencia a la autoridad," *Psiquis* 2, 212–221.

Moos, R., Kopell, B., Melges, F., Yalom, I., Lunde, D., and Clayton, R. (1969), "Fluctuations in symptoms and moods during the menstrual cycle," *Journal of Psychosomatic Research* 13, 37–44.

Muldoon, S. and Carrington, H. (1951), *The Phenomenon of Astral Projection*, Rider & Co., London.

Muller, J. (1995), *Adam Smith in His Time and Ours: Designing the Decent Society*, Princeton University Press.

Nikiforakis, N. (2010), "Feedback, punishment and cooperation in public good experiments," *Games and Economic Behavior* 68(2), 689–702.

North, D. (1990), *Institutions, Institutional Change and Economic Performance*, Cambridge University Press.

Nove, A. (1987), *The New Palgrave Dictionary of Economics*, Stockton, New York, chapter "Socialism," pp. 398–407.

Ohem, A. (1986), "Face the beast and fear the face: animal and social fears as prototypes for evolutionary analyses of emotion," *Psychophysiology* 23(2), 123–145.

Okun, A. (1975), *Equality and Efficiency: The Big Tradeoff*, The Brookings Institution, Washington, DC.

Olsen, M. (1982), *The Rise and Decline of Nations: Economic Growth, Stagflation, and Social Rigidities*, Yale University Press, London.

Ostrom, E. (1990), *Governing the Commons: The Evolution of Institutions for Collective Action*, Cambridge University Press, New York.

O'Sullivan, A., Sheffrin, S., and Perez, S. (2010), *Economics: Principles, Applications and Tools,* sixth edn., Pearson Education, Upper Saddle River, NJ.

Otte, M. (2007), *Der Crash Kommt – Die neue Weltwirtschaftskrise und Wie Sie Sich Darauf Vorbereiten,* Ullstein, Berlin.

Ouchi, W. (1978), "The transmission of control through organizational hierarchy," *Academy of Management Journal* 21(2), 173–192.

Paabo, S. (2003), "The mosaic that is our genome," *Nature* 42, 409–411.

Padgett, J. and Mclean, P. (2011), "Economic credit in Renaissance Florence," *The Journal of Modern History* 83(1), 1–47.

Pardo, J. and Schneider, F., eds. (1996), *Current Issues in Public Choice,* Edgar Elgar, Cheltenham, UK.

Pareto, V. (1906), *Manual of the Political Economy,* reprint edn., Augustus M. Kelley, New York. 1971 translation of 1927 French edition.

Parkin, F. (1971), *Class Inequality and Political Order,* Praeger, New York.

Paulus, P. (1980), *Psychology of Group Influence,* Lawrence Erlbaum, Hillsdale, NJ.

Pellizzari, M. (2010), "Do friends and relatives really help in getting a good job?," *Industrial and Labor Relations Review* 63(6), 494–510.

Petrongolo, B. and Pissarides, C. (2001), "Looking into the blackbox: a survey on the matching function," *Journal of Economic Literature* 39, 390–431.

Pettit, P. (2001), *The Economic World View: Studies in the Ontology of Economics,* Cambridge University Press, chapter 5.

Phelan, P. (1995), "Incest and its meaning: the perspectives of fathers and daughters," *Child Abuse and Neglect* 19(1), 7–24.

Phelps, E. (1999), "The global crisis of corporatism," *Wall Street Journal,* March 25.

Piccione, M. and Razin, R. (2009), "Coalition formation under power relations," *Theoretical Economics* 4(1), 1–15.

Piccione, M. and Rubenstein, A. (2007), "Equilibrium in the jungle," *The Economic Journal* 117(522), 883–896.

Pierson, C. (1996), *The Modern State,* Routledge, London.

Pissarides, C. (1990), *Equilibrium Unemployment Theory,* Basil Blackwell, Oxford.

Podolny, J. and Page, K. (1998), "Network forms of organisation," *Annual Review of Sociology* 24, 57–76.

Porat, M. (1977), "The information economy, volume 1: definitions and measurement," Technical Report, Washington DC.

Posner, E. (2000), "Law and social norms: the case of tax compliance," *Virginia Law Review* 86(8), 1781–1820.

(2002), *Law and Social Norms,* Harvard University Press.

Pratt, C. (2007), *An Encyclopedia of Shamanism*, Vol. II, The Rosen Publishing Group, New York.

Pritzker, B. (1998), *Native Americans: An Encyclopedia of History, Culture, and Peoples*, Vol. I, illustrated edn., ABC-Clio, Santa Barbara, CA.

Pugh, M. (1978), *Electoral Reform in War and Peace 1906–1918*, Routledge and Kegan Paul, London.

Putnam, R. (1993), *Making Democracy Work: Civic Traditions in Modern Italy*, Princeton University Press.

Quiggin, J. (2010), *Zombie Economics: How Dead Ideas Still Walk Among Us*, Princeton University Press, Oxfordshire.

Radner, R. (1992), "Hierarchy: the economics of managing," *Journal of Economic Literature* 30(3), 1382–1415.

Rauch, J. (2001), "Business and social networks in international trade," *Journal of Economic Literature* 39, 1177–1203.

(2010), "Does network theory connect to the rest of us? A review of Matthew O. Jackson's social and economic networks," *Journal of Economic Literature* 48(4), 980–986.

Ray, L. (2007), *Globalization and Everyday Life*, Routledge, New York.

Relethford, J. (2001), *Genetics and the Search for Modern Human Origins*, Wiley, New York.

Reuben, E. and van Winden, F. (2008), "Social ties and coordination on negative reciprocity: the role of affect," *Journal of Public Economics* 92(1–2), 34–53.

Ricardo, D. (1817), *Principles of Political Economy and Taxation*, Dent, London.

Riley, G. (1991), *Divorce: An American Tradition*, Oxford University Press, New York.

Ritzmann, F. (1999), *Wirtschaftswissenschaft als Hobby und Beruf*, Rüegger, Chur.

Roberts, B. and Rodriguez, A. (1997), "Economic growth under a self-interested central planner and transition to a market economy," *Journal of Comparative Economics* 24, 121–139.

Robinson, D. (2003), *A Legal and Ethical Handbook for Ending Discrimination in the Workplace*, Paulist Press, New York.

Robinson, M. (2010), "An empirical analysis of engineers' information behaviors," *Journal of the American Society for Information Science and Technology* 61(4), 640–658.

Rockenbach, B., Sadrieh, A., and Mathauschek, B. (2007), "Teams take the better risks," *Journal of Economic Behavior and Organisation* 63(3), 412–422.

Rogers, C. (1999), *The Wars of Edward III: Sources and Interpretations*, Boydell and Brewer, Suffolk.

Rohwer, S. and Ewald, P. (1981), "The cost of dominance and advantage of subordination in a badge signalling system," *Evolution* 35(3), 441–454.

Rosati, D. (1994), "Output decline during transition: a reconsideration," *Economics of Transition* 2, 419–441.

Rosch, E. and Lloyd, B., eds. (1978), *Cognition and Categorization*, L. Erlbaum Associates, Hillsdale, NJ.

Rosenhan, D. and Mantell, D. (1967), "A replication of the Milgram study," Technical Report, Educational Testing Service, Princeton.

Rousseau, J.-J. (1762), *Du Contract Social; ou Principes du Droit Politique*, Marc Michel Rey, Amsterdam.

Routledge, B. and von Amsberg, J. (2003), "Social capital and growth," *Journal of Monetary Economics* 50, 167–193.

Rubinstein, A. (2005), "Discussion of behavioral economics," in W. N. R. Blundell and T. Persson, eds., *Advances in Economics and Econometrics: Theory and Application*, Vol. II of *Ninth World Congress*, pp. 246–254.

Russell, B. and Brittan, S. (1938), *Power: A New Social Analysis*, George Allen and Unwin Ltd., London.

Sadalla, E., Kenrick, D., and Vershue, B. (1987), "Dominance and heterosexual attraction," *Journal of Personality and Social Psychology* 52, 730–738.

Samuelson, L. (1997), *Evolutionary Games and Equilibrium Selection*, MIT Press, Cambridge, MA.

Samuelson, P. (1938), "A note on the pure theory of consumer behaviour," *Economica* 5(17), 61–71.

(1950), "The problem of integrability in utility theory," *Economica* 17(68), 355–385.

(1983), *Foundations of Economic Analysis*, illustrated edn., Harvard University Press, Cambridge, MA.

Samuelson, P. and Nordhaus, W. (2010), *Economics*, nineteenth edn., McGraw-Hill Irwin, New York.

Sandmo, A. (2005), "The theory of tax evasion: a retrospective view," *National Tax Journal* 58(4), 643–663.

Schermerhorn, R. (1961), *Society and Power*, Random House, New York.

Schulte-Ruther, M., Markowitsch, H., Shah, N., Fink, G., and Piefkea, M. (2008), "Gender differences in brain networks supporting empathy," *NeuroImage* 42, 393–403.

Schumpeter, J. (1934), *The Theory of Economic Development*, Oxford University Press.

Seabright, P. (2000), *The Vanishing Rouble: Barter Networks and Non-Monetary Transactions in Post-Soviet Societies*, Cambridge University Press.

Segrin, C. and Nabi, R. (2002), "Does television viewing cultivate unrealistic expectations about marriage?," *Journal of Communication* 52(2), 247–263.

Sen, A. (1985), "Goals, commitment and identity," *Journal of Law, Economics and Organisation* 1, 341–355.

(1988), *On Ethics and Economics*, Wiley-Blackwell, New Jersey.

Seuss, D. (1973), *Did I Ever Tell You How Lucky You Are?*, Collins Childrens Books, Random House, New York.

Sexton, R. (2011), *Exploring Economics*, fifth edn., Cengage Learning, Mason, OH.

Shanab, M. and Yahya, K. (1978), "A cross-cultural study of obedience," *Bulletin of the Psychonomic Society* 11(4), 267–269.

Sidak, J. (2006), "A consumer-welfare approach to network neutrality regulation," *Journal of Competition Law and Economics* 2(3), 349–474.

Simmel, G. (1964), *Conflict, and the Web of Group Affiliations*, Free Press of Glencoe, Macmillan, London.

Simon, H. (1953), "Notes on the observation and measurement of political power," *Journal of Politics* 15, 500–516.

(1991), "Organizations and markets," *The Journal of Economic Perspectives* 5(2), 25–44.

Slemrod, J. (2007), "Cheating ourselves: the economics of tax evasion," *Journal of Economic Perspectives* 21(1), 25–48.

Smith, A. (1759), *The Theory of Moral Sentiments*, 1984 reprint edn., Liberty Fund, Indianapolis.

(1776), *The Wealth of Nations*, Everyman's Library, London.

Smith, J., Howitt, W., and Cassell, J. (1857), *John Cassell's Illustrated History of England: From the Earliest Period to the Reign of Edward the Fourth*, W. Kent and Co., London.

Smith-Mckoy, S. (2001), *When Whites Riot: Writing Race and Violence in American and South African Cultures*, University of Wisconsin Press.

Sobel, J. (2002), "Can we trust social capital?," *Journal of Economic Literature* 40, 139–154.

(2005), "Interdependent preferences and reciprocity," *Journal of Economic Literature* 43, 392–436.

Spencer, G. (1969), "Religious networks and royal influence in eleventh-century south India," *Journal of the Economic and Social History of the Orient* 12(1), 42–56.

Spitz, R. (1945), "Hospitalism – an inquiry into the genesis of psychoanalytic conditions in early childhood," *Psychoanalytic Study of the Child* 1, 53–74.

(1946), "Hospitalism: a follow-up report on investigation described in volume 1, 1945," *Psychoanalytic Study of the Child* 2, 113–117.

Sprott, W. (1958), *Human Groups*, Penguin Books, London.

Squire, L., Berg, D., Bloom, F., du Lac, S., Ghosh, A., and Spitzer, N. (2008), *Fundamental Neuroscience*, third edn., Academic Press, London.

Stenberg, C., Campos, J., and Emde, R. (1983), "The facial expression of anger in seven-month-old infants," *Child Development* 54(1), 178–184.

Stern, P. (1995), "Why do people sacrifice for their nations?," *Political Psychology* 16(2), 217–235.

Sternberg, R. and Weis, K. (2006), *The New Psychology of Love*, Vail-Ballou Press, New York.

Stevenson, O. (1998), *Neglected Children: Issues and Dilemmas*, Blackwell, Oxford.

Stigler, G. (1961), "The economics of information," *Journal of Political Economy* 69(3), 213–225.

(1971), "The theory of economic regulation," *The Bell Journal of Economics and Management* 2(1), 393–397.

Stone, G. (2011), *Core Microeconomics*, second edn., Worth Publishers, New York.

Summers, L. (1986), "Some skeptical observations on real business cycle theory," *Federal Reserve Bank of Minneapolis Quarterly Review* **Fall**, 23–27.

Sung, K. (2001), "Elder respect: exploration of ideals and forms in East Asia," *Journal of Aging Studies* 15, 13–26.

Sutter, M. (2009), "Individual behavior and group membership: comment," *American Economic Review* 99(5), 2247–2257.

Swaan, W. and Lissowaska, M. (1992), "Enterprise behaviour in Hungary and Poland in the transition to a market economy: individual and organizational routines as a barrier to change," in W. Blaas and J. Foster, eds., *Mixed Economies in Europe: An Evolutionary Perspective on their Emergence, Transition and Regulation*, Edward Elgar, Aldershot, pp. 69–102.

Swan, E. (2007), "Blue-eyed girl? Jane Elliott's experiential learning and anti-racism," in M. Reynolds and R. Vince, eds., *The Handbook of Experiential Learning and Management Education*, Oxford University Press, pp. 202–220.

Tajfel, H. (1969), "Cognitive aspects of prejudice," *Journal of Social Issues* 25(4), 79–97.

(1982), *Social Identity and Intergroup Relations*, Cambridge Uni- versity Press, New York.

Tajfel, H., Billing, M., Bundy, R., and Flament, C. (1971), "Social categorization and intergroup behaviour," *European Journal of Social Psychology* 1(2), 149–178.

Taylor, J. and Weerapana, A. (2010), *Principles of Economics*, sixth edn., Cengage Learning, Mason, OH.

Teiwes, F. and Sun, W. (1999), *China's Road to Disaster: Mao, Central Politicians and Provincial Leaders in the Unfolding of the Great Leap Forward, 1955–1959*, Armonk, New York.

Templeton, A. (2002), "Out of Africa again and again," *Nature* 416, 45–51.

The Holy Bible (1974), authorized King James version edn., New American Library, New York.

The Talmud of the Land of Israel, Volume XI: Shabbat (1991), University of Chicago Press. Translated by J. Neusner, 1991.

Theus, K. (1994), "Subliminal advertising and the psychology of processing unconscious stimuli: a review of research," *Psychology and Marketing* 11, 271–290.

Thompson, R. (1994), "Emotion regulation: a theme in search of a definition," in N. Fox, ed., *The Development of Emotion Regulation: Biological and Behavioural Considerations (Monographs of the Society for Research in Child Development)*, Vol. LIX, pp. 25–52.

Thompson, R. and Goodvin, R. (2005), "The individual child: temperament, emotion, self and personality," in M. Bornstein and M. Lamb, eds., *Developmental Science: An Advanced Textbook*, Lawrence Erlbaum Associates, Mahwah, NJ.

Torgler, B., Schneider, F., and Schaltegger, C. (2009), "Autonomy, tax morale, and the shadow economy," *Public Choice* 144(1–2), 293–321.

Townsend, J. (1989), "Mate selection criteria: a pilot study," *Ethology and Sociobiology* 10, 241–253.

Townsend, J. and Levy, G. (1990), "Effects of potential partners' physical attractiveness and socioeconomic status on sexuality and partner selection," *Archives of Sexual Behaviour* 19(2), 149–164.

Tucker, I. (2010), *Economics For Today*, seventh edn., Cengage Learning, Mason, OH.

Turner, J., Hogg, M., Oakes, P., Reicher, S., and Wetherell, M. (1987), *Rediscovering the Social Group: A Self-Categorization Theory*, Basil Blackwell, Oxford.

Urgesi, C., Aglioti, S., Skrap, M., and Fabbro, F. (2010), "The spiritual brain: selective cortical lesions modulate human self-transcendence," *Neuron* 65(3), 309–319.

420   *References*

Van Praag, B. and Frijters, P. (1999), "The measurement of welfare and
    well-being: the Leyden approach," in D. Kahneman, E. Diener, and
    N. Schwarz, eds., *Well-being: The Foundations of Hedonic Psychology*,
    Russell Sage Foundation, New York.
Vaughn, G., Tajfel, H., and Williams, J. (1981), "Bias in reward allocation in
    an intergroup and interpersonal context," *Social Psychology Quarterly*
    44(1), 37–42.
Vega-Redondo, F. (2003), "Building up social capital in a changing world,"
    Journal of Economic Dynamics and Control **30**(11), 2305–2338.
Verspagen, B. (2002), "Evolutionary macroeconomics: a synthesis between
    neo-Schumpeterian and post-Keynesian lines of thought," *The Elec-
    tronic Journal of Evolutionary Modeling and Economic Dynamics*
    (1007). Retrieved from http://ideas.repec.org/a/jem/ejemed/1007.html
    on November 1, 2012.
Viscusi, W., Huber, J., and Bell, J. (2011), "Promoting recycling: private
    values, social norms, and economic incentives," *American Economic
    Review* **101**(3), 65–70.
Vitebsky, P. (1995), *Shamanism*, Duncan Baird Publishers, London.
Voland, E. and Engel, C. (1990), "Female choice in humans: a conditional
    mate selection strategy of the Krummhorn women (Germany, 1720–
    1874)," *Ethology* **84**(2), 144–154.
Vollenweider, F., Gamma, A., Liechti, M., and Huber, T. (1998), "Psycho-
    logical and cardiovascular effects and short-term sequelae of MDMA
    ('Ecstasy') in MDMA-naïve healthy volunteers," *Neuropsychopharma-
    cology* **19**, 241–251.
von Neumann, J. and Morgenstern, O. (1947), *Theory of Games and
    Economic Behavior*, second edn., Princeton University Press.
Vromen, J. (2008), "Economics and philosophy: more than having fun
    and making fun," Technical Report, Board of Erasmus, University of
    Rotterdam.
Vyasa, K. (1896), *The Mahabharata of Krishna-Dwaipayana Vyasa, Book
    13, Part 1*, Bibliobazaar, South Carolina. Translated by K. M. Ganguli,
    2008.
Waal, F. D. (1996), "Macaque social culture: development and perpetuation
    of affiliative networks," *Journal of Comparative Psychology* **110**, 147–
    154.
Walras, L. (1874), *Elements d'Economique Politique Pure*, Orion Editions,
    Illinois. Translation as *Elements of Pure Economics* by William Jaffe,
    1954.
Weber, M. (1922), *Wirtschaft und Gesellschaft*, Bedminster Press, Tuebin-
    gen, Germany.

(1923), *General Economic History*, reprint edn., Cosimo Inc., New York. 2007 reprint of 1927 English translation by Frank Hyneman Knight.

Weichenrieder, A. (1996), "Fighting international tax avoidance: the case of Germany," *Fiscal Studies* 17, 37–58.

Wellman, B. (1983), "Network analysis: some basic principles," *Sociological Theory* 1, 155–200.

Whaples, R. (2009), "The policy views of American Economic Association members: the results of a new survey," *Econ Journal Watch* 6(3), 337–348.

White, E. (1990), "The stock market boom and crash of 1929 revisited," *The Journal of Economic Perspectives* 4(2), 67–83.

Whitworth, S. (2004), *Men, Militarism, and UN Peacekeeping: A Gendered Analysis*, Lynne Rienner Publishers Inc., London.

Wiese, H. (2009), "Applying cooperative game theory to power relations," *Quality and Quantity* 43(4), 519–533.

Williamson, J. (2011), *Trade and Poverty: When the Third World Fell Behind*, MIT Press, Boston.

Williamson, O. (1985), *The Economic Institutions of Capitalism*, Free Press, New York.

(1991), "Comparative economic organization: the analysis of discrete structural alternatives," *Administrative Science Quarterly* 36(2), 269–296.

Wilson, D. (2002), *Darwin's Cathedral: Evolution, Religion and the Nature of Society*, University of Chicago Press.

Winters, L., McCulloch, N., and McKay, A. (2004), "Trade liberalization and poverty: the evidence so far," *Journal of Economic Literature* 42, 72–115.

Wintrobe, R. (2006), *Rational Extremism: The Political Economy of Radicalism*, Cambridge University Press.

Wittfogel, K. (1957), *Oriental Despotism: A Comparative Study of Total Power*, Yale University Press.

Wolfgang, J., Rocher, M., and Sutter, M. (2009), "Group polarization in the team dictator game reconsidered," *Experimental Economics* 12(1), 26–41.

Wood, J. (1984), *Adam Smith: Critical Assessments*, Routledge, London.

Yamagishi, T., Gillmore, M., and Cook, K. (1988), "Network connections and the distribution of power in exchange networks," *American Journal of Sociology* 93(4), 833–851.

Young, H. (1993), "The evolution of conventions," *Econometrica* 61, 57–84.

(1998), *Individual Strategy and Social Structure: An Evolutionary Theory of Institutions*, Princeton University Press.

Yu, L. (1893), *The Analects of Confucius*, Oxford University Press Inc., New York. Translated by C. Huang, 1997.

Zahn-Waxler, C. (2000), *Wisconsin Symposium on Emotion: Vol I. Anxiety, Depression and Emotion*, Oxford University Press, chapter "The early development of empathy, guilt and internalization of responsibility: implications for gender differences in internalizing and externalizing problems."

Index

40-Hour Famine, 24

abstractions, *see also* beliefs
  emotional bonds with, 138–139,
    328–329
  underpinning circles of reciprocity,
    157, 203–204, 308, 320–323
Africa, 24, 132, 192, 276, 306
aim of the book, 29–30, 51, 72–73,
    334
altruism, 4, 18–19, 24, 58–60, 153
America
  Declaration of Independence, 158
  President, 310–311
analog reasoning, 32–34
animals, *see also* cows, power
  social, 133–134, 138–139
apprenticeships, *see* qualifications,
    education, wage–work contract
army recruits, 77–78
Asian crisis, 281–282
attachment (emotional), 60
  of men to children, 140
Australia, 44, 315–318
  Aborigines of, 183

babies
  as scientists, 110
  confiscation of by Ottomans, 189
bakery, 231–234
bananas, 315–318
bankruptcy, 280–281
beer factory, 274
beliefs, *see also* expectations,
    abstractions
  consideration of by economists, 156
  consideration of by sociologists, 214
  examples of, 118–119
  malleability of, 117–119
  role in love, 87–88

  role in power, 123–124
body language, 121–122, 272
Bollywood, 82
brain
  as a storytelling machine, 92–93
  damage, 92
  physiology, 91–92
  train metaphor for the, 93, 98
bribing the unseen, *see* reciprocity
business links, *see* contacts

Caligula, 127
cannibalism, 43
Capgras syndrome, 96
categorization theory, 102–106, 145,
    207–209
caviar, 115
centralized economies, *see* economic
    systems (comparative)
change management, *see* leadership,
    groups (social)
cheap talk, 11, 14, 160, 331, 340
childbirth, 80–81, 107, 137, 140
children
  development of love program in,
    96–98
  emotional development in, 98–101
  role of in the family, 165–166
  starving, 105
China
  ancient, 167
  modern, 261–262, 272, 288
church, *see also* circles of reciprocity
  doctrine of, 46, 83
  history of, 83–84
circles of reciprocity, 29
  examples of, 155
  large, 154–157, 202–204
  leadership in, 157, 283–284
  small, 152–153, 198–199, 278–279

423